ETHNIC PSYCHOLOGY:
Research and Practice with Immigrants, Refugees, Native Peoples, Ethnic Groups and Sojourners

ETHNIC PSYCHOLOGY:
Research and Practice with Immigrants, Refugees, Native Peoples, Ethnic Groups and Sojourners

*Selected Papers from the North American Regional
IACCP Conference on Ethnic Psychology,
held in Kingston, Canada,
August 16-21, 1987*

Edited by J.W. Berry & R.C. Annis

*Published for the International Association
of Cross-Cultural Psychology*

SWETS & ZEITLINGER B.V. AMSTERDAM / LISSE   1988

SWETS NORTH AMERICA INC. BERWYN, PA | PUBLISHING SERVICE |

This volume was published with the assistance of funds provided by Multiculturalism Canada.

Library of Congress Cataloging in Publication Data

North American Regional IACCP Conference on Ethnic Psyochology (1987 : Kingston, Ont.)
Ethnic psychology: research and practice with immigrants, refugees, native peoples, ethnic groups and sojourners, selected papers from the North American Regional IACCP Conference on Ethnic Psychology held in Kingston, Canada, August 18-21, 1987 / edited by J.W. Berry & R.C. Annis.
p. cm.
Published for the International Association of Cross-Cultural Psychology.
Bibliography p.
ISBN 90265 09685
1. Ethnopsychology--Congresses. 2. Ethnicity--Psychological aspects Congresses. 1. Berry, John W. II. Annis, R.C.
III. International Association of Cross-Cultural Psychology.
IV. Title.
GN502.N67 1987
155.8--dc19   88-36891 CIP

CIP-GEGEVENS KONINKLIJKE BIBLIOTHEEK, DEN HAAG

Ethnic

Ethnic psychology : research and practice with immigrants, refugees, native peoples, etnic groups and sojourners : selected papers from the North American Regional IACCP Conference on Ethnic Psychology, held in Kingston, Canada, August 16-21, 1987 / ed. by J.W. Berry & R.C. Arnis. - Berwyn : Swets North America ; Lisse : Swets & Zeitlinger
Published for the International Association of Cross-Cultural Psychology. - Met lit. opg.
ISBN 90-265-0968-5 geb.
SISO 414.9 UDC 159.922.2 NUGI 716
Trefw.: cross-culturele psychologie.

Omslag ontwerp H. Veltman
Gedrukt bij Offsetdrukkerij Kanters B.V., Alblasserdam
© Copyright 1988 J.W. Berry en Swets & Zeitlinger, Lisse.

ISBN 90 265 0968 5

CONTENTS

INTRODUCTION

J.W. Berry & R.C. Annis

In 1985, on behalf of the International Association for Cross-Cultural Psychology, Lars Ekstrand organized a very successful European Regional Conference at Malmo, Sweden. This event, which culminated in the production of a volume entitled "Ethnic minorities and immigrants in cross-cultural perspective" (Ekstrand, 1986), stimulated substantial discussion on both theoretical and applied issues concerning ethnic minorities and immigrants. This European conference also served to heighten awareness of the need for social policy makers, as well as psychologists, to better understand the psychological issues pertaining to Immigrants, Native Peoples, Ethnic Groups, Refugees and Sojourners. This perceived need in turn led a number of people to suggest that a North American Regional conference be held and also be devoted to this same theme. John Berry and Ron Samuda served as co-chairmen of the Organizing Committee, Bob Annis as chairman of the Scientific Programme Committee, and Uichol Kim and Rudy Kalin as co-chairmen of the Local Arrangements Committee[1]. Partial funding was provided by the Canadian Secretary of State for Multiculturalism, to whom we offer our thanks.

During the conference over 100 papers were presented on a variety of topics relating to ethnic psychology (see Cross-Cultural Psychology Bulletin, 1987, Vol. 21, No. 3, 5-11, for a copy of the full programme). Most papers were concerned with research and practice in North America, but some were focussed on experience elsewhere. Hence, the cross-cultural flavour of the conference derived not so much from the traditional comparative approach that is the hallmark of cross-cultural psychology, but from the intercultural phenomena that take place when people from different cultures come into contact and interact in multicultural societies (Berry, 1986).

The term ethnic psychology is intended to include all those psychological phenomena that appear in societies where individuals and groups remain culturally distinct from one another (Berry, 1985). The usual topics include such issues as acculturation, adaptation, stress, identity, ethnic relations, assessment, education, counselling and therapy in groups such as immigrants, refugees, Native Peoples, ethnic groups and sojourners. The thrust of the present volume is to show that these issues and peoples can best be understood using the perspectives and tools rooted in our experience as cross-cultural psychologists, rather than the more conventional approach (that largely ignores culture) found in most of the psychological literature on the topic of "minorities".

This volume contains selected papers chosen to illustrate these themes and approaches. Necessarily many fine papers had to be excluded, and we apologize to those presenters whose work could not be included here. The volume is organized into five sections, beginning with some general issues that set the sociocultural and policy stage for work in ethnic psychology, and continuing with a series of more focussed sections dealing with particular phenomena and issues.

In the first section two major invited addresses are presented that illustrate the contrast between official multicultural policy and programmes in Canada, and some of the problems that attend these community and governmental initiatives. On the one hand there is a statement of a vision or ideology that guides the management and evolution of cultural diversity in the country, and on the other there is a critical analysis of some of the practical difficulties (particularly in the domain of schooling; see also Samuda, Berry and LaFerrière, 1983) that accompany their implementation. These contrasting presentations are themselves evidence of a healthy pluralism in thought and action, and serve to alert the reader to the wide range of positions that can be taken when working in the area of ethnic psychology. As in the case of the Malmö conference volume (in which the opening section focussed on the Swedish experience), this attention to the Canadian situation is intended to introduce conference delegates and readers to current thinking in the host country. However, this Canadian focus may also be justified on the grounds that Canada was the first country to officially adopt a multicultural policy, and it has been a model, to some extent, for other countries seeking to go the pluralist route.

The second section is concerned with how individuals negotiate their way into life in a plural society. Whether one is an immigrant, a refugee or a visitor, one engages in contact with other cultural groups, possibly experiences conflict, and eventually arrives at some form of resolution. The concept of <u>acculturation</u> is used to refer to this process, and that of <u>psychological adaptation</u> is the term used to identify the long-term outcome of this acculturation process. Earlier generalizations about the inevitable negative psychological consequences of acculturation have given way to more variable views: some individuals can and do move successfully between cultures, while others are virtually destroyed by the process. The particular outcome is dependent upon a host of factors that have been identified in the literature (Berry & Kim, 1988), and further evidence is provided in this section for a variety of acculturating groups.

The third section deals with a related issue: how individuals maintain or change their personal and ethnic identity during the course of acculturation. Once again, earlier generalizations - that there is likely to be large scale identity change and confusion - seems to be no longer accepted. With more refined methods and instruments now in use, and with a better theoretical understanding of the variability in acculturation, a range of outcomes is now being found among individuals who deal daily with two or more cultures.

The fourth section is concerned with one of the longest-standing issues in cross-cultural psychology: how to validly assess individuals who are culturally different from the culture of the test-maker or the test standardization group. Since Samuda's (1975) pioneering book, this issue has been at the forefront of work with ethnic groups in plural societies, and remains one of the great unsolved problems today.

The fifth section continues a concern with the application of research in an attempt to find solutions to social and psychological problems in plural societies. Included are a concern for intergroup relations, the migration plans of youth, and intercultural therapy and substance abuse.

We hope that this volume of selected proceedings will serve as both a reminder and a partial record of the presentation and discussions that took place in Kingston during a very hot week in August 1987. We intend it to be one link in a continuing chain of events in the Association that will make the work of cross-cultural psychologists more relevant to the needs of the variety of cultural groups who have come to live, learn and work together in plural societies.

References

Berry, J.W. (1985). Cultural psychology and ethnic psychology: A comparative analysis. In I. Reyes-Lagunes and Y. Poortinga (Eds.), From a Different Perspective. Lisse: Swets and Zeitlinger, pp.3-15.

Berry, J.W. (1986). Multiculturalism and psychology in plural societies. In L.H. Ekstrand (Ed.), Ethnic minorities and immigrants in a cross-cultural perspective. Lisse: Swets and Zeitlinger, pp. 35-51.

Ekstrand, L.H. (Ed.) (1986). Ethnic minorities and immigrants in cross-cultural perspective. Lisse: Swets and Zeitlinger.

Samuda, R. (1975). Psychological testing of American minorities: Issues and consequences. New York: Harper & Row.

Samuda, R., Berry, J.W. & Laferrière, M. (Eds.) (1983). Multiculturalism in Canada: Social and Educational Perspectives. Toronto: Allyn and Bacon.

Note

[1] In addition to those who chaired committees, a great deal of work was contributed by members of those committees. We wish to thank all whose efforts made the conference possible, and in particular we wish to recognize Pat Brown, Effie Ginsberg and Floyd Rudmin for their major contributions to local arrangements and Audrey Bailey for her assistance in preparing the manuscript for publication.

Part I

MULTICULTURALISM:
POLICIES AND CONTRADICTIONS

MULTICULTURAL POLICY AND PRACTICE IN CANADA

Gilbert H. Scott
Director General, Multiculturalism

Canada is a vast country blessed with abundance. We are rich in natural and human resources. Assuredly, we are a significant part of the global village, and are eager participants in forums of this kind. For the benefit of our visitors from abroad, I should mention that according to the 1981 census, Canada's population is a little over 24 million. 25% are from ethnic backgrounds other than British or French. The latter represents 40% and 27% respectively, of the total population. The 8% remaining reported themselves as having multiple ethnic origins.

These are but cold statistics. The human side of these figures is revealed in the everyday lives of ordinary Canadians. In some schools in Vancouver, Toronto, and Montreal over 50% of the children belong to an ethnic group other than French or English. The extent to which these children find their ethnocultural backgrounds reflected in the school curriculum gives a clear message as to how "Canadian" is defined. If young Canadians grow up safe in the knowledge of their geographic and cultural citizenry the leap to becoming world citizens, with a global perspective, is much more assured.

As the world approaches the 21st century, clear and open communication lines between nations, on all manner of interests, be they vested or otherwise, are essential. I see the work of the International Association for Cross-cultural Psychology, and this forum in particular, as an example of the kind of international sharing which increases understanding and co-operation between nations. The Association's symposiums are particularly important because they not only provide a window on how nations are rising to meet social challenges, but, because they are rooted in academic discipline and scholarship, they also help to light the way, revealing what choices and workable options are available for social policy-makers.

Multi-cultural and multi-racial nations like Canada are confronted by the apparent paradox of having to reconcile two seemingly, contradictory ideals: pluralism and cohesion. I would like to outline how multiculturalism, as a practical instrument of government, may be used to unite these diverse concepts. In so doing, I should acknowledge the contribution of researchers such as yourselves, for without your work, and that of others, upon which to draw, I would have no case.

In Canada, fifteen or twenty years ago there was little interest in ethnicity outside of academia. To most other people it was just a word in the dictionary. However, what was once a paucity of research has become an ever-increasing addition to our knowledge about what Canada and Canadians are all about. Ethnicity is a relatively new concept and we are all indebted to researchers who have added so much to our understanding of the pluralistic dimension and socio-cultural development of Canada. The Canadian vocabulary is now enriched by words such as "Ethnocultural", referring to groups and organizations which struggle to come to terms with the inter-relationships between ethnicity and culture.

As you are all no doubt aware, there are differing schools of thought on the efficacy of a federal multiculturalism policy that attempts to unite the two concepts of national unity and the social cohesion of diverse cultural and racial elements, and to do so, moreover, within the bilingual framework of Canada's two official languages. However, it is becoming increasingly clear that the philosophical underpinnings of multiculturalism have a strong theoretical basis that is now being investigated with increasing vigour. The net result is that researchers, such as the Association's Past-President, John Berry, are able to tell policy-makers that they are at least, "on the right track" (Berry, 1984). The importance of this kind of encouragement and guidance from those among you who consider yourselves to be cross-cultural psychologists and ethnic psychologists, as well as from others in related disciplines, cannot be under-estimated. Of course, it is essential if multiculturalism policy is to retain its integrity and dynamism.

One of the most important aspects of the multiculturalism policy is the nature and extent of its universality. Although narrowly interpreted to emphasize cultural retention, in its first awakening, during the early 1970's, the policy as originally conceived, has shown in its evolution over the past 15 years, that it is versatile and flexible enough to serve Canadians in a variety of ways. The original four objectives are: cultural retention, cultural sharing and inter-group understanding, removal of discriminatory barriers, and provision for the acquisition of an official language. Recently, an attempt was made to translate them to reflect the current environment. It was found that they could equally be expressed as:

8

Societal Adaptation: To foster within Canadian society, respect
for the multicultural/multi-racial nature of the nation and
capacity to serve and reflect Canadians of all cultures.
Heritage Enhancement: To promote the enhancement of
ethnocultural heritages as integral and evolving forms of the
Canadian experience, and finally,
Integration: To assist immigrants and members of ethnocultural
and racial groups to function effectively as Canadians.
The Secretary of State and Minister responsible for Multiculturalism
sums it up more eloquently, and certainly more succinctly, when he
speaks of equality, diversity, and community, these being in his
words the "essence of Canadian citizenship".

This concept of citizenship lies at the heart of multiculturalism
policy, and vice versa. As such, multiculturalism stands as a model
for intercultural harmony and societal cohesion. It promotes
equality of opportunity for full participation in Canadian society
for all, irrespective of race, colour or creed. Equally as
important, it promotes not merely tolerance of cultural diversity,
but an acceptance and true appreciation for it.

Over the years, the multiculturalism sector has worked in partnership
with many educators, researchers and community groups to promote
these concepts. Some examples of these partnerships are:

- support for community-based, ethnocultural organizations with
  a mandate to advocate on behalf of their respective
  constituencies;
- working with publishers and invididual authors to ensure that
  learning materials more accurately and completely reflect the
  reality of our multicultural and multiracial society;
- support for race relations initiatives within existing
  institutions of the justice and health care system;
- working with faculties of education and teachers' and
  trustees' organizations to assist in the development of
  sensitization programs for teachers, and trustees;
- supporting scholarly research;
- working with universities to establish chairs of ethnic
  studies and fellowships; and
- working with heritage language schools to enhance heritage
  language learning. The multiculturalism sector financially
  assists about 1,000 supplementary schools across Canada.
  There are about 125,000 students in more than 8,000 classes
  across the country and 62 languages are being taught.

I am sure that some of you will recognize yourselves in these
partnerships. For example, Ron Samuda's writing and research on
multiculturalism issues is well-known at home and abroad (Samuda,
1983; Samuda, Berry and Laferrière, 1984). His work on intelligence
assessments of school-age children has enlightened many to both the
power of streaming and that of the school curriculum to shape a
child's self-image.

The impetus provided by research for policy implementation and renewal is vital. However, it must be admitted that, for the most part, the multiculturalism movement has been fuelled essentially by governments, minority groups and academics. Other Canadians have remained largely on the periphery. One of the challenges for Canada is to make multiculturalism <u>all</u> <u>Canadian</u>. However, there is some reason for optimism. According to one survey, 75% of respondents feel "favourably disposed to the idea of multicultural, mutually tolerant, and diverse society". (Berry, Kalin and Taylor, 1977)

More and more, those involved in multiculturalism have been insisting that one way of helping to ensure national receptivity towards multiculturalism is to provide a firm legislative base. To our credit, this has been done to a significant extent. Section 27 of the Canadian Charter of Rights and Freedoms affirms the importance of Canada's multicultural heritage in the degree that the Charter "shall be interpreted in a manner consistent with the preservation and enhancement of the multicultural heritage of Canadians". Proposed legislation in the form of a Multiculturalism Act, which the Secretary of State and Minister responsible for Multiculturalism has committed himself to table and which was recently recommended by the Parliamentary Standing Committee on Multiculturalism, will provide additional notice for all Canadians, and indeed for the rest of the world, that a concern for social justice is part of the fabric of Canadian society.

In a shrinking world, this recognition has an extension beyond our borders. A multicultural Canada, standing for cultural and ethnic equality, provides an excellent role model for other pluralistic societies. Indeed, the Australian Commissioner on Community Relations, the Honourable A.J. Grassby, said in 1981 during the fourth Canadian Conference on Multiculturalism, when speaking of Australia's multicultural society, "I am pleased to say that your (Canada's) example gave us inspiration and we are still following in your footsteps".

I would not wish to convey a false impression by dwelling on Canada's achievements. There is no room for complacency. We are too far away from an acceptable reduction of differential group treatment and their underrepresentation in our institutions, to be beguiled by false optimism. Until multiculturalism becomes a way of life, a way of thinking for all Canadians, we cannot say that we have progressed beyond a state of "readiness". To go further requires individual and collective will and the concerted effort of scholars, educators and community-based groups and organizations.

As scholars, cross-cultural, and ethnic psychologists, your contribution goes well beyond academic dialogue. Successive Canadian governments have recognized this so that over the past 15 years, federal multiculturalism policy has encouraged the activities of a number of organisations devoted to research, exchange and publication. Some examples of these are: Canadian ethnic studies research institutes and centres at universities across Canada; the Multicultural History Society of Ontario; the Jewish Historical Society of Canada; the Central and East European Studies Association of Canada; the Canadian Asian Studies Association; the Mennonite Historical Society of Canada; and the Canadian Ethnic Studies Association.

In recent years, ethnic studies has been the focus of significant, new research which is being undertaken by people who often have links to a group, and so possess special insight into it, but who also have the academic training necessary for perspective and critical analysis. These researchers are also well versed in Canadian history as a whole, and are therefore able to analyse the objectives behind immigration policies, the economic forces affecting settlement patterns, the attitudes of Canadians toward immigrants and so forth. It is heartening to note that Canadian scholars who are attempting to analyse the nature of Canadian national identity, are taking an interest in the role ethnicity has played and continues to play. We need the answers to many research questions related to psychological functioniong and cross-cultural interaction. Clearly, one cannot legislate attitudes. Science, though some may dispute it, does have a social responsibility; and the social sciences, in particular could lead us further in finding practical solutions to attitudinal change.

One of the main tenets of Canadian multicultural policy is equality in terms of sociocultural rights. This has remained central over the years but, clearly, we need to know much more about differences in the psychology of women and men from different ethnic and cultural backgrounds. Without this knowledge, guess work becomes a poor substitute for assurance.

One certainty we do have is that the enhancement of socio-cultural rights is not a responsibility assigned to any particular level of government or any type of interest-group. It is of fundamental importance to all of us, everywhere in the world. Increasing public awareness and understanding the issues are responsibilities that we must all share.

In this age which possesses the means to destroy civilization as we know it, we desperately need to develop adequate mechanisms for co-operation and participatory action, not only in matters pertaining to world peace and disarmament, but as well, and perhaps more importantly, in matters pertaining to augmenting the social, cultural and economic conditions which are prerequisites for peace.

During his plenary lecture at the 1985 conference of the International Association for Cross-Cultural Psychology, the Under Secretary of State for Sweden, Jonas Widgren (1986) ended on a note of hope. He pointed to the world's youthful vanguard of resistance to social injustice of all kinds as good cause for optimism.

I would like to suggest that this conference should begin on that note of optimism. Inevitably, during discussions over the next few days, world problems will be centre stage, and rightly so. In the Canadian context, Thomas Berger (1981) has spoken of our "fragile freedoms", how at times in our history we have found it acceptable to remove rights from indentifiable groups and communities. Redressing past injustices and ensuring the continued momentum of multiculturalism are the challenges ahead. Entrenching multiculturalism in the constitution and in the forthcoming multiculturalism act provides Canada with a strong legislative base upon which we can build, and I am optimistic that as a country we will rise to the challenge.

At the global level there is also optimism. Youth world wide hold dear the expectancy of a better world to come. We all have an obligation to keep working towards that ideal.

REFERENCES

Berger,T. (1981). Fragile Freedoms: Human Rights and Dissent in Canada. Toronto: Clarke Irwin.

Berry, J.W. (1984). Multicultural policy in Canada: A social psychological analysis. Canadian Journal of Behavioural Science, 16, 353-370.

Berry, J.W., Kalin, R. & Taylor, D.M. (1977). Multiculturalism and Ethnic Attitudes in Canada. Ottawa: Supply and Services.

Samuda, R. (1983). Cross-cultural testing within a multicultural society. In S.H. Irvine & J.W. Berry (Eds.) Human Assessment and Cultural Factors. New York: Plenum.

Samuda, R., Berry, J.W. & Laferrière, M. (Eds.) (1984). Multiculturalism in Canada: Social and Educational Perspective. Toronto: Allyn & Bacon.

Widgren, J. (1986). Immigrants and ethnic minorities in Europe. In L. Ekstrand (Ed.). Ethnic Minorities and Immigrants in a Cross-Cultural Perspective. Lisse: Swets & Zeitlinger.

CANADIAN DUALISM AND PLURALISM: TENSIONS, CONTRADICTIONS AND EMERGING RESOLUTIONS

John Mallea
President, Brandon University

COMPETING MODELS OF CANADIAN SOCIETY, CULTURE AND EDUCATION

Three broad and competing sets of assumptions about what constitutes or should constitute authentic models of contemporary Canadian culture and society can be identified: monoculturalism, biculturalism and multiculturalism. Monoculturalism stresses uniformity and finds expression in both anglo-conformity and franco-conformity; biculturalism is rooted firmly in the concept of English-French duality; and multiculturalism emphasizes broader notions of pluralism.

Each model has its supporters and a more or less well-defined ideology and matrix of concepts, ideas and images. Each is associated with one or other of three positions on language: unilingualism, bilingualism and multilingualism. Each influences the stances taken by majority and minority groups on issues in the politics of culture. And each has exerted considerable influence over the governance, goals and content of public education.

The presence of these three competing versions of what constitutes the legitimate Canadian cultural model has resulted inevitably in tensions, struggles and conflicts. At different times, and in different settings, linguistic strife, racial tensions and religious struggles have formed central leitmotifs in the history of Canadian politics, culture, and schooling.

In this paper, I focus on the contradictions and tensions that arise out of the competition between dualism and pluralism. These contradictions and tensions, I believe, underly major issues of language, culture, ethnicity and race. They are particularly well illustrated in Canada's federal policy of "Multiculturalism Within a Bilingual Framework", and provincial policies of multicultural education.

With the support of all three major Canadian political parties, this policy was introduced in 1971. In presenting it in the federal Parliament, former Prime Minister Trudeau rejected firmly the monocultural or assimilationist model. It was, he declared, an undesirable and unacceptable goal for Canadian society: "there cannot be one cultural policy for the Canadians of British and French origin, another for the original peoples and yet a third for all others. For although there are two official languages, there is no official culture, nor does any ethnic group take precedence over any other. No citizen or group of citizens is other than Canadian, and all should be treated fairly" (Trudeau, 1971: 1).

The above policy of "Multiculturalism Within a Bilingual Framework" expressed support for a number of goals: the preservation of basic human rights, the elimination of discrimination, the encouragement of cultural diversity, the strengthening of citizen participation, and the reinforcement of Canadian identity. It aimed at helping create a sense of identity, belonging and individual freedom of choice; these aims in turn were to form the basis of national unity. Ethnic loyalties, it was stressed, need not and usually did not, detract from wider loyalties to community and country.

Initial reception of the policy "Multiculturalism Within a Bilingual Framework" was at best mixed. Anglophones and a variety of other ethno-cultural groups appeared to favour it (Berry, Kalin and Taylor, 1977; Burnet, 1981), whereas Francophones expressed views ranging from lack of enthusiasm (Painchaud, 1976) to outright rejection (Rocher, 1972). The most vocal opposition to this policy was voiced by those francophones in Quebec who claimed that the new policy distorted both the historical and sociological realities of Canadian life. Canada, they argued, possessed two main cultures and two official languages, and as culture and language were indivisible, to juxtapose multiculturalism and bilingualism was contradictory.

The policy was also considered to be politically dangerous, in that it undermined the already slender faith of French-Canadians that the federal government was willing and able to protect their language and culture (Mallea, 1977). Other critics considered the policy suspect on political grounds. As Reitz (1980) points out, ostensibly its political objective is the promotion of national unity, but more partisan political objectives have been charged. For example, it has been suggested that oppositional elements that might resist and challenge those things which hurt and oppress are marginalized (Thomas, 1984). The result is that minority ethno-cultural groups have been unable to establish organizations and institutions which could compete in any serious way with those of the two official language groups (Wardhaugh, 1983).

Most analysts of multiculturalism are rightly critical of the lack of conceptual clarity surrounding the term. There is, too, a strong sense that its intellectual foundations are shaky, resulting in a need for more full-blown, scholarly analyses. These concerns apply with equal if not more weight to the field of multicultural

education. Is multicultural education a socio-political instrument
for ensuring cooperation by granting limited concessions? Is it
designed to realize democratic ideals or is it another form of social
control (Barton and Walker, 1983)? Is the cultural capital that
minority children bring to school to be viewed as different but
valid, or inappropriate and deficient? Are multicultural educational
materials included for therapeutic purposes? Do these materials
celebrate individual social mobility but ignore ethnic
stratification? Do they stress consensus and avoid dealing with
conflict (Manicom, 1984)? Do multicultural education policies assume
that knowledge will reduce prejudice and discrimination? Do their
priorities recognize and legitimize cultural differences while
failing to deal with racism at the institutional, structural and
individual level (Patel, 1980), or as some argue, do current
approaches help maintain the myth about subordinate groups as
"problems to be studied", while leaving institutional and structural
inequalities intact (Augustine, 1984)?

Tensions between majority-minority relations, social cohesion and
control,. and individual and collective rights have historically
exerted a major influence upon Canadian schooling. They continue to
do so. They pose, in particularly acute form, what elsewhere has
been termed the pluralist dilemma in education (Bullivant, 1981).
This dilemma arises in large part out of the need to strike an
appropriate balance between the educational needs and aspirations of
minority and majority groups. Canadian school systems, for example,
are expected, at one and the same time, to respond to the realities
of cultural diversity while promoting overarching goals, social
cohesion and national integration. This task has never been an easy
one. Schools reflect a society's goals and while they "can help to
develop and transmit certain political orientations that must be
shared, within a certain range of variations, by most members of any
ongoing system," (Easton, 1975: 311) many difficulties obviously
arise in the absence of consensus over what these orientations are or
should be.

The three competing models of Canadian society, culture and schooling
each had their impact on our public education systems. During the
1960s and 1970s, despite being rejected at the policy level
assimilation continued to exert an influence on practice; while
multiculturalism attracted some attention and support. But of the
three models it was bilingualism and biculturalism that dominated
events, and efforts to translate this model into programmatic,
institutional and structural forms met with considerable opposition
(Sylvestre, 1980). In a number of provinces, applications of the
bilingual-bicultural model in schools were strongly opposed by
Anglophone majorities. Some liberalization of "what were in 1966
very restrictive policies with respect to minority language
education" in Ontario, Manitoba and New Brunswick (Rideout, 1977:
132) took place, but progress elsewhere was slow. Only in New
Brunswick, Canada's only officially bilingual province, could it be
said that considerable progress was made.

The absence of substantial progress in institutional and structural terms undoubtedly fueled efforts to enshrine official language educational rights in a new Canadian Constitution. In 1981, these efforts were rewarded with the inclusion of minority language educational rights in the Canadian Charter of Rights and Freedoms, which formed part of the Constitution Act (1982). Interpretations of Section 23 of the Charter, "Minority Language Educational Rights" are still being developed. Notwithstanding the fact that access to minority language education is now a constitutional right, rather than a provision subject to the possibility of legislative change, the translation of this right into practice has encountered difficulty. Why is this the case? Why have the bilingual-bicultural model, and the legislative and constitutional efforts to implement it, experienced such difficulty in gaining acceptance?

Conclusive answers are not available, but a number of problems with this bilingual-bicultural model can be identified. To begin with, the model's assumptions do not adequately reflect the demographic, economic and political changes that have occurred in Canada since Confederation, but especially since World War II. As a result, the concepts and terminology employed in the model are of limited applicability. Concepts such as "charter groups" and "founding peoples" for example are considered suspect and are frequently rejected out of hand. Native peoples consider the concept of "founding peoples" to be inaccurate, inappropriate and even insulting. Members of minority racial and ethno-cultural groups, particularly in Western Canada, dislike both this term and the concept of "charter groups". They also resent the appellation "other ethnic groups", which to them smacks of marginalization, subordinate status, and second-class citizenship.

THE LIMITS OF TRADITIONAL THEORY

Given the above problems, it is reasonable for policy-makers to look to scholars for assistance and to assume, in particular, that the social science would have something of value to offer. There are, however, at least five major reasons why traditional explanatory theory offers limited aid in helping resolve the tensions, contradictions and dilemmas inherent in education in multiracial, multicultural and multilingual societies.

First, there are the inherent limitations of social science theory itself. The dialectic between the universal and particular cannot be resolved by appeal to any all-encompassing set of principles; instead it must be worked out generation by generation in the context of the day (Itzkoff, 1969). Second, in that racially and culturally diverse societies "are characterized in part by the co-existence of autonomous but non-complementary sub-societies which do not share common values, what coherence exists cannot be fully accounted for by value consensus" (Watson, 1982). Third, theories of multi-ethnic societies are inadequate as a statement of what constitutes the arena of political contention and decision-making. They lack a theory of

power and fail to examine power relations, decision-making, and
policy formulation at the local community level in terms of the
broader societal structure of power (Halebsky, 1976). Fourth, such
theories frequently ignore the tensions between political democracy
and economic inequality (Giroux, 1983). Fifth, and most
particularly, they rarely analyse schooling except in terms of the
very limited context of cultural differences. Consequently, they
fail to confront the importance of power differentials and the
ordering of power relations in the structuring of state-aided public
education.

Rarely have the questions of schooling in multi-ethnic societies been
examined in socio-economic, political, institutional and structural
terms. Existing studies, moreover, have been conducted largely from
the viewpoint of the majority or dominant group. Studies undertaken
from the point of view of minority or subordinate groups are
virtually non-existent. On the contrary, prevailing theories of
schooling have stressed the school's role in cultural transmission
and emphasized notions of neutrality, stability and consensus.

The cumulative impact of these and related limitations is severe.
Explicit theoretical and conceptual frameworks are employed only
infrequently and normative ideological statements abound. The need
to search for and apply new theoretical concepts and frameworks is
apparent. Fortunately, these concepts exist and are to be found in
contemporary sociological theory dealing with inter-group relations
and the nature of schooling.

INTER-GROUP RELATIONS REVISITED

Probably the most valuable macro-analysis of inter-group relations to
be found in the theoretical literature in recent years is that
provided by R. A. Schermerhorn in Comparative Ethnic Relations: A
Framework for Theory and Research (1970). Observing that the central
purpose of any general sociological theory is to postulate the
essential nature of social interaction, he grounds his theory in the
argument that inter-group relations are to be seen "as a special case
of societal relations in their broadest and most generic sense,
rather than as a separate and unrelated field of inquiry" (p. 17).

The contributions of structural-functionalism and power-conflict
theory to the understanding of inter-group relations, he argues, are
limited. The former suffers from the proclivity of functionalists
and systems analysts to emphasize symmetrical relationships, a
preference that has led them to place a selective emphasis on
congruence, mutuality, complementarity and organic balance. These
theorists adopt the view that societies can only persist when total
system needs are satisfied. Priority is accorded to these needs, and
structures established which are characterized by stability and
predictability. Their primary function is maintenance of the
existing system. Whether they are good or bad in terms of individual
preferences or partial group standards is less important. Not

surprisingly, therefore, this approach has generally worked to support preservation of the status quo.

Traditional power-conflict theory is based on the concept of the inherent scarcity of means, with attempts to control these means resulting in open or concealed conflicts requiring the application of power to attain and maintain control. Efforts to resolve these conflicts result in the development of unequal power relations. These relations are not fixed, and continued contestation for control leads to emphasis being placed on change rather than preservation of the status quo. Conflicts between groups of unequal power, Schermerhorn points out, are not necessarily destabilizing. They can also engender integrative bonds which possess system characteristics of their own (Schermerhorn, 1970).

Schermerhorn does not recommend dispensing altogether with structural-functionalism or systems analysis. Rather he considers the two theoretical approaches to be alternatives that have greater or lesser relevance at different points in dialectical analysis. In his view, they are not dichotomous intellectual systems, nor for explanatory purposes must an either/or choice be made.

The adoption of Schermerhorn's dialectical approach possesses three mutually reinforcing advantages. First, it keeps the analyst face to face with the concrete realities of social situations, it underlines their fluidity and complexity, and it serves to correct the one-sidedness of narrow explanations. Second, it does not bolster any particular ideological position; it is "a weapon that can be used against all ideologies, an empirical sort of probing that asks whether unsuspected dualities are lurking in our answers - sometimes leading to affirmative, sometimes to negative replies" (1970: 49). And third, it makes an important analytical distinction between culture and structure:

> Culture signifies the ways of action learned through socialization, based on norms and values that serve as guides or standards for that behaviour. Social structure, on the other hand, refers to "the set of crystallized social relationships which its (the society's) members have with each other which places them in groups, large or small, permanent or temporary, formally organized or unorganized, and which relates them to the major institutional activities of the society, such as economic and occupational life, religion, marriage and the family, education, government and recreation. (Schermerhorn, 1970: 80)

Moreover, as Singleton (1977) points out, by adopting a dialectical approach to analyses of schooling in a plural society, the intimate relationship between culture and politics is reinforced, and the interlocking roles of symbols (the language of instruction, for example) and power is revealed.

CONTEMPORARY FORMS OF PLURALISM

The distinction between culture and structure underlines the importance of the analytical differences between cultural, normative, political, and socio-economic pluralism. Cultural pluralism, the form of pluralism most often invoked in connection with schooling, refers to the presence of racial and ethnic groups possessing languages and/or other cultural norms and values which differentiate them from the dominant group in a society. Normative pluralism, usually expressed in ideological terms, refers to the realm of goals and objectives such as the toleration or appreciation of cultural differences. Political pluralism refers to the existence of a multiplicity of autonomous groups and associations (including but not restricted to those possessing an ethnocultural base) that exert pressure on the initiation, formulation, and implementation of public policy. Structural pluralism refers to the presence of institutions and structures reflecting racial and cultural diversity. These range from a situation where complete duplication of services is provided to a situation where racial and ethnic groups participate in a number of common institutions, but also continue to maintain those which reflect their own distinctive cultural features. A fifth form, socio-economic pluralism, is crucially important to the analysis of schooling in a multi-racial, multicultural and multilingual society.

Cultural Pluralism. Cultural pluralism is an imprecise concept. It is employed loosely in the theoretical literature and some difficulty has been experienced also in defining it in the literature on education (Gibson, 1976). Most writers who employ the concept suggest that it goes beyond objective cultural differences (Van den Burghe, 1973). Other interpretations have considered policies of cultural pluralism to be dysfunctional (Wardaugh, 1983) or to obscure more important social problems (Bullivant, 1981). In Canada, the concept is used frequently without benefit of definition. According to McLeod (1979), since no ethnic group forms an outright majority, and since neither Anglo- nor Franco-Canadians settled and developed the land in certain regions, cultural pluralism has been considered a suitable social and cultural policy for Canadians, albeit one that has frequently been ignored (Wardaugh, 1983). For the purposes of this paper, cultural pluralism can be defined as the presence of racial and ethnic groups whose language, religion and/or other traditional norms and values are embodied in patterns that differentiate them from the dominant group.

Normative or Ideological Pluralism. The ideological system, since it coordinates and structures all other cultural and social systems, has been described as the most vital element of a society's culture. Normative ideologies, moreover, are a fundamental part of every society and serve as important sources of cohesion and unity. In federal societies, normative or ideological pluralism is a widely acknowledged principle, one that is based on the premise that all groups that continue to interact with each other develop normative regularities and system interdependencies (Schermerhorn, 1970).

In Canada, normative or ideological pluralism is an acknowledged principle of government with normative ideals forming the basic "software" of politics. Yet despite their importance, they have rarely been the subject of critical scrutiny.

Even more rare is an assessment of the normative goals of educational systems, whose role in the stabilization of ideological systems is widely acknowledged (Smolicz, 1979). Ideologies are expressed routinely in educational policies; these ideologies are primarily a set of ideas and beliefs about society located in concrete educational practices (Giroux, 1983), and they exert considerable influence over individuals and groups. There can be no question, moreover, that the dominant ideology shapes the culture and structure of public schooling.

Institutional and Structural Pluralism. According to Schermerhorn, "culture and social structure are virtual Siamese twins, with each implicated in the other. So if a cultural group has its own special set of norms, they will ipso facto define certain institutions or patterns that separate the members of that group structurally from adjacent groups, at least in some minimal way" (1970: 124). Multi-ethnic societies are, by definition, societies that possess plural institutions and structures, and these institutions reflect the different degrees of power, wealth and knowledge possessed by dominant and subordinate ethnic groups. Canadian society, like other societies, consists of a system of institutionalized relations, with the different institutional forms together making up the social, political and economic structures. Identifiable racial and ethnic groups exercise dominant control over these structures, and the status of the culture of a subordinate group is related directly to its status in the economic and political structure (Bullivant, 1981: 72). For these reasons, it is essential for any sociological analysis of culture to concern itself with the analysis of educational institutions and of the forms of cultural production they promote and legitimize (Williams, 1981).

Political Pluralism. Political pluralism refers to the multiplicity of autonomous groups and associations (including those possessing a racial and ethno-cultural base), that bring pressure to bear on the development and implementation of political decisions. Ideally, autonomous pressure groups and the web of private links which citizens develop within the family, neighbourhood and voluntary associations, serve to mediate between the individual and the state (Townsend, 1983). Schermerhorn suggests further that in addition to preventing the state "or even any private source of power from gaining monopolistic weight, they help to train citizens in the political skills necessary for carrying on the democratic process; they accustom men to accept the legitimacy of opposition" (Schermerhorn, 1970: 123).

Research on ethnicity and education has largely conceived of politics and school systems intersecting at but one major point: the

20

socialization of ethnic minorities to the dominant culture (Wirt, 1979). Or, as is more frequently the case, it has been expressed in terms of nation-building. That is, ethnicity has been seen as a categorical reference rather than a political process and ethnic groups have been treated as static systems which constrain the political integration of nations (Singleton, 1977). Such treatments have led to calls for a statement of the theoretical relationship between the political system and school policy as they affect cultural integration (Wirt, 1979), and between multicultural education and the political framework within which it operates and by which it is conditioned (Mitter, 1984). According to one prominent critic, we need to examine schools "not only with reference to their existing connections with other agencies in the fields of production and cultural production, it also means tracing historically the ever-changing pattern of connections" and grounding the fight for control of schooling among competing political and socio-economic forces and their accompanying educational theories (Giroux, 1981: 80).

In Canada, such calls for alternative theoretical frames focusing on the relationships among race, ethnicity and the politics of schooling are now being heard (Dahlie et al., 1981). Martel (1984) has asked whose interests are being served by existing power structures in education? And Moodley (1981, 1983, 1984) has called for multicultural education to be politicized in an effort to improve the chances for school success of children from immigrant and ethno-cultural minority backgrounds.

Socio-economic Pluralism. Socio-economic differences, one of the most important forms of differentiation affecting individuals and groups in racially and ethnically plural societies is usually referred to in terms of social and ethnic stratification. Yet no general theory of ethnic stratification exists and social and ethnic stratification are frequently treated as though they were virtually synonymous (Shibutani and Kwan, 1965). However, as Glazer amd Moynihan (1975) have suggested, ethnicity may well be shown to be as important a phenomenon as social class in determining educational outcomes, and by extension, one's position in the socio-economic hierarchy.

Studies of the relationship between ethnic and social stratification in Canada are of recent origin (Porter 1965), and even the broad outlines are subject to fairly wide-ranging discussion and interpretation. Relationships among ethnicity, social class and education are even unclear and less researched than relationships between ethnic and social stratification. Porter (1965) and Clement (1975) have strongly criticized the belief that Canadian society is a meritocracy, or that its educational system provides equal opportunity for all. Both scholars have concluded that the educational system helps preserve the status quo. For example, Clement is sceptical that educational reform can bring about fundamental structural change in the absence of more widespread economic and political change (1975).

One of the most ambitious pieces of quantitative research analyzing the differences between racial and ethnic groups on measures of educational attainment was that conducted by Herberg (1980). His study examined the educational performance of thirteen racial and ethnic groups in five Canadian cities over a period of time. Great differences were observed in the educational attainment among ethnic groups in the same city; the relative value placed on formal education appeared to vary greatly among ethnicities within the same social environment; and each ethnic group--and likely each one in each city--seemed to be characterized by a unique set of internal social values and relations influencing the functions of formal education within that group in its social-geographic context. Given this degree of relativity, and the limited nature of current research, one can express only the most tentative conclusions on group specific relationships between ethnicity, social stratification and educational attainment. However, sufficient evidence is available to indicate that the relationship varies between groups and that the "vertical mosaic" is not as fixed and rigid as some authors have suggested (Young, 1987).

CONTEMPORARY THEORIES OF CULTURE AND EDUCATION

Theorists critical of traditional sociological theories of education are insistent that educational systems are not as autonomous as many previous commentators believed. They argue that schools are part of a much larger, interlocking pattern of institutions, structures and processes (political, economic, social and cultural), and that such patterns exert considerable influence and control over the role and practice of schooling. For example, Raymond Williams observes that: "The common prescription of education, as the key to change, ignores the fact that the form and content of education are affected, and in some cases determined, by the actual systems of (political) decisions and (economic) maintenance" (cited in Apple, 1979: 27, 28). The school's relationship to the broader political and economic system is also informed by a complex set of differential power relations. In effect, the dominant racial, cultural and linguistic groups in a society exercise considerable control over the governance, administration curricula and practices of public schools.

The result of this control is that a series of conscious selections are made from a larger cultural tradition in which the knowledge, skills and values of the dominant group are prominently featured. The hierarchical structure and organization of the curriculum reflects these judgements and the differential allocations of time, resources and status accorded various subjects of study confirm them. Alternative curricular forms (for example those advanced by subordinate ethno-cultural groups) are treated as either supplementary activities or excluded altogether. Why this is so is rarely made explicit; assumptions remain tacit, as do epistemological consensus-oriented, and uncritically supportive of existing economic, political, ideological and intellectual frameworks (Pratt, 1975).

Theories of culture generally find their basis in one or the other of three ideological traditions: conservative, liberal-democratic or Marxist. The first assumes that culture is largely static and to be conserved; the second that the individual, (and individual expression), is the key element in the production of culture; and the third, that the economic structure is of central importance in its formation. All three traditions consider culture to be a central concept in any comprehensive theory of society and that public institutions such as schools play a central role in the production and reproduction of culture.

Culture has been defined in a variety of ways in the social sciences and traditionally these definitions have stressed the transmission of culture. Implicit in these definitions is the view of culture as relatively stable and unchanging. These relatively unproblematic definitions of culture have come under considerable criticism of late and the ·necessity to re-think the links between culture, economic and political power, especially the power of dominant groups to exercise control over cultural institutions like the school, has been stressed (Bourdieu and Passeron, 1977). Williams (1981) has called for the development of a political economy of culture, and Giroux (1981) has emphasized the need to politicize the concept of both culture and schooling.

Two of the most significant theoretical contributions to the critical sociology of education over the last two decades involve reappraisals of the theory of culture and its relationship to the school. These are reproduction theory and resistance theory.

Advocates of reproduction theory reject any notion of the educational system as a closed and neutral system in which all children receive equal treatment and exposure to the same formal culture irrespective of background. On the contrary, they view education as a permeable system, one deeply affected by the cultural and socio-economic resources children bring to the school. Thus to treat students as though they are equal, when in reality they are not, only permits and encourages the impact of the differences in these resources. From their perspective, school success, which liberal-democratic theory views as the outcome of objective and open competition, is the result of an unequal contest and is better explained by the school's acceptance, distribution and legitimation of a socially-determined cultural capital.

Resistance theory argues that culture and knowledge are also mediated and produced in the school (Giroux, 1981). Resistance is an active process involving interactions between lived experiences and the institutions and structures that attempt to shape them. It is a political act involving actors, processes and structures internal and external to the educational system. And it directs attention to the ways in which minority individuals and groups "can find a voice and maintain and extend the positive dimensions of their own cultures and histories" (Giroux, 1983: 111). Classroom relations, moreover, are not always static. Schools serve frequently as sites of opposition and resistance to the dominant culture (Willis, 1983) and conflicts possess their own dynamism along racial and ethnic as well as class lines (Breton, 1979).

The most developed theory of resistance in education, and one that stresses the important role played by minority groups in resisting dominant group interpretations of culture and schooling can be found in Giroux's _Theory and Resistance in Education_ (1983). Traditional theory (both conservative and liberal) is roundly criticized for its tendency to view schools merely as instructional sites, and for its inability to see their importance as contested cultural and political sites. Marxist and neo-marxist theories of schooling are found too abstract in that they reduce resistance to a form of political style, and fail to situate it within specific political contexts and movements. Reproduction theorists are criticized for their virtual exclusion of theories of resistance in their analyses of schooling. They are criticized for employing models of domination that are inherently static and a scholar such as Bourdieu is criticized for his failure to acknowledge the importance of resistance in his analysis of cultural production and reproduction.

These two critical theories of culture and education, while drawing largely upon power-conflict perspectives of group relations, also recognize the value of some forms of structural analysis. Herein lies one of the sources of their strength. Another is the group of five inter-related and associated concepts which possess considerabe explanatory power in the analysis of schooling in plural societies.

Cultural Capital. The first of these five concepts is that of cultural capital, and is perhaps best understood by way of analogy to that of human and physical capital. By viewing culture as a valuable resource, the control over form and content of which is contested, we can better understand current conflicts over schooling. As is well known, the question of which specific knowledge, belief systems, values and patterns of behaviour are to be selected for transmission by schools is problematic. Not only is it a question of what culture and what heritage is to be reproduced (Hodgetts, 1968), but also whose culture and whose heritage (Werner, 1974). That certain types of values, knowledge and skill are more highly rated than others in public school systems is not in doubt. Why this is so, why such hierarchies exist, and the assumptions and criteria on which they rest, is much less clear. However, the concept of cultural capital, when linked with the concepts of cultural hegemony and cultural reproduction, strongly suggests that the process of selection and hierarchical ordering which takes place is largely determined by the exercise of power by the dominant cultural group, and therefore the curriculum reflects this group's preferred content, values and traditions. Language is a clear case in point. With very few exceptions, the language of instruction in a community is the

24

language of the dominant or majority group. Schools reinforce the
role of language in mediating relationships between dominant and
subordinate groups. In doing so, they help produce, reproduce and
legitimate differential relations among majority and minority, racial
and ethno-cultural groups.

Cultural Hegemony. The assertion of cultural hegemony in the field
of public education has been discussed by a number of critical social
theorists, prominent among whom are Bourdieu and Passeron (1977).
These authors defined cultural hegemony as the imposition by the
dominant group of a specific cultural design based on its possession
of power, whereby the group's culture is reproduced and distributed
through a variety of institutions including the school.
Subsequently, Giroux (1981: 23) defined cultural hegemony as "the
successful attempt of a dominant class to utilize its control over
the resources of the state and civil society, particularly through
the use of the mass media and the educational system, to establish
its view of the world as all inclusive and universal". Cultural
hegemony is neither fixed nor unchanging. Rather, dominant groups
need to renew continually their hegemony, authority and control and
they do so in the face of efforts by subordinate groups (including
racial, cultural and linguistic groups) to resist these forms of
domination.

Cultural Reproduction. Cultural reproduction, refers to the efforts
by dominant and subordinate groups alike to transmit their knowledge,
values, belief systems and behavioral norms from one generation to
the next. This dynamic process is intimately connected to the larger
process of reproduction in which the social, economic and political
characteristics of a group are reproduced. It is also related
inseparably to the reproduction of relations between dominant and
subordinate racial, ethnic and linguistic groups, which are the
result of direct and indirect applications of power by the dominant
group. "Mainstream" culture is largely determined by these
relations, and is compatible with the cultural tradition of the
dominant group, as well as being the outcome of both desired and
deliberate continuity of practice. "Mainstream" culture is
reproduction in action.

Cultural Legitimation. The fourth concept of the five concepts,
cultural legitimation, suggests that claims of legitimacy for school
curricula and practices are largely derived from the relative amount
of authority and power possessed by the dominant cultural group
(Schermerhorn, 1970). Schools and school curricula not only transmit
and distribute the cultural capital of the dominant group, they
legitimize it also by conferring on it qualities of objectivity,
neutrality, and even universality. Therefore, questions of societal
integration are intimately related to questions of legitimacy. Such
conferral of legitimacy cannot be taken for granted. The arbitrary
imposition of knowledge and culture is resisted frequently by
minority groups, and as a result, the cultural legitimation of the
process of schooling must be reworked continually as conditions and

inter-group relations undergo modification and change.

Cultural Resistance. The fifth concept is that of cultural resistance. Sociologists and political scientists in Canada, even when they have focused on the dysfunctional aspects of educational systems, have neglected to explain why they seem to work to the advantage or certain groups and not others. For the most part, their explanations have not been pursued "in terms of the groups that make up society, the source of their power, and the contradictions that these involve . . . they do not conceive of resistance on the part of those who are disadvantaged by the operation of the system" (Murphy, 1979:50 italics added). Giroux concurs; defining culture as "lived antagonistic relations" situated within a complex of socio-political institutions and social forms that limit as well as enable human action. Culture represents a mediating link between a system of power relations and educational processes and outcomes (1981: 26-29). It is patently obvious, therefore, that schools are contested cultural and political sites. The creation and implementation of public educational policy are by definition political acts; and as political acts, moreover, they are frequently met with resistance by racial, ethnic and linguistic minority groups.

EMERGING RESOLUTIONS: ABORIGINAL RIGHTS

The explanatory potential of combining concepts and theories drawn from the critical sociology of culture and schooling can best be understood by examining a concrete example of efforts to resolve the current contradictions and tensions inherent in dualism and pluralism. The example chosen is that of aboriginal self-government.

Indeed, perhaps no single issue better illustrates the contested nature of culture and schooling in Canada than the controversial constitutional debates over the nature of aboriginal self-government. In particular, it provides valuable insights into the contradictions and tensions arising from competing models of dualism and pluralism. It underscores the fact that the nation's public educational institutions, structures and systems are centrally located in the nation's legal, economic, political and social framework. It confirms the contested nature of culture and illuminate the struggle between dominant and subordinate cultural groups over the control, content and process of schooling.

All four aboriginal peoples' organizations (the Assembly of First Nations, the Inuit Committee on National Issues, the Native Council of Canada, and the Metis National Council) view self-government as an inherent right. Moreover, and this point needs to be emphasized, all four advocate self-government within the Canadian political system (Hawkes, 1985). Furthermore, while there is no agreement on specifics, the aboriginal peoples generally believe that in order to survive as distinct cultures or peoples, they need land-based self-government. This means reaffirming and reinforcing their power to exist as distinct collectivities, and requires the power to exercise their collective rights. They want these powers not only to protect native identities, but also to enable them to improve social and public services by exercising control over matters such as education, language and other cultural areas (Boisvert, 1985).

It is important to remember that there are currently two major thrusts in the efforts to establish aboriginal self-government: policy-making processes of the state and the enhanced autonomy for aboriginal peoples to manage their own affairs. The "first important variable involved with forms of self-government for the aboriginal peoples is the authority function--the kind and degree of authority that are recognized within the political system" (Boisvert, 1985: 17). It is generally agreed, however, that the concept of authority includes issues of education, language and culture as well as those of land title, resources and economic development.

The history of schooling for the aboriginal peoples in Canada, while containing instances of success, is for the most part a record of continuing,˙ systematic failure (Berry, 1971). Since 1867, the federal government and its agents have abrogated the right of aboriginal governments to make all decisions affecting their people. First the church, and later the state, established residential or boarding schools for native students which detached them from their communities, families, culture, language, belief systems and life-styles. Within their walls, native children were isolated, proselytized and introduced to the presumed benefits of Euro-Canadian civilization, all in an effort to eradicate and replace their indigenous culture and language.

Only over the last twenty-five years has the structural pattern of native schools operated by the churches, but funded primarily by the state, been set aside. As recently as the early 1980's, fifty-four percent of Indian children commute to provincial and private schools from their homes on the reserves (C.E.A., 1984). Assimilationist practices (especially in the area of language), while not overtly sanctioned at the policy level, were vigorously pursued (Tschanz, 1980). Indian participation on school boards is rare, and is generally limited to membership on native advisory committees (the power of appointment resting with the school board), or to native education councils on the reserves. The majority of school boards enrolling native children do not have a policy regarding native representation. In some school boards the need for native content and instruction in the native languages is receiving much-needed attention, but it is all too clear that in many others nothing is being done (C.E.A., 1984: 84).

The failure of these assimilationist efforts of schools to replace native languages and cultures is frequently explained in the literature by means of deficit theory. It is argued that native children fail to achieve conventional academic success because they are culturally and linguistically deficient (McShane & Berry, 1988).

Rarely are explanations couched in terms of the inability of the school system to provide an education that builds on, and reinforces, the cultural capital the children already possess. Nor are the efforts of native communities to resist cultural impoverishment and replacement taken into account. Yet this resistance helps to explain the persistence of native cultures in the face of assimilationist pressures, and contributes to our understanding of native efforts to reassert their treaty and aboriginal rights (Berry, 1980).

The rejection by the native peoples of assimilationist and officially bilingual models of Canadian society and schooling was dramatically revealed by the publication in 1972 of a seminal document Indian Control of Indian Education by the National Indian Brotherhood. Within its pages that the Royal Commission on Bilingualism and Biculturalism's view of Canada, that British and French cultures should dominate in the public schools, was resisted most explicitly and vigorously. In its place, an alternative philosophy of schooling was presented. This philosophy stressed that the school's primary responsibility towards native children was to promote and reinforce their own cultural identity. Native children needed to learn their own history, values, customs and language, if they were to take pride in their identity, and, if these goals were to be achieved, the hegemonic control of the white majority must be set aside. Authority for native education was to be placed firmly in the hands of the native peoples themselves.

More recently, calls for self-government in education for aboriginal peoples have reached their most sophisticated expression (if not widespread implementation) in the Northwest Territories, the population of which is composed of four major cultural groups: Inuit, Dene, Metis and Euro-Canadians. Yet even here, it should be noted, the overall governance of the school system resides in the hands of the Northwest Territories' Department of Education, and innovative developments fall into the category of administrative bodies possessing delegated, but limited executive powers.

In the Northwest Territories, "bilingualism" is interpreted to mean both official and aboriginal languages and this usually means Inuktitut-English, Slavey-English, Dogrib-English, Loucheux-English, Chipewyan-English or Inuvialuktun-English. Multiculturalism is stressed and, in an attempt to satisfy the many language development needs, the government has recognized the rights of communities to decide on native language programs and how they should be developed. In addition, normative curriculum outcomes have included the expectation that a high school graduate would be able to demonstrate "a knowledge of his/her own cultural background and an understanding of the multicultural, multi-ethnic nature of the Northwest Territories in particular, and of Canada in general" (Northwest Territories Department of Education, 1978: 1).

To reinforce these rights and goals, a number of innovative structures have been constructed. Depending on local and regional conditions, the local education authority may be either a community education committee, a community education society, or a regional educational society or authority. For example, in the Baffin region, Community Education Councils replaced committees and societies, and a Divisional Board of Education replaced the Baffin Regional Educational Society.

These new structures are all community-based and are designed to ensure that minority cultures shape the policies, curricula, staffing and operating procedures of publicly-funded schools. As such, they are being watched carefully by aboriginal groups and their organizations, both within the Northwest Territories and beyond. Attention is also being paid to the question of fiscal control. According to one knowledgeable observer, working models of aboriginal education require guarantees in both primary and subordinate legislation to prevent distortion of appropriate policies and procedures. According to Couture (1979) the "absolute democratization of Indian Education can only be possible under terms of absolute control of funding; the bottom line to all current transfer-to-local control projects is that the feds still hold the purse strings". Without control of these purse strings, it will be difficult if not impossible to establish "functional democracy" as opposed to the "guided democracy" of the past.

Changes such as those described above, while marking slow but positive progress in the development of aboriginal powers in education, are minor when compared to the possibilities inherent in current constitutuional debates concerning aboriginal self-government. Presently, these controversial discussions are focussing on the forms aboriginal self-government would take vis-a-vis existing governments. Three approaches are currently being discussed: delegation, devolution, and constitutional entrenchment.

The first, delegation, is unpopular with many of the native peoples; there are, as well, limits to delegation in Canadian federalism. The second, devolution, lies somewhere mid-way between delegation and constitutional entrenchment; it suggests turning responsibility for managing their own affairs over to the native peoples, and "implies an irrevocability to transfers of jurisdiction which is absent from the delegation model" (Boisvert, 1985: 72). The third, constitutional entrenchment, which is unacceptable to several provincial governments, involves amending the Constitution to recognize collective rights such as the right of aboriginal peoples to educate their own children, speak their own language, control their own membership and manage their own collective property.

What powers, authority and models of aboriginal self-government will follow are questions to which the answers vary considerably. The aboriginal peoples, being no more homogeneous than other Canadians, have no single model in mind. There are many possible forms of models, and their jurisdictional scope may vary widely depending upon the history and traditions of the groups involved (Boisvert, 1985).

Local ethnic government with dependent powers primarily of an administrative nature, of which existing Indian band governments are an example, is clearly not practical. In this model, local government powers would be essentially administrative and confined to such areas as culture, education and language, funded for the most part through conditional grants.

Local ethnic government with semi-autonomous powers, some of which are legislative, is a model being explored currently in Quebec. The preferred option of three of the four national aboriginal peoples' organizations is local ethnic government with substantial autonomy. This model most closely approximates the model recommended in the report of the House of Commons Special Committee on Indian Self-Government, popularly known as the Penner Report. This report recommended that, in addition to entrenching the right of Indian people to self-government in the Constitution, Indian First Nations governments with substantial legislative powers should be recognized through an Act of Parliament (Hawkes, 1985).

Despite the difficulties in reaching agreement, a number of significant points have already emerged. The most important of these is the political recognition at the governmental level, of the necessity for aboriginal peoples to possess some form of self-government if they are to participate in Canadian economic, political and social life, while at the same time, possessing the necessary autonomy and self-determination to develop their cultures. There is considerable evidence, too, that "the drive of aboriginal peoples for self-government will not be snuffed out. Failure would merely strengthen their resolve. Demands on governments to recognize aboriginal rights to self-government will not decrease, but rather they will increase. Public opinion and support for aboriginal peoples will not fall away, but will grow" (Hawkes, 1985: 97).

There is no going back. Now the focus is on establishing new institutions so that aboriginal peoples can make their own collective decisions. These include: local aboriginal governments; regional government; municipal government; national aboriginal special purpose bodies; band council government; aboriginal representation in national and regional governments; and even regional aboriginal governments in which aboriginal laws could be made paramount, and concurrent in at least specific fields such as cultural, social and educational policy. There is, moreover, no reason why experiments with all of these forms could not be carried out simultaneously to meet different situations across the country. Any attempt to apply "universal" models, processes or legal instruments would be ill-advised. Further, flexible approachs will have to be developed so as to accommodate diverse structures and allocations of policy responsibility (Hawkes, 1985), particularly where cultural, linguistic and educational policy is concerned.

CONCLUSION

The issue of aboriginal rights raises fundamental questions about the meaning of democratic pluralism in Canada. The matters raised, the questions involved, the processes, structural models and institutional forms under discussion -- all possess implications beyond their immediate consideration. They go to the heart of subordinate group concerns regarding their participation, or rather lack of it, in policy-setting and decision-making. They lie at the centre of minority group struggles to exercise control over the future development of their culatures, and, in a very direct manner, they pose questions of what is to be understood in Canada by individual, parental and group rights in public education. For example, what right does a racial, cultural, linguistic and ethnic majority group have to exist as a distinct collective within our political system? What rights do such groups have to protect their collective identities? What forms of participation are guaranteed in our legal, economic, political, social and public educational systems to ensure that these rights can be exercised? What structures, especially in the area of publicly-funded education, flow from the expression of these democratic rights in a dual and plural Canada?

Neither the assimilationist model of Canadian majority-minority relations, the dualist or bilingual-bicultural model, nor the hybrid multicultural- bilingual model, has offered much room for the continuance of native cultures. The current unequal distribution of economic and political powers, buttressed by white-dominated legal structures and social institutions, have further marginalized aboriginal cultures, languages and identities.

Publicly-funded educational systems have reinforced this process by placing litle or no value on the cultural capital native students bring to school. As the historical record reveals, however, aboriginal peoples have repeatedly resisted such deficit theories of cultural capital, vigorously opposed racially-biased models of schooling, and repeatedly drawn attention to the contradictions they contain.

Today, aboriginal peoples are systematically contesting the authenticity and legitimacy of current forms of public schooling, and the models of Canadian dualism and pluralism from which they are derived. They are insisting that their collective rights in this arena receive much greater political recognition than hitherto; new forms of governance are being introduced; and innovative educational structures are being established. New institutional forms are being developed, and differentiated school curricula and hiring patterns are more in evidence.

Such questions and the responses they have elicited in efforts to resolve the contradictions and tensions of Canadian dualism and pluralism are not restricted to questions of aboriginal rights. They are also central to the political and legal struggles of official and non-official language groups. Special interest group politics in education is gaining ground, and traditional structures are being modified and alternatives substituted. Majority group governance of publicly-funded systems of schooling is successfully being challenged. Institutional and curricular innovations are assuming a wide variety of forms in a variety of different contexts and locales (Mallea, 1984).

To date, however, these developments are largely unknown, rarely appreciated and frequently misunderstood. Why this is so remains to be investigated. And the explanatory power of the sociological theories discussed in this paper have much to offer in this regard. First, they stress the dialectical relationship between the universal and the particular, incorporate contributions from systems analyses and power-conflict theory, and recognize the impact of differential power relations in public education. Second, the articulation and application of the several forms of pluralism help explain the limitations of normative pluralism which to date has formed the basic "software" of Canadian politics. Dualism, it can be seen, is one form of pluralism and is capable of varying definitions and interpretations. Race and ethnicity are treated as important variables in their own right, and the reductionist tendency to subsume ethnic stratification under social stratification requires vigorous challenge.

These theories also reveal school systems for what they are: part of a much larger framework of economic, political and culatural systems. School systems are neither closed nor neutral systems. They are contested cultural and political sites within which existing relations and curricular content are often resisted and opposed. This resistance, moreover, is increasingly expressed in political terms, thereby underlining the fact that the resolution of the contradictions and tensions in our publicly-funded systems of education is primarily a political issue. Similarly, they point up the fact that studies of Canadian schooling have been conducted mainly from the perspective of dominant, not subordinate groups. To reverse this approach, to view schooling and its outcomes from the vantage point of minority groups, is essential if our understanding of theory as well as practice is to be advanced.

Finally, the utilization of concepts such as cultural hegemony, reproduction and legitimacy can be particularly useful in conducting in-depth analyses of internal processes of the school. Schooling is lived experience, and by combining these concepts and integrating them with the contributions of ethnographic studies, we can enhance our ability to resolve the contradictions and tensions inherent in current models of Canadian dualism and pluralism.

REFERENCES

Anisef, P. (1975). Consequences of ethnicity for educational plans among grade 12 students. In A. Wolfgang (Ed.), The education of immigrant students: Issues and consequences. Toronto: Institute for Studies in Education.

Apple, M. W. (1979). Ideology and curriculum. London: Routledge and Kegan Paul.

Augustine, J. (1984). Black studies or black-white studies? Currents, Fall.

Barton, L. & Walker, S. (Eds.). (1983). Race, class and education. London: Croon Helm.

Berry, J.W. (1971). Educational Opportunity for The Ontario Indian Population. Toronto: Commission on Post-Secondary Education.

Berry, J.W. (1980). Native peoples and the larger society. In R.C. Gardner & R. Kalin (Eds.), A Canadian Social Psychology of Ethnic Relations. Toronto: Methuen.

Berry, J.W., Kalin, R. & Taylor, D.M. (1977). Multiculturalism and Ethnic Attitudes in Canada. Ottawa: Supply and Services.

Boisvert, D. A. (1985). Forms of aboriginal self-government (Aboriginal peoples and constitutional reform, Background Paper No. 2). Kingston: Queen's University, Institute of Intergovernmental Relations.

Bourdieu, P. & Passeron, J.C. (1977). Reproduction in education, society and culture (R. Nice, Trans.). London: Sage Publication. (Original work published 1977).

Breton, R. et al. (1979). From a different perspective: French Canada and the issue of immigration and multiculturalism. TESL Talk.

Bullivant, B. (1981). The pluralist dilemma in education: six case studies. Sydney: Allan & Unwin.

Burnet, J. (1981). Multiculturalism ten years later. History and Social Science Teacher, Fall.

Canadian Education Association. (1984). Recent developments in native education. Toronto: Author.

Clement, W. (1975). The Canadian corporate elite: An analysis of economic power. Toronto: McClelland & Stewart.

Councils of Ministries of Education. (1978). Social sciences programs in Canada as of 1978-1979. Toronto: Author.

Couture, J. E. (1979). Secondary education for Canadian registered Indians, past, present, future: A commentary. Ottawa: Department of Indian and Northern Affairs.

Dahlie, H. (1983). Confessions of an immigrant's daughter. Canadian Ethnic Studies, 15(1).

Easton, E. (1957). The function of formal education in a political system. The School Review, 65(3).

Gibson, M. A. (1976). Approaches to multicultural education in the U.S.: Some concepts and assumptions. Anthropology and Education Quarterly, 7(4).

Giroux, H. A. (1981). Ideology, culture and the process of schooling. Philadelphia: Temple University Press.

Giroux, H. A. (1983). Theories of reproduction and resistance in the new sociology of education: A critical analysis. Harvard Educational Review, 53(3), 257-293.

Glazer, N. and Moynihan, D. (1975). Ethnicity: Theory and Experience. Cambridge: Harvard University Press.

Halebsky, S. (1976). Mass society and political conflict: Toward a reconstruction of theory. Cambridge: Harvard University Press.

Hawkes, D. C. (1985). Aboriginal self-government: What does it mean? Peoples and constitutional reform. Symposium conducted at The Institute of Intergovernmental Relations, Queen's University.

Herberg, E. N. (1980). Education through the ethnic looking-glass: Ethnicity and education in five Canadian cities. Unpublished doctoral dissertation, University of Toronto.

Hodgetts, A.B. (1968). What culture? What heritage? Toronto: The Ontario Institute for Studies in Education.

Hodgetts, A. B. and Gallagher, P. (1978). Teaching Canada for the 80's. Toronto: The Ontario Institute for Studies in Education.

Itzkoff, S. W. (1969). Cultural pluralism and American education. Scranton: International Textbook Company.

Karabel, J. and Halsey, A. H. (1976). The new sociology of education. Theory and Practice, 3(4).

King, A. J. C. (1968). Ethnicity and school adjustment. Canadian Review of Sociology and Anthropology, 5(2).

Mallea, J. R. (1977). Quebec's language policies: Background and response. Quebec: Les Presses de l'Université Laval.

Mallea, J. R. (1984). Cultural diversity in Canadian education: A review of contemporary developments. In R. Samuda, J.W. Berry & M. Laferrière (Eds.), Multiculturalism in Canada: Social and educational perspectives. Toronto: Allyn and Bacon.

Manicomn, A. (1984, October). Ideology and multicultural curriculum. Race, ethnicity and education: Critical perspectives Symposium, Toronto.

Martel, A. (1984). When the sunne shineth, make hay: Studies in perspective and power for Alberta minorities and the Canadian charter of rights and freedoms. Race, ethnicity and education: Critical perspectives Symposium, Toronto.

McLeod, K. A. (1979). Multiculturalism, bilingualism and Canadian institutions. Toronto: University of Toronto, Guidance Centre, Faculty of Education.

McLeod, K. A. (1979). Schooling for diversity; Ethnic relations, cultural pluralism, and education. TESL Talk.

McShane, D. & Berry, J.W. (1988). Native North American abilities. In S.H. Irvine & J.W. Berry (Eds.), Human abilities in cultural context. New York: Cambridge University Press.

Ministry of Supply and Services. (1981). Canadian charter of rights and freedoms. Ottawa, Canada. Author.

Mitter, W. (1984, July). Multicultural education in the perspective of comparative education. Considerations concerning conceptual and thematic foundations. Annual conference of the European Comparative Education Society, Würzburg.

Moodley, K. A. (1984). The ambiguities of multicultural education. Currents, Fall.

Moodley, K. A. (1981). Canadian ethnicity in comparative perspective. In J. Dahlie and T. Fernando (Eds.), Ethnicity, power and politics in Canada. Toronto: Methuen.

Moodley, K. A. (1983). Canadian multiculturalism as ideology. Ethnic and Racial Studies, 6(3).

Murphy, R. (1979). Sociological theories of education. Toronto: McGraw-Hill Ryerson.

Northwest Territories Department of Education: Education Programs and Evaluation Division. (1978). Philosophy of education in the Northwest Territories. Northwest Territories: Author.

Painchaud, R. (1976, February). The Franco-Canadians of Western Canada and multiculturalism. Second Canadian Consultative Conference on Multiculturalism, Ottawa.

Patel, D. (1980). Dealing with interracial conflict: Policy alternatives. Montreal: Institute for Research on Public Policy.

Porter, J. (1965). The vertical mosaic: An analysis of social class and power in Canada. Toronto: University of Toronto Press.

Pratt, D. (1975). The social role of school textbooks in Canada. In E. Zureik and R. Pike (Eds.), Socialization and values in Canadian society: Vol. 1, Carleton Library No. 84. Toronto: McClelland and Stewart.

Reitz, J. B. (1980). The survival of ethnic groups. Toronto: McGraw-Hill Ryerson.

Rideout, E. B. (1977). Policy changes of the ten Canadian provinces between 1967 and 1976 with respect to second-language learning and minority language education, as expressed in acts, regulations, directives, memoranda and policy statements of provincial departments and ministries of education. Department of the Secretary of State.

Rocher, G. (1972). Les ambiguités d'un Canada bilingue et multiculturel. Presented to the Canadian Sociology Association, Montreal.

Schermerhorn, R. A. (1970). Comparative ethnic relations: A framework for theory and research. New York: Random House.

Singleton, J. (1977). Education and ethnicity. Comparative Education Review, 21(2/3).

Shibutani, T. and Kwan, K. M. (Eds.), (1965). Ethnic stratification: A comparative approach. New York: Macmillan.

Smith, M. G. (1965). The plural society in the British West Indies. Berkeley: University of California Press.

Smolicz, J. J. (1979). Culture and education in a plural society. Canberra: The Curriculum Development Centre.

Smooha, S. (1978). Israeli pluralism and conflict. London: Routledge and Kegan Paul.

Sylvestre, P. F. (1980). Penetang: L'Ecole de la resistance. Ottawa: Editions Prise de Parole.

Thomas, B. (1984). Principles of anti-racist education. Currents, Fall.

Townsend, R. G. (1983). Orwell and the politics of equity. Journal of Educational Equity and Leadership, 3(3).

Traub, R. E. et al., (Eds.), (1976). Openness in schools: An evaluation study. Toronto: Ontario Institute for Studies in Education.

Trudeau, P. E. (1971, October). Federal government's response to book IV of the Royal Commission on bilingualism. Ottawa: House of Commons.

Tschanz, L. (1980). Native languages and government policy. London: University of Western Ontario, Centre for Research and Teaching of Canadian Native Languages.

Van den Burghe, P. (1973). Pluralism. In J. J. Honigmann (Ed.), Handbook of social and cultural anthropology. Chicago: Rand McNally.

Wardhaugh, R. (1983). Language and nationhood: The Canadian experience. Vancouver: New Star Books.

Watson, G. L. (1982). Social theory and critical understanding. Washington: University Press of America.

Williams, R. (1981). Culture. Glasgow: Fontana.

Willis, P. (1983). Cultural reproduction and theories of reproduction. In L. Barker and S. Walker (Eds.), Race, class and education (pp.107-138). London: Croon Helm.

Wirt, F.M. (1979, February). The stranger within my gate: Ethnic minorities and school policy in Europe. Comparative Education, 23(1).

Young, J.C. Ed. (1987). Breaking the mosaic, ethnic identities in Canadian schooling. Toronto: Garamond Press.

Werner, W. et al. (1974). Whose culture? Whose heritage? Ethnicity within social studies curricula. Vancouver: Centre for the Study of Curriculum and Information, Faculty of Education, University of British Columbia.

Part II

ACCULTURATION AND
PSYCHOLOGICAL ADAPTATION

ACCULTURATION AND PSYCHOLOGICAL ADAPTATION: A CONCEPTUAL OVERVIEW

J.W. Berry

Throughout the world, a process of culture contact and change has been taking place for millenia, and continues at an ever-increasing pace. In the past, conquest and enslavement were common, while nowadays migration (both voluntary and enforced) is the predominant experience. Individuals and groups must somehow deal with this process in all its dimensions: political, economic, cultural, social and psychological. In this chapter, the concepts of acculturation and adaptation will be employed to describe and analyse this overall chain of events from initial contact to the eventual outcome for individuals in their new society.

ACCULTURATION

A central concept in this chapter is that of acculturation; the process is represented schematically in Figure 1. Acculturation is a term which has been defined as culture change that results from continuous, first hand contact between two distinct cultural groups (Redfield, Linton and Herskovits, 1936). While originally proposed as a group-level phenomenon, it is now also widely recognized as an individual-level phenomenon, and is termed psychological acculturation (Graves, 1967). At this second level, acculturation refers to changes in an individual (both overt behaviour and covert traits) whose cultural group is collectively experiencing acculturation. It is important to note here that, while mutual changes are implied in the definition, in fact most changes occur in the non-dominant group (culture B) as a result of influence from the dominant group (culture A). It is on these non-dominant (or acculturating) groups that we will focus in trying to understand how people adapt psychologically during acculturation.

What kinds of changes may occur as a result of acculturation? First, physical changes may occur: a new place to live, a new type of housing, increasing population density, urbanization, more pollution

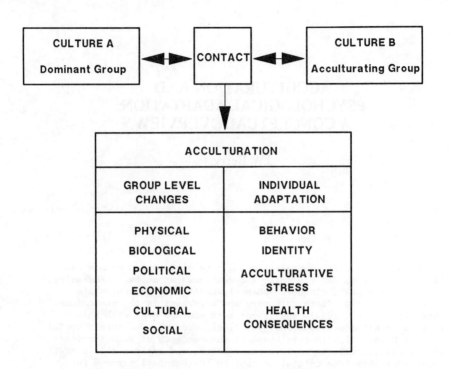

Figure 1. The Process of Acculturation and Adaptation

etc. Second, biological changes may occur: new nutritional status, and new diseases (often devastating in force). Third, political changes occur, usually bringing the non-dominant groups under some degree of control, and usually involving some loss of autonomy. Fourth, economic changes occur, moving away from traditional pursuits toward new forms of employment. Fifth, cultural changes (which are at the heart of the definition) necessarily occur: original linguistic, religious, educational and technical institutions become altered, or imported ones take their place. Sixth, social relationships become altered, including intergroup and inter-personal relations. Finally, numerous psychological changes occur at the individual level. Changes in behaviour are well-documented in the literature (see Berry, 1980 for a review); these include values, attitudes, abilities and motives. Existing identities and attitudes change and new ones develop: personal identity and ethnic identity often shift away from those held prior to contact, and views about how (and whether) one should participate in the process of acculturation emerge (see Berry, Kim, Power, Young & Bujaki, 1986); other attitudes (such as intergroup attitudes and lifestyle preferences) also change and develop during acculturation.

Stress phenomena, and related pathology, both appear during acculturation (see Berry, Kim, Minde & Mok, 1987). It is in these domains where much of the present concern lies, including the psychological, social and physical health consequences of acculturation. While these negative and largely unwanted consequences of acculturation are not inevitable, and while there are also opportunities to be encountered during acculturation, it is nevertheless the case that serious problems do appear in relation to acculturation (Berry and Kim, 1988). It is our view that these problems reside in the interaction between the two groups in contact, and that· they can be managed and ameliorated by identifying their specific source.

ADAPTATION

As employed here, adaptation is the generic term used to refer to both the process of dealing with acculturation and the outcome of acculturation (Dubos, 1965) It is proposed that there are different strategies of adaptation (as a process) that lead to different varieties of adaptation (as an outcome). For the individual, three such strategies have been identified (Berry, 1976). These have been termed adjustment, reaction, and withdrawal, and may be defined in the following way. In the case of adjustment, changes in the organism are in a direction which reduces the conflict (that is, increases the congruence or fit) between the environment and the organism by bringing it into harmony with the environment. In general, this strategy is the one most often intended by the term adaptation and may indeed be the most common form. In the case of reaction, changes are in a direction which retaliates against the environment; these may lead to environmental changes which, in effect, increase the congruence or fit between the two, but not by way of cultural or behavioural adjustment. In the case of withdrawal, change is in a direction which reduces the pressures from the environment; in a sense, it is a removal from the adaptive arena, and can occur either by forced exclusion or by voluntary withdrawal. It is important to note that the third strategy (withdrawal) is often not a real possibility for those being influenced by larger and more powerful cultural systems. And for the second strategy (reaction), in the absence of political power to divert acculturative pressures, many acculturating peoples cannot successfully engage in retaliatory responses. Thus, individual change in order to adapt to the context (some form of the adjustment strategy of adaptation) is often the only realistic alternative.

Parallelling these differing strategies of adaptation, there are varying ways in which individuals can acculturate. Corresponding to the view that adjustment is not the only strategy of adaptation, we take the view that assimilation is not the only mode of acculturation. This position becomes clear when we examine the framework proposed by Berry (1984). The model is based upon the observation that in culturally plural societies, individuals and groups must confront two important issues. One pertains to the maintenance and development of one's cultural distinctiveness in society; it must be decided whether one's own cultural identity and customs are of value and should be retained. The other issue involves the desirability of inter-ethnic contact, deciding whether relations with the larger society are of value and should be sought. These are essentially questions of attitudes and values and may be responded to on a continuous scale, from positive to negative. For conceptual purposes, however, they can be treated as dichotomous ("yes" or "no") decisions, thus generating a fourfold model (see Figure 2) that serves as the basis for our discussion. Each cell in this fourfold classification is considered to be an acculturation option (both a strategy and an outcome) available to individuals and to groups in plural societies. These four options are Assimilation, Integration, Separation and Marginalization.

When the first question is answered "no", and the second is answered "yes", the Assimilation option is defined, namely, relinquishing one's cultural identity and moving into the larger society. It can take place by way of absorption of a nondominant group into an established dominant group, or it can be by way of the merging of many groups to form a new society, as in the "melting pot" concept. In a detailed analysis of this form of acculturation, Gordon (1964) distinguishes a number of sub-varieties or processes; most important among these are cultural or behavioural assimilation, in which collective and individual behaviours become more similar, and structural assimilation, in which the non-dominant groups participate in the social and economic systems of the larger society. This is clearly the variety that most closely resembles the adjustment form of adaptation.

The Integration option implies some maintenance of the cultural integrity of the group (that is, some reaction or resistance to acculturative pressures) as well as the movement to become an integral part of a larger societal framework (that is, some adjustment). Therefore, in the case of Integration, the option taken is to retain cultural identity and move to join with the dominant society. In this situation, there are a number of distinguishable ethnic groups, all cooperating within a larger social system. Such

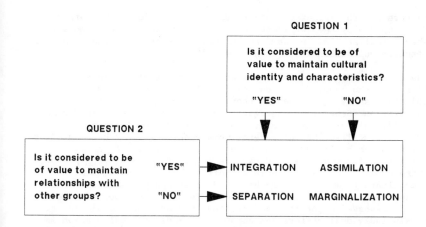

QUESTION 1

Is it considered to be of value to maintain cultural identity and characteristics?

"YES" "NO"

QUESTION 2

Is it considered to be of value to maintain relationships with other groups?

"YES"   INTEGRATION   ASSIMILATION

"NO"   SEPARATION   MARGINALIZATION

Figure 2. Four Modes of Acculturation

an arrangement may occur where there is some degree of structural assimilation but little cultural and behavioural assimilation, to use Gordon's terms.

When there are no substantial relations with the larger society, accompanied by a maintenance of ethnic identity and traditions, another option is defined. Depending upon which group (the dominant or nondominant), controls the situation, this option may take the form either of Segregation or of Separation. When the pattern is imposed by the dominant group, segregation to keep people in "their place" appears. On the other hand, the maintenance of a traditional way of life outside full participation in the larger society may be desired by the acculturating group and thus lead to an independent existence, as in the case of separatist movements (that is, reaction followed by withdrawal). In our terms, Segregation and Separation differ mainly with respect to which group or groups have the power to determine the outcome.

Finally, there is an option that is difficult to define precisely, possibly because it is accompanied by a good deal of collective and individual confusion and stress. It is characterised by striking out against the larger society and by feelings of alienation, loss of identity, and what has been termed acculturative stress (Berry & Annis, 1974). This option is Marginalization, in which groups lose cultural and psychological contact with both their traditional culture and the larger society (either by exclusion or withdrawal). When imposed by the larger society, it is tantamount to ethnocide. When stabilized in a nondominant group, it constitutes the classical situation of marginality (Stonequist, 1937).

The model in Figure 2 can be employed at four distinct levels. First, at the level of the dominant or larger society, national policies can be identified as those encouraging Assimilation, Integration, Separation/Segregation or Marginalization. In Canada, the official policy is clearly towards Integration (termed "multiculturalism" by the Federal Government), while other societies' policies can be identified as being toward various alternatives, using this framework. Second, at the level of acculturating groups, these communities can articulate their wishes and goals, and communicate them to their members and to the larger society. Third, at the level of individuals, attitudes toward these four alternatives can be assessed using standard attitude measurement techniques, to obtain individual preferences about which mode of acculturation is most desirable (see Berry et al., 1986, for a review of some empirical studies of acculturation attitudes). And, fourth, similar attitudes among individuals in the dominant society about how others should acculturate can be measured.

ACCULTURATING GROUPS

Although many of the generalities found in the literature about the effects of acculturation have been based on a single type of group, it is clear that there are many kinds of acculturating groups, and adaptations may vary depending upon this factor. In the review by Berry & Kim (1988), five different groups were identified including Immigrants, Refugees, Native Peoples, Ethnic Groups and Sojourners (see Figure 3). Among them there are variations in the degree of voluntariness, movement and permanence of contact, all factors which might affect the psychological adaptation of members of the group. Those who are voluntarily involved in the acculturation process (e.g., Immigrants) may experience less difficulty than those with little choice in the matter (e.g., Refugees and Native Peoples), since their initial attitudes toward contact and change may be more positive. Further, those only temporarily in contact and who are without permanent social supports (e.g., Sojourners) may experience more problems than those more permanently settled and established (e.g., Ethnic Groups). These distinctions suggest some important variations in how individuals will adapt during acculturation.

DOMINANT GROUPS

Variations in dominant groups also exist, and these variations may have implications for the adaptation of acculturating people. First, there are clear variations in the degree to which there is tolerance

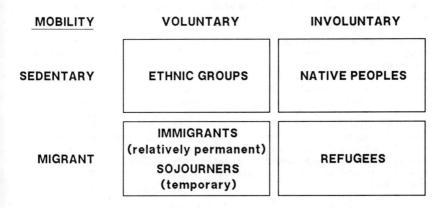

VOLUNTARINESS OF CONTACT

MOBILITY	VOLUNTARY	INVOLUNTARY
SEDENTARY	ETHNIC GROUPS	NATIVE PEOPLES
MIGRANT	IMMIGRANTS (relatively permanent) SOJOURNERS (temporary)	REFUGEES

Figure 3. Five Types of Acculturating Group

for the maintenance of cultural diversity. As Murphy (1965) has noted, tolerant (pluralist, multicultural) societies do not generally force individuals to change their way of life, and usually have established ethnic social support groups to assist individuals in the acculturation process. In contrast, assimilationist societies place more pressures on acculturating individuals to change, and often lack social supports for them. Both of these factors have clear implications for the social and mental health of acculturating individuals.

Second, even in relatively pluralistic and tolerant societies, all ethnic groups are not equally accepted; variations in ethnic attitudes in the larger society (including levels of prejudice and acts of discrimination) are well-documented for Canada (Berry, Kalin & Taylor, 1977), and for many other countries. The mental health effects of such intolerance (exhibited as rejection, antagonism, and conflict) have been suggested early on in the literature (e.g., Jahoda, 1960; WHO, 1983), but have not been well-studied up till now.

ACCULTURATIVE STRESS

The concept of stress has had wide usage in the recent psychological and medical literature (e.g., Lazarus, 1980; Selye, 1976), and it has sparked considerable controversy as well (e.g., Antonovsky, 1979; Selye, 1975). For the purposes of this chapter, stress is considered to be a generalized physiological and psychological state of the organism, brought about by the experience of stressors in the environment, and which requires some reduction (for normal functioning to occur), through a process of coping until some satisfactory adaptation to the new situation is achieved.

The concept of acculturative stress refers to one kind of stress, that in which the stressors are identified as having their source in the process of acculturation; in addition, there is often a particular set of stress behaviours which occur during acculturation, such as lowered mental health status (specifically confusion, anxiety, depression), feelings of marginality and alienation, heightened psychosomatic symptom level, and identity confusion. Acculturative stress is thus a phenomenon that may underlie a reduction in the health status of individuals (including physical, psychological and social aspects). To qualify as acculturative stress, these changes should be related in a systematic way to known features of the acculturation process, as experienced by the individual.

In a recent review and integration of the literature, Berry and Kim (1988) attempted to identify the cultural and psychological factors which govern the relationship between acculturation and mental health. We concluded that clearly, mental health problems often do arise during acculturation; however, these problems are not inevitable, and seem to depend on a variety of group and individual characteristics which enter into the acculturation process. That is, acculturation sometimes enhances one's life chances and mental health, and sometimes virtually destroys one's ability to carry on; the eventual outcome for any particular individual is affected by other variables that govern the relationship between acculturation and stress. This conception is illustrated in Figure 4. On the left of the figure, acculturation occurs in a particular situation (e.g., migrant community or native settlement), and individuals participate in and experience these changes to varying degrees; thus, individual acculturation experience may vary from a great deal to rather little. In terms used currently, acculturating individuals experience varying "life change events". In the middle, stressors may result from this varying experience of acculturation; for some people, acculturative changes may all be perceived as stressors, while for others, they may be benign or even seen as opportunities. On the right, varying levels of acculturative stress may become manifest as a result of acculturation experience and stressors.

The first crucial point to note is that relationships among these three concepts (indicated by the solid horizontal arrows) are probabilistic, rather than deterministic; the relationships are likely to occur, but are not fixed. The second crucial point is that these relationships all depend upon a number of moderating factors

48

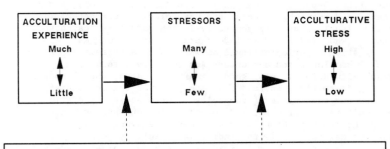

Figure 4. Factors Relevant to Acculturative Stress

(indicated in the lower box), including the nature of the larger society, the type of acculturating group, the mode of acculturation being experienced, and a number of demographic, social and psychological characteristics (including coping abilities) of the group and individual members. That is, each of these factors can influence the degree and direction of the relationships between the three variables at the top of Figure 4. This influence is indicated by the broken vertical arrows drawn between this set of moderating factors and the horizontal arrows.

One of these moderating factors, as we have already seen, is the nature of the host or larger society: is there a pluralist or multicultural ideology (with attendant tolerance for cultural diversity), or is there an assimilationist ideology (with pressures to conform to a single cultural standard)? As we have noted, arguments, and some evidence, exist (e.g., Murphy, 1965) that social and psychological problems may be less among acculturating persons in plural societies than in assimilationist ones.

Other variables identified by Berry and Kim (1988) were the nature of the acculturating group (Immigrants, Refugees, Native Peoples, Ethnic Groups and Sojourners), modes of acculturation (Assimilation,

Integration, Separation/Segregation and Marginalization), and a
variety of demographic, social and psychological characteristics of
the individual. These are generally in the domain of "psychosocial
factors" (WHO, 1979) and include characteristics such as
pre-migration experiences (such as war, torture or famine), prior
cultural knowledge and encounters (essentially a form of
"pre-acculturation"), age, gender, marital status, social supports, a
sense of "cognitive control" that one has over the acculturation
process, and the degree of congruity between one's expectations about
the acculturation process, and the realities one has encountered
during the process. Of particular importance among these
psychological factors is the individual's ability to cope with
acculturative experience; individuals are known to vary widely in how
they deal with major changes in their lives (Lazarus & Folkman,
1984), resulting in large variation in the level of stress
experienced. Many other factors appear in the literature, but in our
review these seemed to be the most theoretically relevant, and
empirically-consistent, predictors of acculturative stress.

CONCLUSIONS

This conceptual overview is intended to provide a framework for
understanding how individuals adapt during the process of
acculturation. It may also serve as a general introduction to many
of the chapters that follow in this section. The essential message
is that there are likely to be wide individual and group differences
in how people work their way between cultures. We, as cross-cultural
psychologists, should be prepared to make our concepts and
instruments as wide-ranging as the phenomena we are likely to
encounter when studying and serving acculturating individuals.

REFERENCES

Antonovsky, A. (1979). Health, Stress and Coping. San
   Francisco: Jossey-Bass.

Berry, J.W. (1976). Human Ecology and Cognitive Style: Comparative
   Studies in Cultural and Psychological Adaptation. London: Sage.

Berry, J.W. (1980). Social and cultural change. In: H.C. Triandis
   and R. Brislin (Eds) Handbook of Cross-cultural Psychology, Vol.
   5, Social, Boston: Allyn and Bacon.

Berry, J.W. (1984). Cultural relations in plural societies:
   Alternatives to segregation and their sociopsychological
   implications. In N. Miller and M. Brewer (Eds) Groups in
   Contact. New York: Academic.

Berry, J.W. & Annis, R.C. (1974). Acculturative stress. Journal of Cross-cultural Psychology, 5, 382-406.

Berry J.W., Kalin, R. & Taylor, D.M. (1977). Multiculturalism and Ethnic Attitudes in Canada. Ottawa: Government of Canada.

Berry, J.W. & Kim, U. (1988). Acculturation and mental health. In: P. Dasen, J.W. Berry and N. Sartorius (Eds) Health and Cross-cultural Psychology: Towards Applications. London: Sage.

Berry, J.W., Kim, U., Minde, T., & Moke, D. (1987). Comparative studies of acculturative stress. International Migration Review, 21, 491-511.

Berry, J.W., Kim, U., Power, S., Young, M. & Bujaki, M. (1986). Acculturation attitudes in plural societies. Unpublished paper under review.

Berry, J.W., Trimble, J. & Olmeda, E. (1986). The assessment of acculturation. In: W.J. Lonner & J.W. Berry (Eds), Field Methods in Cross-Cultural Research. London: Sage.

Dubos, R. (1965). Man Adapting, New Haven: Yale University Press.

Gordon, D. (1972). Assimilation in American Life. New York: Oxford University Press.

Graves, T. (1967). Psychological acculturation in a tri-ethnic community, South-western Journal of Anthropology, 23, 337-350.

Jahoda, M. (1960). Race Relations and Mental Health. Paris: UNESCO.

Lazarus, R.S. (1980). Psychological stress and adaptation: some unresolved issues. In: Selye's Guide to Stress Research, 1. Edited by H. Selye. New York: Van Nostrand Reinhold.

Lazarus, R.S. & Folkman, S. (1984). Stress Appraisal and Coping. New York: Springer.

Murphy, H.B.M. (1965). Migration and the major mental disorders: A reappraisal. In: M.B. Kantor (Ed.). Mobility and Mental Health. Springfield: Thomas.

Murphy, H.B.M. (1977). Migration, culture and mental health. Psychological Medicine, 1, 677-684.

Redfield, R., Linton, R. & Herskovits, M.J. (1936). Memorandum on the study of acculturation. American Anthropologist, 38, 149-152.

Selye, H. (1975). Confusion and controversy in the stress field. Journal of Human Stress, 1, 37-44.

Selye, H. (1976). The Stress of Life (Rev. Ed.). New York: McGraw-Hill.

Stonequist, E.V. (1937). The Marginal Man, New York: Scribner.

World Health Organization (1979). Psychosocial factors and health: New programme directions. In: P. Ahmed & G. Coelho (Eds.), Towards a New Definition of Health, New York: Plenum.

World Health Organization (1983). Apartheid and Health. Geneva: WHO.

REFUGEE ADAPTATION:
BASIC RESEARCH ISSUES AND APPLICATIONS

W.B. Emminghaus
Refugee Department
German Red Cross
Bonn, FR Germany

In the development of cross-cultural psychology at least two approaches can be distinguished. First, there is a scientific interest in the question whether "psychological laws", as developed in European and European-derived countries, can be regarded as really universal (see Triandis 1980, IACCP 1983). This aspect can be conceived of as that of a self-governing process of scientific development. Second, psychologists are called upon to contribute to the solution of problems that arise in society itself for other (e.g. economic, political) reasons. For example, the increase in the numbers of encounters between members of different countries can be regarded as such an external reason. There is a considerable amount of "migration" in part short-term (as in tourism and student exchange programs), and in part long-term (as in work migration and in the case of the world refugee problem).

Although practical work cannot and should not be conceived as purely application of theory, problems that arise from these migratory movements challenge theory formation and can be seen as (external) incitement conditions for the (internal) development of science. Both aspects, the internal logic of scientific theory-building, as well as the claims implicitly or explicitly expressed by society, can be regarded as important issues in the development of science (see Kuhn 1962). They do not, however, always merge, since practical problems call for immediate action and theory-building is engaged in long-range reflection. Very often the most complex problems have to be given priority in practical work, whereas scientific efforts, such as experimentally oriented research, have to look for rather simple cases to investigate clear-cut theoretical interrelationships.

In this respect, it may not be accidental that most of the psychological research on groups in culture-contact situations has been done with exchange students and that refugees, in spite of their number, have not yet assumed an important position in cross-cultural psychology (Berry & Kim, 1988). Since they form persons suffering in intercultural contexts, it seems to be justifiable to examine the situation of this group more carefully, explaining their life conditions and posing questions for theory formation in cross-cultural psychology in general. These might be influential for more basic issues and for other groups in bi-cultural settings as well.

The cross-cultural psychologist in the field of application has an intermediate position between theory and practice. On the one hand, theoretical knowledge has to be examined regarding its usefulness for practical purposes, and on the other hand the practitioner can be used by scientists as a resource person for real-life situations. These situations do not actually present themselves as psychological ones, but need to be interpreted as such. For the society, refugees quite often form just one marginal group that could be approached as others by both practitioners and researchers.

In this chapter we want to present the refugee's situation as comprehensively as possible, including the social and political context, and to apply a psychological frame-work. We will see that a modified understanding of concepts from cross-cultural psychology and an extension of research efforts will then be required. The Federal Republic of Germany has been chosen as a well-suited context for this analysis, since there is a unique constellation of different refugee groups in this country.

CULTURE-SHOCK, CROSS-CULTURAL ENCOUNTERS, AND INTER-CULTURAL CONFLICTS

There are different approaches in psychology regarding the conceptualization, as well as the treatment of, disturbances in psychological well-being. At least two vantage points can be differentiated for the refugee problem, that of a clinician working in a bi-cultural situation and that of the social-psychological approach of a cross-cultural psychologist seeing refugees just as one (especially disadvantaged) group in a culture-contact situation. The terms <u>culture shock</u> and <u>inter-cultural conflict</u> stand for these approaches respectively.

<u>Culture-Shock: The Traditional View</u>. Psychologists as practitioners very often adhere to the specialization of clinical psychology which has a considerable affinity with mental hospitals and clinics. Refugee assistance is no exception, and an overlap of psychiatric and psychological issues is only natural: in earlier times Pedersen (1949), for instance, used the term "refugee neurosis", when describing severe psychopathological reactions; much more common, and broader in its meaning, is the term "culture shock" coined by Oberg (1960) to comprise the difficulties engendered when an individual enters a different culture. Whereas for Pedersen paranoid reactions can be found quite regularly in refugees, the core of Oberg's concept of culture shock is "the anxiety that results from losing all our familiar signs and symbols of social intercourse" (1960, p. 177); in any case someone subjected to such experiences can be seen as "a sick

person with a mild or severe case of culture shock as the case may be" (1960, p. 189). For Foster (1962) "culture shock is a mental illness" and he describes it as "a malady, an occupational disease of people, who has been suddenly transplanted abroad" (cf Arnold 1967, p. 53). The conceptualizations mentioned so far are clearly of psychiatric origin. The authors themselves have a medical background, apply a medical model of explanation, or follow a model that is connected with medicine (e.g., psychoanalysis). Epidemiological studies on migrants, including refugees, also very often follow a mental illness model that is derived from a medical analysis.

Within psychology this mental illness model has been much criticized for its emphasis on (1) internal conditions in the diagnosis of psychological disturbances, (2) the treatment of the affected individual alone, who (3) is labeled as ill, adopting the appropriate social role. Critics of that model traditionally can be found in (social-) learning theory, which attributes a more important influence, in the areas of assessment and treatment, to the social environment (e.g., Kanfer & Phillips, 1970; Tharp & Wetzel, 1969).

This general discussion has had its concomitants in the area of culture-contact situations. Furnham & Bochner (1982), for instance, discard the traditional view of culture shock and apply Argyle's approach of social skill learning for training sojourners in a culturally new environment. Higginbotham & Tanaka-Matsumi (1981) explicitly follow Tharp & Wetzel (1969) and redefine culture shock for their purpose of counselling across cultures by analyzing "specific experiences and behaviors of the individual in a new environment". An agreement seems to exist that the social environment has to be taken into account systematically in order to explore and to treat the difficulties that someone experiences when entering a strange culture. How this inclusion is to be made still remains an open question: for instance, is the "natural environment" that learning theories claim to include sufficient for the systematic and adequate consideration of cultural environment, and can the resulting difficulties in culture-contact situations traditionally subsumed under the term culture shock be explained? The refugee's situation in particular seems to call for an approach that focuses more on an interactional relationship between culture and individual that could be named cross-cultural encounter.

Cross-Cultural Encounters: Inter-Actions. According to the definition given by the United Nations High Commissioner for Refugees (UNHCR) a refugee is any person, who "owing to a well-founded fear of being persecuted for reasons of race, religion, nationality or political opinion, is outside the country of his nationality, or owing to such fear, is unwilling to avail himself of the protection of that country" (cf Goldschmidt & Boesch 1983, p. 17). This definition formulated for the purpose of international law implies that a person is not just living in a new natural and social environment that one has to adapt to or that one has to relearn.

Rather, one finds oneself the target of influences stemming from the surrounding social environment. This becomes obvious also by emphasizing, as Kunz (1973, 1981) does, that refugees are _pushed_ out of a country rather than being (as supposedly other migrants are) _pulled_ to a country of destination, or when the involuntariness of migration is made the defining psychological criterion for refugees (see Berry et al., 1987). The importance of (home and host) culture becomes most evident in Boesch's description of the refugee's situation as one changing "from expulsion to hospitality" (1983, p. 53). Culture then has to be seen as actively contributing to the psychological problems as well as to the psychological well-being of the refugee.

The interrelationship between culture and the individual has been widely discussed in cross-cultural psychology. The specific kind of interaction in the refugee's case might lead to a better understanding of the clinical problems as well. In his metamethodological analysis Eckensberger (1979) differentiated five metaphysical models conceptualizing the relationship between individual and environment. One of his touchstones was the explanatory power of a theoretical approach for the concept of culture itself. His conclusion is that within _action theories_ both individual _and_ culture can be conceptualized. The opposition of environment and individual is overcome thereby, since man, by realizing his goals, is changing his environment which, in turn, may alter his goals. This model assumes a _dialectical_ relationship between individual and culture and presupposes the concept of a _reflexive human being_.

We follow this point of view in principle, but know from theoretical analysis and practical experience that in the refugee's situation the confrontation between individual and culture is not, in fact, nullified. Instead, it is - to use Hegel's notion - _aufgehoben_, which includes both that it is revoked _and_ preserved. Action theory should be termed here more adequately as a theory of _inter-action_, and both culture and individual seen as agents. This means that culture is following goals as the individual does, is choosing between alternative means, is calculating consequences of actions (intended and unintended) and can be seen as responsible for its actions. In the case of correspondence between the respective goals, then, there is also in fact no confrontation between individual and culture; there are, however, incompatibilities, which we would like to emphasize here for the case of refugees so that _conflicts_ are not rare. Refugees have been (a) excluded from participation in the home country, and (b) are subjected to regulations in the host country. There is nothing like a relationship based on mutual consent between the refugee and his cultural environment anymore. The core of the problem then is not one of individual culture shock, but one of conflict-laden encounters between culture and individual. Such conflicts may already arise in the home culture; but also in the host country situation the difficulties, as seen from this interactional point of view, are due more to the fact that someone becomes (or is kept) alienated by a culture or society, than simply to the fact of being alien in an unknown environment.

<u>Locus of Conflict: Situation in the Host Country</u>. The situation in the host country is (since it is a bi- or multi-cultural one) of specific interest for the cross-cultural psychologist and, in addition, the action field for the psychologist as a practitioner. When the refugee arrives in the host country there is, of course, relief about having successfully escaped the persecution by his respective home country. Very soon this experience is followed by frustration and difficulties, and psychological help may be needed. From a cross-cultural point of view, the inter-actions between host country and the refugee have to be examined. The main points are summarized in Table 1 in which there are different kinds of refugee groups, (only one of which has the refugee status according to UNHCR) that can be found in the Federal Republic of Germany, and the legal regulations that are applied to members of the respective groups. We restrict ourselves here to those regulations that have some impact on the individual's aspirations or needs.

Legal regulations as described in the table have to be interpreted <u>bi-directionally</u>: for the <u>individual</u> they form opportunities for, or barriers against, the pursuit of their goals, for the <u>society</u> they are the means for the realization of specific political goals. These political intentions and their manifestations in laws and administrative regulations are named here (in part also by political leaders) as <u>deterrent</u> for asylum-seekers, as <u>receptive</u> for bona-fide refugees, and as <u>integrative</u> for recognized refugees. For a specific group of refugees who are seen to be Germans by law, (i.e. resettlers/*Volksdeutsche*, from Eastern and South-Eastern European countries, and also for migrants from the GDR) <u>support</u> or even <u>compensation</u> is aimed at. Individuals may pass through different legal statuses, a process that very often takes a long time (up to seven years). The well-being of the refugee will be dependent to a large extent on the progress he makes in these legal matters.

Changes in the process of acculturation, lasting many years, have been reported in the relevant literature, and the contribution of features of the dominant or host country has been acknowledged (see Furnham & Bochner, 1986; Berry & Kim, 1988). Our inter-actional approach can be seen as an extension of these analyses by focusing on the conflict <u>between</u> individual and society (instead of intrapersonal conflicts alone), and by identifying legal regulations as the locus of conflict.

Oberg's observation that "you talk as if the difficulties are more or less created by the people of the host country for your special discomfort" (1960, p. 178), therefore, should not be taken too lightly as a perceptual distortion leading to a diagnosis of culture shock as a mental illness. As can be seen in the case of the refugees, (but might also be true, even if less obvious, for other groups as well) it can also be an adequate description of the

Table 1: Refugee versus Society: Legal Regulations as Locus of Conflict Between Society's and Individual's Intentions for Refugee Groups with Different Legal Status (Federal Republic of Germany)

Legal Status	Intentions of Individual (Needs)	Law Regulations		Intentions of Society (policy)
		Barrier for Individual	Means of Society	

Asylum-Seeker	Shelter
	Food
	
	Freedom of Movement
	
	Family Unity
	
	Education of Children
	
	Working/Labour
	
	Health Care
		Temporary Residence Permit:
		- Assembly Camp
		- Collective Feeding as a Rule
		
		- Locally Restricted
		
		- Nuclear Relationships
		  guaranteed, not from home
		
		- No Obligation, nor Right
		  for School/Kindergarten
		
		- Not before 5(1) year waiting
		  Social Welfare
		
		- Generally Reduced to Minimum
				(administrative facilitation)
				" deterrent "

"bona fide" Refugee (recognized, but still pending)	Freedom of Movement Shelter Working/Labour	Temporary Residence Permit: - Exceptions of Restrictions - Decentralized/Private - Permitted, but as Not-Advantaged Foreigner		"receptive"
Refugee(UNHCR) (granted asylum) also: quota refugees	Freedom of Movement Work/Labour Family Unity Schooling	Travel Document for Refugees: - Residence Permit Unlimited - Work Permit Equivalent to Citizens - Unification also from Abroad/ Home Country - Obligatory (Right and Duty)		Integration

Resettlers "Volksdeutsche" Migrants from GDR ('Zuwanderer')	the same as above	Citizen Passport:
		- all Rights of Citizens, Recognition
		  of Claims Acquired in Country of
		  Origin
				Support/Compensation

societal reality. Our argument might become clearer if we consider
that individuals from the same culture may adopt different legal
statuses, and that individuals coming from different countries are
subsumed under the same legal category.
The refugee then can be seen from two vantage points: regarding
their country of origin, they can be ranked on a dimension of
cultural distance (see Table 2), where asylum-seekers form the most

Table 2: Culture distance and legal/political distance
as two "dimensions" of the situation of refugees
from different countries (examples)

		Groups	Dimension A: Cultural distance (ref. home culture/ country of origin)		
			"near"	"inter-mediate"	"far"
Dimension B: Legal and political distance (ref. host culture/ country of residence)	supportive	RESETTLERS (Volksdeutsche)	Poland Czecheslovakia Romania	USSR	
	integrative	REFUGEES(UNHCR) (also quota refugees)	Poland Romania Hungary	Turkey Iran Afghanistan Ethiopia	Sri Lanka Ghana ⟨Vietnam⟩ ⟨Cambodia⟩
	deterrent	ASYLUM-SEEKERS	Yugoslavia Romania Poland	Turkey Iran Afghanistan Ethiopia	Vietnam Cambodia
	recruited	GUEST WORKERS (non-refugees)	Yugoslavia Italy	Turkey Maroc	Korea Philip-pines

distant, resettlers the nearest group. The relative contribution of
the two "factors" to the refugee's well-being still has to be
investigated. This can be done by comparing individuals from the
same country of origin, but with a different legal status (Vietnamese
refugees vs Vietnamese asylum-seekers, asylum-seekers vs resettlers
from Poland are examples) and by comparing refugees from different
countries with the same legal status (e.g. Vietnamese vs Polish
asylum-seekers) and combinations thereof (see also Berry et al.
1987).

CONFLICT SOLUTION AND INTER-CULTURAL ENCOUNTERS

There is, as we have tried to show, considerable evidence that the
problems of refugees have their origins in, or at least are sustained
by, the (conflict-laden) inter-action with the host society. It
seems to be evident to us that the resentment of strangers that is
often regarded as an expression of xenophobia, is also at least in
part dependent on legal ascriptions and political evaluations; one
example is the changes in the attitude towards the Vietnamese
refugees, who were welcomed by the German citizens in 1979, but now
are (as asylum-seekers) discredited as "welfare refugees". It is an
open question whether policy can be seen as a rationalization for
xenophobia (see Boesch, 1983), or whether xenophobia is a consequence
or concomitant of the exclusions manifested in political decisions.
Conflicts do exist, however, with the society and its members. The
goals pursued are not compatible in every respect, and the legal
situation demonstrates that quite impressively.

Conflict solution as the goal of psychology. Within the general
theoretical frame-work of action theory one aim of empirical research
is to predict favourable and unfavourable events and to suggest
actions fostering positive outcomes. The truth of empirical research
has to be construed by a consensus of scientists as regards their
terminology and their goal of scientific action (Werbik 1974, p. 17).
The choice of a specific question and the proposal of specific
actions need to be justified by a criterion that is different from
the plea for truth. We follow Werbik (1974, pp. 45ff), who
explicitly presents conflict solution as the goal of psychology as a
science and in application. Every situation in which two people
pursue incompatible goals is called an "interpersonal conflict", and
a conflict solution is attained by changing the situation in such a
way that both can reach their goals without hindering the other in
the attainment of his goal. This mode of analysis can be transferred
to the situation of the refugee in the host country, since it can be
interpreted as one of inter-action with the refugee and the country
as conflicting agents.

Werbik suggests three main principles for conflict solution, namely a
principle of deliberation (*Beratungsprinzip*) and a principle of
morality (*Moralprinzip*). Whereas the former implies that everyone in
the conflict gets the opportunity to express his wishes and goals
freely and without restrictions (the emergence of internal conflicts

by suppressing own desires is meant to be avoided by that), the content of the latter is normative, encouraging both partners to find or construct superordinate goals that are apt to fulfill their aspirations, but avoids the original incompatibility (the external conflict is meant to be solved by that). These two principles together form a third, the principle of conflict solution (Konfliktlösungsprinzip) and can, from our point of view, be employed in the solution of inter-cultural conflicts of the refugee as well. For culture-contact situations Bochner (1982, p. 16) and Klineberg (1982, p. 53) follow a similar line of reasoning by their emphasis on equal status and superordinate goals as major pre-requisites for arriving at better relations. Culture contacts that fulfill these conditions can justly be called inter-cultural encounters and should replace inter-cultural conflicts.

Levels of intervention. From the theoretical framework presented so far we can conclude that the balancing of the interests of the country and of the individual has to be pursued. This is a goal that is difficult to attain. In culture development all the meaningful powers of the society contribute to the pursuit of a goal of this kind. Psychological interventions must find their place within this process, being aware of their limited possibilities but taking the chances that nonetheless are given. In therapeutic social work it has been suggested that levels of intervention are differentiated according to their goals. Three intervention types of different scope are presented, namely causal goals, compensatory goals, and props (see Linden & Hoffmann, 1976). This differentiation originally was made to take into account the modifiability of the individual, which may vary according to the seriousness of his disturbance, his age, and other variables of this kind. With regard to our issue of "refugee in host-country" the problem is not located in the individual alone. It is not (or at least not predominantly) a deficiency in the means of the individual that has to be considered, but the resistance and threats stemming from outside, i.e. the societal conditions. The graduation of the scope of interventions then should be oriented at the barriers erected for the individual by society. A causal approach, therefore, is to be directed at the level of policy and institutions, a compensatory approach is best directed at the administration to influence the application of the law, or at the interpersonal level, where inter-cultural encounters can be fostered to remove interindividual misunderstandings and resentment; an intervention that could be named as offering props takes the situation as given (in a way that natural conditions can be taken as givens) and tries either to enhance the frustration tolerance of the individual or teach him some coping skills. Different activities of the psychologist and of other professionals (e.g. social workers) and volunteers in practical refugee assistance can be subsumed under one of these headings; all forms of intervention have their respective value and realize different types of encounter and conflict-solution (see Table 3). We will give some examples here; a more comprehensive presentation can be found elsewhere (see Emminghaus, 1988).

Level of Intervention	Type of Encounter	Type of Solution
CAUSAL (policy)	<u>society-minority</u> considerate law-making by political parties in parliaments	<u>multiculturalism</u> protection of minorities, equal participation in society
COMPENSATORY (administration)	<u>society-individual</u> law application by individual officials	<u>balancing of interests</u> settlement of single cases as exceptions
(inter-actional)	<u>individual-individual</u> functional equivalence of culture-specific actions	<u>understanding and sympathy</u> mutual tolerance and and acceptance of differences
"PROPS" (actional)	<u>individual</u> deficiencies in means and personal effectiveness in coping	<u>adaptation</u> learning a new (social) environment

<u>Props</u>. Refugees are supported individually and encounters are of only minor importance. First aid activities in securing the basic facilities of life belong in this category. As a cross-cultural psychologist, during training sessions or in individual meetings, one just informs the refugee about the way one should behave in order to get positive consequences or avoid negative ones in a new social environment. Argyle's social skills training can be placed here, the goal of which is to master social situations (see Furnham & Bochner 1982, p. 165). Argyle has developed his theory following the paradigm of perceptual and motor skills and therefore it may not be a surprise that social and cultural reactions are only considered as feedback for the effectiveness of skills applied and (mutual) interactions are represented only marginally. The same might apply to the approach of Tharp and Wetzel (1969) and its application to culture-contact situations by Higginbotham & Tanaka-Matsumi (1981), since the "natural environment" that they intend to include is analysed only in terms of reinforcing events, without giving any systematic value to the interactive quality of culture-individual relationships.

The psychologist then is the one with the knowledge of the host country and his task is mainly one of "teaching". Examples from our practical work are (a) reminding refugees of the importance of written (vs oral) communication in our country, (b) emphasizing the importance of time limits in legal and everyday matters, (c) explaining rules in the camp or in private accommodation (e.g. times of rest) and (d) in general teaching them to meet the expectations that inhabitants of the host country might have regarding the style of conversation (e.g. keeping eye contact adequately, keeping the right bodily distance). On the other hand, (and this is a more clinical aspect) the refugee is supported when he is likely to break down. This means that psychologists are (a) offering individual counselling, (b) initiating withdrawal treatment in the case of alcoholism and the acquisition of control behaviors, (c) enhancing resistance strength of psychosomatically affected or depressive persons (e.g. through sports).

All these examples are seen as just props, since they do not influence the inter-action direction. The knowledge of the cross-cultural psychologist is needed; as an expert, he can give information about how to adapt to the new environment. In this realm he is not employed to facilitate bi-directional inter-actions, but to shape culturally adequate action. The refugee, by learning new skills, becomes "less visible" and remains marginal in the host country.

Compensatory Goals: Interpersonal Encounters. Within the scope of compensatory interventions interpersonal encounters are initiated. This approach represents more than mere adaptation, but less than an essential change (which has to be made on a political level). The compensatory approach is directed at inter-actions with individuals. These form inciting conditions for a mutual understanding that is based on a respectful appreciation of two different culture-specific ways of acting rather than an adaptation on the part of the refugee. Some examples from the practical experience of a cross-cultural psychologist are: the elucidation of phenotypically different conversation styles to illustrate that although a conversation may start with personal matters in Asian cultures and more distant topics in Western cultures, both styles serve the same genotypically superordinate goal, namely the expression of respect for the conversation partner; and pointing to the fact that the indirect approach of Asians as well as "coming to the point soon" as Westerners do, both are shown to be equivalent insofar as the common goal of tension relief in conversation is concerned.

Cross-cultural psychologists also prepare formal situations that are meaningful for different participating culture-groups (including Germans as inhabitants of the host country), and an exchange of different culture-dependent meanings is prompted. Examples are cooking activities, table manners, and children's parties. Again commonalities in meaning behind manifest differences are made obvious, such as (a) that different ingredients for meals serve the same goal aiming at healthy nourishment in differing climatic environments, (b) that table manners serve the common goal of showing peacefulness and separating food-taking from other tabooed areas such

as toilet-habits (keeping left hand below the table) or sexuality
(keeping both hands on the table), (c) that leaving something on the
plate (as Japanese do), or clearing it completely (as Germans do)
serve the same goal, namely to show gratefulness and satisfaction to
the cook; (d) during children's play activities, parents of different
cultural origin are made to recognize that differing forms of child-
rearing are just culture-specific efforts to reach an optimal balance
of the dependence-independence antagonism.

Within all these areas the cross-cultural psychologist assumes the
role of a mediator who has to make sure that everyone can express
themselves and give explanations for their cultural habits. All of
these ways of acting have their respective value, taking common goals
as a reference point of evaluation, and new ones can be elaborated
such as arriving at interdependence as a solution of the dependence-
independence issue in child-rearing. Just as academic cross-cultural
psychologists are struggling with matters of <u>functional equivalence</u>
in finding suitable indicators for psychological constructs (e.g.
Sears, 1961), refugees and inhabitants of the host country, as "naive
cross-cultural psychologists", detect culture-specific actions as
different but equivalent means serving one common goal. The cross-
cultural psychologist in the role of a consultant is just a
facilitator of such constructive communication. These examples
should be seen as only compensatory, since the conflict analyses and
solutions of this kind are done on an interpersonal level where the
solution of the basic antagonism of individual vs society cannot be
approached. Neither assimilation (suppressing the idiosyncrasies of
the refugee), nor segregation (no interconnections are fostered) are
aimed at, but the respectful recognition of at least two ways of life
and the broadening of the respective action potential. This approach
is extended by including key persons in different areas such as
teachers and kindergarten personnel, staff members of hospitals and
officials of welfare offices, who are supervised by psychologists.

<u>Compensatory Goals: Refugees vs Administration</u>. Legal regulations
that are seen here as the core of the refugee's difficulties are
applied by officials in adminstration. There is always some leeway
for the specific case that can be used in favour of the refugee and
his needs. Examples from the cross-cultural practical work referring
to some of the restrictions named in Table 1 are: (a) the extension
of the claim of family unification of asylum-seekers, including the
different meaning of extended (vs nuclear) family in most of the
third world cultures, (b) the permission of a common residence for
husband and wife, for couples not (yet) married in terms of civil
marriage, but according to traditional rites, and (c) the exception
from residence restrictions for participation in culture-specific
occasions such as circumcision rituals, menarche celebrations,
funerals or other family affairs.

The cross-cultural psychologist as a practitioner again is fostering
the mutual understanding of refugees and German officials. He tries
to attain benevolence for the refugee, disclosing pan-human and

64

humanitarian aspects in cultural peculiarities. If the wishes
of the refugee cannot be fulfilled (as is often the case), this is
explained by the psychologist who supplies information about the laws
and their reasons. The refugee thereby is prevented from developing
paranoic ideas and from attributing the restrictions personally to
himself. The aspirations of the individual and the necessities of
the administration are to be balanced in this type of encounter.

Causal Goals: Influencing Policy. Since it follows from our analysis
that the refugee's problem stem from laws and their derivation from
policies, politicians should be approached as well. Psychologists
sometimes evaluate policies (see Berry, 1984, with regard to
multiculturalism in Canada), but as practitioners they have to
influence policies as well. Examples from the cross-cultural
psychologist's practical work are (a) the participation in expert's
hearings of different political parties and parliamentary factions
with the purpose of influencing processes of opinion formation, (b)
the regular supply of information to key political figures indicating
the effects of the laws on individual refugees, and (c) the
establishment of a lobby in favour of refugees in parliament and
political parties.

The cross-cultural psychologist must have considerable knowledge
about the general interrelationship of culture and individual, of
majority and minority in interaction. In encounters of this type,
policy-makers and refugee-groups are involved. The cross-cultural
psychologist as a mediator has to take into account the claim of the
society to keep its integrity, as well as the claim of the individual
group or person to retain or achieve their integrity. This forms a
common goal, although on different levels, and can be appreciated as
such.

PRACTICAL REFUGEE WORK AND CROSS-CULTURAL PSYCHOLOGY

The relationship of refugee assistance (analyzed and done by
psychologists in practical work and scientific cross-cultural
psychology) is seen here bi-directionally. As a practitioner in this
field the psychologist can make use of the results that have been
collected in scientific research; this practical field and its target
group, however, can be taken as a scientific challenge for
conceptualizations on a theoretical level, too:
1. As we have tried to show, the theoretical analysis of the
refugee's situation from the practitioner's point of view is likely
to lead to a change at least in focus as regards the understanding of
the interrelationship between individual and culture.
2. It also calls for a consideration of conflict-solution as the goal
of psychology: universality of culture-specifics in actions are to be
the practitioner's goal, rather than universality of empirical
relations, as in the traditional cross-cultural approach.
3. We have tried to present refugee aid as a professional field for
cross-cultural psychologists, requiring, however, an inclusion of
social work and legal matters. The latter, therefore, have been

included in our atheoretical re-analysis within a psychological framework.
4. The role of the cross-cultural psychologist in practice is manifold. This can be demonstrated most easily in the case of refugees as the most disadvantaged group in a culture-contact situation. Sometimes the psychologist is a trainer for culture learning, sometimes he is a consultant in the overlapping area of culture and politics. His knowledge can be regarded as a valuable and indispensable addition to that of clinical psychologists, who are more likely led to a misinterpretation of conflicts in a bi-cultural setting as an intra-individual conflict, or even mental illness.
5. Moreover, the analysis of the refugee's situation could be valuable to induce a re-consideration of other groups, migratory or sedentary, in bi-cultural settings. From the point of view presented here, the analysis of the differences between these groups regarding their psychological well-being (or "acculturative stress, see Berry et al, 1987) could be broadened, giving more attention to the whole situation and political issues.
6. In spite of their interdependence, a disparity between science in research and art in practical work, however, will remain: practical intervention needs a creative and responsible application of theoretical knowledge for the single case which often is lost in efforts of scientific psychology. Recently, an adoption of a clinical attitude has been requested also for scientific cross-cultural psychology (Eckensberger, 1987). The notorious tension between theory and practice remains, but this could be made more fruitful for both sides. Thus, Kurt Lewin's well-known dictum that "there is nothing more practical than a good theory" is still true. From the perspective of the practitioner who tries to establish conflict free interactions by intercultural encounter for the mutual enrichment of two partners, however, Lewin's statement can be complemented by quoting John MacMurray: "All meaningful knowledge is for the sake of action, and all meaningful action is for the sake of friendship." (1957, p. 15)

REFERENCES

Arnold, C.B. (1967). Culture shock and a Peace Corps Field Mental Health Program. Community Mental Health Journal, 3, 53-60.

Berry, J.W. (1984). Multicultural policy in Canada: A social psychological analysis. Canadian Journal of Behavioural Science, 16, 353-370.

Berry, J.W. & Kim, U. (1988). Acculturation and mental health. In P.R. Dasen, J.W. Berry & N. Sartorius (Eds.), Health and cross-cultural psychology: Towards applications. Newbury Park: Sage.

Berry, J.W., Kim, U. & Minde, T.E. (1987). Comparative studies of acculturative stress. International Migration Review, 21, 491-511.

Bochner, S. (1982). The social psychology of cross-cultural relations. In S. Bochner (Ed.), Cultures in contact: Studies in cross-cultural interaction. Oxford: Pergamon Press, pp. 5-44.

Boesch, E.E. (1983). From expulsion to hospitality: A psychologist's look at the refugee problem. In E.E. Boesch & A.M.F. Goldschmidt (Eds.), Refugees and development. Baden-Baden: Nomos, pp. 53-74.

Eckensberger, L.H. (1979). A metamethological evaluation of psychological theories from a cross-cultural perspective. In L.H. Eckensberger, W.J. Lonner & Y. Poortinga (Eds.), Cross-cultural contributions to psychology. Lisse: Swets & Zeitlinger, pp. 255-275.

Eckensberger, L.H. (1987). Boesch's dynamic action theory - a bridge between theory and practice, between general laws and contexts? Arbeiten der Fachrichtung Psychologie, 113. Saarbrücken: Universität des Saarlandes.

Emminghaus, W.B. (1988). From first aid in emergency to intercultural encounters: A comprehensive view. In League of Red Cross and Red Crescent Societies (Ed.), Hand of Humanity. Dordrecht: Martinus Nijhoff.

Foster, G. (1962). Traditional cultures and the impact of technological change. New York: Harper & Row.

Furnham, A. & Bochner, S. (1982). Social difficulty in a foreign country: An empirical analysis of culture shock. In S. Bochner (Ed.), Cultures in contact. Oxford: Pergamon Press, pp. 161-198.

Furnham, A. & Bochner, S. (1986). Culture shock: Psychological reactions to unfamiliar environments. London: Methuen.

Goldschmidt, A.M.F. & Boesch, E.E. (1983). The world refugee problem. Refugees and development. In E.E. Boesch & A.M.F. Goldschmidt (Eds.), Refugees and Development. Baden-Baden: Nomos, Pp. 15-51.

Higginbotham, H.N. & Tanaka-Matsumi, J. (1981). Behavioral approaches to counselling across cultures. In P. Pedersen, J.G. Draguns, W.J. Lonner & J.E. Trimble (Eds.), Counselling Across Cultures. Honolulu: University of Hawaii Press, pp. 247-274.

IACCP (1983). Constitution and by-laws. International Association for Cross-Cultural Psychology.

Kanfer, F.H. & Phillips, J.S. (1970). Learning foundations of behavior therapy. New York: John Wiley & Sons.

Klineberg, O. (1982). Contact between ethnic groups: A historical perspective of some aspects of theory and research. In S. Bochner (Ed.), Cultures in contact: Studies in cross-cultural interaction. Oxford: Pergamon Press, pp. 45-55.

Kuhn, T.S. (1962). The structure of scientific revolutions. Chicago: University of Chicago Press.

Kunz, E.F. (1973). The refugee in flight: Kinetic models and forms of displacement. International Migration Review, 7, 125-146.

Kunz, E.F. (1981). Exile and resettlement: Refugee theory. International Migration Review, 15, 42-51.

Linden, M. & Hoffmann, N. (1976). Erhöhter therapeutischer Anspruch und verschenkte therapeutische Chance: Kausale, kompensierende und korsettierende Therapie. In P.A. Fiedler & G. Hörmann (Eds.), Therapeutische Sozialarbeit. Münster: Deutsche Gesellschaft für Verhaltenstherapie, pp. 57-74.

MacMurray, J. (1957). The self as agent. London: Faber & Faber.

Oberg, K. (1960). Cultural shock: Adjustment to new cultural environments. Practical Anthropology, 7, 177-183.

Pedersen, S. (1949). Psychopathological reactions to extreme social displacements (refugee neuroses). Psychoanalytic Review, 26, 344-354.

Sears, R.R. (1961). Transcultural variables and conceptual equivalence. In B. Kaplan (Ed.), Studying personality cross-culturally. New York: Harper & Row, pp. 445-455.

Tharp, R.G. & Wetzel, R.J. (1969). Behavior modification in the natural environment. New York: Academic Press.

Triandis, H.C. (1980). Preface. Handbook of cross-cultural psychology. Boston: Allyn & Bacon.

Webik, H. (1974). Theorie der Gewalt. Eine neue Grundlage für die Agressionsforschung. München: Fink.

INDIVIDUALISTIC AND COLLECTIVE INTEGRATION STRATEGIES AMONG IMMIGRANTS: TOWARD A MOBILITY MODEL OF CULTURAL INTEGRATION

Fathali M. Moghaddam
McGill University
Montreal, Canada

Over the last two decades, two research areas that could potentially increase our understanding of immigrants and the process of immigration have made strong advances. These two research areas have up to now not had much contact or exchange of ideas or paradigms. One is the area of intergroup relations, which has relied heavily on laboratory research (Brown, 1988; Billig, 1976; Doise, 1978; Tajfel, 1978; Taylor & Moghaddam, 1987; Turner, 1987; Worchel & Austin, 1996), and gained particular importance in Europe (Moghaddam, 1987). The second area is concerned with exploring integration processes among immigrants, focusing particularly on the "ethnic revival" witnessed recently in numerous societies (Darroch & Marston, 1987; Glazer & Moynihan, 1976; Olzak, 1983; Smith, 1979). Historically, this second research domain has been field oriented and of particular importance in the United States, Canada, Australia, and other immigrant receiving countries. While there are fundamental conceptual reasons why these two research areas should be closely related, in practice there has been very little contact between them.

The objective of this paper is to introduce a number of concepts that could make a modest contribution by suggesting mutually constructive exchanges in basic ideas between the two areas. In the process it is hoped that we can arrive at a better understanding of the behavior of immigrants as disadvantaged group members.

Both the experimentally oriented area of intergroup relations and the field oriented area of research on integration processes among immigrants share a central concern for understanding the reactions of disadvantaged group members to perceived inequality. A major challenge for students of intergroup relations has been to explain the conditions under which a disadvantaged group member will accept the situation, attempt to improve his or her position through individual action, or try to participate in some kind of collective action against perceived injustice (Taylor & Moghaddam, 1987).

Immigrants also represent a disadvantaged group, and the study of

69

integration processes among immigrants can be viewed as an attempt to
understand the behavior of both disadvantaged and advantaged group
members. For example, will the immigrant attempt some kind of an
individualistic strategy for improving his/her position, such as
moving toward assimilation into the majority group, or will he/she
attempt to use the heritage culture as a focus for mobilizing the
ethnic minority against perceived injustice? A group of us at McGill
have recently carried out a number of studies focusing on the behavior
of disadvantaged groups, adopting the experimental laboratory methods
dominant in intergroup relations (Moghaddam & Stumborg, 1988; Taylor,
Moghaddam, Gamble, & Zellerer, 1987; Wright, Taylor, & Moghaddam,
1988) as well as the field approach prevalent in research on immigrant
integration strategies (Lambert, Mermigis, & Taylor, 1986; Lambert &
Taylor, in press, Moghaddam & Taylor, 1986; Moghaddam, Taylor, &
Lalonde, 1987; Moghaddam, Taylor, & Lalonde, in press, Taylor, Wright,
Moghaddam, & Lalonde, 1988). Two major themes emerge from our
research, and both of these concern the strategies individual
immigrants adopt in order to improve their situation. First, whether
the disadvantaged group member adopts a "normative" or a "non-
normative" strategy. Second, whether the individual attempts to take
individualistic or collective action. Using these dimensions,
normative/non-normative and assimilation/heritage culture maintenance,
we present a preliminary model of integration strategies among
immigrants.

TOWARD A MOBILITY MODEL OF INTEGRATION STRATEGIES

The major assumption underlying the mobility model of integration
strategies is that immigrants are motivated to improve their life
conditions and to "get ahead" in the adopted land. In this context,
"getting ahead" involves, among other things, the betterment of both
economic conditions and social status. The alternative strategies
available to immigrants for trying to improve their conditions of life
can be conceived as lying at some point in a space delimited by two
vectors (figure 1). The first vector has as its polar extremes total
assimilation and total heritage culture maintenance. Assimilation
requires that the immigrant abandon the heritage culture and take on
the mainstream culture. Similarly, heritage culture maintenance at
its extreme involves the immigrant retaining important aspects of the
heritage culture, including the heritage language.

In this connection, it is useful to introduce a distinction made by
Taylor (1987) between the three domains of public, community, and
private life. For our purpose, the private domain includes all
activities that occur inside the home. The community domain refers to
any social context outside the home where the ethnic ingroup is in a
numerical majority, such as ethnic shops, ethnic restaurants, and
cultural centers for minorities. The term public domain denotes all
social contexts outside the home where the ethnic group is in a
numerical minority, such as government buildings and schools. Total
assimilation involves the immigrant adopting the language and culture
of the majority group, even in the private domain. Thus, conversation
between family members in the immigrant's home would take place in
English, for example, rather than in the heritage language. At the
other extreme, total heritage culture maintenance involves maintaining

important aspects of the heritage culture and speaking the heritage language even in the public context, such as in banks and schools.

The extreme poles of the second vector are total normative and total non-normative behavior. For the purposes of this discussion, normative behavior includes all activities that are endorsed by the majority group as being appropriate behavior for minority group members and implicitly or explicitly support the existing intergroup power hierarchy. An important example of normative behavior is the upward mobility of a select "token" sub-group of disadvantaged group members into the advantaged group. Several theories of intergroup relations predict that when the way is open for talented members of the disadvantaged group to work their way up to the advantaged group, these new "token" group members will become particularly staunch supporters of the existing intergroup power hierarchy (Taylor & Moghaddam, 1987). Having "made it" according to the rules of the system, these individuals become strong supporters of the dominant group's system.

The term non-normative behavior refers to activities that are not endorsed by the majority group as being appropriate behavior for minority group members and potentially work toward a change in the existing intergroup power hierarchy. For example, a minority group member who succeeds in gaining entrance into the advantaged group may decide to take advantage of his new position to mobilize the disadvantaged group and lead an attack on the existing intergroup power hierarchy, through block voting, boycotting, and striking, for example.

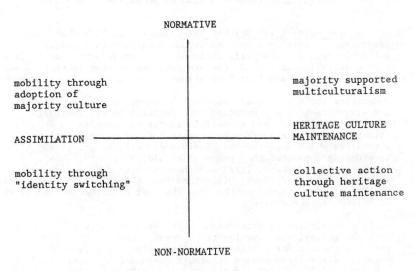

Figure 1: Diagramatical representation of the mobility model, with the four main mobility strategies identified.

As illustrated in figure 1, the mobility strategies available to
immigrants can be categorized as being   (1) normative/assimilation,
(2) normative/heritage culture maintenance,   (3) non-
normative/assimilation,   (4) non-normative heritage culture
maintenance. We shall discuss each of these four categories, giving
examples of behavior that falls within each category.

(1) Normative/Assimilation. Assimilation is probably the most
normative integration strategy for immigrants, because in terms of
consequences it leads to minimal threat to the status quo. The
"melting-pot" ideology that historically has been dominant in the
United States is in line with normative assimilation. While this
ideology has received explicit support from successive U.S.
administrations, researchers also have assumed that various processes,
particularly urbanization and industrialization, would eventually lead
to the assimilation of ethnic minorities (Parkin, 1979).
Consequently, taking on the "American way" among immigrants seems to
have received political support from the majority group, and also
assumed to be inevitable by various researchers.

The so-called "rise of ethnicity" in recent years has forced
researchers to seriously reassess the assimilationist assumption
(Glazer & Moynihan, 1976; Olzak, 1983). The vitality of numerous
ethnic cultures prevalent in major North American cities is attracting
research attention (Driedger, 1987; Maldonado & Moore, 1985), as is
the challenge of ethnic conflict at the international level (Boucher,
Landis, & Clark, 1987). One consequence of these developments is the
increased focus on just treatment for ethnic minorities as
collectivities, as reflected in debates on affirmative action
programs.

(2) Normative/Heritage Culture Maintenance. In 1972 the Trudeau
government officially committed Canadian society to a policy of
multiculturalism. Australia followed the example of Canada in 1976.
Multiculturalism is a bold, new and adventurous step in that it seems
to go against certain long-held assumptions concerning human behavior.

Underlying the drive toward cultural homogeneity in the United States
and elsewhere is the assumption that cultural heterogeneity is
potentially divisive and a possible source of weakness in society.
This reasoning is supported by a major body of psychological
literature which suggests that individuals will be positively biased
toward outgroups that they perceive as similar (Brown, 1984).
Freudian theory (Freud, 1921) and the theory of frustration and
aggression (Dollard, Doob, Miller, Mowrer, & Sears, 1939) both imply
that dissimilar others are the ones who most often become the target
of "displaced aggression".

While the "similarity-attraction" hypothesis receives a wide range of
both theoretical and experimental support, there is also support for
the idea that, under certain conditions, similarity leads to a
negative disposition toward others (Moghaddam & Stringer, 1988; Taylor
& Metee, 1972). Tajfel and his associates (Tajfel, 1978, 1984; Tajfel
& Turner, 1986) have presented evidence in support of their
proposition that individuals are motivated to achieve positive

distinctiveness. Social identity theory suggests that the more an outgroup is seen as similar, the greater the threat to the distinctiveness of ingroup identity (Tajfel & Turner, 1986). From this perspective, there are potential merits to having dissimilar groups in society.

The policy of multiculturalism also assumes that cultural heterogeneity has benefits, but that these can be reaped only if all ethnic groups feel confident and secure in their own identity (Berry, 1984; Berry, Kalin, & Taylor, 1977; Lambert et al., 1986). Thus, feeling confident and proud of one's own heritage culture and ethnic identity is assumed to lead to more positive attitudes toward dissimilar others. A more basic assumption underlying multiculturalism policy is that ethnic minorities are motivated to retain their heritage cultures (Moghaddam & Taylor, 1987). In the context of this discussion, it is important to keep in mind that the institutional support provided to minority groups to help them retain the heritage culture, in the form of government grants, access to publicity materials and information, for example, is established and controlled by the majority group.

(3) <u>Non-Normative/Assimilation</u>. In certain cases individual immigrants might adopt an assimilationist integration strategy involving individual mobility, at the same time as they attempt to "get ahead" through non-normative behavior. That is, an immigrant could attempt to achieve social mobility within mainstream society, an acceptable goal, but not abide by the means to achieve these goals that are acceptable to the majority group. In extreme cases, an immigrant might use the rules of the system to work against the system, and to make personal progress at the expense of majority group members.

An example would be an ethnic group member who switches hats, becoming a "visible minority" or a "mainstreamer", depending on the needs of the occasion. In some situations, it might benefit the individual to take on the identity of an ethnic group member in order, for example, to participate in affirmative action programs, or to contribute to "reverse discrimination" (Dutton & Lennox, 1974) movements against majority group members.

In other situations, it could be more beneficial for the same individual to become a "mainstreamer", to demonstrate that he/she can function effectively within the cultural norms of the majority group. An example would be an ethnic group member who is employed as a middle-level manager in a company whose management is almost exclusively majority group members, but the main body of whose workers are immigrants. When interacting with the management of the company, the ethnic manager might blend in as much as possible to the majority culture, use the language and terminology of the majority group, and emphasize his achievements in terms of majority group values. He might, for instance, emphasize the prestige schools he graduated from, the football team he played for, and the high-status majority group members he personally knows. The objective of this self-presentation exercise would be to show that he is a success according to the rules set by the majority group. However, the same "ethnic" manager might revert to his ethnic identity when negotiating with the ethnic workers of the company, so that he could increase his influence among the workers.

The extent to which these kinds of switches in identity take place is probably associated with a number of personality variables. For example, those who score high on the traits of self-monitoring (Snyder, 1974), public self-consciousness (Feningstein, Scheier, & Buss, 1975), and machiavelianism (Christie & Geis, 1970) probably would be likely identity switchers. However, the ultimate goal of an individual who adopts a non-normative form of assimilation is to improve his or her own individual position, and not the position of the ethnic collectivity.

(4) Non-Normative/Heritage Culture Maintenance. The non-normative form of heritage culture maintenance involves the ethnic group using the heritage culture as a means of achieving greater group cohesion in order that the ethnic ingroup becomes more successful in challenging the majority group. The objective of this challenge would be to change the existing intergroup power hierarchy, so that the ethnic minority could achieve higher social status and economic power. The classic example of this kind of collective action in recent years has been the Black Power movement, that eventually led to greater freedom and parity in some areas for blacks (Killian, 1984).

Theories of intergroup relations provide several predictions concerning the conditions in which an ethnic group would adopt non-normative heritage culture maintenance (Taylor & Moghaddam, 1987). An assumption explicit in several of the theories, including the Five-Stage Model (Taylor & McKirnan, 1984) and elite theory (Pareto, 1935; Prewitt & Stone, 1973), is that individuals will attempt first to achieve mobility on an individual basis, and only resort to collective action when they perceive the system to be closed and the way up into the advantaged group to be blocked. Social identity theory (Tajfel & Turner, 1986) makes the prediction that the system would have to be perceived as being both illegitimate and unstable before individuals resort to collective action. Realistic conflict theory (Sherif, 1966) assumes the roots of collective action to lie in incompatible group interests. These differences might be set aside if the groups adopt a superordinate goal, such as "peaceful coexistence", but mis-perceptions and mis-attributions might lead to a spiral of "destructive conflicts" (Deutsch, 1985). The general picture that theories of intergroup relations impart is that collective action is resorted to only: (a) after individual mobility is blocked, (b) the interests of the two group are perceived as incompatible, (c) the system is perceived to be illegitimate, (d) and also unstable enough so that there is a real possibility that collective action would lead to changes in the intergroup power hierarchy.

Resource mobilization theory adds another precondition for effective collective action: the availability of various resources, such as expert personnel, access to the mass-media and campaign funding (Killian, 1984; Tilly, 1978). Such resources have become available increasingly to some ethnic minorities. This is because some immigrant groups have gained economic power in the second sector of the "dual economy" (Averitt, 1968; Galbraith, 1979) and helped establish the various "ethnic economic enclaves" thriving in North America (Kim, 1981; Wilson & Martin, 1982). Ethnic economic enclaves provide an economic springboard for the political activities of ethnic minorities, but they also help strengthen ethnic awareness and shape ethnic identity.

Portes (1984) has defined ethnic awareness as, "...the perception by members of a minority of the social distance separating them from the dominant group and the existence of discrimination based on racial or cultural differences" (p. 384). In a number of studies, we have found evidence that such an awareness exists among visible minority immigrant groups (Moghaddam & Taylor, 1987; Moghaddam, Taylor, & Lalonde, in press), but the preference for individualistic mobility strategies and the prevalence of the belief that the system is not altogether closed, diminishes the possibility for non-normative collective action. Even a remote possibility that individuals could move from a disadvantaged to an advantaged group seems to be effective in orienting disadvantaged group members toward individual rather than collective action in the face of perceived injustice (Wright, Taylor, & Moghaddam, 1988). This preference for individual action on the part of disadvantaged group members, together with innovative new forms of discrimination adopted by the advantaged group, such as "symbolic racism" (Isaac, Mutran, & Stryker, 1980; Kinder & Sears, 1981), help maintain power disparities.

Concluding Comments. The ethnic revival documented internationally in recent years (Smith, 1979) has involved a shift of behavior among ethnic minorities, away from assimilation and normative behavior toward heritage culture maintenance and non-normative behavior. One consequence of this has been greater emphasis on collective action by ethnic minorities, who seek greater parity with, and independence from, majority groups. These developments have led not only to research attention on the "ethnic revival", particularly among field oriented researchers in North America (Olzak, 1983), but also they have stimulated research on minority group behavior among experimentally oriented researchers in Europe (Moscovici, Mugny, & Van Avermaet, 1985). There is a need, however, for closer contact between researchers concerned with intergroup relations and those focusing on ethnic minorities in the field. This paper represents an attempt at this form of rapprochement.

Finally, this discussion has focused on individualism and collectivism in relation to social mobility and the strategies individuals adopt to improve their position in the social hierarchy. In contrast to this stands another body of research that is concerned mainly with cross-cultural differences in individualism-collectivism (Hofstede, 1980; Triandis, Bontempo, Villareal, Asai, & Lucca, 1988). There is need for synthesis between this cross-cultural research on individualism-collectivism, and research on individualistic-collective mobility strategies among minority groups.

REFERENCES

Averitt, R. T. (1968). The dual economy: The dynamics of the American industry structure. New York: Norton.

Berry, J. W. (1984). Multiculturalism policy in Canada: A social psychological analysis. Canadian Journal of Behavioural Science, 16, 353-370.

Berry, J. W., Kalin, R., & Taylor, D. M. (1977). Multiculturalism and ethnic attitudes in Canada. Ottawa: Supply and Services Canada.

Billig, M. G. (1976) Social psychology and intergroup relations. London: Academic Press.

Boucher, J., Landis, D., & Clark, K. A. (Eds.). (1987). Ethnic conflict: International perspectives. Newbury Park, CA.: Sage.

Brown, R. J. (1984). The role of similarity in intergroup relations. In H. Tajfel (Ed.), The social dimension (pp. 603-623). Cambridge: Cambridge University Press.

Brown, R. J. (1988). Group processes. Oxford: Basil Blackwell.

Christie, R., & Geis, F. L. (Eds.) (1970). Studies in Machiavelianism. New York: Academic Press.

Darroch, A. G., & Marston, W. G. (1987). Patterns of urban ethnicity. In L. Dreidger, (Ed.), Ethnic Canada (pp. 111-137). Toronto: Copp, Clark & Pittman.

Deutsch, M. (1985). Distributive justice: A social psychological perspective. New Haven: Yale University Press.

Doise, W. (1978). Groups and individuals: Explanations in social psychology. Cambridge: Cambridge University Press.

Dollard, J., Doob, L. W., Miller, N. N., Mowrer, O. H., & Sears, R. R. (1939). Frustration and aggression. New Haven: Yale University Press.

Driedger, L. (Ed.) (1987). Ethnic Canada. Toronto: Copp, Clark & Pittman.

Dutton, D. G., & Lennox, V. L. (1974). Effect of prior "token" compliance on subsequent interracial behavior. Journal of Personality and Social Psychology, 29, 65-71.

Feningstein, A., Scheier, M. F., & Buss, A. H. (1975). Private and public self-consciousness: Assessment and theory. Journal of Consulting and Clinical Psychology, 43, 522-527.

Freud, S. (1921). Group psychology and the analysis of the ego. London: Hogarth Press.

Galbraith, J. K. (1971). The new industrial state. New York: Mentor.

Glazer, N., & Moynihan, D. P. (1970). Beyond the melting pot. Cambridge, MA.: MIT Press.

Hofstede, G. (1980). Culture's consequences. Beverly Hills, CA: Sage.

Isaac, L., Mutran, E., & Stryker, S. (1980). Political protest orientations among black and white adults. American Sociological Review, 45, 191-213.

Killian, L. M. (1984). Organization, rationality, and spontaneity in the Civil Rights movement. American Sociological Review, 49, 770-783.

Kim, I. (1981). New urban immigrants: The Korean community in New York. Princeton: Princeton University Press.

Kinder, D. R., & Sears, D. O. (1981). Prejudice and politics: Symbolic racism versus racial threats to the good life. Journal of Personality and Social Psychology, 40, 414-431.

Lambert, W. E., Mermigis , & Taylor, D. M. (1986). Greek Canadian's attitudes towards own group and other Canadian ethnic groups. Canadian Journal of Behavioural Science, 18, 35-51.

Lambert, W. E., & Taylor, D. M. (in press). Assimilation versus multiculturalism: The views of urban Americans. Sociological Forum.

Maldonado, L., & Moore, J. (Eds.) (1985). Urban ethnicity in the United States: New immigrants and old minorities. Newbury Park, CA.: Sage.

Moghaddam, F. M. (1987). Psychology in the three worlds: As reflected in the crisis in social psychology and the move toward indigenous Third World psychology. American Psychologist, 42, 912-920.

Moghaddam, F. M., & Taylor, D. M. (1987). The meaning of multiculturalism for visible minority immigrant women. Canadian Journal of Behavioural Science, 19, 121-136.

Moghaddam, F. M., Taylor, D. M., & Lalonde, R. N. (1987). Individual and collective integration strategies among Iranians in Canada. International Journal of Psychology, 22, 301-313.

Moghaddam, F. M., Taylor, D. M., & Lalonde, R. N. (in press). Integration strategies and attitudes toward the built environment: A study of Haitian and Indian immigrant women in Montreal. Canadian Journal of Behavioural Science.

Moghaddam, F. M., & Stumburg, B. (1988). Responses to perceived inequality in conditions of procedural and distributive justice/injustice. Paper presented at the Canadian Psychological Association Conference, Montreal.

Moghaddam, F. M., & Stringer, P. (1988). Out-group similarity and intergroup bias. Journal of Social Psychology, 128, 105-115.

Moscovici, S., Mugny, S. G., & Van Ameraet (Eds.) (1985). Perspectives on minority influence. Cambridge: Cambridge University Press.

Olzak, S. (1983). Contemporary ethnic mobilization. Annual Review of Sociology, 9, 355-374.

Pareto, V. (1935). The mind and society: A treatise on general sociology, 4 vols. Hillsdale, N.J.: Erlbaum.

Parkin, F. (1979). Marxism and class theory: A bourgeois critique. New York: Columbia.

Portes, A. (1984). The rise of ethnicity: Determinents of ethnic perceptions among Cuban exiles in Miami. American Sociological Review, 49, 383-397.

Prewitt, K., & Stone, A. (1973). The ruling elites: Elite theory, power, and American democracy. New York: Harper & Row.

Sherif, M. (1966). Group conflict and cooperation: Their social psychology. London: Routledge & Kegan Paul.

Smith, A. D. (1979). Nationalism in the twentieth century. Oxford: Martin Robertson.

Snyder, M. (1974). The self-monitoring of expressive behavior. Journal of Personality and Social Psychology, 30, 526-537.

Tajfel, H. (1978). Differentiation between social groups: Studies in the social psychology of intergroup relations. London: Academic Press.

Tajfel, H. (Ed.) (1984). The social dimension 2 vols. Cambridge: Cambridge University Press.

Tajfel, H., & Turner, J. C. (1986). The social identity theory of intergroup behavior. In S. Worchel & W. G. Austin (Eds.), Psychology of intergroup relations (pp. 7-24). Chicago: Nelson-Hall.

Taylor, D. M. (1987) Understanding ethnic diversity from a social psychological perspective. Paper presented at the Regional Conference of the International Association for Cross-Cultural Psychology, Kingston.

Taylor, D. M., & McKirnan, D. J. (1984). A five-stage model of intergroup relations. British Journal of Social Psychology, 23, 291-300.

Taylor, D. M. & Moghaddam, F. M. (1987). Theories of intergroup relations: International social psychological perspectives. New York: Praeger.

Taylor, D. M., Moghaddam, F. M., Gamble, I., & Zellerer, E. (1987). Disadvantaged group responses to perceived inequality: From passive acceptance to collective action. Journal of Social Psychology, 127, 259-272.

Taylor, D. M., Wright, S. C., Moghaddam, F. M., & Lalonde, R. N. (1988). The personal/group discrimination discrepancy: Perceiving my group, but not myself, to be the target for discrimination. Unpublished manuscript, McGill University.

Taylor, S. F., & Metee, D. R. (1971). When similarity breeds contempt. Journal of Personality and Social Psychology, 20, 75-81.

Tilly, C. (1978). From mobilization to revolution. Reading, MA.:Addison-Wesley.

Triandis, H., Bontempo, R., Villareal, J., Asai, M., & Lucca, N. (1988). Individualism and collectivism: Cross-cultural perspectives on self-group relationships. Journal of Personality and Social Psychology, 54, 323-338.

Turner, J. C. (1987). Rediscovering the social group: A self-categorization theory. Oxford: Basil Blackwell.

Worchel, S., & Austin, W. G. (1986). Psychology of intergroup relations. Chicago, Ill.: Nelson-Hall.

Wilson, K., & Martin, W. A. (1982). Ethnic enclaves: A comparison of Cuban and black economies in Miami. American Journal of Sociology, 88, 135-160.

Wright, S. C., Taylor, D. M., & Moghaddam, F. M. (1988). Responding to membership in a disadvantaged group: From acceptance to collective protest. Unpublished manuscript, McGill University.

MARITAL AND ACCULTURATIVE STRAIN AMONG INDO-CANADIAN AND EURO-CANADIAN WOMEN

James A. Dyal, Ludmila Rybensky and Moira Somers
University of Waterloo
Waterloo, Canada

As with most of the major decisions in our lives the decision to pull up roots and move to a new country has both positive and negative consequences. It is probably fair to say that in spite of all of the negatives, most immigrants to North America will affirm that, all things considered, they are glad that they made the decision to immigrate. They are likely to say that even if they have had to face innumerable problems which are unique to their status as immigrants, they also have opportunities which have made their lives richer, fuller, and more successful than they would have been at home.

While acknowledging the positive consequences of immigration, psychologists have tended to focus their research on the stresses and negative sequelae. This focus is understandable in terms of possible applications in helping to relieve unnecessary stress as well as in terms of our historical orientation toward behavioral/emotional problems and their alleviation. Our own work over the past several years has certainly exemplified this focus on the stress and distress which accompany acculturation (Dyal and Dyal, 1981; Dyal and Chan, 1985). However, preoccupation with the simple stress-distress relationship provides a limited perspective at best. As a consequence we have increasingly focused on what we regard as a more positive theme, namely the personal and social resources which the individual has available to buffer and alleviate the stress-distress relationship (Dyal, 1980; Dyal and Bertrand, 1985).

Another characteristic of much of the acculturative stress literature is that it seems to focus exclusively on acculturative stressors as though they were the only stressors operating in the lives of immigrants. Indeed, it may be less important to differentiate acculturative stressors than it is to examine the ways in which a variety of stressors function in both acculturating and non-acculturating samples.

Furthermore it is apparent that the impact of a particular stressor will depend on the type of distress measure which is being considered; it is important to include distress measures which are specific to a particular stressor as well as measures of more general mental health status.

The present research was designed with these considerations in mind. We have thus measured in acculturating (Indo-Canadian women) and non-acculturating (native born Euro-Canadian women) samples three types of stressors (marital strain, stressful life events, and acculturative strain); four coping resources which could serve as potential moderators (coping strategies, social support, locus of control, and acculturation support); and four aspects of distress (marital distress, depressive symptoms, psychosomatic symptoms, and acculturative distress). In addition, several situational characteristics were evaluated: culture (Euro-Canadian vs Indo-Canadian), age, length of marriage, age when married, years since immigration, education of subject, education of husband, number of children at home, income, number of organizations joined, and religion (Christian vs non-Christian).

The rationale for focusing on women immigrants has been developed previously by Dyal and Dyal (1981) and Dyal and Rybenski (1987). The extensive literature which documents gender differences in emotional problems and reported distress, may reflect the fact that by virtue of differential role demands women are both exposed to a greater variety of stressors and are less adequately equipped with the more efficacious coping strategies (Pearlin and Schooler, 1978; Menaghan, 1982). We hypothesize that the addition of acculturative strain to ongoing life stress may result in immigrant women being even more distressed than their counterparts in their adoptive country.

Immigrant women's experience has too often been neglected or subsumed under that of men. As a consequence it is not surprising to find few studies which have examined the process of acculturative stress and distress from the perspective of women. Nonetheless, the research which is available supports the view that women may be particularly vulnerable to acculturative and marital strain (Dyal and Dyal, 1981). For example, Masuda, Lin and Tazuma (1980) while investigating the possible link between stress and illness in immigrants, suggested that although immigrants as a group may not be a high-risk group for illness, the women in this group may be exceptions. Other researchers (Roskies et al., 1975; Naditch and Morrissey, 1976; Selyan, 1978, and Dyal and Chan, 1985) report that female immigrants experience greater adjustment difficulties than do males.

Menaghan (1982) has provided an extensive panel design which has examined the effects of several situational characteristics, marital strain and coping strategies on marital distress and later marital problems for a large representative sample in Chicago. The major features of Menaghan's results were that: (1) marital strain was (a) higher for women than men, (b) higher for those respondants who had been married longer, (c) strongly related to the type of coping strategy which was used; (2) four coping strategies significantly influenced marital distress with negotiation and optimistic comparisons reducing distress and selective ignoring and resignation increasing distress.

The present study permits an extension of the results obtained with the American sample used by Menaghan, to a sample of Euro-Canadian women and a sample of East-Indian immigrant women in Canada. Over and above the test of the generalizability of Menaghan's results, we can determine the degree to which cultural differences may operate to influence the level of marital problems, the types of coping strategies which are used, the level of distress experience, and the relationships which exist among these variables. Of particular interest will be the possible moderating effects among the coping resources and the possibility that marital strain and acculturation strain interact to exacerbate the stress-distress relationship.

Method

Subjects. A sampling frame of 326 households of East-Indian origin and 308 households of Euro-Canadian origin was randomly selected from the Kitchener-Waterloo telephone directory. Selection of the East-Indian participants was based on a list of names of East-Indian origin (Indian and Pakistani) constructed by Naidoo (1985).

An introductory letter describing the research and soliciting their participation was sent to the wife in each of these households; this was followed by a telephone screening interview to determine the subjects' suitability and willingness to participate. Members of the East-Indian immigrant group had to be foreign-born whereas the comparison subjects were born in Canada of Euro-Canadian heritage. One hundred thirty East-Indian women and 125 Euro-Canadian women were both suitable and willing to participate. They were sent a confidential, self-administrated set of questionnaires, accompanied by a letter further delineating the nature of the study. Additionally, to eliminate any anxiety as well as to ensure participants' cooperation, the leaders of various clubs and organizations in the East-Indian community were approached to support participation in the study among their membership. Completed questionnaires were returned by 70 (54%) of the East-Indian subjects and 92 (75%) of the Euro-Canadian sample. For the East-Indian sample 83% were employed outside the home and 90% had children at home; comparable figures for the Euro-Canadian sample were 90% and 76%. Other relevant demographics for the East-Indian and Euro-Canadian samples respectively were: age, 36.2 and 37.8; years married, 15.1 and 15.6; age of marriage 21.6 and 22.1; number of children at home, 1.9 and 1.6.

Psychometric Instruments. The marital strain scale consisted of nine items from the marital problems scale constructed by Menaghan (1982). They reflected the subjects' judgements of the amount of "marital inequity" (e.g., "My husband expects more from me than he is willing to give".) and "marital distance" (e.g., "My husband seems to bring out the best in me".) which existed in their marriage. The acculturation strain scale consists of 15 problem areas which potentially place demands on coping resources for the immigrant. They include such items as 'Loss of your cultural/religious identity', 'Longing for familiar people and things from your home country', 'Lack of traditional respect for parents/elders by South Asian children in Canada'. Each item was rated on a six point scale from 'extreme' to 'none at all' with regard to the amount of tension or strain associated with that problem. The scale was adapted from a previous scale constructed for use with South-Asian women by Naidoo (1985).

The four coping resource domains were: (1) coping strategies, (2) social support, (3) locus of control, and (4) acculturation support.. The 13 items used by Menaghan (1982) to measure four coping strategies were used in the present study. These were: negotiation (e.g., "How often do you sit down to talk things out?"); optimistic comparison (e.g., "How often do you appreciate your own marriage more after seeing what other marriages are like?"); selective ignoring (e.g., "How often do you try to overlook your husband's faults and pay attention only to good points?"); and resignation (e.g., "How often do you just keep your hurt feelings to yourself?").

The social support scale was the Instrumental-Expressive Support Scale constructed by Lin, Dean and Ensel (1979). The scale consists of 26 items which reflect lack of support in four areas: (1) 'monetary problems', (2) 'excessive demands', (3) 'lack of companionship', and (4) 'communication problems'.

The acculturation support scale utilized a six point Likert scale to provide measures of: (1) 'perceived cultural support' ('opportunities') (e.g., "Compared to Canada-born, white Canadians, South Asian immigrants have an equal opportunity for success in Canada".); (2) level of co-ethnic friendship (e.g., "How many South Asian friends can you really talk with about things that are important to you?"); (3) other friendships (e.g., "How many times have you had friends who are not South Asian visiting in your home in the past month?"); (4) peer group acceptance (e.g., "My South Asian friends appreciate me as I am."); and (5) alienation from Canadian culture (e.g., "Living in Canada does not give me the opportunity to be the kind of person I would like to be.").

The locus of control measure was the IPC scale constructed by Levenson (1981). It consists of three subscales reflecting 'internality', 'powerful others', and 'chance'.

Distress was measured in four domains: (1) psychosomatic symptoms, (2) depressive symptoms, (3) marital distress, and (4) acculturation distress. Psychosomatic symptom formation was indexed by the Langner Scale (Langner, 1962). The CES-D scale (Radloff, 1977) was used to provide a measure of non-clinical depression. Marital distress was measured by an eight-item, six-step Likert scale, constructed by Menaghan (1982) to measure the amount of distress associated with daily marital life. Acculturative distress was measured by a similar scale in which the referent was "the pleasures and problems of your daily life as a South Asian immigrant to Canada".

Results

A detailed presentation of the results of this study will be reserved for future research reports. For the present we wish to indicate the general tenor of the most salient findings obtained through a series of multiple regression analyses which were conducted separately for the two stressors of marital strain and acculturative strain[1].

Impact of Marital Strain. The multiple regression analyses conducted on the marital strain data were of two sorts. First, we conducted a set of single stage analyses in which the variables at each conceptual level are used as predictors of each of the subsequent variables. For example, situational (demographic) variables are first used to predict marital strain; then, in a separate equation, they are used as predictors of coping strategies and again in a separate equation to predict the distress measures. Marital strain is then used to predict the coping strategies and then the distress measures and finally the coping strategies are used as predictors of the distress measures. We will describe only the salient features of the single stage analyses in

[1]The original conference presentations (Dyal and Rybensky, 1987; Dyal and Somers 1987) provide somewhat more detailed information including comparisons of the mean levels of performance of the two cultural groups on all of the variables. These reports may be obtained from the first author.

order to present the more parsimonious model based on net sequential effects.

Considering first the relationships of situational characteristics to subsequent variables in the single stage analyses we found number of years of marriage to be the only significant predictor of marital strain (.28)[2], with marital strain increasing with marital duration. Furthermore, the likelihood of using negotiation as a coping strategy decreases (.22) while the tendency to use resignation increases with length of marriage (.28).

Analysis of the direct effects of marital strain on conceptually subsequent variables revealed that with increases in marital strain there is reduction in the use of negotiation (-.72) and optimistic comparisons (-.66) and an increase in the use of selective ignoring (+.31) and resignation (+.61). As would be expected all three distress measures are positively related to marital strain (.47, .45 and .47 for marital distress, depression and psychosomatic symptoms respectively).

The coping strategies relate differently to each of the measures of distress. Negotiation is negatively related to both marital distress (-.31) and depression (-.23) but does not influence psychosomatic symptoms. Optimistic comparison is negatively related to both marital distress (-.24) and psychosomatic symptom formation (-.21). The more the individual uses resignation the greater the distress as manifested by psychosomatic (.20) and depressive symptoms (.23). Selective ignoring was unrelated to any of the distress measures.

Since these single-stage analyses do not take into account the variance attributable to conceptually prior or subsequent stages we conducted the multiple stage analyses to get at the net sequential effects. In this analyses we entered successively in a single equation, the situational variables, then marital strain, and then the coping strategies to predict the distress measures. The regression weights from these sequential analyses represent the effects of a given variable net of all of the preceding variables in the equation. The results for the combined sample are presented in Fig. 1.

The level of marital strain clearly has the strongest predictive relationship to three distress measures. In the case of marital distress only income level and negotiation add significant predictive increments. In the case of depression the number of organizations to which the person belongs adds significantly to the prediction of depressive symptoms. And in the case of neurotic symptoms, education of the husband and number of children at home add significant net effects. Only the coping strategy of negotiation was a significant predictor of acculturative distress.

When we break down these effects for the combined sample into effects for each cultural group we obtain some interesting similarities and differences. While marital strain is the primary predictor of marital distress for both groups, the income effect is due entirely to the Euro-Canadians and the negotiation effect applies only to the East-Indians. In the case of the depressive symptoms, the marital strain effect is confined to the East-Indians whereas the income effect was again specific to the Euro-Canadians. Only marital strain predicts neurotic psychosomatic symptoms for both cultural samples. While the

[2] Values are standardized regression weights for the whole sample.

woman's educational level and the number of children at home
significantly influence symptom formation for the Euro-Canadians only.

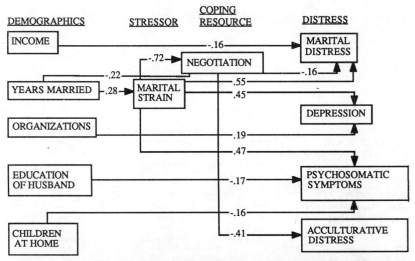

Figure1. <u>Overall Descriptive Model Based on Sequential Forward Net Effects.</u>
Derived from Multiple Regression Analyses in which the variables at
each successive stage are added to the variable list from the previous
stage. All analyses are based on the combined sample except
'acculturative distress' which applies to the Indo-Canadian sample only.

We have prepared comparable analysis of the net predictive power of
the locus of control factors and the social support variables but we
will not present them here in order to provide a comparison of the
relative impact of the three different types of coping resources.

<u>Relative Impact of Resources for Coping with Marital Strain.</u> Combined
scores based on Z transformations were computed to represent each of
the coping resources. These scores were then entered into a stepwise
multiple regression equation which included marital strain as the
stressor. The results for the two cultural groups and the combined
sample are presented in Table 1.

The most salient features of these results are as follows: (a) for
the Indo-Canadian sample marital strain is the primary predictor of
marital distress, depressive symptoms and psychosomatic symptoms but
for the Euro-Canadians its effects are limited to marital distress; (2)
for the Indo-Canadians the coping resource of locus of control was the
most consistent predictor of distress, being significant for all four
of the distress measures. The direction of the effect was that greater
externality goes with greater distress; (3) for the Euro-Canadians in
contrast social support was the most consistent and strongest coping
resource; and (4) in no case was the coping effectiveness variable
significantly related to any of the distress measures.

Table 1. Relative impact of marital strain and coping resources on four distress measures for the Euro-Candian, Indo-Canadian and combined samples (Standardized regression weights).

Predictor	Euro-Canadian	Indo-Canadian	Combined
DV = Marital Distress			
Marital Strain	.711***	.654****	.686****
Social Support	-.443***		-.286****
Locus of Control	.164*	.200*	.169**
Coping Effectiveness			
R^2 =	.645****	.464****	.552**
DV = Depressive Symptoms (CES-D)			
Marital Strain		.657****	.165*
Social Support	-.562****	-.369***	-.571****
Locus of Control	-.287**	-.201*	-.279**
Coping Effectiveness			
R^2 =	.390****	.570****	.416****
DV = Psychosomatic Symptoms (Langner)			
Marital Strain		.553**	.240**
Social Support	-.483****	-.219*	-.294***
Locus of Control	.239*	.227*	.218**
Coping Effectiveness			
R^2 =	.285****	.388****	.319****
DV = Acculturative Distress			
Marital Strain			
Social Support		-.349***	
Locus of Control		.364***	
Coping Effectiveness			
R^2 =		.320****	

* .05   ** .01   *** .001   **** .0001

Stress Moderator Effects. We then asked whether there was any evidence that the coping resources served to moderate the impact of marital strain on distress. We sought evidence with regard to probable moderator effects through the use of multiple regressions in which the stressor was entered into the equation first, followed by the coping resource and then the cross-product of these two variables was entered. Significant effects associated with the stressor or with the coping resource can be regarded as additive main effects whereas a significant cross-product indicates a non-additive interaction. The precise nature of the interaction can then be determined by substituting appropriate beta weights in the regression equations. If increases in the moderator variable (eg. coping resource) are accompanied by decreases in the strength of the relationship between the stressor and the distress then the moderator serves as a buffer. On the other hand if the stress-distress relationship increases with increases in the coping resource then the moderator functions as an exacerbater.

We ran such moderator analyses for each of the cultural groups separately and combined using each of the coping resources as the potential moderator. As would be expected from the previous analyses both social support and locus of control provided strong and consistent main effect relationships to all distress measures for both groups;

however, in no instance was the cross-product interaction term
significant for locus of control or social support. That is, these
coping resources have a direct effect on distress but they did not
serve to moderate the relationshop between marital strain and any of
the distress measures.

We ran such moderator analyses for each of the cultural groups
separately and combined using each of the coping resources as the
potential moderator. As would be expected from the previous analyses
both social support and locus of control provided strong and consistent
main effect relationships to all distress measures for both groups;
however, in no instance was the cross-product interaction term
significant for locus of control or social support. That is, these
coping resources have a direct effect on distress but they did not
serve to moderate the relationship between marital strain and any of
the distress measures.

On the other hand consistently significant interactions were
obtained for marital strain and coping effectiveness. The nature of
the interactions were such that with increase in marital strain those
people who tend to use the more positive coping strategies of
negotiation and optimistic comparison actually have a more rapid
increase in marital distress than do those who rely relatively less on
them. That is, at high levels of marital strain even the normally more
efficacious coping strategies no longer serve to reduce distress but
rather increase it. It's as though the person has given her best shot
and since those efforts haven't reduced the marital inequity and
distance the marital distress is heightened even more.

Impact of Acculturative Strain. The statistical details of the results
of the net sequential analysis with acculturative strain as the
stressor will be presented in subsequent research reports. For the
present we will simply present a verbal summary and graphic
representation (Figures 2 and 3) of the most salient features of these
results. Furthermore, it should be recognized that the relative impact
of acculturative strain and situational characteristics will depend on
which coping resources are in the equation. Nonetheless acculturative
strain was a consistant predictor of acculturative distress, marital
distress and psychosomatic symptoms. In all analyses psychosomatic
symptoms tended to increase with age and to decrease with number of
organizational memberships. In the equation containing social support
as the coping resource, religion was related to acculturative distress
such that East-Indian women who were Christian were more distressed
than those who maintained their traditional religion.

The primary results for each of the coping resources are as follows:
(1) Only the positive coping strategies of negotiation and optimistic
comparison were significantly related to the distress measures. The
results of this analysis are presented graphically in Figure 2; (2)
Among the locus of control factors control by 'powerful others' was
positively related to acculturative distress and psychosomatic
symptoms; the perception of control by 'chance' was positively related
to depressive symptoms; (3) Among the social support variables
'communication problems' was highly predictive of all four distress
measures while 'lack of companionship' was significanlty related to
marital distress and "excessive demands" were predictive of depressive
symptoms (Figure 3); (4) Using acculturation support as the coping
resource only 'alienation from Canadian culture' predicted overall
acculturative distress.

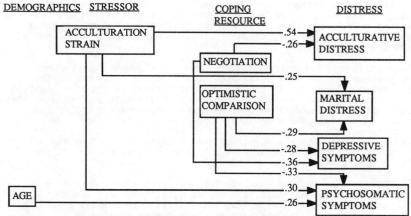

Figure 2. Significant sequential net effects (standardized regression coefficients) predicting distress with acculturation strain as the stressor and coping strategies as the coping resource.

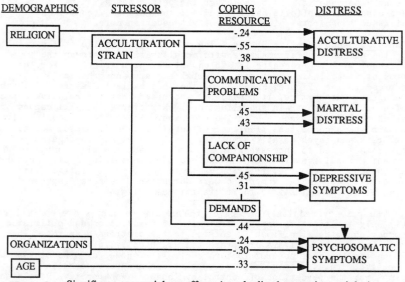

Figure 3. Significant sequential net effects (standardized regression weights) predicting distress with acculturation strain as the stressor and social support as the coping resource.

Relative Impact of Resources for Coping with Acculturative Strain.
While the above sequential net effect analyses provide a description of
the effectiveness of each coping resource relative to the situational
characteristics and acculturative strain, it was also desirable to
determine the impact of the coping resources relative to each other.
As noted in the discussion of marital strain this comparison was based
on composite scores computed for each coping resource. These coping
resource scores were then entered into a free entry step-wise multiple
regression. The results, presented in Table 2, indicate that the
coping resources were most effective in predicting acculturative
distress and depressive symptoms, where they account for about half of
the variance (R^2 = .506 and .477 respectively). Acculturation strain
accounts for an additional 37% of the variance in acculturative
distress with social support and locus of control adding increments of
9% and 5% respectively.

Table 2: Comparison of effectiveness of coping resources with
acculturative strain as the stressor.

Stressor/ Coping Response	Distress			
	Marital Distress	Acculturative Distress	Depressive Symptoms	Psychosomatic Symptoms
Acculturative Strain	.309**	.607***	-	-
Social Support	-.452**	-.307**	-.602***	.460***
Locus of Control	-	.238*	.217*	.274*
Coping Effectiveness	-.265**	-	-.281**	-
Accult. Support	-	-	-	-
R^2	.358****	.506****	.477****	.282****

* = .05; ** = .01; *** = .001; **** = .001

Social support is the strongest predictor of depressive symptoms
accounting for 36% of the total variance. Coping effectiveness added a
significant increment of 7% and locus of control an additional 4%.

Slightly over one third (R^2 = .358) of the variance of marital
distress was attributable to our strain and coping variables, with
social support accounting for 20% and acculturative strain and coping
effectiveness accounting for increments of 8% and 6% respectively.
Similarily social support accounted for 20% of the variance of
psychosomatic symptoms while locus of control added a significant
predictive increment of 7%.

Combined Effects of the Stressors. We were also interested in testing
the combined effects of the two content specific stressors - marital
strain and acculturative strain. First we wished to determine if they
were indeed providing independent additive effects on the distress
measures, and secondly to test the possibility that the strains may
interact to provide an exacerbation of their independent effects. The
results of the relevant moderator analyses are presented in Table 3.

It can be seen that while marital strain provides the primary
influence on marital distress (45% of the variance), acculturative
strain adds a significant independent contribution of 6%. Similarly,
the primary determinant of acculturative distress is acculturation
strain (37% of the variance) but marital strain adds a reliable

independent effect (5%). In neither case was there a significant interaction of the two strains in predicting marital or acculturation distress. On the other hand, when the more general, symptom-oriented measures of distress are considered, marital strain and acculturation strain do provide a significant interaction over and above their additive effects. The nature of the interaction is such that the addition of acculturation strain to marital strain results in an exacerbation of the distressing effects of marital strain.

Table 3. Significant standardized regression weights indicating independent and interactive effects of acculturative strain and marital strain on distress.

	Distress			
Stressor	Marital Distress	Acculturative Distress	Depressive Symptoms	Psychosomatic Symptoms
Marital Strain	.654****	.230**	.613****	.506****
Acculturative Strain	.245**	.607****	.328**	.311**
MS x AS	-----	-----	1.040*	.916[b]
R^2	.470****	.390****	.474****	.337****

(b) = .07; * = .05; ** = .01; *** = .001; **** = .0001

Discussion

Marital Strain. There is a lot of data here and we are still trying to assimilate it, so let us simply point out a few of the themes in the data which we believe to be particularly interesting in terms of cultural differences.

1. First, is the unhappy theme of the effects of marital duration - as marital duration increases the amount of marital strain increases, the probability of using negotiation as a coping strategy decreases and the probability of using resignation increases. A debilitating scenario relating these variables can be readily seen. As length of marriage increases marital strain increases in part because conflicts are not resolved and successful conflict resolution becomes less likely because the more effective coping strategy of negotiation is used less and the less effective strategy of resignation is used more. These factors represent a tight little vicious circle which results in more distress and more marital problems.

Similar relationships between strain, coping strategies and marital distress were reported by Menaghan (1982) for Americans. In the present study the debilitating effects of marital duration applies to the Euro-Canadian sample only. None of these relationships hold for the East-Indian immigrants; length of marriage does not increase marital strain, or change the probability of using the various coping strategies or increase marital distress.

In this context it should be noted that the East-Indians tend to use resignation as a coping strategy significantly more often than the Euro-Canadians (Dyal and Rybensky, 1987). It could be reasonably speculated that there are several aspects of Indian culture which would support the greater tendency of Indian women to use resignation as a coping strategy - including a traditional caste structure and a social structure which emphasizes lack of social mobility and may predispose toward a resigned acceptance of the status quo. In addition the fatalistic theme in religion is apparent. The argument would be that since these cultural features provide a more normative context for the use of resignation it may be a more effective coping strategy for the East-Indians than for the Canadians.

In addition to these cultural features, another factor which may be operating to predispose the East-Indians to utilize the more passive, less problem solving oriented coping strategies is their tendency to be more externally oriented with regard to the role of powerful others and chance factors in controlling their lives. We have previously observed that

"The Karma countries of the East provide a particularly promising context in which to search for cultural differences in the moderator effects of LOC. For example, if immersion in a Karma-oriented Zeitgeist fostered a "giving up" problem dissolution approach to anxiety-driven problem behaviors (Fogle & Dyal, 1983), then externality might in fact serve to reduce the stress of negative life events for Asians, whereas internality moderates life stresses for control-oriented cultures such as those of North America." (Dyal, 1984, p 284).

A compatible conceptualization has been proposed by Weitz et al. (1984) who differentiate primary and secondary control. In the latter case 'vicarious' control may be obtained through indentifying and aligning oneself with powerful others, or an 'illusory' secondary control may be attained by accomodating or accepting fate. As noted by Partridge (1987) "...the term "illusory" reflects the North American bias against accepting existing realities peacefully, but in fact it is a highly adaptive strategy when one can in reality, expect to have very little primary control." (p. 14).

The relationship between locus of control and coping strategies may be usefully considered in the context of Bandura's self-efficacy theory (Bandura, 1986). This approach would recognize that when an individual's belief system emphasizes the control of chance and powerful others, we have an expectancy which is likely to foster feelings of low self-efficacy. Such perceived inefficacy is likely to be associated with less persistant efforts to solve problems and with coping strategies which involve emotion-focused coping rather than problem-focused coping. The tendency for East-Indian women, who are high on 'chance' and 'powerful others' scales to use more resignation and less negotiation is of course congruent with a self-efficacy interpretation. For the Euro-Canadians externality operates to increase resignation but has no significant effect on the problem solving strategy of negotiation.

2. The only other situational variable to produce interesting cultural differences is income. It will be recalled that although the educational level of the East-Indians was significantly higher than that of the Euro-Canadians, their annual income was significantly lower. In spite of this disparity, annual income and the social

support variable of 'money problems' were significantly related to
marital distress and depression for the Euro-Canadian women but not for
the East-Indians. These relationships can be understood in the context
of relative deprivation theory under the assumption that the East-
Indians have available constant and salient reminders of their economic
position in Canada relative to what they would have had in India. This
form of psycho-economic coping strategy involves a type of optimistic
comparison vis a vis reference groups in India as well as across time
from arrival in Canada. Although Pearlin et al. (1981) have found that
such positive comparisons, along with a devaluation of the importance
of money do not operate directly to reduce depression, they do serve to
decrease perceived economic strain, and to increase feelings of mastery
and self esteem which in turn influence depression.

3. The level of marital strain is by far the strongest predictor of
marital distress for both cultural groups. This finding is consistent
with the results of Menaghan with Americans. On the other hand
inclusion of distress measures other than marital distress reveals that
marital strain influences depressive and psychosomatic symptoms for the
Indo-Canadians but not for the Euro-Canadians. This differential
cultural effect illustrates the importance of using a variety of
distress indicators in evaluating the effects of any stressor.

Acculturative Strain. The most salient finding regarding coping
strategies is that negotiation is negatively related to all measures of
distress. It should be recalled that all of the coping strategy
measures were specified in the context of coping with marital problems.
The fact that the use of negotiation to deal with marital strains is
also associated with reduced acculturative distress may reflect a
generalized tendency to deal with stressors in a problem-focused as
opposed to an emotion-focused manner and it is this generalized
tendency rather than a specific coping strategy which accounts for the
significant association of negotiation and acculturative distress.

Among the social support variables the most consistently strong
predictor of all distress measures was 'communication problems'. In
their validation studies of the social support instrument Lin et al
(1979) also had found 'communication problems' to be significantly
related to depressive symptoms for an American sample. The present
results show that for these Indo-Canadian women 'communication
problems' are strongly associated with acculturative and marital
distress as well as psychosomatic symptom formation. It should be
remembered that the pervasive and strong effects of 'communication
problems' on acculturative distress are over and above the effects of
acculturation strain.

Numerous studies have implicated locus of control as being
functionally related to a variety of measures of emotional distress for
mainstream Euro-American samples (Dyal, 1984) and more recently for
samples of Asian-American immigrants to Seattle (Kuo and Tsai, 1986).
The direct relationships between control by 'chance' events and by
"powerful" others on depression and acculturative distress extends the
applicability of these findings to Indo-Canadian women.

It is also of interest that only external control by 'powerful
others' was significantly related to several components of the coping
resources involved in acculturative support, for example, greater
control by powerful others was negatively related to perceived
opportunity (r=-.22; p=.03), to number of non-Indian friends (r=-.30;
p=.006) and positively related to alienation from Canadian culture

(r=.38; p=.001). The important contribution of 'powerful others' to acculturation strain, acculturative distress and acculturative support highlights the vulnerability of immigrants to host nationals and coethnics who are often in control of many aspects of the immigrants' life.

It also suggests that such 'vicarious secondary control' through identification with powerful others may not be a particularly efficacious coping strategy in the context of the demands of acculturating to a western culture.

The only component of the acculturation support scale which was a significant predictor of acculturative distress net of the effects of acculturative strain was 'alienation from Canadian culture'. It is understandable that a person who feels alienated from a culture in which she is required to live would indeed manifest other aspects of emotional distress associated with being an immigrant to Canada. On the other hand it is surprising to us that other components of the acculturation support scales were not related to acculturative distress either as a main effects or in interaction with acculturative strain. It is unclear at this point whether the lack of effect is due to psychometric inadequacies or is a real effect.

Relative Efficacy of the Coping Resources. Both in the case of acculturative strain as the stressor and analysis of marital strain, we find the two most effective coping resources to be social support and locus of control. In contrast, coping effectiveness failed to predict acculturative distress and psychometric symptoms and acculturative support was unrelated to any distress measure.

These results are consistent with a substantial literature on locus of control and social support based primarily on American non-immigrant samples. Furthermore, recent work by Kuo and Tsai (1986) has extended the relevance of both of these variables to the adjustment difficulties and depressive symptoms of Asian-American immigrants.

It should also be noted that the effects of these coping resources on distress in the context of acculturation strain is uncomplicated by interactions with the strength of the stressor. That is, the lack of social support and an external locus of control contribute independently to acculturative distress and neither buffer or exacerbate the effects of high acculturation strain.

From the point of view of immigrant adjustment it is heartening to recognize that coping resources involving social support and internal locus of control can reduce the impact of acculturative strain on psychopathological symptom formation. From the point of view of the researcher this type of finding reaffirms the importance of including coping resources in our analyses of the consequences of acculturative strain. From the perspective of the acculturating immigrant, the stress researcher and the practicing clinician, it is important to recognize that marital strain and acculturation strain may impact distress in either an independent additive manner as in the case of marital and acculturative distress, or they may interact to exascerbate distress, as in the case of depression and psychosomatic symptoms. The complexity of these effects supports our contention of the importance of simultaneously evaluating the additive and interactive contribution of several stressors to a variety of distress measures in future research on acculturative stress.

References

Bandura, A. (1986). Social foundation of thought and action: A social cognitive theory. Englewood Cliffs, N.J. Prentice-Hall Inc.

Dyal, J.A. (1980). Psychosocial mediation of acculturative stress. Paper presented at the Fifth International Conference, International Association for Cross-Cultural Psychology. Bhubaniswar, India.

Dyal, J.A. (1984). Cross-cultural research with the locus of control construct. In H.M. Lefcourt (Ed.) Research with the locus of control construct. Vol 3. Extensions and limitations. New York: Academic Press.

Dyal, J.A. & Bertrand, S. (1985). A search for moderators of acculturative stress: Sensation seeking, self-acceptance and locus of control among Trinidadian students. Paper presented at the annual convention of the Canadian Psychological Association, Halifax, Nova Scotia.

Dyal, J.A. and Chan, C. (1985). Stress and Distress: A study of Hong Kong Chinese and Euro-Canadian students. Journal of Cross-cultural Psychology, 16, 447-466.

Dyal, J.A., & Dyal, R.Y. (1981). Acculturation, stress and coping: Some implications for research and education. International Journal of Intercultural Relations, 5, 301-328.

Dyal, J.A. & Rybensky, L. (1987). Marital strain and distress among Indo-Canadian and Euro-Canadian women. Paper presented at the First Regional North American Conference of the International Association for Cross-cultural Psychology. Kingston, Ontario, Canada.

Dyal, J.A. & Somers, M. (1987). Acculturative stress and distress among Indo-Canadian women. Paper presented at the First Regional North American Conference of the International Association for Cross-cultural Psychology. Kingston, Ontario, Canada.

Fogle, D. and Dyal, J.A. (1983). Paradoxical giving-up and the reduction of sleep performance anxiety in chronic insomniacs. Journal of Psychotherapy: Theory, Research and Practice, 20, 21-30.

Kuo, W.H. and Tsai, V-M. (1986). Social networking, hardiness, and immigrants mental health. Journal of Health and Social Behavior, 27, 133-149.

Levinson, H. (1981). Differentiating among internality, powerful others and chance. In H. M. Lefcourt (Ed.) Research with the Locus of Control Construct. Vol. 1. Assessment methods. New York, Academic Press.

Lin, N., Dean, A. & Ensel, W.M. (1979). Development of social support scales. Paper presented at the Third Biennial Conference on Health Survey Research Methods. May 16-18. Reston, Virginia.

Menaghan, E. (1982). Measuring coping effectiveness: A panel analysis of marital problems and coping efforts. Journal of Health and Social Behavior, 23, 220-234.

Naditch, M.P. and Morrisey, R.F. (1976). Role stress, personality, and psychopathology in a group of adolescent immigrants. Journal of Abnormal Psychology, 85, 113-118.

Naidoo, J. C. (1985). A cultural perspective on the adjustment of South Asian Women in Canada. In I.R. Lagunes & Y.H. Poortinga (Eds.), From a different perspective: Studies of behavior across cultures, (pp. 76-92). Lisse, The Netherlands: Swets and Zeitlinger.

Partridge, K. (1987). How to become Japanese: A guide for North Americans. Kyoto Journal, 4, 12-15.

Pearlin, L., & Schooler, C. (1978). The structure of coping. Journal of Health and Social Behavior. 18, 2-21.

Pearlin, L., Lieberman, M.A., Menaghan, E. & Mullan, J. T. (1981). The stress process. Journal of Health and Social Behavior, 22, 337-356.

Radloff, L.S. (1977). The CES-D scale: A self-report depression scale for research in the general population. Applied Psychological Measurement, 1, 385-401.

Roskies, E., Lida-Miranda, M.L., & Strobel, M.G. (1975). The applicability of the life events approach to the problems of immigration. Journal of Psychosomatic Research, 19, 235-240.

Selyan, A.A. (1978). The immigrant experience: Who cares? Canada's Mental Health, 76, 2-4.

Weisz, J.R., Rothbaum, F.M. & Blackburn, T.C. (1984). Standing out and standing in: The psychology of control in Japan. American Psychologist, 39, 955-969.

DIPLOMATIC WIVES:
ACCULTURATIVE STRESS IN SHORT-TERM MULTIPLE SOJOURNERS IN ZIMBABWE

Kathleen Myambo
University of Zimbabwe
Harare, Zimbabwe

Pamela O'Cuneen
European Economic
Commission
Brussels, Belgium

The social psychology of cross-cultural relations represents a major area of investigation in cross-cultural psychology and recently entire volumes have been devoted to the psychological effects of culture contact (e.g., see Bochner, 1982; Brislin, 1981; and Klineberg and Hull, 1979). The major groups of persons studied in relation to culture contact have been short-term sojourners, such as foreign students and contract workers, and immigrant populations who settle permanently and become faced with the problem of assimilating into the culture of the receiving country. One group of sojourners who have been largely ignored in the sojourn literature are those who experience culture contact through short-term multiple sojourns, interspersed with short-term multiple periods of residence in their home countries. This group is best typified by the members of the diplomatic corps and it is the wives of members of the diplomatic corps who are the subjects of this study.

The wives of diplomats differ from the subjects of previous culture contact studies in several important respects. As part of the Diplomatic Corps of various countries, they move from one country to another, spending in each an average of three years, returning to their home country for six months to three years, and then going abroad again. They thus fall outside the categories of both the single-episode, short-term subjects, and the long-term permanent migrant population. In addition, the important element of choice is diminished as individuals in this group have little part in deciding where their next posting will be. Finally, by sojourning in the role of spouse, subjects are exposed to the stresses and strains of cultural adaptation without the motivation of a work role and the instrumental adaptation which the work role demands.

The research literature on culture contact has been mainly a-theoretical but has been dominated by the major concepts of culture shock (Oberg, 1960) and reverse culture shock (Gullahorn and Gullahorn, 1963). The concept of culture shock refers to the disorientation and confusion which results when a person enters a second culture and familiar cues are absent. This then results in feelings of loss, confusion over roles and role expectations and feelings of lack of control. Reverse culture shock can occur when an individual returns to his home culture after a sojourn and finds that either he/she has changed, or the home culture has changed, and there is no longer a great deal of shared experience and shared expectancies between the individual and home culture.

In spite of the fact that the research literature on culture contact is mainly a-theoretical, models of the adaptation or adjustment process of the sojourner in the new culture have been put forward by Smalley (1963), Adler (1975) and Bochner (1982). Smalley (1963) proposed an adjustment hypothesis which included four stages of culture shock. The first stage was labelled as the stage of fascination during which the sojourner is filled with enthusiasm and excitement. This stage is quickly replaced by a stage of hostility which results when the sojourner realizes that he/she is unable to solve problems in familiar ways. The third stage in this model is the stage of improvement and adjustment during which challenges are viewed in a less intense manner and the new culture is beginning to be understood. The fourth and final stage is one of biculturalism, and this stage is marked by a full understanding of host cultural norms and a feeling of being at home.

Adler (1975) produced a variation on the traditional model of culture shock by expanding Smalley's model to five stages and emphasizing the positive value of transitional experiences in personal growth. The five stages of this model share certain common ground with Smalley's model and differ most notably in the end result in that the sojourner does not merely gain a state of successful functioning but attains a final state of independence in which cultural relativism is reached and cultures are seen simply as acceptable alternatives.

Bochner's (1982) model of the psychological outcomes of culture contact for individuals can be summarized in four possibilities. One possibility is that the individual can reject the home culture and embrace the second culture, resulting in "passing" or a loss of ethnic identity. A second possibility is for the individual to reject the host culture and exaggerate the home culture. This results in a chauvinistic attitude which can lead to nationalism and racism. A third option for the individual is to vacillate between the two cultures, remaining marginal to both and suffering the conflict and identity confusion which are inherent in vacillation. A final option which an individual might pursue is that of mediation in which the individual synthesizes both cultures and experiences personal growth as a result.

The application of these models to the present study is difficult to hypothesize as these models have been based on short-term, one-time sojourners or long-term immigrant populations. The subjects of this study, being the wives of diplomats, are expected to participate in the host culture and yet their participatory role is predefined for them as "representing the culture" of their home country. Hence, the role in which they perform is that of reinforcing their own cultural identity. In addition to the predefined role set out for these subjects, the length of the sojourn, being for a two to three year period, may force the subjects to leave the host culture before the stage of biculturalism (Stage 4) is reached. It may be that these subjects experience fascination (Stage 1), hostility (Stage 2) and improvement (Stage 3) within each host culture and then move on to a new host culture to begin the process again. The period between sojourns may be marked by reverse culture shock when the individual returns to the home culture between foreign assignments.

THE RECEIVING CULTURE

The study presented in this paper was conducted in Harare which is the capital city of Zimbabwe. Zimbabwe (formerly Rhodesia) is located in south central Africa and is a front line state bordering with South Africa. Zimbabwe became independent from Britain in 1980 and Robert Mugabe became and still remains the first black Prime Minister. Prior to 1980, a fifteen year civil war ensued between the white "settler" minority and the indigenous black population.

Zimbabwe, like many ex-colonial societies, contains two main groups, the "Europeans" (Whites) and the "Africans" (Blacks). Since independence the two cultures have begun to merge and previously closed social groups, such as sport and social clubs, have opened membership to all racial groups. Presidential directives have ensured that educational opportunities, job advancement and residence in former "all-white" areas are available to members of all races.

Since the opening up of the country to international influences in 1980, more than 56 countries have set up diplomatic missions in Harare and the urban community has become increasingly pluralistic. The pluralistic nature of the society and the pronounced British origins of the Whites in the country should be kept in mind in interpreting the result of this study. In addition, in terms of climate, life-style, political stability and a government policy of "non-racialism", Zimbabwe is categorized by most Foreign Service personnel as an "easy" posting.

METHOD

Subjects. The subjects in this study consisted of 23 women, ranging in age from 27 to 55 years, all of whom were the wives of members of the Diplomatic Corps to Zimbabwe. Subjects were selected who either spoke English as a first language or who spoke English as a second language for six years or longer. As such, the subjects were drawn from the Australian High Commission, the Canadian High Commission, and the Delegation of the Commission of the European Community.

The original number of women who met the language criteria was 32, but of these, eight were either on leave or in such close proximity to leave that they found it inconvenient to participate. An additional subject declined to be interviewed as she felt it would be too upsetting as her children had just departed for boarding school abroad.

Interviewer. All interviews were conducted by a 41-year old Diplomatic wife who originated from an English-speaking British Commonwealth country. At the time of the investigation, the interviewer had several years of experience as a secondary school teacher and was a final year student in the psychology degree program at the University of Zimbabwe.

Apparatus. An interview schedule consisting of several sections was developed from the research literature on sojourners. The schedule consisted of questions on demographic data, information on best friends and companions, activities both within Zimbabwe and in the home culture, a 21-item general level of adjustment questionnaire, and an open-ended question on stress and coping during culture contact.

A general level of adjustment questionnaire was designed to yield a measure of adjustment to culture contact and diplomatic role. Subjects were asked to rate themselves on a scale from 1 to 5 between two extremes of reaction, from negative to positive. This questionnaire resulted in the General Adjustment Score (GAS). The topics covered in the questionnaire included culture shock, reverse culture shock, family situation, work role, identity, local involvement in social affairs, friendships and perceived control. During the open-ended discussion which took place towards the conclusion of the interview, each subject was asked to rate her satisfaction with her present lifestyle on a scale from 1 to 10 and this was taken as a measure of subjective satisfaction, yielding the Subjective Satisfaction Score (SSS).

RESULTS

Demographic Data. The sample, though English speaking, varied in nationality. Of the 23 subjects, 17 were British nationals, three were Australian, one was German, one was American and one was Brazilian. While a mixture of nationalities does not represent an ideal sample, Harare offers a relatively small Diplomatic Community compared with larger cities. All subjects fulfilled the linguistic requirements of the study and travelled under conditions which were sufficiently similar to enable valid comparisons to be made.

Subjects ranged in age from 27 to 55 years with a mean age of 39.39 (S.D. = 7.01). Four per cent of the sample were in the 25-30 year age group, 56 per cent of the sample were in the 31-40 year age group, 31 per cent of the sample were in the 41-50 year age group, and 9 per cent were in the 51-55 year age group.

All of the women had completed secondary education. One had a Ph.D., one an M.A., six possessed Bachelor's degrees in Arts or Education, two had partially completed B.A. degrees, and the other four had training in nursing, journalism, primary teaching and music. Nine of the women had no diplomas or post-secondary qualifications.

Three of the women were childless and the maximum number of children in any family of those interviewed was three. The subjects had a mean number of 2.1 children (S.D. = 0.85). Of the 29 children, seven were of pre-school age and at home with the mother, 20 were in school in Zimbabwe, and two were at school abroad.

The number of years spent in diplomatic life ranged from 1.5 to 18 years, with a mean of 9.80 (S.D. = 3.93). The number of foreign postings ranged from one to six, with a mean of 3.48 (S.D. = 1.57). At the time of the interviews, subjects had been resident in Zimbabwe for a period ranging from one month to 4 years, 5 months, with a mean residency of 1.47 (S.D. = 1.13) years.

Of the total sample of 23, 22 women spoke at least one language other than English. Fifteen subjects spoke one or more languages other than English fluently, all of which had been learned or improved during previous postings. Although English is the official language in Zimbabwe five of the subjects had begun lessons in the local Shona language or had firm intentions of doing so.

Four subjects worked full or part-time in Zimbabwe, two for their own High Commissions, one on an unpaid voluntary basis, and one on a special part-time teaching assignment for a government institution. A number of women expressed dissatisfaction with employment restrictions imposed by the Zimbabwean Government on diplomatic wives and felt that their satisfaction would be significantly increased if they were allowed to use their training in full or part-time employment. Only one subject had never worked and she had married halfway through a university degree in Veterinary Science.

Social Network. The Social network of subjects was measured by using the Best Friends Check List and the Companions Check List as developed by Furnham and Bochner (1982) in their study of overseas students in Britain. Subjects were asked to describe their three best friends, both in Zimbabwe and in their home country, in terms of their age, sex, nationality and occupation and these data are shown in Table 1.

Table 1: Friendship networks both in Zimbabwe and home country expressed as percentage of total friends. N = 23.

	In Zimbabwe	In Home Country
Zimbabweans	54.8 (N = 12)	-
Co-national	19.4 (N = 34)	76.4 (N = 55)
Other Foreign	25.8 (N = 16)	23.6 (N = 17)
Total	100.00 (N = 62)	100.00 (N = 72)

The subjects listed 62 friends in Zimbabwe and 72 in their home countries. Of the 62 friends in Zimbabwe, 60 were female and two were male. Zimbabwean friends accounted for 55 per cent of the total friendships. One woman described no friends in Zimbabwe and two subjects reported exclusively Zimbabwean friendships. Thirteen women described no co-national friends and no subject had an exclusively co-national network. The number of friendships reported within the diplomatic circle in Zimbabwe was eight (12.9%).

In addition to describing friends, subjects were asked to describe the companions with whom they performed 12 everyday activities both in Zimbabwe and in their home country. Both in Zimbabwe and in their home countries, activities tended to be conducted by subjects on their own (46.5 per cent of activities in Zimbabwe and 36.6 per cent in their home country). The next largest number of activities were carried out with the subject's husband (26.8 per cent versus 17.4 per cent) and only a small percentage of activities were carried out with a companion (17.4 per cent versus 15.3 per cent). In all but two activities which involved a specific hobby, the companions cited were also cited as friends on the Best Friends Check List.

Multiple regression analyses. Two step-wise multiple regression equations using demographic factors as predictors of the General Adjustment Score (GAS) and the Subjective Satisfaction Score (SSS) were carried out. In the first analysis, demographic predictors of subjects' scores on the general adjustment questionnaire, which measured adjustment to culture contact and diplomatic role, were evaluated. None of the demographic predictors reached significance at either the .05 or .01 level of significance. Demographic predictors of the subjective satisfaction scores (SSS) were then analyzed. None of the demographic predictors reached significance in this analysis.

Two further step-wise multiple regression equations were conducted. The first equation was conducted to ascertain the individual items on the general adjustment questionnaire that best predicted the General Adjustment Score (GAS). Item 10, involvement in local European affairs, entered the regression equation first, resolving 35 per cent of the variance in the mean adjustment score, $F (1,18) = 9.71$, $p < .01$. It was followed by Item 17, reaction of family and friends to stories of travel, which explained another 15 per cent of the variance, $F (2,17) = 8.40$, $p < .01$. Item 16, changes in family and friends back home, entered the regression equation third, accounting for an additional 13 per cent of the variance, $F (3,16) = 9.14$, $p < .01$. Item 13, choice over next posting, entered the regression equation fourth, explaining another 11 per cent of the variance in the mean satisfaction score, $F (4,15) = 10.77$, $p < .01$.

A further step-wise multiple regression analysis was conducted to determine which individual items from the general adjustment questionnaire best predicted the Subjective Satisfaction Score (SSS). Item 5, seeing themselves as helpful to their husband's career, entered the regression equation first, explaining 58 per cent of the variance in the Subjective Satisfaction Score, $F (1,18) = 25.04$, $p < .01$. It was followed by Item 7, the attitude that travel enhanced the quality of family life, which resolved a further 14 per cent of the variance, $F (2,17) = 21.87$, $p < .01$. Item 13, choice in the next posting, entered the regression equation third accounting for another 6 per cent of the variance, $F (3,16) = 18.43$, $p < .01$.

DISCUSSION

The demographic data clearly show that subjects in this study are a mature, well-travelled and culturally experienced group of persons. The results of the study which have only been partially reported here due to shortage of time, show that all subjects experienced some aspects of culture shock phenomena and had developed numerous coping strategies for dealing with the sojourn experience. All subjects were basically satisfied with their present life-style.

The social network of the subjects, showing mainly friendships with members of the host culture, is clearly distinct from that of Furnham and Bochner's study on foreign students which showed that these students mainly had friendship networks which consisted of compatriots.

The results of the step-wise multiple regression analysis on the general adjustment questionnaire show that adjustment was greatest in subjects who were involved in local European social affairs. The majority of local "Europeans" in Zimbabwe are distinctly British in origin and the majority of subjects in this study were also British in origin or from a British Commonwealth country. These data show that subjects' adjustment was closely related to having a social network of persons similar to themselves with whom they could identify. Secondly, adjustment was greatest in persons who did not experience reverse culture shock, i.e., persons who arrived in their home country for home leave and found that family and friends were fascinated by their travel stories and did not appear to have "changed" during the subjects sojourn. Finally, adjustment was related to the experience of "perceived control", that is, those who felt that they had a choice over their next posting were generally better adjusted.

The results of the multiple regression analysis on the subjects' subjective level of satisfaction is associated with identification with the husband's career and a positive attitude towards the international travel which is an inherent part of his career. Additionally, perceived control over the choice of the next posting is linked to personal satisfaction.

The results of this study, taken as a whole, clearly show that adjustment and satisfaction in short-term multiple sojourners is linked to the sojourners' subjective identification with the role in which they travel and feelings of perceived control. It is suggested that further research on this group look more closely at the issue of identity and perceived control as the key issues in predicting satisfaction and adjustment.

REFERENCES

Adler, P. (1975). The transitional experience. An alternative view of culture shock. Journal of humanistic psychology, 15(4), 13-23.

Bochner, S. (Ed.). (1982). Cultures in contact: Studies in cross-cultural interaction. Oxford: Pergamon Press.

Brislin, R.W. (1981). Cross-cultural encounters: Face to face interaction. Oxford: Pergamon Press.

Furnham, A. and Bochner, S. (1982). Social difficulty in a foreign culture: an empirical analysis of culture shock. In S. Bochner (Ed.) (1982). Cultures in contact: Studies in cross-cultural interaction. Oxford: Pergamon Press.

Gullahorn, J. T. and Gullahorn, J. E. (1963). An extension of the U-curve hypothesis. Journal of social issues, 19(3), 33-47.

Klineberg, O. and Hull, W.F. (1979). At a foreign university: An international study of adaptation and coping. New York: Praeger.

Oberg, K. (1960). Cultural shock: Adjustment to new cultural environments. Practical anthropology, 7, 177-182.

Smalley, W. (1963). Culture shock, language shock, and the shock of self discovery. Practical anthropology, 10, 49-56.

ACCULTURATION ATTITUDES AND STRESS OF WESTERNERS LIVING IN JAPAN

Kate Patridge
Kwansei Gakuin University
Nishinomiya, Japan

Within the field of cross-cultural psychology, most of the existing research on acculturation has been carried out in pluralistic societies such as Canada or Australia, with the focus on "minority groups", many (though not all) of which may be termed "third world". The resulting understanding of the acculturation process has therefore been rather limited. A more universal understanding of the phenomenon could be developed by comparing existing data with information about the acculturation of "first world" minorities living in non-pluralistic societies. In line with this approach, the purpose of the pilot study reported here was to begin to investigate the acculturation experience of English-speaking Westerners living in Japan.

The Japanese population of about 130 million forms an overwhelmingly continuous and daily contact for the less than 35,000 English-speaking foreigners (from various countries) who are estimated to live in Japan. The Japanese are a highly homogeneous racial and cultural group who have kept themselves insulated from most outside influences for almost all but the past 150 years of their recorded history. An example of the Japanese attitude to foreigners ("gaijin", alien) is shown in the treatment of the Korean ethnic population living in Japan. Even though many Korean families have been in Japan for several generations, Korean individuals are legally treated as "aliens" who are subject to more or less the same immigration laws and restrictions as temporary foreign visitors, and they are treated with considerable and very real social and economic discrimination by the Japanese. "White" foreigners in Japan are less subject to such discrimination, but they also are not allowed full participation in Japanese society, both legally and socially.

The largest concentration (an estimated 30,000) of English-speaking foreigners in Japan is in the Tokyo area, followed by an estimated 3,000 in the Osaka/Kobe/Kyoto area, and the largest proportion of all these Westerners is American. Using Berry's (Berry et al., 1986) system of classification, the Westerners in Japan are primarily sojourners and immigrants; that is, they moved voluntarily into Japan, either temporarily or permanently. In some cases (e.g., certain groups of English-language teachers, certain business people), these foreigners (mainly American) have been invited by the Japanese. However, in the majority of cases, they have come to Japan on their own volition, for reasons ranging from economic necessity to curiosity.

As mentioned above, English-speaking Westerners in Japan are a definite minority, comprising less than 35,000 in a population of 130 million. While there are pockets of concentration of Westerners living close together, both in Tokyo and in Kobe, it is typically only the wealthier business and diplomatic people who can afford to live in these "ghettoes", and many others are scattered throughout major urban areas. Recent increases in the cost of living in Japan appear to be resulting in a decline in the number of Westerners posted to Japan on business. On the other hand, English teaching continues to be a growing business (in fact it is about the only type of work that is freely available to foreigners), and the Japanese government has recently started to import young English-language teachers from the West, on a short-term basis. There is also an increase in the numbers of Western men and women who are marrying Japanese nationals and coming to live permanently in Japan. In general, a growing number of Westerns are coming to "seek their fortunes", one way or another in Japan.

English-speaking Westerners in Japan have formed their own national associations, as well as multinational business and social associations. There are several English-language weekly and monthly magazines, as well as a number of daily newspapers published in English by the major Japanese newspapers. However, there could not be said to be any kind of organized response or policy to acculturation, except perhaps on an issue-focused, temporary basis.

The purpose of the present research was to begin a descriptive study of the lives of Western residents in Japan, including their experience of acculturative stress, and their attitudes towards acculturation.

METHOD

Subjects. There was a total of 84 subjects, divided into two groups. Group 1 consisted of the Western spouses of Japanese nationals (mainly immigrants), while Group 2 consisted of Western English teachers living in Japan and not married to Japanese (mainly sojourners).

Group 1 consisted of 62 subjects, 84% women and 16% men, all of whom were married to Japanese spouses. The female subjects in this group were all recruited by a request for volunteers placed in the monthly newsletter of the Association of Foreign Wives of Japanese, a support and social group founded about 15 years ago. These subjects thus were not a representative sample of foreign spouses of Japanese, but rather a particular group who were socially oriented enough to join such an organization. The male subjects in Group 1 were recruited individually.

Group 2 consisted of 22 subjects, 68% female and 32% male, all of whom were English teachers who were not married to Japanese. This group was recruited through contacts with three English-language schools in Osaka.

Assessment Instruments. All subjects were given or sent an 11-page questionnaire, along with a self-addressed and stamped return envelope. The questionnaire consisted of:
a) an adapted version of the Berry and Kim Acculturation Attitudes Scale (Kim, 1984). Appended to this scale were two questions aimed at determining the subjects' views of the attitude of Japan, as a host culture, to minority groups. All items were answered on a 5-point Likert scale.
b) a Background Information form, including questions about age, place of birth, sex, marital status, nationality of spouse and children, length of residence in Japan, reasons for being in Japan, planned length of stay in Japan, current work, Japanese language ability, and a question concerning the best and worst things about living in Japan.
c) the Cawte Acculturative Stress Scale (Cawte et al., 1968), consisting of 10 somatic stress symptoms and 10 psychological symptoms, with an adapted 5-point Likert response scale. Appended to this scale were two questions related to subject satisfaction with life in Japan, and strategies used by the subject to cope with the stress of life in Japan.

RESULTS

Group 1 Demographic Data. The average age of this group was 36.7 years, with a range from 22 to 64 years. Of the 62 subjects (52 female, 10 male), the majority (61%) were American, followed by British (13%), Canadian (10%), European (8%), South East Asian (5%) and Australian (3%). Thus this group was in fact not restricted to Western English-speaking foreigners (81%), although all subjects were proficient in English.

The average length of residence in Japan was 9.7 years, with a range from 6 months to 29 years. In terms of how long these subjects were planning to stay in Japan, 68% could be classified as "immigrants", as they were intending to stay in Japan indefinitely; 23% did not know how long they would stay. The remaining 9% of subjects in this group were split evenly between those intending to leave within 1 year, and those intending to stay for between 6 to 15 years.

These bi-cultural marriages had an average of 1.5 children each, and most of these were attending Japanese rather than international (English-language) schools. (This may reflect both a commitment to life in Japan, as well as financial considerations, since international schools are very expensive.) Almost all of the children had dual nationality.

Given the presence of Japanese-speaking children in most of these homes, it is perhaps not surprising to find a high proportion (77%) of these subjects who reported speaking Japanese moderately well or excellently, but only 34% reported being able to read Japanese at these levels. Both English and Japanese were used in 38% of subjects' homes, English only was used in 32%, and 5% reported using Japanese only.

Over 70% of these subjects had a B.A. or higher degree, and over half (52%) reported working as English teachers. Nineteen percent reported being "housewives only", with a small number of other occupations such as translating or business. The main reason given by this group for being in Japan was related to being married to a Japanese (78%).

Group 2 Demographic Data. The average age of subjects not married to Japanese was 32.9 years, with a range from 22 to 77 years. Of the 22 subjects (15 female, 7 male), over half (55%) were American, followed by British (14%), Australian (9%), and 9% (2 subjects) who were born in Japan but raised in the U.S.A.

The average length of residence in Japan for this group was 4.7 years (although the mode was 0.5 years), with a range from 1 month to 33 years. This group consisted mainly (68%) of sojourners, that is, subjects who were planning to stay in Japan for less than 6 years, and most for not more than 3 years. In this group, 23% could be classified as immigrants, planning to stay indefinitely, and 9% did not yet know how long they would stay. Most subjects (83%) in this group were single.

Almost two-thirds (64%) of this group reported speaking no Japanese at all, or at a poor level, with the percentage of moderate to good readers of Japanese being only 18 . English was used in 73% of these subjects' homes, 18% used English and Japanese, and 9% (the two born in Japan), used only Japanese.

This was a well-educated group, with 90% having a B.A. or higher degree, and all of the subjects were working as English teachers. The main reasons reported by this group for coming to Japan were: for work or money (36.4%); for adventure and curiosity (31.8%); and to learn about Japanese culture and language (27.3%).

Acculturation Attitudes. Table 1 gives the pattern of average scores

for each of the four acculturation attitudes, across the two groups.
The immigrant group (Group 1) scored highest on Integration, followed
by Separation, Marginalization and Assimilation. The sojourner group
(Group 2) also scored highest on Integration, but this was followed
instead by Assimilation, Separation and Marginalization. Thus Assimilation was least preferred by the immigrants but somewhat favored by
the sojourners. In a t-test, the immigrant group was significantly
higher on Integration than the sojourner group (p = .0085), while the
higher average score on Assimilation for the sojourner group
approached significance (p = .0910).

The internal consistency of the Acculturation Attitudes Scale was
assessed using Cronbach's alpha, as follows: Integration alpha, .73;
Assimilation alpha, .73; Separation alpha, .75; Marginalization alpha,
.68. There were no particularly "bad" items. Multiple regression
analyses were performed to determine if there were any variables that
would predict acculturation attitude, but results here were inconclusive.

Table 1
Acculturation Attitudes Scores

		Group 1	Group 2
Integration			
	Mean	4.2	4.0
	S.D.	0.34	0.56
Assimilation			
	Mean	2.0	2.2
	S.D.	0.41	0.49
Separation			
	Mean	2.2	2.1
	S.D.	0.49	0.52
Marginalization			
	Mean	2.2	2.1
	S.D.	0.45	0.44

Japan is interested in maintaining the diversity and differences of
its minority groups (1 = Strongly disagree, 5 = Strongly agree).

	Group 1	Group 2
Mean	2.4	2.2
S.D.	1.49	1.51

Japan is interested in maintaining positive relations with its
minority groups (1 = Strongly disagree, 5 = Strongly agree).

	Group 1	Group 2
Mean	2.2	1.9
S.D.	1.02	1.10

Acculturative Stress. Table 2 gives the average scores for both groups on the Acculturative Stress Scale. There were no significant differences between the two groups in any of the stress results. There was also no significant difference between the two groups in terms of their level of satisfaction with life in Japan, with both groups showing a relatively high degree of satisfaction.

Table 2
Acculturative Stress Scores

	Group 1	Group 2
Overall Stress Score		
Mean	2.04	1.95
S.D.	0.423	0.553
Somatic Stress Score		
Mean	1.93	1.88
S.D.	0.461	0.600
Psychological Stress Score		
Mean	2.15	2.03
S.D.	0.511	0.589
Life Satisfaction Score		
Mean	3.76	3.81
S.D.	0.803	0.873

However, within the overall subject sample, there was a definite pattern of stress symptoms that both groups reported. This pattern included raised scores for the following symptoms, in descending order of emphasis: Getting angry when told by someone else what to do; Often being annoyed or irritated by others; Feeling tired and exhausted when getting up in the morning; Having stiff muscles and joints; Feeling unhappy and depressed. Four of these six symptoms are from the psychological stress scale, suggesting that this is a somewhat psychologically-minded group of subjects, as would be expected from a mainly American sample.

In terms of reliability, Cronbach's alpha for the Somatic Stress portion of the scale was .72, and that for the Psychological Stress portion was .83, both in the acceptable range.

Multiple regression analyses were performed to determine which variables would predict somatic and psychological stress. For somatic stress, the multiple correlation coefficient was R = .45, with the two main predictors being the acculturation attitudes of Marginalization

(B = .39) and Separation (B = .24). For psychological stress, the multiple correlation coefficient was R = .45, with the three main predictors being Marginalization (B = .32), Age (B = -.24) and Education Level (B = .21).

In other words, an acculturation attitude of Marginalization was definitely associated with higher levels of acculturative stress, and this replicates the findings of Berry et al. (1987) with other subject groups. Also implicated were the Separationist attitude, being younger, and being more educated, although these variables were not particularly related to each other.

A principal component factor analysis was performed to determine the pattern of variables. Four interpretable factors were found, using a varimax rotation. Factor I, a "sojourner" factor, brought together subjects in the sojourner group who had lived in Japan for a short time (factor loading -0.87), were younger (-0.79), could speak Japanese reasonably well (0.63), and were in Japan for the money and/or adventure (0.48). Factor II, a "stress" factor, included somatic stress (factor loading 0.81) and psychological stress (0.73), and the acculturation attitudes of Marginalization (0.68) and Separation (0.60). Factor III, an "Assimilation" factor, included a denial of the use of English media (factor loading 0.78), Assimilationist attitudes (0.56), and the belief that Japan dislikes minorities (0.39) (which is a good reason for trying to be assimilated). Factor IV, a "Separation" factor, included a low score in Integration (factor loading -0.77), a lack of use of Japanese media (0.69), membership in the sojourner group (0.51), Separationist attitudes (0.37), and being male (0.32).

The best aspects of life in Japan. The two most frequent responses here were: the challenge and stimulation of learning about a new culture in contrast with one's own, and the personal safety and security of life in Japan. Other benefits included: meeting good people, the civility and kindness of the Japanese, good pay and good work opportunities and conditions, and Japanese aesthetics and food.

The worst aspects of life in Japan. Although the question was not phrased as such, it seems likely that many of the things that subjects disliked about Japan also represented sources of stress for them. These items were classified into three loose groups: psychological, physical and miscellaneous dislikes. The major psychological dislikes were: complaints about and problems with Japanese people, isolation and homesickness, problems related to being a foreigner in Japan, and the struggle to communicate. The major physical dislikes were: crowding and lack of space, high prices, pollution and related problems, and the weather. Miscellaneous dislikes included the education system, and commuting and travel problems.

Strategies for coping with stress. Subjects were asked to describe their "greatest help or comfort in coping with the stress of living in Japan". Coping strategies were loosely classified into three categories: social coping, cognitive coping, and rest and relaxation. The most frequently mentioned source of help or comfort was social: friends, spouse and/or family (81 responses). Cognitive coping strategies were next (27 responses), with the main themes appearing to be related to a confident self-image (e.g., "I'm a coper"), adjustment strategies (e.g., "I just try to be myself and not strain too hard to adjust to Japanese society"), or to a sustaining religious belief system. Rest and relaxation strategies included hobbies and pasttimes such as reading, movies, gardening, exercise and spending time at home.

DISCUSSION

The results of this pilot study begin to outline a picture of the acculturation experience of Western sojourners and immigrants in Japan. In spite of a perception of the Japanese as being disinterested, if not unwilling, to allow for the integration of Westerners into society, most of the subjects in this study, both immigrants and sojourners, favored an acculturation attitude of Integration. The contrast between the ideal and the reality suggests a potent source of stress for these individuals, and it would be interesting to investigate how long-term residents have been able to achieve a sense of integration in the face of this contrast.

For immigrants whose children are attending Japanese schools, the ideal of integration is particularly understandable. However, among the sojourners there was also a group with an acculturation attitude of Assimilation, suggesting that these adventurous younger people were willing to forego their own cultural identities and try to immerse themselves in the Japanese experience for the short time they planned to be in Japan.

Although there were no significant differences between the two groups in terms of Acculturative Stress, the specific pattern of stress symptoms across both groups is interesting, although its significance is not clear. As in other studies (e.g., Berry, Kim, Minde & Mok, 1987), high stress levels were associated with an acculturation attitude of Marginalization, although Separation was also implicated. It would seem to be important to investigate the precursors and development of the acculturation attitudes. For example, an interesting question is whether some Marginalized people were "marginalized" before going to Japan (or any other host country), or whether this is merely one stage in the process of acculturation, for certain people. In addition, it would be useful to examine the particular coping strategies of each attitudinal group, since the high stress levels of Marginalized people may be associated with poor coping strategies, in contrast to the hardier groups (Integration and Assimilation).

Japan is a country of contrast and paradox, and this is reflected in the likes and dislikes of the subjects in this study. A large proportion of subjects complained about various aspects of the Japanese personality, and were unhappy with the cramped, overcrowded conditions. On the other hand, subjects strongly appreciated the stimulation and opportunities for learning in such a completely different culture, as well as the personal safety and security of life in Japan. The paradox is also reflected in the fact that although every subject had several major complaints, and many reported substantial levels of stress, the average level of satisfaction with life in Japan was high.

This descriptive study has provided a first look at the acculturation and texture of life of English-speaking Westerners living temporarily or permanently in Japan. A major dynamic in this experience is the desire for integration into a non-pluralistic culture that has no historical precedent for absorbing "outsiders". One issue that deserves further study, and that is likely to present a major challenge for integration-seeking Westerners in Japan, particularly those from the United States and Canada, is how to adapt their ideals of assertiveness and individualism to the cooperative and collectivist context of Japan.

REFERENCES

Berry, J.W., Kim, U., Minde, T. & Mok, D. (1987). Comparative studies of acculturative stress. International Migration Review, 21, 491-511.

Berry, J.W., Kim, U., Power, S., Young, M. & Bujaki, M. (1986). Acculturation attitudes in plural societies. International Review of Applied Psychology.

Berry, J.W., Trimble, J.E. & Olmedo, E.L. (1986). Assessment of acculturation. In W.J. Lonner & J.W. Berry (Eds.), Field Methods in Cross-Cultural Research. Beverley Hills: Sage.

Cawte, J., Bianchi, G.N. & Kiloh, L.G. (1968). Personal discomfort in Australian Aborigines. Australian and New Zealand Journal of Psychiatry, 2, 69-79.

Kim, U. (1984). Psychological acculturation of Korean immigrants in Toronto: A study of modes of acculturation, identity, language and acculturative stress. Unpublished master's thesis, Queens University, Kingston, Ontario.

SOCIAL INTEGRATION STRATEGIES OF HAITIAN AND INDIAN IMMIGRANT WOMEN IN MONTREAL

R.N. Lalonde
York University
Toronto, Canada

D.M. Taylor and F.M. Moghaddam
McGill University
Montreal, Canada

When arriving in a new host country, an immigrant can be socially disadvantaged in many ways. The newly arrived immigrant typically lacks financial, emotional (e.g., social support), and cognitive (e.g., knowledge of social bureaucracy) resources. Much of immigrants' social disadvantage, however, stems from their minority status. Their ethnicity, race, colour, religion, language and/or dress will often distinguish them from the host country's culture. Given the drawbacks associated with a minority position, the process of integration for the immigrant is a challenging one. The purpose of this paper is to examine immigrant integration from an intergroup relations perspective by focussing on different approaches to social integration. More specifically, an individual approach to integration will be contrasted with a collective approach.

In the North American context two general strategies for immigrant integration underlie current social policies: one is an assimilationist strategy that follows from the melting pot philosophy of the United States, the other is a heritage culture maintenance strategy as espoused by Canada's policy of multiculturalism. These two strategies represent two behavioral options for integration: assimilation involves an individual strategy where immigrants leave their group to join the majority group, whereas multiculturalism involves a collective strategy where immigrants remain within their original group. Moghaddam, Taylor & Lalonde (1987) have noted that theories of intergroup relations would view these behavioral strategies as two options available to socially disadvantaged group members attempting to improve their social status. While many studies have examined immigrant integration, research has only begun to study integration in terms of social psychological theories of intergroup relations.

Two intergroup theories that are particularly relevant to the study of immigrant integration are Social Identity Theory (Tajfel & Turner, 1979)

114

and the Five-Stage Model of intergroup relations (Taylor & McKirnan, 1984). These theories assume that individuals desire to belong to advantaged social groups, and that under certain conditions, individual and collective strategies are options available to socially disadvantaged individuals who desire a change in their social status.

Social Identity Theory (Tajfel & Turner, 1979) assumes that individuals, in order to enhance their self-esteem, strive to achieve a positive social identity by belonging to positively valued groups. To determine if their ingroup provides them with a positive social identity, they will make social comparisons between their own group and relevant outgroups. The theory predicts that when an individual fails to achieve a positive social identity there will be a desire for change. One method for creating change is individualistic: for example, the individual attempts to move in the social hierarchy by leaving the ingroup and joining the advantaged group. An alternative approach is collectivistic, that is, to work with the ingroup in order to improve its status. These strategies represent two different stages in Taylor and McKirnan's (1984) Five Stage Model of intergroup relations. According to this model, talented members of a disadvantaged group individually attempt to gain entrance into an advantaged group. If these members fail to pass into the advantaged group they are likely to attribute their failure to an unjust social hierarchy (e.g., a discriminating advantaged group) and will attempt to mobilize their fellow disadvantaged ingroup members into taking collective action.

While many social scientists have used the individual-collective distinction (Hofstede, 1980; Hui & Triandis, 1986; Kluckhohn & Strodtbeck, 1961; Mead, 1967; Triandis, Leung, Villareal & Clack, 1985; Triandis et al., 1986), it has only recently been extended to the study of immigrant integration. Moghaddam et al. (1987) used the distinction to study Iranian immigrants attempting to establish a new life in Canada. Although their questions were formulated at a general level, they uncovered some interesting findings. Individuals for whom heritage culture maintenance was more important, as compared to those for whom it was less important, were more likely to favour a collective approach to social integration over an individual approach. This was also reflected by their greater likelihood of belonging to an Iranian cultural organization and by the greater importance they ascribed to establishing contacts within their ingroup community. It would seem, therefore, that the individual-collective distinction made by intergroup theories, represents a beneficial approach to the study of immigrant integration.

Moghaddam et al. (1987), however, raised a concern in their study. Their Iranian sample was relatively advantaged compared to other immigrant groups in that it was highly educated and not as visible. Some of their previous work examining South Asian immigrant women had suggested that an immigrant's visibility represents a potentially important barrier for individual integration into a new society (Moghaddam & Taylor, 1987). The present study, therefore, focussed on two groups of highly visible immigrant women: Haitians and Indians. If visible immigrant women are ghettoized within their group, they may not perceive an individual approach as a successful integration strategy, leaving collective action as the viable alternative.

In order to test the theoretical utility of the individualism-collectivism distinction for the study of immigrant integration, a number of predictions were made on the basis of Social Identity Theory and the Five Stage Model A first set of hypotheses was directed at testing the conditions required for the different types of social integration orientations. Both the Five Stage Model and Social Identity Theory predict that social injustice can lead to collective action; as a result, it was hypothesized that perceptions of discrimination and social barriers imposed by outgroups would be related to stronger support of a collective integration strategy. This prediction assumes that both Haitian and Indian women cannot easily dissociate themselves from their groups and that a collective strategy would be the most salient alternative when faced with discrimination. A second prediction follows from the Five Stage Model which states that it is the more talented members of a disadvantaged group that will attempt individual social mobility strategies; thus it was hypothesized that individuals who perceived themselves as possessing more personal ability would more strongly endorse an individual integration strategy. Finally, both Social Identity Theory and the Five Stage Model argue that social comparison is a basic psychological precess involved in intergroup relations (Taylor & Moghaddam, 1987). While there is no direct relationship between the outcome of social comparisons and a particular strategy for social change in these models, it was expected that there would be some type of relationship between the social comparison process and an immigrant's integration strategy.

A second set of hypotheses addressed certain behaviors that should be related to integration strategies. It was predicted that individuals adopting a more collective approach to social integration would be more motivated to retain their ethnic identity, more likely to establish contacts within their own community, more desirous of living in an ethnic neighborhood, and more likely to participate in their ethnic community, than individuals having a more individual orientation to integration.

A final hypothesis was put forward with respect to integration strategies. Triandis et al. (1985) suggested that individuals in collectivist cultures are more likely to receive social support. Furthermore, there is evidence indicating that social support acts as a buffer of life-change stresses (Cohen & Hoberman, 1983). Given that immigrating to a new country is a major life stressor (Berry, 1986), it was predicted that individuals supporting a collectivist strategy would show less signs of stress than immigrants favouring an individualistic strategy. This hypothesis is consistent with Kim and Berry's (1986) view that individuals in a multicultural society should experience less acculturative stress than individuals in a society having an assimilation policy.

METHOD

Respondents. Participants in this study consisted of 136 Haitian and
108 Indian immigrant women living in Montreal. The mean ages of the
samples were 35.12 and 32.83 for the Haitian and Indian women
respectively. The Haitian women had been living in Montreal for an
average of 10.93 years and 80% of them were Canadian citizens. The
average years of residence for the Indian sample was 13.61 with 81%
having Canadian citizenship. While the profile of the two samples
differed with respect to their level of education (i.e., the Indian
women had attained higher levels than the Haitian women), each sample
seemed to adequately reflect their respective population profiles in
Montreal (c.f., 1981 Canadian population census). An important
demographic difference between these populations is their numbers. As
of 1981, Haitians represented 4.24% of incoming immigrants to the
Montreal region, whereas Indians accounted for 1.34%. Moreover, from
1981 to 1985 there were close to five times more Haitians than Indians
immigrating to the Montreal area, thus making Haitians a more visible
immigrant group than Indians.

Materials. The present research was part of a large scale project
addressing immigrant integration. The following variables are those
most pertinent to the present study. Questions were formulated to be
answered on a 9 point scale ranging from definitely no to definitely
yes, unless indicated otherwise. Given this study was a preliminary
investigation of integration orientations, many of the variables were
assessed with single items. When multiple items were used to measure a
variable, Cronbach alpha reliability coefficients are reported.

Social integration strategy: Two questions, which had been successfully
used by Moghaddam et al. (1987), were used to assess integration
strategies. Both questions began with the phrase 'In order for me to
get ahead in Canada it is important that ...'. One question stressed
working individually ("I go it alone, rather than acting as part of the
Haitian/Indian community"), whereas the other question emphasized a
collective strategy ("I work with others in the Haitian/Indian
community, rather than go it alone").

Perceived discrimination: Measures of group discrimination and
individual discrimination were assessed by aggregating responses on
three items. The respondent was asked the extent to which her ethnic
group was discriminated against on the basis of race, culture, and being
newcomers ($\alpha=.80$) and the extent to which she had personally been
discriminated against on the basis of the same attributes ($\alpha=.77$).

Social barriers and perceived ability: Respondents were asked to what
extent Canadian society (outgroup barrier), the Indian or Haitian
community (ingroup barrier), and their personal qualities (perceived
ability) 'make it easy for you to get ahead in Canada'. Responses were
given on a scale ranging from 'very difficult' to 'very easy'.

Relative social standing: To assess the distinctiveness of the ingroup in terms of social standing, respondents were asked to compare the treatment of their ingroup in Canada relative to specific outgroups, using a scale ranging from 'much worse than' to 'much better than'. Social comparisons were made with majority groups (i.e., English and French Canadian: $\alpha=.93$), and with other minority groups (i.e., Italian, Haitian/Indian, Lebanese, Jewish, Greek: $\alpha=.80$).

Motivation for culture retention: Eight items assessed motives for heritage culture maintenance. A principle components factor analysis revealed that three items (i.e., culture seen as part of personality, more confidence in getting ahead within ethnic community, hope of someday returning to homeland) defined the primary factor which was labelled "motivation for purposes of identity". These items were aggregated into a single measure ($\alpha=.58$).

Community contacts: Three questions were asked to determine the importance of developing contacts in certain communities (Anglophone, Francophone, and Haitian/Indian) in order to get ahead in Canada.

Importance of ethnic neighborhood. Five items were combined to assess the importance given to an ethnic neighborhood ($\alpha=.76$). They included reporting a large number of the ingroup in one's neighborhood, and giving importance to being as close as possible to ingroup friends, ingroup shops, relatives, and religious or cultural centres.

Participation in ethnic community: Respondents were asked to rate the extent to which they participated in events organized by their ethnic community on a scale ranging from 'not at all' to 'to a great extent'.

Stress symptoms: An abbreviated 17 item version of the Hopkins Symptom Checklist ($\alpha=.88$) was used as an indicator of psychological distress (Derogatis, Lipman, Rickels, Uhlenhuth & Covi, 1974). This measure asked respondents how often they felt a number of different symptoms (e.g., headaches, insomnia, nausea).

Procedure. Respondents were interviewed in their homes by a trained interviewer of their own sex and ethnicity. A structured interview procedure was used where interviewers were responsible for asking questions and recording responses. The respondent was asked to provide an answer on the basis of a prescribed scale from a booklet that was given to the respondent. Interviews with Haitians were based on a French questionnaire, whereas interviews with Indian women were based on an English questionnaire. A back translation procedure was used to ensure equivalency of the two forms.

RESULTS AND DISCUSSION

Group differences in integration strategies. In order to determine if the Indian and Haitian samples differed with respect to their preferred integration strategies, responses to the two questions assessing strategies were analyzed using a two factor (Sample by Strategy) ANOVA.

There was a significant main effect for strategy ($F(1,240)=39.23$, $p<.001$) which was subsumed under a significant sample by strategy interaction ($F(1,240)=20.94$, $p<.001$). A post-hoc analysis of the cell means ($p<.01$) revealed that while the Indian women preferred an individual strategy to a collective strategy ($M=5.95$ vs. $M=3.34$), there was no significant difference in preference for the Haitian women ($M=4.88$ vs $M=4.47$). A further analysis of the means revealed that the Haitian sample showed a significantly stronger preference for collective action than the Indian sample, whereas a reversed pattern of results was found for the individual approach.

Although both of the samples represent immigrant groups who may be additionally disadvantaged because of their physical visibility, it is apparent from the results that they do not perceive a collective strategy as their only mode of integration. The preference for an individual orientation by the Indian sample is particularly interesting, given that recent work by Triandis et al. (1986) reported that India was one of the more collectivistic countries that they examined. The present sample, therefore, can be considered to be somewhat at odds with the Triandis data. A number of potential explanations for the discrepancy exist. First, it is possible that the individualism-collectivism distinction made by Triandis is unrelated to the present distinction; this seems unlikely, however, given the nature of the items used by Triandis (e.g., If the group is slowing me down, it is better to leave it and work alone). A more compelling reason would be that individuals who emigrate have different orientations than individuals who remain in a country; the act of emigrating, in itself, can be considered the expression of an individualistic orientation. Finally, a collective strategy for integration may not be as salient for Indian women in Montreal, given their relatively small number.

Correlates of integration strategy. The two items assessing integration orientation were combined into a single measure, such that high scores were indicative of a collective integration orientation. Pearson product moment correlations were computed between the resulting collective integration index and the other variables in order to test the proposed hypotheses. The results of these analyses are presented in Table 1. It can be noted the pattern of results remained the same when the integration items were examined separately.

It was predicted that perceptions of discrimination and outgroup social barriers would be related to the endorsement of a collective strategy. This hypothesis received only weak support, with only one of six correlations being significant, namely a correlation between individual discrimination and integration orientation for the Indian women. It is possible that no relationships were found between ratings of discrimination and integration strategies because discrimination was examined at a very general level (i.e., on the basis of race, culture, being a newcomer, social barriers). In order to adequately test the hypothesized relationship, future research should assess instances of discrimination directed at behaviors characterizing attempts at changing social status (i.e., being refused a job, a promotion, an apartment in a different neighborhood).

While barriers imposed by Canadian society were not related to integration orientation, it can be seen in Table 1 that perceived ingroup barriers were negatively correlated with integration orientation for both samples. In other words, individuals who perceived their ethnic ingroup as making it difficult for their advancement favored an individual strategy, whereas individual favoring a more collective strategy saw the ingroup as a facilitator for their getting ahead.

Table 1. Correlates of integration orientation of visible immigrant women.

	HAITIANS	INDIANS
MOTIVES OF INTEGRATION STRATEGY		
Individual discrimination	-.11	.22 *
Group discrimination	-.07	-.01
Canadian social barriers	.08	-.13
Ingroup barriers	.33 ***	.40 ***
Perceived personal ability	-.23 **	-.14
Social standing relative to majority	.08	-.06
Social standing relative to minority	.32 ***	.24 *
BEHAVIORS INVOLVED IN INTEGRATION		
Motivation for identity retention	.22 **	.41 ***
Ingroup contacts	.51 ***	.52 ***
English Canadian contacts	-.27 **	-.02
French Canadian contacts	-.20 *	-.07
Importance of ethnic neighborhood	.22 *	.47 ***
Participation in ethnic community	.30 ***	.16
CONSEQUENCE OF STRATEGY		
Hopkins Symptom Checklist	-.34 ***	-.01

*** p<.001   ** p<.01   * p<.05

It was predicted that individuals having the most ability would prefer an individual strategy. This hypothesis received support from the Haitian sample, but not from the Indian sample. This was an encouraging result given that the measure of ability was a single item self-report measure. The absence of a relationship for the sample of Indian women may be due to restriction of range in actual ability: seventy-five percent of the Indian sample received some educational training beyond high school. It would be beneficial in future research to operationalize a measure that would clearly identify the more talented individuals in a group.

The results pertaining to social comparisons and integration strategies are particularly informative. Theories of intergroup relations that focus on disadvantaged groups usually assume that members of these groups focus on the advantaged groups for purposes of social comparison. When comparisons were made with the "advantaged groups" (majority Canadians), however, there were no significant relationships with integration orientation for either sample. There were significant relationships, for both samples, between integration orientation and social comparisons made with other "disadvantaged groups" (minority Canadians), indicating that individuals favoring a collective integration strategy are more likely to see themselves as better off than other minorities. While these results are somewhat at odds with intergroup theories, they are in line with the Festinger's (1954) original theory of social comparison, which postulated that social comparisons occur only when others are similar to oneself. Given that the other disadvantaged groups were more pertinent with regard to the selection of an integration orientation, it seems that social psychological theories of intergroup relations would be richer if they integrated these other groups within their frameworks. Recent sociological work on resource mobilization and competitive ethnic relations may be particularly enlightening with regard to such extensions (e.g., Olzak, 1986).

A first finding with respect to behaviors related to integration was that the motivation to retain ethnic identity was significantly related to a integration orientation for both samples; individuals having a stronger desire to retain their ethnic identity were more likely to favor a collective approach for getting ahead in Canadian society. This result lends credence to the idea of linking the policy of multiculturalism (i.e., heritage culture maintenance) with a collective strategy for immigrant integration.

It was found, as hypothesized, that a collective orientation was positively related to the perceived importance of establishing ingroup contacts for purposes of gaining an advantaged position. The idea that a collective orientation would be negatively related to creating outgroup contacts was supported only for the Haitian sample. As hypothesized, attributing importance to living in an ethnic neighborhood was related to a collective integration orientation for both samples. Finally, it was found that Haitian women who participated more actively

in their ethnic community were more likely to favor a collective
orientation, thus replicating the findings of Moghaddam et al. (1987).

A final result of interest in this study was the significant negative
correlation between scores on the Hopkins Symptom Checklist and
integration orientation for Haitian women. This relationship suggests
that Haitian women who prefer a more individual integration strategy are
more likely to report symptoms that are characteristic of psychological
distress. While this result suggests that one's integration strategy
can have important consequences, its generalizability is limited given
that it was not obtained for the sample of Indian women.

GENERAL DISCUSSION

The study's major contribution is in demonstrating that the distinction
made by theories of intergroup relations regarding individual and
collective forms of behavior in response to social disadvantage is
relevant to the study and understanding of immigrant integration. Many
of the predictions concerning individual and collective forms of
behavior made by Social Identity Theory (Tajfel & Turner, 1979) and the
Five-Stage Model of intergroup relations (Taylor & McKirnan, 1984), were
supported within the context of immigrant integration.

The present study also points to the importance of studying immigrants
from different cultures while focussing on the particular
characteristics of their new social milieu. Indian women in Montreal
were found to be more individually oriented in their integration
strategies than were Haitian women. It was suggested that the
demographic characteristics of the Indian population in Montreal may
have precluded a more collective strategy. This interpretation is
speculative and future research should further test the idea that
individuals from immigrant groups that are more strongly represented are
more likely to engage in collective integration strategies.

There are of course some limitations in the present study. Perhaps the
most important limitation lies in the measurement of integration
orientation, which was assessed using only two items. While the measure
that was used did prove to be informative in the present study and in
past research (Moghaddam et al., 1987), future research would benefit
from a more psychometrically sound measure. The recently developed
measure of individualism-collectivism developed by Triandis and his
colleagues (Triandis et al., 1986) should prove to be useful as a
general measure of individualism-collectivism. Along these lines, we
are presently developing a multidimensional measure of integration
orientation that directly addresses the process of immigrant
integration.

Finally, while immigrant integration strategies can conceptually be
viewed as either individualistic or collective, these strategies are not
mutually exclusive. An individual may adopt a variety of behaviors that
would characterize both strategies in order to respond to the demands of
different situations (i.e., collectivistic in social behaviors, but

individualistic in economic behaviors). The adoption of an interactionist perspective is one of the many challenges facing psychologists studying immigrant integration.

REFERENCES

Berry, J.W. (1986). Multiculturalism and psychology in plural societies. In L. Ekstrand (Ed.), Ethnic minorities and immigrants in a cross-cultural perspective (pp.35-51). Lisse: Swets & Zeitlinger.

Cohen, S. & Hoberman, H.M. (1983). Positive events and social support as buffers of life change stress. Journal of Applied Social Psychology, 13, 99-125.

Derogatis, L.R., Lipman, R.S., Rickels, K., Uhlenhuth, E.H. & Covi, L. (1974). The Hopkins Symptom Checklist (HSCL): A measure of primary symptom dimensions. In P. Pichot (Ed.), Psychological Measurements in Psychopharmacology, 7, 79-110.

Festinger, L. (1954). A theory of social comparison processes. Human Relations, 7, 117-140.

Hofstede, G. (1980). Culture's consequences: International differences in work-related values. Beverly Hills: Sage.

Hui, C.H. & Triandis, H.C. (1986). Individualism-collectivism: A study of cross-cultural researchers. Journal of Cross-Cultural Psychology, 17, 225-248.

Kim, U. & Berry, J.W. (1986). Predictors of acculturative stress: Korean immigrants in Toronto, Canada. In L.H. Ekstrand (Ed.), Ethnic minorities and immigrants in a cross-cultural perspective (pp. 159-170). Lisse: Swets & Zeitlinger.

Kluckhohn, F. & Strodtbeck, I. (1961). Variations in value orientations. New York: Harper & Row.

Mead, M. (1967). Cooperation and competition among primitive peoples. Boston: Beacon.

Moghaddam, F.M. & Taylor (1987). The meaning of multiculturalism for visible minority immigrant women. Canadian Journal of Behavioural Science, 19, 121-136.

Moghaddam, F.M., Taylor, D.M. & Lalonde, R.N. (1987). Individualistic and collective integration strategies among Iranians in Canada. International Journal of Psychology, 22, 301-313.

Olzak, S. (1986). A competition model of ethnic collective action in American cities, 1877-1889. In S. Olzak & J. Nagel (Eds.), Competitive ethnic relations (pp. 17-46). N.Y.: Academic Press.

Tajfel, H. & Turner, J. (1979). An integrative theory of intergroup conflict. In W.G. Austin & S. Worchel (Eds.), The social psychology of intergroup relations (pp. 33-47). Monterey: Brooks-Cole.

Taylor, D.M. & McKirnan, D.J. (1984). A five-stage model of intergroup relations. British Journal of Social Psychology, 23, 291-300.

Taylor, D.M. & Moghaddam, F.M. (1987). Theories of intergroup relations: International social psychological perspectives. New York: Praeger.

Triandis, H.C., Bontempo, R., Betancourt, H., Bond, M., Leung, K., Brenes, A., Georgas, J., Hui, C.H., Marin, G., Setiadi, B., Sinha, J.P.B., Verma, J., Spangenberg, J., Touzard, H. & de Montmollin, G. (1986). The measurement of etic aspects of individualism and collectivism across cultures. Australian Journal of Psychology, 38, 257-267.

Triandis, H.C., Leung, K., Villareal, M.J. & Clack, F.L. (1985). Allocentric versus idiocentric tendencies: Convergent and discriminant validation. Journal of Research in Personality, 19, 395-415.

Note. The authors would like to thank the women who participated in this study and R.A. Schuller for her helpful comments on an earlier version of this paper.

IMMIGRANTS' MENTAL HEALTH AND SOCIAL RELATIONS IN MONTREAL

Jean-Claude Lasry
Université de Montréal
Montréal, Canada

A clear relationship has been established between stressful life events and illness (WEISS et al., 1957; KISSEN, 1958; RAHE et al., 1964; BROWN & BIRLEY, 1968; PAYKEL et al., 1969; SOMMER & LASRY, 1984). Those life events (e.g., divorce, unemployment, moving, financial difficulties, etc.) necessitate a certain amount of social readjustment, which has been calibrated by HOLMES & RAHE (1967).

Further studies have evidenced the mediating impact of the social environment between stress and illness. Social support will attenuate the stress experienced, whereas lack of social support will contribute to illness, physical or mental (COBB, 1976; DEAN & LIN, 1977; KAPLAN et al., 1977). D'ARCY & SIDDIQUE (1984) have, for example, shown that mothers who reported a low level of social support, exhibited a relatively high level of symptomatology.

As SCHAEFFER et al. (1981) point out, researchers do not distinguish between the social network and the social support that members derive from it. Social support can come either directly from individual members of the network or indirectly from organizations within the network. LIN et al. (1979) and BIEGEL et al. (1980) have shown that community attachment can be of great significance for mental health, respectively for Chinese-Americans and for "ethnics" descending from Southern and Eastern Europe. An ethnic community - based network is a better predictor of psychiatric symptoms than life events.

In a study on the psychological adaptation of Vietnamese refugees in Canada, BERRY & BLONDEL (1982) also showed that links to an established ethnic community is crucial for mental health. They even predict that "adaptation problems may be especially difficult and prolonged", without the presence of an established social network involving ethnic community organizations.

KUO & TSAI (1986) elaborate on the social networking of immigrants. Rather than being "uprooted and transplanted vegetables", immigrants work actively to reestablish their disrupted social networks. KUO & TSAI's study assessed social network and support, and found them to be correlated to psychological symptoms. Their findings reinforce the argument that strong social support is imperative for good mental health, and that strong ethnic ties are beneficial to psychological well-being and definitely not harmful.

COCHRANE & STOPES-ROE (1977) compared the psychological adjustment of Indian, Pakistani and Irish immigrants in England. Whereas immigrants in this study presented "more cohesive family situations" than the English born, only Indian immigrants presented a significant negative correlation between support from family members and psychological symptoms.

Using a different type of mental illness assessment, i.e. mental hospital admissions rather than symptom checklists in community surveys, MUHLIN (1979) proved that there was a strong inverse relationship between the density of an ethnic group in a community and the rate of mental illness among the group. He did show that cultural isolation was related to psychiatric hospitalization rates for the foreign-born living in New York.

In previous papers, we have reported on the assessment of mental health in a Montreal immigrant population and found it to be related to length of stay in the country, and to gender of the respondent (LASRY, 1977; LASRY & SIGAL, 1976). The objective of the present paper is to devise an index of social relations and to relate it to the immigrants' mental health, controlling for pertinent variables such as length of stay, gender and education. We hypothesize that the better the social relations, the lower the psychiatric symptomatology.

METHODOLOGY

Subjects - Immigrants from North Africa (Morocco, Algeria, Tunisia), of Jewish religion, have been interviewed to assess their adaptation in Montreal. Sampling was stratified by length of residence in the country, which ranged from 2 to 15 years at time of study. Procedures have been described fully elswewhere (LASRY, 1981).

Average length of stay in Canada was 6.8 years, while mean age for men was 37.1, and for women, 35.1. Total number of respondents was 469 (258 men, 211 women), representing 82 single persons and 387

Table 1: Percentage distribution on the four questions composing the Social Relations Index

		MEN (N=258)	WOMEN (N=211)	TOTAL (N=469)
1. Have you encountered some difficulty in making friends in Montreal?				
(1) Yes (5) No	(1)	31.0%	38.4%	34.3%
	(5)	69.0%	61.6%	65.7%
2. Are your current friends members of your family, friends from your childhood, or new friends?	(1)	5.4%	9.0%	7.0%
	(3)	5.4%	7.6%	6.4%
(1) No friends (4) Childhood	(4)	24.4%	22.7%	23.7%
(3) Family (5) New friends	(5)	64.7%	60.7%	62.9%
3. Do you find it easy or difficult to get along with most of your colleagues?	(1-2)	8.9%	3.7%	6.6%
(1) Very difficult (4) Easy	(3)	10.9%	6.2%	8.7%
(2) Difficult (5) Very easy	(4-5)	62.4%	50.7%	57.1%
(3) So so (0) No colleagues	(0)	17.8%	39.3%	27.5%
4. Do you find it easy or difficult to get along with your boss or your supervisor?	(1-2)	8.9%	5.2%	7.2%
(1) Very difficult (4) Easy	(3)	9.7%	8.1%	8.9%
(2) Difficult (5) Very easy	(4-5)	65.5%	47.4%	57.4%
(3) So so (0) No boss	(0)	15.9%	39.3%	26.4%

married ones. Both spouses of 199 families were interviewed separately, excluding 11 Canadian-born spouses from the study.

Instruments: 1- <u>Mental Health</u>: The Mental Health score is derived from the pathognomonic answers to a list of 22 psychiatric symptoms devised by LANGNER (1962). This checklist has been widely used in community studies, differentiating well between normal and psychiatric cases (COCHRANE et al., 1977; PRINCE et al., 1967). ENGELSMANN et al. (1972) carried out a cluster analysis of this scale, and identified three clusters: Anxiety (5 items), Depression (5 items) and Psychosomatic Complaints (8 items), leaving four items unclassifiable. We modified slightly the translation made for a Quebec study by PRINCE & MOMBOUR (1967).

2- <u>Social Relations</u>: The four questions retained to assess social relationships (MILLER, 1970) were asked both of male and female respondents. A question evaluating participation in voluntary organizations was dropped, since it was asked only of men.

TABLE 2: Mental Health Score (Langner) according to the immigrants' Social Relations Index

SOCIAL RELATIONS INDEX	DISTRIBUTION OF THE SOCIAL RELATIONS INDEX			MENTAL HEALTH AVERAGE		
	Men	Women	Total	Men*	Women*	Total*
1.00-2.50	6.6% (17)	10.9% (23)	8.5% (40)	7.6	9.4	8.7
2.51-3.50	23.3% (60)	26.1% (55)	24.5% (115)	5.2	6.7	5.9
3.51-4.50	43.0% (111)	36.5% (77)	40.1% (188)	3.5	5.5	4.3
4.51-5.00	27.1% (70)	26.5% (56)	26.9% (126)	3.2	5.5	4.0
$\bar{X}$	4.01	3.87	3.95	4.1	6.1	5.0
(N)	(258)	(211)	(469)			

* F is significant at $p < .001$

The index of Social Relations is the mean of the four questions. The higher the score, the better the social relations. Table 1 presents the percentage distributions to each item, with their scoring.

The first question deals with the difficulty the immigrants encountered in making friends in Montreal: only one third of the subjects stated they did have some difficulty. The next question establishes the type of friends made, whether they are members of the family, friends from childhood (in North Africa) or whether they are new friends. Over 60% agreed with the last alternative.

The last two questions assess the ease of the relationships at work, with colleagues and with a boss. The answers to those two questions are quite similar. About 7% find their social interaction at work difficult or very difficult, while about 2/3 of men and half of the women find their work relationships easy or very easy.

RESULTS

Table 2 presents the distribution of the Social Relations index, according to the respondent's gender. For all, independently

TABLE 3: Mental Health Score according to type of Friends

TYPE OF FRIENDS	MEN**		WOMEN		TOTAL*	
	$\bar{X}$	(N)	$\bar{X}$	(N)	$\bar{X}$	(N)
No friends	6.1	(14)	6.8	(19)	6.5	(33)
Friends from family	4.9	(14)	6.9	(16)	6.0	(30)
Friends from childhood	5.0	(63)	5.8	(48)	5.3	(111)
New friends	3.5	(167)	6.1	(128)	4.6	(295)

** F is significant at $p < .01$ * F is significant at $p < .05$

TABLE 4: Mental Health Score according to the way the immigrants get along with their colleagues

GETTING ALONG WITH COLLEAGUES	MEN**		WOMEN**		TOTAL**	
	$\bar{X}$	(N)	$\bar{X}$	(N)	$\bar{X}$	(N)
No colleagues	4.7	(46)	7.2	(83)	6.3	(129)
(Very) Difficult	5.4	(23)	8.9	(8)	6.3	(31)
So So	4.5	(28)	5.5	(13)	4.9	(41)
(Very) Easy	3.6	(161)	5.2	(107)	4.2	(268)

TABLE 5: Pearson correlations between the Social Relations Index and the Mental Health Scale, and its three clusters

SUBJECTS	MENTAL HEALTH SCALE	ANXIETY CLUSTER	DEPRESSION CLUSTER	PSYCHOSOMATIC CLUSTER
Men (N= 258)	.30	.25	.28	.27
Women (N=211)	.27	.11*	.40	.20
TOTAL (N= 469)	.30	.19	.35	.24

* Except this figure, all r_s are significant at $p < .001$

of gender, the average Social Relations score hovers around 4, a sign of a good social adjustment (the scale ranges from 1 to 5). Only one third of the respondents manifest a score lower than 3.50.

The mental health score is also presented in Table 2, in relation to the Social Relations index. Regardless of gender, the worse the social relations, the greater the number of psychiatric symptoms (p <.001). In fact, the immigrants who have difficult social relations (,< 2.50) report a mean number of psychiatric symptoms higher than the cut-off point of 7, suggested by LANGNER as defining impaired persons (1962). As has been previously shown (GOVE & TUDOR, 1973; TAILLEFER & LASRY, 1987), the women in our study exhibit a greater number of symptoms than men (6.1 vs 4.1, p <.001).

The intensity of the symptomatology is linked to the type of friends (Table 3). When men state they have no friends, their mental health score is significantly worse than those who have friends (p < .01). When they have friends, who are either from their family or their childhood, their number of symptoms is still higher than those who made new friends in Montreal (5.0 vs 3.5).

Although the differences are non-significant, the trends are similar for women. It is interesting to note that their symptomatology is equivalent, whether they have no friends or have only family members as friends. The better mental health level for our female respondents is associated with having friends from childhood or having made new friends in Montreal.

The social relationships established at work also have an influence on the mental health level (see Table 4). The easier it is for the immigrants to get along with their colleagues at work, the better their level of mental health.

Table 5 shows that the correlation between social relations and the global mental health scale is around .30. This correlation is highest with the Depression cluster, particularly for women (r=.40).

DISCUSSION

According to the Social Relations index devised (mean of 4.0, on a scale of 1 to 5), the Jewish immigrants from North Africa have made a fairly good social adjustment in Montreal. Two thirds of them state they encountered no difficulty in making friends, most of those being new acquaintances made in Montreal. At work again, the majority finds it easy to get along with their colleagues and with their supervisor. We have previously shown that the colleagues and the supervisors preferred by the Jewish immigrants from North Africa are the French Canadians, members of the Quebec majority hosting the immigrants (LASRY, 1983). This attraction towards the host population reflects their social integration and adjustment in Montreal.

Our general hypothesis is confirmed. There is a correlation, albeit moderate, between social relations and mental health. Even when pertinent variables like length of stay or education are controlled, the partial correlations are quite similar to the zero order ones. Difficult social relations then are accompanied by a higher psychiatric symptomatology, particularly depressive symptoms for women. The importance of this correlation is enhanced by the fact that we have previously noticed that "depression seems to be a minor feature in our immigrants' reaction to adaptation" (LASRY, 1977).

One could argue that the immigrants have poor social relations because of mental illness. This is rather unlikely when taking into account the evaluation and selection process immigrants go through, before being accepted in Canada: mentally ill persons are refused entry as immigrants.

It follows then that the difficulty faced by the immigrants in their social adaptation is causing psychiatric symptoms, particularly depression. Our results lend support to the argument made by immigrants' organizations that their activities facilitate the social adaptation and the greater well-being of their members; this argument is also confirmed by the data from BIEGEL et al. (1980), BERRY & BLONDEL (1982) and KUO & TSAI (1986).

REFERENCES

BERRY, J.W. & BLONDEL, T. (1982). Psychological adaptation of Vietnamese refugees in Canada. Canadian Journal of Community Mental Health, 1: 82-88.

BIEGEL, D., NAPARSTEK, A. & KHAN, M. Social support and mental health: An examination of inter-relationship. Paper presented at the 88th Annual Meeting of the American Psychological Association, Montreal, 1980.

BROWN, G.W. & BIRLEY, J.L.T. (1968). Crises and life changes and the onset of schizophrenia. Journal of Health and Social Behavior, 9: 203-214.

COBBS, S. (1976). Social support as a moderator of life stress. Psychosomatic Medicine, 38, 300-314.

COCHRANE, R. A comparative study of the adjustment of Irish Indian and Pakistani immigrants to England. Paper presented at the British Psychological Society Conference, the Mahesh Desai Memorial Lecture. Nottingham, England, 1979.

COCHRANE, R. & STOPES-ROE, M. Psychological and social adjustment of Asian immigrants to Britain: a community survey. Social Psychiatry, 1977, 12: 195-206.

COCHRANE, R., HASHMI, F. & STOPES-ROE, M. Measuring psychological disturbance in Asian immigrants to Britain. Social Sciences and Medicine, 1977, 2: 157-164.

D'ARCY, C. & SIDDIQUE, C.M. (1984). Social support and mental health among mothers of preschool and school age children. Social Psychiatry, 19: 155-162.

DEAN, A. & LIN, N. (1977). The stress-buffering role of social support. The Journal of Nervous and Mental Disease, 165: 403-417.

ENGELSMAN, F., MURPHY, H.B.M., PRINCE, R., LEDUC , & DEMERS, H. (1972). Variations in responses to a symptom check-list by age, sex, income, residence and ethnicity. Social Psychiatry, 7: 150-156.

GOVE, R. & TUDOR, F. (1973). Adult sex roles and mental illness. American Journal of Sociology, 78: 812-835.

HOLMES, T.H. & RAHE, H. (1967). The social readjustment rating scale. Journal of Psychosomatic Research, 11: 213-218.

KUO, W.H. & TSAI, Y.M. (1986). Social networking, hardiness and immigrant's mental health. Journal of Health and Social Behavior, 27: 133-149.

KAPLAN, B., GORE, S. & CASSEL, J. (1977). Social support and health. Medical Care, 15: 47-58.

KISSEN, D.M. (1958). Some psychosocial aspects of pulmonary tuberculosis. International Journal of Social Psychiatry, 3: 252.

LANGNER, T.S. (1962). A twenty-two item screening score of psychiatric symptoms indicating impairment. Journal of Health and Human Behavior, 3: 269-276.

LASRY, J.C. (1983). Sephardim and Ashkenazim in Montreal. Contemporary Jewry, 6: 27-33.

LASRY, J.C. A Francophone Diaspora in Quebec, in M. WEINFELD, W. SHAFFIR & I. COTLER (Eds.). The Canadian Jewish Mosaic, pp. 221-240. Toronto: Wiley, 1981.

LASRY, J.C. (1977). Cross-cultural perspective on mental health and immigrant adaptation. Social Psychiatry, 12: 49-55.

LASRY, J.C. & SIGAL, J.J. (1976). L'influence sur la santé mentale de la durée de séjour, de l'instruction, du revenu personnel et de l'âge chez un groupe d'immigrants. Revue Internationale de Psychologie Appliquée, 25: 215-222.

LIN, N., ENSEL, W.M., SIMEONE, R.S. & KUO, W. (1979). Social support, stressful life events and illness: a model and an empirical test. Journal of Health and Social Behavior, 20: 108-119.

MILLER, D.C. (1970). Handbook of research design and social measurement (2nd Ed.). New York: David McKay.

MUHLIN, G.L. (1979). Mental hospitalization of the foreign-born and the role of cultural isolation. International Journal of Psychiatry, 25: 258-266.

PAYKEL, E.S., Myers, J.K., DIENELD, M.N., KLERMAN, G.L. (1969). Life events and depression. A controlled study. Archives of General Psychiatry, 21: 753-760.

PRINCE, R.H., MOMBOUR, W., SHINER, E.V., & ROBERTS, J. (1967). Abbreviated techniques for assessing mental health in interview surveys: an example from central Montreal, Laval Médical, 38: 58-62.

PRINCE, R. & MOMBOUR, W. (1967) A technique for improving linguistic equivalence in cross-cultural surveys. International Journal of Social Psychiatry, 13: 229-237.

RAHE, R.H., MEYER, M., SMITH, M., KJAER, G. & HOLMES, T.H. (1964). Social stress and illness onset. Journal of Psychosomatic Research, 8: 35-44.

SCHAEFER, C., COYNE, J.C. & LAZARUS, R.S. (1981). The health-related functions of social support. Journal of Behavioral Medicine, 4: 381-405.

SOMMER, D. & LASRY, J.C. (1984). Personality and reactions to stressful life events. Canada's Mental Health, 32: 19-20.

TAILLEFER, S.C. & LASRY, J.C. (1987). Marital status, gender and mental health. Canadian Psychology, 28, 2a:602.

WEISS, E., DLIN, B., ROLLIN, H.R., FISCHER, H.K. & REPLER, C.R. (1957). Emotional factors in coronary occlusion. Archives of Internal Medicine, 99: 628.

LIFE EXPERIENCES, STRESS AND ADAPTATION OF IMMIGRANT ADOLESCENTS

Amado M. Padilla
Stanford University
Stanford, U.S.A.

In an effort to empirically examine the effects of exposure to various life change events in conjunction with normative developmental changes in children and adolescents, a series of studies have attempted to identify and measure childhood/adolescent stress (Coddington, 1972; Yeaworth, York, Hussey, Ingu & Gordman, 1980; Newcomb, Huba & Bentler, 1981; Gad & Johnson, 1980; Lewis, Siegel & Lewis, 1984; Mechanic, 1983). Unfortunately, few studies have examined the stress process among groups of immigrant children or adolescents. Those children or adolescents who are culturally and ethnically different face additional adaptive demands which may place them at higher risk for the development of psychological or behavioral problems. Indeed, numerous studies suggest immigrant and refugee individuals suffer from greater rates of psychological disturbances as compared with non-immigrants. (Dyal & Dyal, 1981; Warheit, Vega, Auth, Meinhardt, & 1985; Westermeyer 1986).

These higher rates of psychological disorders have been postulated to be the result of an inability to adapt to a combination of numerous psychosocial changes. Given the fact that immigrants must in fact adapt to a multitude of critical sociocultural changes, a stressful life events paradigm may offer an effective conceptual framework from which to study the impact of sociocultural change. In general, life change events which are appraised as being stressful have been found to play a significant role in the precipitation of physical as well as psychological disorders, particularly if other mediating variables such as personal resources, social supports and coping behaviors are examined (Bloom, 1985).

Sandler and Block (1979) examined the relationship between stressful life events and maladjustment in 134 children from inner-city schools and reported a positive relationship between stressful events and maladjustment. Research which examines the extent to which immigrant status places children/adolescents at greater risk for developing emotional or behavioral difficulties is lacking. In addition to the need to examine and clarify prevalence and incidence of behavioral/emotional problems among various sub-groups of Hispanic children and adolescents, new approaches toward assessment of psychosocial stress factors are needed which may be specific to these youth and which may predispose them to behavioral and emotional problems.

Early empirical work with children conducted by Coddington (1972), following a methodology similar to that used by Holmes and Rahe (1967), used life change units (LCU) to weigh the amount of adjustment required by each adolescent life change. A similar approach has more recently been utilized (Yeaworth et al., 1980). Some criticisms of this approach have been raised (Byrne & Whyte, 1980; Cervantes & Castro, 1985) particularly since individual differences in the experience and appraisal of the stressfulness of a given event are likely (Lazarus & Folkman, 1984). Others (Lewis et al., 1984) criticize early adolescent stress researchers in their attempts to generate lists of stressful life events based on adult perceptions. Lewis and colleagues also criticized earlier adolescent stress research for not considering continuous stressors such as prolonged parental conflict or, as Newcomb et al. (1981) suggest, poor socio-economic conditions.

In an attempt to construct a meaningful stress scale for pre-adolescents, Lewis et al. (1984) took an ethnographic approach where individual and group interviews were conducted with 5th and 6th graders of similar ages from white, middle-class backgrounds.   In this fashion, the investigators were able to construct a set of 22 stressful items which were subsequently pre-tested, refined to 20 items, and then used in a larger study of 2,400 5th graders. Lewis and colleagues speculate that there are strains in childhood that "may not be appreciated by adults," and therefore recommend a similar approach toward item generation in future child/adolescent stress research.

Within the general body of empirical investigation on adults, there has been an emerging body of work focusing on ethnic minority groups, particularly Hispanics (Pine, Padilla & Maldonado, 1985; Vega & Miranda, 1985; Castro et al., 1986). Unfortunately, while empirical work with adult Hispanic groups is beginning to flourish, there exists a dearth of information concerning Hispanic childhood/adolescent stress.

Newcomb, Huba and Bentler (1986) did include a sample of Hispanic adolescents in their study of the impact (or desirability) of life change events in relation to demographic variables and previous exposure to these events. The perceived desirability of 39 life events and occurrence of these events was reported by a sub-sample of 153 Hispanics.

Newcomb and colleagues found a significant multivariate difference between the four ethnic groups sampled. When Hispanics and Blacks were compared, significant differences emerged on three cluster scales: Deviance, Relocation and Distress. Hispanic adolescents perceived Deviance items (e.g., trouble with the law; stole something valuable; trouble in school) and Distress items (e.g., pimples on face; got therapy; thought about suicide) as significantly more desirable (less stressful) than the Black sample. Black adolescents reported Relocation items (e.g., parents changed jobs; changed schools; family moved) as significantly more desirable than the Hispanic sample. In comparing Hispanic adolescents with the White and Asian sub-samples, no significant differences on cluster scales emerged. Similarly, when the rho rank-order correlation coefficient was computed there was a high degree of relative rank ordering of the 39 events between the four sub-samples (.96 to .99). For the entire sample, got or gave V.D. was reported as the most undesirable event, regardless of previous exposure. For Hispanic adolescents this item was followed by death in the family, family accident or illness, serious accident or illness and parent abused alcohol. In all cases except one (given medication by a physician), exposure to the event increased the desirability (reduced stress appraisal) of the event relative to those adolescents who had not experienced the event. Relative rank-ordering of events between the experienced and inexperienced subjects was highly correlated (rho=.89). The investigators conclude that the life-event appraisal process is influenced by an adolescent's ethnic background and therefore ethnicity must be considered an important moderator when evaluating the impact of life events.

A second study of Hispanic children was conducted by Yamamoto and Byrnes (1984) in which 167 Hispanic fourth, fifth and sixth graders were compared with 88 Anglo American children on a previously developed, 20-item life event scale. Hispanic children were found to report a markedly higher incidence of events such as academic retainment (28% vs. 14%), poor report card (62% vs. 39%), and being sent to the principal (63% vs. 48%). The Hispanic children rated the events, giving a class report and not making 100 on a test, as being markedly more stressful when compared to the Anglo American children. The authors suggest that Hispanic children may find the tasks of schooling and its individually competetive settings harder to handle than other children.

The precise ethnic composition of the Hispanic sub-samples in each of the two previously cited studies was not reported, making results difficult to interpret. Cervantes and Castro (1985) argue for more systematic stress research where Hispanic sub-population differences are controlled. The exposure, appraisal and outcome of stressful events vary greatly depending on generational status, ethnic subgroup membership, English vs. Spanish language proficiency and socioeconomic status. For instance, events reported as being highly stressful for immigrant Salvadoran adolescents may be quite different than those reported by third generation (native-born) Mexican American adolescents.

Given the utility of examining childhood/adolescent stress, the current study aimed at identifying culturally-specific potentially stressful events for a group of Mexican immigrant adolescents. Impressionistic reports suggest that higher levels of psychological distress in immigrants may be related to the trauma of relocation, conflicts in cultural attitudes and beliefs, language difficulties and lowered socioeconomic conditions (Derbyshire, 1980; Nicol, 1974; Shuval, 1982).

A second aim of this study was to examine the reliability and possible validity of a specially constructed instrument, the Hispanic Children's Stress Inventory (HCSI), to assess psychosocial stressors in an immigrant population of Mexican children/adolescents. This instrument was designed to tap stressors that may be specific to the life experiences of adolescent immigrants who are not proficient in English, knowledgeable of U.S. cultural patterns, and whose family unity may be disrupted. Current stress measures for adolescents are not sensitive to the particular type of events that immigrants may experience (e.g., difficulty in communicating in English). An attempt was made in the construction of this instrument to synthesize current methodologic considerations in the development of a stress scale specific for Hispanic youth.

Another aim of the current investigation was to examine both gender and age differences in the exposure to and appraisal of potentially stressful events among Mexican immigrant adolescents. Finally, the study aimed at replicating earlier findings related to the reduction in the appraisal of stress following previous exposure.

METHODOLOGY

Subjects. Participants in the study were 242 first generation, Mexican-born adolescents sampled from three high schools and two junior high schools in the Los Angeles County area. A total of 131 males and 111 females participated in the study. The five selected schools are located in areas which have at least 20% to 30% of Hispanic residents within their boundaries. All participants were solicited from English as a Second Language (ESL) courses. Participants were first given a parental consent form and upon completion of this were administered a series of questionnaires in groups of 40-50. Since many of the participants had obtained varied levels of education in Mexico prior to migration the age range of students in grades 7 through 12 was broad (12-21). Those few participants either younger than 13 or older than 19 were excluded from the current study, resulting in 242 participants.

Instruments. The Hispanic Children's Stress Inventory (HCSI) was utilized in the present study. The HCSI was developed in a methodology similar to Lewis et al. (1984) where small group semi-structured interviews were initially conducted with 20 Hispanic children in an effort to generate a preliminary set of psychosocial stress items specific for this population. A content analysis of the tape interview material was conducted by three Hispanic judges. Following this content analysis an initial version of the inventory with 24 items representing both chronic stressors and discrete events was prepared. In an initial pilot study of 125 fifth and sixth grade Hispanic children a Cronbach's coefficient apha of .80 was estimated. A test of concurrent validity revealed the HCSI to correlate significantly (r=.74; p   .01) with the Lewis et al. (1984) Feel Bad Scale, which would suggest the HCSI to tap a dimension of stress somewhat similar yet possibly culturally distinct from that measured in the Feel Bad Scale.

For the present study, the HCSI instructions for administration and scoring were slightly modified. For each item respondents were asked first to report whether or not they had experienced the event over the past year. Secondly, respondents were asked to indicate on a 5-point Likert scale their appraised stress for each particular item. The appraisal response categories ranged from 1 to 5 (1=not at all stressful; 2=minimally stressful; 3=moderately stressful; 4=very stressful; 5=extremely stressful). Respondents were asked to rate each event in terms of how much stress the event created for them (in the case of occurrence) or to indicate how much stress it would cause should it be experienced. In this fashion a distinction could be made between appraised stress as a function of experience.

In an effort to further evaluate the psychometric properties of the HCSI, a concurrent validity measure, the Piers-Harris Self-Concept Scale (1984) was included in the current study.

The Piers-Harris Children's Self-Concept Scale is an 80 item, self-report inventory which assesses self-concept in children and adolescents (Piers, 1984). Self-concept is defined by the authors of the scale as a "relatively stable set of self-attitudes reflecting both a description and an evaluation of one's own behavior and attributes" (pg. 1). Based on the notion that children cannot be characterized simply by an overall level of self-concept but may view themselves quite differently across different areas, the authors developed six separate cluster scales. These cluster scales examine areas of relative strengths and weaknesses including problematic behaviors, intellectual and school status, physical appearance and attributes, anxiety, popularity, and general feelings of happiness. The Piers-Harris measure was selected as a criterion measure given its breadth in assessing multidimensional aspects children/adolescent self-esteem. Further, the Piers-Harris has been found to be significantly related to other measures of childhood psychopathology and intelligence (Piers, 1984), therefore, serving as a valid criterion measure when administered along with the Hispanic Children's Stress Inventory. Low total scores on the Piers-Harris as well as low subscale scores refelcted less self-esteem.

In addition to the HCSI a demographic questionnaire which included a self-assessment of English language proficiency was administered. All instruments were translated and administered in Spanish to all respondents.

RESULTS

Phase 1. A first step in analyzing the results of the current study was to estimate the reliability of the HCSI with this group of Mexican adolescents. Cronbach's Alpha was computed for all $\underline{Ss}$ resulting in an internal consistency coefficient of .92 in the assessment of discrete and chronic stressors. A second step in the psychometric analysis of the HCSI was to assess the validity of the scale through correlational procedures. There exists no current definitive measure of psychosocial stress in Latino adolescents, therefore, the Piers-Harris Children's Self-Concept Scale was conceptualized as most relevant to the establishment of concurrent and/or construct validity of the HCSI. Analyses here consisted of correlating the two sets of scores using the Pearson Product-Moment Correlation Coefficient. The total HCSI score was found to correlate significantly and negatively (r=-.23, $\underline{p}$=.001) with the total Piers-Harris score, as well as with five of the six cluster scales. Since low scores on the Piers-Harris are reflective of less self-concept, or a tendency toward personal problems/difficulties in each specific domain, the results suggest that as HCSI scores increase (greater perceived psychosocial stress) problems in overall self-concept with related problems also tend to increase. Of particular interest is the highly significant correlation (r=-.25, $\underline{p}$=.001) between the total HCSI Score and the Anxiety sub-scale. The Anxiety sub-scale is a cluster of 14 items described as reflecting general emotional disturbances and dysphoric mood. The initial finding suggests an increase in subjective distress with increases in scores on the HCSI for this immigrant sample.

Phase 2 - Following psychometric evaluation of the HCSI a second step in analyzing the results of the HCSI was to evaluate the degree of appraised stressfulness for each of the 24 items. This was done by rank ordering of the items from most to least stressful for the total sample. The most stressful item for this immigrant sample was "Parents getting sick and going to the hospital" (X=3.8). This was followed by "Having family member arrested" (X=3.6), "Living in a poor neighborhood where there is crime" (X=3.4), "Father or Mother drinking" (X=3.3) and "Leaving friends and relatives behind when moving" (X=3.3). Other items rated as constituting rather high levels of stress revolved around economic conditions, "Parents not making enough money to pay the bills" (X=3.2), language differences, "Not understanding the teacher when she explains something in English" (X=3.0), "When kids make fun of the way you speak English" (X=3.0), and school problems, "Getting in trouble at school" (X=3.0).

Consistent with other findings in the area of adolescent stress, those items occurring most frequently were not necessarily those constituting the highest levels of stress. For example, while "Making new friends at school" was the most frequently occurring event for this sample (82.2%), the event was appraised as being minimally stressful (X=2.2). The second most frequent occurring item "Having to go to church" (65%) revealed a similar relationship where it too was appraised as being minimally stressful (X=2.1). Conversely, many of the items were reported to be experienced by large percentages of the adolescent sample and were also appraised as being quite stressful. Events such as "Parents getting sick..." (50.8%), "Having family member arrested" (40.8%), "Leaving relatives and friends when moving" (64.6%), "Parents not making enough money..." (43.6%), and "Not understanding teacher...", (64.9%) exemplify this finding.

The next step in examining the data was to determine whether there existed a difference between our male and female respondents in their appraisal of stressfulness of the 24 items. Possible gender differences were tested using t-tests on each item. Overall, the female respondents differed significantly in the appraisals on 10 items, in all cases appraising the items as more stressful than did the males. For the entire sample a total mean HCSI score was computed (X=67.84). A total score was also computed for males (X=64.80) and for females (X=71.27), the difference here being significant (p=.01).

An analysis was also conducted to determine the differences in the rank-ordering of the items by males as opposed to females. A Spearman Rho coefficient was computed on stress appraisal rankings resulting in rho=.96. Therefore, male and female adolescents have a very high degree of agreement in the ranking of the stressfulness of the items, even though female respondents have higher stress ratings on many of the items their relative ranking of items is very consistent with the relative ranking of males.

It was also necessary to determine whether subjects appraised the items differently depending on whether or not they had experienced the event in the past year. The percent of subjects indicating that they had or had not experienced the event along with mean appraisal scores for each item was examined next. Analysis showed that the appraisal ratings were significantly higher on all but 3 items for Ss who indicated that they had recently experienced the event. The 3 items for which no significant differences were found were "Making new friends at school," "Having to go to church," and "Not having enough Latino friends." Again using Spearman's Rho, a high degree of agreement in the ranking of the events for the experienced and inexperienced was found (rho=.85).

Because the respondents of this study were all immigrants to the United States we also sought to determine whether length of residence and self-ratings of English language proficiency were related to the perception of stress. Respondents were dichotomized into those that had been in the United States for less than 1 year (N=98) or over 1 year (N=139) and then t-tests were computed on the appraisal ratings of each item. Only the item "Moving from one neighborhood to another" was significant (p=.05) with Ss residing in the U.S. longer than 1 year rating the item as more stressful (X=3.4) than Ss living in the U.S. less than 1 year (X=2.9).

As for English Language proficiency, Ss were dichotomized into two groups: poor English (N=176) vs. good English (N=64) ability. Again computing t-tests on the stressfulness appraisal ratings between the two groups, findings revealed significant differences on only 4 items. The 4 items all of which were rated as more stressful by the Poor English Group were as follows: "Making new friends at school," "When you speak in one language and your friends answer in another," "Parents getting sick and going to the hospital," and "Having family member arrested." Surprisingly, only one of these items was related to language. The item "Not understanding teacher when she explains something in English" was rated as more stressful (X=3.3) by the Poor English Group than the Good English speakers (X=3.0) but the difference failed to reach statistical significance. In addition, the item "When kids make fun of the way you speak English" showed no difference in appraisal ratings (3.4 vs. 3.5) between the two language ability groups.

A final set of comparisons that were carried out had to do with the variable of age. Respondents were divided into 3 age groups: 13 to 14 year olds (N=47), 15 to 16 year olds (N=77) and 17 to 19 year olds (N=117). Using ANOVA procedures each item was then examined to determine whether there were differences in either the occurrence of the event in the past 12 months or in the appraisal ratings between the 3 age groups. Three items ("Having to go to church," "Being pressured by friends to get into fights," "Pressure to speak only English at home") were found to show a significant decrease in the occurrence of the event in the past year with age. For instance, 81% of the youngest group of Ss but only 56% and 65% of the two older groups reported having to go to church. With regard to speaking English at home, 35% of the youngest and 21% and 11% respectively of the next two age groups reported this event as occurring recently. Although differing significantly (p=.05) in the occurrence of these three events, the groups did not differ in their stress appraisals of these items. The single item that differed significantly among the three groups on stress appraisal was the item "When kids make fun of the way you speak English." For this item, the two older groups had a mean stress rating of 3.1 whereas the young Ss' mean rating was 2.6.

DISCUSSION

The study of childhood/adolescent mental health can be greatly enhanced by the use of new theoretical and methodological approaches such as that provided by the stress-illness paradigm (Cervantes & Castro, 1985). This is particularly true for children and adolescents who migrate to this country, often facing the task of adapting to a new set of socio-linguistic norms. The present study attempted to shed some light on the process of acculturative adaptation and stress as experienced by adolescents who have recently immigrated from Mexico.

Results from this study demonstrate the need for investigating culturally specific life events, something that to date has been neglected in the childhood/adolescent research. In line with thinking about Mexican cultural values and the importance placed on family unity (Ramirez & Arce, 1981; Staples & Mirande, 1980) we found a significant number of the most stressful items from the HCSI to revolve around family concerns, and more specifically the disruption of family unity. With the exception of the item "Living in a neighborhood where there is crime," the six most stressful items as rated by our sample revolved around disruptions to family unity. This is in rather sharp contrast to findings with majority-group adolescents who report more personalized events as constituting the highest levels of reported stress (Coddington, 1972; Yeaworth et al., 1980). A true comparison of earlier findings, however, is difficult in that items included in the HCSI were not asked in previous studies, nor was it our intent to replicate findings through the use of existing adolescent stress measures. Remember that the items employed in this study were generated from semi-structured interviews with Mexican children similar to those that constituted the sample of this study and were not taken from existing scales of adolescent stress.

In addition to items related to family disruption we also found language differences to constitute rather high levels of stress as reported by our sample (e.g., Not understanding teacher when she explains something in English; When kids make fun of the way you speak English). When analyzing the data on the basis of self-ratings of English proficiency alone, it appears that items reflective of necessitated contact with the majority culture group, such as managing parental sickness and hospitalization and contact with legal/court officials as reflected in the item "Having family member arrested" are significantly more stressful for those who have little proficiency in English. In all, it appears that the current study provides preliminary evidence for the identification of culturally-specific stress themes for adolescent Mexican immigrants. However, more research is clearly called for especially comparisons with majority group adolescents.

Aside from the issue of ethnicity our results were quite similar to previous findings with respect to gender differences. Overall females appraised events as constituting greater levels of stress when compared with their male peers. These results may coincide with clinical observations which describe females generally as being more willing to express emotions and to discuss problems. Given the high degrees of agreement in the rank ordering of items as a function of their relative stress, it simply appears that our female respondents were more expressive in their stress appraisals. A finding distinctly different from that reported by Newcomb et al. (1985) was the fact that our "experienced" subjects reported significantly higher levels of stress than "inexperienced" subjects. While others argue that experience of an event requires mastery, adaptation and coping, it may be that recent immigrant adolescents are at a loss when trying to cope with chronic stressors such as family disruption and language differences. These stressors require a great deal of adaptive effort and hence may be anticipated to be more stressful when there is some previous exposure to such circumstances. Obviously, needed are studies which investigate the coping repertoire or lack thereof of immigrant children and adolescents in adjusting to such chronic and pervasive stressors (note that a large percentage of respondents report experiencing both family disruptors and language difficulties).

Also surprising was that in the construction of the scale, stressors pertaining to school performance did not emerge as problematic for our Mexican respondents. The only school related item "Not understanding teacher when she explains something in English" which received a stress appraisal rating of 2.8 for males and 3.2 for females indicates the importance of language as the primary school related stressor. More research is needed that explores other facets of school related stressors relevant to immigrant children and adolescents.

Mention should be made here of the applicability of using the HCSI with Mexican adolescents in future stress research. Used earlier with a younger sample, the HCSI reveals good reliability as reported in our estimate of internal consistency. The HCSI also appears reliable for this older sample. The issue of validity, however, was addressed only indirectly in the present study. While HCSI scores were found to correlate significantly with the Lewis et al. Feel Bad Scale in a younger sample, further work is needed to evaluate the validity of the scale with an adolescent sample. The significant negative correlations that were obtained between the HCSI and five of the cluster scores of the Piers-Harris Self-Concept suggest that the HCSI is a valid measure of stress. However, future research needs to assess direct measures of external criterion validity where other indicators of adolescent stress including behavior/emotional problems are assessed along with the HCSI. Only in this fashion can the HCSI be evaluated for effective use in research and clinical settings as a true measure of culturally specific child/adolescent psychosocial stress.

REFERENCES

Bloom, B.L. (1985). Stressful life event theory and research: Implications for primary prevention. Rockville, Maryland: U.S. Department of Health and Human Services.

Byrne, D. G., & Whyte, H. M. (1980). Life events and myocardial infarction revisited: one role of measures of individual impact. Psychosomatic Medicine, 42, 1-10.

Castro, F. G., Baray-Losk, A., McCreary, C., Cervantes, R., Bolden, D., Bhieh, B., & Gonzalves, R. (1986). Rehabilitation compliance in hand-injured Latino immigrant laborers: A multivariate stress-coping model analysis. The Journal of Compliance in Health Care, 1(2), 111-133.

Cervantes, R. C., & Castro, R. G. (1985). Stress, coping, and Mexican American mental health: A systematic review. Hispanic Journal of Behavioral Sciences, 7, 1-73.

Coddington, R. D. (1972). The significance of life events as etiological factors in the disease of children. I-A survey of professional workers. Journal of Psychosomatic Research, 16, 7-18.

Dyal, J.A., & Dyal, R.Y. (1981) Acculturation, stress and coping. International Journal of Intercultural Relations, 5, 301-328.

Derbyshire, R. L. (1980). Adaptations of adolescent Mexican-Americans to the United States society. In E. B. Brady (Ed.), Behavior in new environments: Adaptations of migrant populations, (pp. 275-290). Beverly Hills: Sage Publications.

Gad, M. T., & Johnson, J. A. (1980). Correlates of adolescent life stress as related to race, SES, and levels of perceived social support. Journal of Clinical Psychology, 9, 13-16.

Holmes, T. H., & Rahe, R. H. (1967). The social readjustment rating scale. Journal of Psychosomatic Research, 11, 213-218.

Lazarus, R., & Folkman, S. (1984). Stress, appraisal, and coping. New York: Springer Publishing Co.

Lewis, C. E., Siegel, J. M., & Lewis, M. A. (1984). Feeling bad: Exploring sources of distress among pre-adolescent children. American Journal of Public Health, 74, 117-122.

Mechanic, D. (1983). Adolescent health and illness behavior: Review of the literature and a new hypothesis for the study of stress. Journal of Human Stress, 9, 4-13.

Newcomb, M. D., Huba, G. H., & Bentler, P. M. (1981). A multidimensional assessment of stressful life events among adolescents: Derivation and correlates. Journal of Health and Social Behavior, 22, 400-415.

Newcomb, M. D., Huba, G. J., & Bentler, P. M. (1986). Desirability of various life change events among adolescents: Effects of exposure, sex, age, and ethnicity. Journal of Research in Personality, 20(2), 207-227.

Nicol, A. R. (1974). The problems faced by young immigrants. Practitioner, 213, (1275), 329-334.

Pine, J., Padilla, A. M., & Maldonado, M. (1985). Ethnicity and life event cognitive appraisals and experiences. Journal of Clinical Psychology, 41, 460-465.

Piers, E.V. (1984). Piers-Harris children's self-concept scale. Revised manual 1984. Los Angeles, CA: Western Psychological Services.

Ramirez, O., & Arce, C. (1981). The contemporary Chicano family: An empirically based review. In A. Baron, Jr. (Ed.), Exploration in Chicano psychology, (pp. 3-28). New York: Praeger.

Sandler, I.N., & Block, M. (1979). Life stress and maladaptation of children. American Journal of Community Psychology, 7, 425-440.

Shuval, J. T. (1982). Migration and stress. In L. Goldberger and S. Breznitz (Eds.), Handbook of Stress: Theoretical and Clinical Aspects, (pp.677-691). New York: The Free Press.

Staples, R., & Mirande, A. (1980). Racial and cultural variations among American families: A decennial review of the literature on minority families. Journal of Marriage and the Family, 42, 887-903.

Vega, W. A., & Miranda, M. R. (1985). Stress and Hispanic mental health relating research to service delivery. (DHHS Publication No. ADM 85-1410). Rockville, MD: U. S. Government Printing Office.

Warheit, G. J., Vega, W. A., Auth, J., & Meinhardt, K. (1985). Mexican-American immigration and mental health: A comparative analyses of psychosocial stress and disfunction. In W. A. Vega & M. R. Miranda (Eds.), Stress and Hispanic Mental Health: Relating Research to Service Delivery, (pp.76-109). Rockville, MD: National Institute of Mental Health.

Westermeyer, J. (1986). Migration and Psychology. In C.L. Williams & J. Westermeyer (Eds.), Refugee mental health in resettlement countries (pp. 39-59). San Francisco, CA: Hemisphere Publishing Corporation.

Yamamoto, K. (1979). Children's ratings of the stressfulness of experiences. Developmental Psychology, 15, 581-582.

Yamamoto, K. & Byrnes, D.A. (1984). Classroom Social Status, Ethnicity, and Ratings of Stressful Events. The Journal of Educational Research, 77, 283-286.

Yeaworth, R., York, J., Hussey, M., Ingu, M., & Gordman, T. (1980). The development of an adolescent life change event scale. Adolescence, 15, 93-97.

Part III

ETHNIC IDENTITY

THE OPERATIONALIZATION OF ETHNIC IDENTITY

Peter Weinreich
University of Ulster at Jordanstown
Newtownabbey
Northern Ireland

An understanding of the sociopsychological processes of the maintenance of ethnic identities within society has hitherto been hampered by
a lack of theoretical concepts concerning identity development and
change, which could be readily operationalized for empirical research
in the field. Sophisticated theorizing about ethnic identity is generally not matched by an operationalization of concepts by means of
which it may be assessed in its variety from group to group and from
one social context to another. In terms of its variety, there are, for
example, contrasts between the variants of Jewish 'identity' in
central Europe prior to World War 2 and those of Israeli Jews born
after the creation of the state of Israel, in which the contrasting
but closely related images of genocide, exodus, and nation building
separate the two kinds. For another example, there are the differences
in the identity structures of people born in Gujerat in the Indian
subcontinent compared with those of Gujerati-speaking Indian-British
born in England, who are separated by migration, education, and
cultural context.

The mismatches between theory and its operationalization are largely
problems of conceptualizing the processes of identity development and
defining the complex of concepts associated with them, so that such
variations in identity may be assessed. These problems will receive
attention in this paper. In addition, it is fundamentally important in
discussing the relationships between ethnic groups that the mode of
theorizing is sensitive to the historical context.

There are, of course, universal facts of life, such as birth and
death, and fundamental needs of life such as sustenance, shelter,
health care and so on, which are the reasons for the creation of
societal institutions and rituals that support the necessary associated activities. Much investment of effort, emotion, and resources goes
into these activities in all communities. But the manner of their
organization, the meaning given to them, and the moral interpretation

of their smooth execution or lapses in their functioning, are constructions from varying cultural perspectives often signifying radically different ways of life. Ethnic identity has to do with identifying with such differing constructions of such universals, which give
people interpretations of life and provide the individual with the
resources and emotional support systems of the community. Any theoretical conceptualization of the processes of identity development must
therefore build in such differing 'value systems' centrally within its
framework.

In practice, identification with a particular construction of universals of life tends to be partial rather than total. The reality in contemporary societies is that with widespread communication systems some
partial identifications are made with others across ethnic boundaries,
so that these boundaries themselves are not always distinct nor rigid.
People do not remain immune to the attractive and statusful characteristics of role models outside the confines of their immediate circles.
They are able to create new definitions of themselves in order to
resolve existential problems that may arise from identifications with
initially 'alien' characteristics.

The stand taken by the Identity Structure Analysis metatheoretical
framework to be presented here is radically opposed to generating
universalistic theories of ethnic identity. No grand universal theory
is feasible, which could explain sociopsychological processes of
ethnic identity maintenance within any one ethnic group in relationship to others across countries and geographical regions. The desire
for a grand theory may arise from a confusion about the relationship
of definition to explanation. Because it is possible to give a definition of ethnic identity, this might suggest that some universal
entity has been identified and therefore requires explanation in terms
of universal processes of its development and maintenance in society.
But people's ethnic identity is not a thing. Rather it is itself a
**complex of processes by means of which people construct and re-
construct their ethnicity.** Furthermore, it is only a part, albeit for
many a strikingly important one, of the totality of their identities. Other aspects, such as gender identity, are also fundamentally
important and involve further complexes of processes of definition and
redefinition.

IDENTITY STRUCTURE ANALYSIS: ITS OPERATIONALISATION

Valuable progress has been made in delineating concepts that are
related to issues of people's self-concepts and identity. The importance that people's identities and self-expression have for behaviour
is recognised in the voluminous literature on these subjects by social
anthropologists, sociologists, psychologists and others, one recent
collection of papers representing these various disciplines being that
edited by Anita Jacobson-Widding (1983).

The perspectives of different social science disciplines naturally
tend to focus on their own specific concerns and preoccupations and

hence typically to locate the concept of identity within their arenas of discourse. Although much referred to, the meaning of the concept is frequently left implicit in their writings. Important insights derive from anthropological and sociological prespectives, but as might be anticipated, the more detailed analysis of the component aspects of identity has tended to be the work of psychologists of various persuasions. The boundaries between the disciplines are not hard and fast. The task of explaining identity processes in society is necessarily an interdisciplinary one, in which relevant concepts drawn from the anthropological and sociological perspectives need to be integrated with those drawn from psychological perspectives. In the cursory synopses that follow, only the most general statement of insights from differing perspectives are given in order that credit may be given to them in the conceptualization of the various parameters of identity to be operationalized.

In the **social anthropological** perspective, issues of one's relationship with one's ancestry and progeny are demonstrated to be of fundamental importance, concerning which there have been detailed investigations explaining the nature of differing kinship structures in various communities (Keesing,1975). Integral aspects of particular kinship patterns are specific gender roles (Tavris and Offir,1977; Rosaldo and Lamphere,1974) and adherence to related value and belief systems. Rituals and rites of passage are community-endorsed events that bond the individual to the community in which particular values and beliefs are re-affirmed (Van Gennep,1960; La Fontaine,1972). In an analysis of the institutionalised ritual of kindergarten birthday parties in contemporary Israel, Weil (1986) demonstrates how the ritual, through its different stages, serves to both individuate the child and reaffirm group identity through common collective participation. Social anthropologists (Ember and Ember,1973; Leach,1976, 1982; Glazer and Moynihan,1975; Cohen,1974) demonstrate the necessity to take account of the concerns of the major events of life and their relationship to the group, encoded in cultural value and category systems, and in its folklore and folk history, which is particularly important for clarifying issues of ethnicity and ethnic identity.

The **sociological symbolic interactionist** perspective stresses that the self is involved with an interactive process with other people which, from moment to moment, is situated in social contexts (Mead, 1934; Blumer,1969; Weigert,1983) that may differ such that actors develop strategies of self-presentation and negotiation with others in terms of situated identities (Goffman,1959; Burke,1980; Alexander and Wiley,1981). This perspective demonstrates the importance of the definitions of self as held by others (the "looking glass self") and the possible internalization of images of the self experienced as though from the viewpoint of the generalized other (Mead,1934). That the person does not in practice generally have direct access to the other's view of self is highlighted by the **psychotherapists** Laing, Phillipson, and Lee in their use of the term 'meta-perspective' to denote one's interpretation of the perspective that another has of self (Laing et al,1966).

There are a number of orientations within psychology dealing with the concepts of self and identity (Burns,1979), but three broadly defined perspectives both add to and relate to the sociological and anthropological insights cited above. They are the **psychodynamic** approach to identity (Erikson,1956,1963,1968; Hauser,1972; Marcia,1980), the **personal construct** theory view of self (Kelly,1955;Bannister and Fransella,1971; Fransella and Bannister,1977), and the **cognitive-affective consistency** orientation to the relationship between self's cognitions of people, their characteristics, beliefs, behaviours, and associated events on the one hand, and the affective connotations these cognitions have for the person on the other (Rosenberg and Abelson,1960; Osgood and Tannenbaum,1955; Festinger,1957).

Working in the **psychodynamic** tradition, from which derives the term "ego-ideal" (or "ideal self-image"), Erikson broke new ground in a number of ways. His approach is developmental over the whole life-span, in which he stresses the gradual integration of identification elements made during childhood and the negotiation, successful or otherwise, of developmental "tasks" throughout life. He draws attention to the synthesis and resynthesis of earlier identifications in the development of identity, in which he emphasizes that people tend not to form total identifications with others, but more usually partial identifications. He stresses continuity of self as being an essential feature of one's identity. A person may be more or less successful in incorporating new identifications satisfactorily. Erikson's clinical observations are concerned with disturbances in identity development. He describes states of identity diffusion, where the person has been unable to resynthesize part identifications and remains adrift in a confused state about self, and states of identity foreclosure, where the person has latched on to a conception of self that forecloses on other possible alternative ones.

Personal construct theory focusses on the construction and reconstruction of self through the organization and reorganization of personal constructs. Such personal constructs are bipolar categories which act as templates by means of which the person is able to interpret self's and others' behaviours, or to 'construe' their actions. In an ideal world, individuals would use their constructs to anticipate events and test such constructions against reality, so that if disconfirmed, they would be reorganized, an informal operation much along the lines of the formal procedure adopted by the scientist (Kelly's view of 'man the scientist'). Whether people's constructs are generally adequate, or inadequate in some respects, they are the category systems that individuals use to give meaning to the world and to differentiate it into familiar perspectives shared with others that they develop within their cultures and subcultures. They are fundamental features of one's identity and encode one's developing life experiences.

Kelly's 'cognitive' approach to individuals requires complementing with the emotional and affect-laden qualities of people's experiences. Constructs are not necessarily solely cognitive categories, but, on the contrary, they may frequently have strong evaluative connotations. In general, there will be poles of the bipolar constructs that are associated with those desirable states to which one aspires and others that represent those features of life one wishes to avoid. Given the evaluative connotations of the constructs one uses to construe others, as well as self, one will have cognitions of others that are also imbued with affective associations (in extreme cases of love or hatred). Studies informed by the **cognitive-affective consistency** theorists demonstrate that cognitive-affective inconsistencies between one's cognitions of another and one's evaluations of these cognitions (for example, a fine fellow doing something despicable) are uncomfortable psychological states. It is essential that in conceptualizing identity the affective dimensions are incorporated in relation to the cognitive categories used by people to interpret others' behaviour and their own experiences.

From the arguments presented above it is apparent that theorizing about identity processes cannot be of the kind where it is possible to construct a universal theory which will account for all the myriad circumstances of people and their states of identity. It is just as evident that there are commonalities of social interaction and expression of states of identity, those of special concern here having to do with ethnic identity, that is, stating one's origins and future aspirations in terms of kith, kin, and ethnic or 'national' grouping.

Conquest, voluntary or forced migration, and other historical circumstances provide the context for ethnic identity processes, in which matters of social structure, power relationships between subordinate and superordinate groups, and perceived political legitimacy of these relationships all feature. There are commonalites of experience for groups of people confronted with similar kinds of societal circumstances. Therefore, what is required for developing theoretical propositions about identity processes, given these commonalities, is not a foreclosed grand theory, but an open-ended metatheoretical framework of concepts and postulates about content, structure, and process pertaining to identity.

Identity Structure Analysis (ISA) is intended as the beginnings of such a metatheoretical framework. It has its origins in earlier work in the conceptualization of cognitive-affective and dissonance processes in the context of identity structure (Weinreich,1969), but has been evolving in a number of respects since then (Weinreich,1976, 1977a,1979c,1980/86,1982,1985a,1985b,1986a,1986b; McCoy,1986). It has been used in a number of empirical studies ranging from the societal (Weinreich,1979a,1979b,1983a,1983b,1985c; Weinreich et al,1987,1988; Liebkind,1983,1984; Kelly,in press; Northover,1987) to the clinical (Saunders, 1975; Harris,1980; Needham,1984; Weinreich et al,1985a).

ISA draws chiefly upon concepts, outlined above, elaborated by the psychodynamic, personal construct theory, symbolic interactionist, and cognitive-affective consistency theory perspectives on self and identity. It is also sensitive to the fundamental social anthropological concern with cultural variations in belief and value systems, so that values hold a pivotal place in the conceptualization of identity structure. A set of formal definitions of basic ISA concepts is given in a manual (Weinreich,1980/86). Their operationalization depends on algebraic procedures applied to raw data collected using custom-designed 'identity instruments'. For convenience these procedures are implemented by way of specially developed computer programs (Weinreich and Gault,1984; Weinreich et al,1985b). Consideration is now given to certain fundamental definitions and postulates of ISA, elaborated in relation to ethnic identity.

THEORETICAL POSTULATES CONCERNING IDENTIFICATION PROCESSES

Definition of identity. The following definition of identity is based on ones by Erikson (1963) and Laing (1961), but places an emphasis on continuity rather than sameness in identity and gives central importance to the process of construal. **One's identity is defined as the totality of one's self-construal, in which how one construes oneself in the present expresses the continuity between how one construes oneself as one was in the past and how one construes oneself as one aspires to be in the future** (Weinreich,1969,1980/86).

Incorporated within this definition are certain important general principles about human behaviour, which are: (1) individuals act as though they possess limited and variable degrees of autonomy and strive to maintain a maximum sense of autonomy; (2) they have a developmental and temporal sense of themselves; and (3) their sense of autonomy and temporal sense of themselves are achieved in relation to their transactions with others.

The concept of identification is an important one in ISA. However, previous use of the term has been ambiguous, the nature of the ambiguity receiving attention in other publications (e.g. Weinreich, 1979a,1979b). Consequently, two distinct modes of identification are detailed. As well as disposing of the ambiguity, the distinction enables an explicit definition to be given of a person's **conflict in identification** with a significant other. The analytic conceptualization of a person's conflicted identifications in this fashion opens the way for the empirical assessment of the patterns of identification conflicts one may have with significant others.

The two modes of identification are distinguished as **empathetic** identification on the one hand, corresponding to the recognition of sameness between self and other, and **role-model** identification on the other, corresponding to a wish to emulate the other. Thus, one's **empathetic** identification with another refers to the degree of perceived similarity between the characteristics, whether good or bad, of that other and oneself. By contrast, one's **role-model** identification refers to the degree to which one might wish to emulate another when the other is a positive role model, or dissociate from the other when a negative role model. The terms **idealistic**-identification and

contra-identification are used to distinguish between positive and negative role models respectively.

Having distinguished between empathetic and role-model identification, it becomes possible to conceptualize a person's conflict in identification in the following manner. One's identification with another may be considered to be **conflicted** when one empathetically identifies, while simultaneously contra-identifying, with that other. In other words, one's identification is conflicted when one experiences similarities between self and the other, while recognizing in that other characteristics from which one would wish to dissociate.

Processes of change and temporal development are the subject of two theoretical process postulates, which emphasise the agentic characteristics of humans (Weinreich, 1983a, 1983b). Whereas Erikson drew attention in general terms to the synthesis and resynthesis of earlier identifications in identity development, these ISA postulates are explicitly concerned with the processes by means of which people attempt to resynthesize their existing identifications and synthesize further ones with those already existing.

POSTULATE 1 **Resolution of conflicted identifications**: When one's identifications with others are conflicted, one attempts to resolve the conflicts, thereby inducing re-evaluations of self in relation to the others within the limitations of one's currently existing value system.

POSTULATE 2 **Formation of new identifications**: When one forms further identifications with newly encountered individuals, one broadens one's value system and establishes a new context for one's self-definition, thereby initiating a reappraisal of self and others which is dependent on fundamental changes in one's value system.

Amplifying on the theme of conflicts in identification, different identity states can be conceptualized. Towards one extreme a person may have strongly conflicted identifications dispersed across several significant others. Such a condition is considered to be a state of **identity diffusion**, equivalent to that clinically described by Erikson. In between, moderate and quite usual levels of identification conflicts are expected to exist in psychologically well-adjusted people. Towards the other extreme, someone who exhibits minimal levels of identification conflict does not in practice acknowledge quite ordinary differentiations between good and bad characteristics, nor recognize that they are often to be found in both oneself and in others. A state of such defensive denial is regarded as the analytic equivalent of **identity foreclosure** as described by Erikson. For convenience the greater or less strength and dispersion of conflicts in identification with various significant others may be regarded as variations in the parameter of 'identity diffusion', so that 'foreclosed' identity states and 'diffused' ones are represented by minimal levels and by high levels of identity diffusion, respectively.

This conceptualization opens the way to a classification of gross variations in identity states, which uses the parameter of **identity diffusion** in conjunction with that of **self-evaluation** as illustrated in Table 1.

TABLE 1: **ISA CLASSIFICATION OF IDENTITY VARIANTS**

Identity diffusion

	High	Moderate	Low
Self-evaluation			
High	Diffuse high self-regard	Confident	Defensive high self-regard
Moderate	Diffusion	Indeterminate	Defensive
Low	Crisis	Negative	Defensive negative

'Diffused' variants range from **identity crisis** to **diffuse high self-regard** and 'foreclosed' ones from **defensive negative** to **defensive high self-regard**. In ordinary cross-sections of adolescents, the most usual identity variants are found to be **indeterminate** and **confident**. The other identity variants are regarded as vulnerable states, falling into three general classes (Weinreich,1986b). In a **negative** identity state, that is, with low or negative self-evaluation, people perceive themselves as lacking in the skills to act in accordance with their values and aspirations. People in a **diffused** identity state are unlikely to be able to resolve all their dispersed identification conflicts to optimum levels simultaneously, hence they would have difficulties in forming clear cut commitments, irrespective of whether they were in a state of diffuse high self-regard, identity diffusion, or identity crisis. Others in a **foreclosed** identity state have undifferentiated appraisals of their social worlds, so are likely to have difficulties in responding to complex relationships and to changed circumstances. Some may think highly of themselves as in a state of defensive high self-regard, whilst others may be in a defensive negative state, but the common characteristic would be an essentially defensive orientation towards the social world.

THEORETICAL POSTULATES CONCERNING CONSTRUCTS

At a more detailed level of analysis, attention is also given to the individual's use of **personal constructs** in evaluating the merits of self and others. A new parameter, **structural pressure**, is defined which estimates the centrality of people's values and aspirations as they are represented by their constructs, or alternatively the uncertainty and evaluative inconsistency with which they hold and use them (Weinreich,1980/86).

In the ISA definition of identity, a central place is given to the person's construal of self. The constructs generally have a cognitive form, by means of which one is able to attribute characteristics, beliefs, and various kinds of behaviour to self and others. They have to a lesser or greater degree evaluative connotations or affective associations. Some of these will have developed in the context of identifications that have strong cultural significance, and the associated cognitions will represent cultural interpretations of behaviours. Their evaluative connotations will signify cultural values.

If the affective associations of the cognitions are aligned consistently with the overall evaluations of self and others, then the structure of cognitions and affects is one of cognitive-affective compatibility, a dynamically stable state. The structural pressures on the constructs are then positive, that is, maintaining a stable state. When, on the other hand, there are inconsistencies between the evaluative connotations of the cognitions and the overall evaluations of self and others, there arise structures of cognitive-affective incompatibilities which are arenas of stress. These are represented by negative structural pressures on the constructs in question. From these considerations the following postulates concerning constructs are derived:

POSTULATE 1 **Core evaluative dimensions of identity:** When the net structural pressure on one of a person's constructs is high and positive, the evaluative connotations associated with it are stably bound. This means that the construct in question acts as a core evaluative dimension of identity in the judgement of self and others, and that it will be resistant to change.

POSTULATE 2 **Conflicted dimensions of identity:** When the net structural pressure on a construct is low, or negative, **as a result of strong negative pressures counteracting positive ones**, the evaluative connotations associated with the construct are conflicted: the construct in question is an arena of stress.

POSTULATE 3 **Unevaluative dimensions of identity:** When the net structural pressure on a construct is low **as a result of weak positive and negative pressures**, the construct in question is without strong evaluative connotations.

The evaluative connotations of the constructs one uses to interpret the world constitute in effect one's value system. Some constructs feature as core evaluative dimensions of identity, but others are uncertain or conflicted, in which case they are uncertain values. Many such uncertain values in a person would indicate uncertain aspirations and a state of identity diffusion.

Ethnic and gender identity: ancestry and progeny. Ethnic identity is only a part of the totality of one's identity. Researchers have established that ancestry, a sense of peoplehood (Dashefsky,1976), and folklore (Dundes,1983) constitute core components of ethnicity. Based on an analysis by Gordon (1964), ethnicity is defined by Dashefsky (1976): **as a shared sense of peoplehood, based on presumed shared socio-cultural experiences, which represents a part of the collective experience of members of an ethnic group.**

Except for the deviant cases of the isolated migrant or the offspring of a mixed marriage, children will tend to identify with others within their ethnic group through day-to-day activities at kindergarten, school, and beyond. They participate in rituals, such as birthdays, and rites of passage, such as primary to secondary school and school to work transitions, marriage, and procreation. They adopt the moral connotations of these events as defined by the ethnic culture in question. Thus, though only a part of one's identity, ethnicity is a most pervasive part. As with the overall definition of identity given above, that of ethnic identity emphasises continuity, rather than sameness, and hence provides for the individual incorporating new identifications and changing conceptions of self in the light of experience. **One's ethnic identity is defined as that part of the totality of one's self-construal made up of those dimensions that express the continuity between one's construal of past ancestry and future aspirations in relation to ethnicity** (Weinreich,1985a,1986a).

One's construal of past ancestry and future aspirations in relation to ethnicity depends on one's construct system, in particular on those features of it that embody cultural values and beliefs. Since one's construct system is itself open to change, this definition closely parallels the observation that "ethnic identities are not natural facts but cultural constructions which are liable to be reconstructed or amended" (Ovesen,1983,p331).

The ISA theoretical orientation is consonant with the view that ethnicity is often (though not necessarily, nor always) used by people as a resource (Wallman,1986). This follows from the above definition of ethnic identity and the process postulates concerning the synthesis and resynthesis of identifications, which recognise a degree of individual autonomy. As a resource in terms of support and information networks, ethnicity may be used in day-to-day practical matters. It may also be used symbolically in maintaining one's integrity of identity under oppression. Whether or not ethnicity dominates in relationships is in part related to what extent social contexts are homo- geneous, rigidly bounded and closed, or heterogenous, permeable and open (Wallman,1986).

Given that gender is deeply implicated in the complex of societal processes and institutions devoted to ancestry, sexual coupling, procreation, and care of progeny, one's gender role is given partic- ularistic meanings by one's ethnicity. That part of one's identity associated with gender can likewise be explicit defined, so that the differing moral conceptions of gender roles may be both located within a particular ethnicity, and contrasted across ethnicities. Hence, **One's gender identity is defined as that part of the totality of one's self-construal made up of those dimensions that express the continuity between one's construal of one's past gender and one's future aspirations in relation to gender** (Weinreich,1986a).

The child of a migrant reaching adulthood may have future aspirations in relation to the connotations of being male or female, which differ from those he or she accepted and identified with as a child. This is of particular importance to migrant offspring of an ethnic group that espouses strong moral prescriptions of one kind (e.g. Islamic) when they form partial identifications with those of another kind (e.g. a secular form of Judeo-Christian). The embeddedness of gender identity with ethnic identity arises as the result of one's identifications with one's kith and kin, in which one gives meaning to one's existence in relation to, one's past biography and one's future aspirations in terms of the desired way of life for oneself and one's progeny.

This approach to conceptualizing identity provides a basic explanation for ingroup 'favouritism' (Tajfel,1981) and allegiance in terms of the processes of identification with those who are perceived to hold power over resources, who for the very young are in the main of one's own immediate kith and kin. However, it also provides an explanation in a straightforward manner of certain people's 'cross-ethnic' identification with others outside their own ethnicity when such others wield control over one's well being, or have desirable attributes to be emulated (Weinreich,1979a).

It can be seen from the foregoing analysis of the development of identity that **acculturation** (Redfield, Linton and Herskovits,1936) is unlikely to be a straightforward process. Individuals may form different complexes of partial identifications with members of their own group and with members of another, and correspondingly the processes of psychological acculturation (Graves,1967) at the individual level may vary substantially. In some instances the overall magnitude and dispersion of resultant identification conflicts may result in diffused identities. In other cases potentially disturbing identification conflicts may not be acknowledged as in foreclosed identities. Thus, some individuals, experiencing acculturative stress (Berry and Annis,1974; Berry and Kim,1985) may at one time or another be in vulnerable identity states. But most individuals will strive to resolve their major identification conflicts and thereby come to redefine themselves and the ways in which they express their ethnicity (Weinreich,1983a).

Everyday ideologies and variations in ethnic identities. The folklore, folk history, and moral prescriptions of an ethnic group amount to an 'everday ideology', or constitute the group's 'social representation' (Farr and Moscovici,1984). Some of it will be in recorded forms in terms of written texts, pictures, music, song and dance, and more latterly in video and sound recordings.

Using the structural pressure index concerning people's evaluative use of constructs, the ISA approach provides a practical tool for ascertaining key elements of everyday ideologies that accompany ethnic identity, so that people with the same ethnic identity, but subscribing to characteristically different ideologies, may be delineated. Examples are 'progressive' and 'orthodox' young Muslims in the Greater Birmingham region of Britain (Kelly,in press) and young rural and urban Blacks in the Sovenga region of South Africa (Weinreich et al,1987,1988). The investigations from which these examples are drawn demonstrate that the existential sense of having an ethnic identity is not synonymous with subscribing to a common ideology, though there will be adherence to certain common propositions basic to the group.

Identity transitions. Rites of passage are ritualistic devices used to provide cultural support for normative identity transitions within a culture. McCoy (1986) defines a transition as "a relatively short period of accelerated change which occurs between two relatively stable periods" in which the "preceding and succeeding stages will be, in some aspects of their structure at least, identifiably different". It is possible for a person to evoke an 'endogenous' transition of one kind, but meet with an 'exogenous' transition of a very different kind (for example, a Muslim girl's endogenous transition in excercising her new free independent identity, by moving in with a boy she loves, and her exogenous transition of becoming shameful and unmarriageable as defined by her own community).

Alter-ascribed and ego-recognized social identities. People may have identities ascribed to themselves by others. A definition of oneself by others in terms of a role in society is one's social identity for these others and is to be distinguished from one's own self conception (Dashefsky,1976). The ascription of a social identity by another may be termed 'alter-ascribed' so as to emphasise that it may not be a recognised or accepted one by oneself: one's 'ego- recognised' social identity may not accord with an alter-ascribed one (Weinreich,1983b). There are innumerable instances of ethnic groups for whom alter-ascribed social identities by powerful people have been derogatory racist definitions, rejected by the groups concerned for whom their ego recognised social identities were revered.

Metaperspectives of self. A distinction has been made between an alter-ascribed identity for oneself and one's ego-recognised identity. It is possible to reject the alter-ascribed identity. However, the extent to which one is aware of the other's definition of self is another matter. There are many instances when one has no direct access to another's view of oneself (that person's direct perspective on self as an alter-ascribed identity). In such cases, one forms metaperspectives of self, which are one's views of the other's view of self (Laing, et al,1966), or one's interpretations of alter-ascribed identities. Thus, threats to identity may be perceived when there are none, and not recognised for what they are when they do exist, which in sectarian ethnic politics such as in Northern Ireland give rise to a minefield of distrust (Weinreich,1983b,1983c).

Threatened versus vulnerable identities. Vulnerable identity states have been described as those in which people have high identity diffusion (diffused identity variants), or very low identity diffusion (foreclosed identity variants), or very low self-evaluation (negative identity variants). An important distinction can be made between **vulnerabilities** in identity development and **threats** to identity. Vulnerabilities are located within people's identity structures. They refer to their difficulties in handling identification conflicts, which get out of hand in diffused identities or are avoided in foreclosed ones, or to their demoralization. Threats to identity are from sources external to oneself. One's personal identity may be threatened by an alter-ascribed one, in which the other attributes characteristics to oneself which are at variance with what one believes about oneself. In the arena of ethnic relations, threatened identities, defined as follows, are generally the social identities associated with roles in society. **One's social identity is threatened when other people view oneself as a member of a social group in ways that are grossly discrepant from one's own view of self as member of that group** (Weinreich,1986b).

Here, the alter-ascribed social identity is a threat to one's ego-recognized social identity. However, derogatory stereotypes or racist attacks on people's identities are likely to be met with very different reactions, depending on whether or not their identities are vulnerable and, if they are, on the nature of the vulnerability.

Situated identities. Symbolic interactionism has documented the changes in self presentation that occur when situations differ, demonstrating the influence of external social definitions given to the actors. A shift in theoretical perspective would emphasize in addition that the individual may actively engage in different identity states according to social context. In the ISA metatheoretical framework, situated identities refer to the different identity states with which people operate when social contexts change and from which they pursue different kinds of action. In an identity state cued into a particular social context, one empathetically identifies with certain people and acts more like them than one does in a different identity state in another social context, when one empathetically identifies with different people. It follows from the ISA definition of identity that a person's 'situated identity' may be defined as follows. **One's identity as situated in a specific social context is defined as that part of the totality of one's self construal, in which how one construes oneself in the situated present expresses the continuity between how one construes oneself as one was in the past and how one construes oneself as one aspires to be in the future** (Weinreich et al,1987).

By contrast with perhaps a too great an emphasis on the situational self in the symbolic interactionist perspective, which tends to suggest a chameleon-like ephemeral notion of identity, the above ISA definition retains the quality of continuity in a person's identity while attending to the reality of changed states in identity. Despite such changed states, the person remains recognisably the same being.

A study of South African young rural and urban Blacks (Weinreich et al,1987,1988) demonstrated major changes in their situational identities when in an Afrikaner context compared with an English-speaking White context, and both of these compared with their 'natural' identity states. Their changed empathetic identifications with context have implications for behaviour. In the Afrikaner context, when they identify with Afrikaners and have vulnerable identities, the young Blacks may engage in behaviour that, from their more robust natural identity states when they identify with fellow Blacks, they would hold to be despicable. In order to protect themselves from identity vulnerability in the Afrikaner context, young urban, more so than rural, Blacks would need to promote solidarity with their own people, and avoid the overpowering sense of the Afrikaner ethos when interacting individually with Afrikaner authority.

EMPIRICALLY GROUNDED THEORETICAL PROPOSITIONS

The above account of the ISA metatheoretical framework has postulated a set of theoretical concepts concerning aspects of 'identity', together with theoretical process postulates concerning people's syntheses and resyntheses of identifications. It has also provided theoretical postulates concerning the constructs by means of which people interpret and evaluate others and themselves within the social context. The application of this framework of concepts and postulates to empirical data collected using appropriately designed identity instruments enables the investigator to generate theoretical propositions about the socio-psychological processes of identity development in the socio-historical and biographical context under investigation.

A set of such empirically grounded theoretical propositions for migrant offspring in Bristol, England, (Weinreich,1983a) is further examined by Kelly (in press) in relation to other migrant offspring in Birmingham and London. Further propositions arising from a study of sectarianism in Belfast, Northern Ireland (Weinreich,1983b,1986a) are presented here for comparison. They demonstrate that, though ethnicity is salient for both migrant offspring in Britain and for adolescents of the two communities in Northern Ireland, it manifests itself quite differently in the respective socio-historical contexts. As stressed before, ethnic identity is not a thing, but a complex of processes by means of which people construct and reconstruct their ethnicity.

1. National allegiance (being **Irish** or **British**) and religious affiliation (being **Catholic** or **Protestant**) on either side of the psychological divide in Ulster generally combine as emotionally charged dimensions of identity. 2. National allegiance and religious affiliation are considerably more dominant as core **evaluative** dimensions of identity than are other important cognitive ones such as gender. 3. Members of the one ethnic group have salient conflicts in identification with the other group. 4. The psychological dynamics related to these salient identification conflicts are generally reciprocally common to members of both ethnic groups, such that their attempted resolution provides the continuing psychological impetus to

the processes sustaining the sectarian conflict. 5. The one identity, while being interdependent with the other, is at the same time **threatening** to the existence of the other. 6. However, the threats to the one identity by the other do not undermine its rationale, nor thereby give rise to self-doubt among its adherents, but instead the pervasive certainties of the two identities are generally accompanied by high self-esteem. 7. The societal pathology of sectarianism is generally not a result of individual psychopathology. 8. Individuals in whom 'nationality' and 'religion' do not combine to form core evaluative dimensions of identity, and who deviate from the norm, are charcterised by special circumstances (such as early childhood outside Ulster), or by emphatic decisions on their part to pursue doctrines contradistinctive to those prevailing in their ethnic group.

Such theoretical propositions are not, of course, complete 'explanations', but serve instead to generate insights that initially go against received expectations. For example, in the Belfast study, the very high selfevaluations of the respondents on both sides of the divide are unexpected on two counts: they do not mirror the dismal media and public images of demoralised riot-torn communities; and they do not support the view that the self-images of members of the subordinate Catholic group are devalued in comparison with those of the superordinate Protestants. Further analysis of the Belfast ISA data indicates that values and beliefs are held differently by the adolescents according to their ethnicity, gender, and level of school achievement. High-achieving Catholic males tend to evaluate their social world in doctrinal terms, while their female counterparts appear to provide impetus to action based in values of political commitment, effort, and confident assertiveness, these perspectives being less prominant in low-achieving Catholic boys and girls (Weinreich,1985c).

CONCLUSIONS

Certain conclusions about the nature of theorising on ethnic identity follow from the arguments presented in this chapter. The **first** is that the notion of devising a grand theory of ethnic identity should be abandoned. There are sound theoretical reasons why this enterprise is in principle untenable. The evidence from the literature on ethnicity, ethnocentrism, and ethnic relations suggests that many researchers are aware that attempts to generate universal grand theories are inappropriate for many of the issues under discussion. The importance and practical necessity of generating theoretical propositions tied in to specific socio-historical contexts is not thereby questioned.The **second** is that the value systems of individuals in the current socio-historical era are centrally important to the derivation of the more limited set of empirically grounded theoretical propositions for the particular ethnic groups in question. The reason why no grand theory is possible is that value systems evolve and change both in relation to individual biographies and in terms of major developments within the socio-historical context. The **third** is that, while ethnic labels appear to give discrete status to people, the make-up of their identities generally contain elements of identification which cross 'ethnic boundaries'. Within a community of people subscribing to a common 'ethnicity' there may be factions adhering to different ideologies. It is important to be aware that ethnic identity is not an entity, but a complex of processes in contemporary time in which people construct from historical 'facts' biographical continuities between their ancestry and their progeny as a group, generally in a wider social context of other ethnic groups. The **fourth** is that gender identity is fundamentally implicated in ethnic identity with the latter's emphasis on ancestry and progeny and the former's association with procreation. The modes of being male and being female are necessarily related to customs and rituals of male and female gender roles, as they are differently defined according to ethnicity. The **fifth** is that, in developing different identity structures, people will relate to others and respond to situations in markedly different ways. The socio-psychological processes in which people engage are not independent of the structure of their identifications and identification conflicts, nor of the structure of their values. Instead, processes are often structure-dependent so that, for example, people with different kinds of identity vulnerabilities, foreclosed or diffused, relate to the social world and threats to identity in differing manners. The **sixth** is that the identity concerns of members of the superordinate and subordinate communities will differ. The ways in which the differential power that exists between them is exercised will, in part, depend on social contexts (in industry, commerce and housing) being heterogeneous and open, or homogeneous and closed (exercised with tolerance, or with antagonism, respectively). The **seventh** is that people, in engaging with different contexts within the social structure, may act with differing situational identities. Their empathetic identifications may change from one situational context to another, such that in some circumstances they may be in identity states of considerable vulnerability, and in others they may be in good adjustment. The **eighth**, which is perhaps ultimately the one most distinctive of human affairs, is that people possess the ability to innovate and to generate redefinitions of their being in the world. While drawing on previous elements of identification, they create contemporary lifestyles and orientations to their own ethnicity and others, which are not necessarily rigidly tied to the past.

Despite the emphasis here on the realities of social change, the concept of identity provides a pivotal link by way of the continuity in the person between the earlier times and the changed later ones. The expectation is that, given the differing socio-historical contexts of different ethnic groups, empirically grounded theoretical propositions that would explain their position in contemporary time can be derived.

Note. This paper is an abbreviated version of:-
Weinreich,P.(In press) Variations in Ethnic Identity: Identity Structure Analysis, in Liebkind,K.(Ed.)**New Identities in Europe: Immigrant Ancestry and the Ethnic Identity of Youth**, Gower Press.

REFERENCES

Alexander,Jr.,C.N. and Wiley,M.G.(1981) Situated activity and identity formation. In Rosenberg,M. and Turner,R.H.(Eds.) **Social Psychology: Sociological Perspectives.** New York:Basic.

Bannister,D. and Fransella,F.(1971) **Inquiring Man:The Theory of Personal Constructs.** Harmondsworth:Penguin.

Berry,J.W. and Annis,R.C.(1974) Acculturative stress. Journal of Cross-Cultural Psychology,5,382-406.

Berry,J.W. and Kim,U.(1985) Acculturation and mental health. In Dasen, P., Berry,J.W. and Sartorius,N.(Eds.) **Applications of Cross-Cultural Psychology to Healthy Human Development.** London:Sage.

Blumer,H.(1969) **Symbolic Interactionism.** Englewood Cliffs:Prentice Hall.

Burke,P.J.(1980) The self:measurement requirements from an interactionist perspective. **Social Psychology Quarterly,**43,18-29.

Burns,R.B.(1979) **The Self Concept:Theory, Measurement, Development and Behaviour.** London:Longman.

Cohen,A.(1974) **Urban Ethnicity.** London:Tavistock.

Dashefsky,A.(Ed.) (1976) **Ethnic Identity in Society.** Chicago:Rand McNally.

Dundes,A.(1983) Defining identity through folklore. In Jacobson-Widding,A.(Ed.) Op cit.

Ember,C.R. and Ember,M.(1973) **Cultural Anthropology.** New York: Appleton Century-Crofts.

Erikson,E.H.(1956) The problem of ego identity. **The Journal of the American Psychoanalytic Association,**4,56-121.

Erikson,E.H.(1963) **Childhood and Society.** New York:Norton.

Erikson,E.H.(1968) **Identity, Youth and Crisis.** New York:Norton.

Farr,R.M. and Moscovici,S.(Eds.) (1984) **Social Representations.** Cambridge:Cambridge University Press.

Festinger,L.(1957) **A Theory of Cognitive Dissonance.** Evanston, Ill.: Row, Peterson.

Fransella,F. and Bannister,D.(1977) **A Manual for Repertory Grid Technique.** London:Academic Press.

Glazer,N. and Moynihan,D.P.(1975) **Ethnicity:Theory and Experience.** Cambridge:Harvard University Press.

Goffman,E.(1959) **The Presentation of Self in Everyday Life.** New York:Anchor.

Gordon,M.M.(1964) **Assimilation in American Life:The Role of Race, Religion, and National Origins.** New York:OUP.

Graves,T.(1967) Psychological acculturation in a tri-ethnic community. **Southwestern Journal of Anthropology,**23,337-350.

Harris,P.D.G.(1980) Identity development in female patients suffering from anorexia nervosa and bulimia nervosa:an application of Weinreich's Identity Structure Analysis. Unpublished M.Psychol. thesis. Liverpool:University of Liverpool.

Hauser,S.T.(1972) Black and white identity development:aspects and perspectives. **Journal of Youth and Adolescence,**1,113-30.

Jacobson-Widding,A.(Ed.) (1983) **Identity:Personal and Socio- Cultural.** Stockholm:Almqvist & Wiksell International. Atlantic Highlands:Humanities Press.

Keesing,R.M.(1975) Kin Groups and Social Structure. New York:Holt, Rinehart and Winston.

Kelly,A.J.D.(in press) Ethnic identification, association and redefinition:Muslim Pakistanis and Greek Cypriots in Britain. In Liebkind, K.(Ed.) New Identities in Europe:Immigrant Ancestry and the Ethnic Identity of Youth. Gower.

Kelly,G.A.(1955) The Psychology of Personal Constructs. New York: Norton.

La Fontaine,J.S.(Ed.) (1972) The Interpretation of Ritual:Essays in Honour of A.I. Richards. London:Tavistock.

Laing,R.D.(1961) The Self and Others. London:Tavistock.

Laing,R.D.,Phillipson,H. and Lee,A.R.(1966) Interpersonal Perception: A Theory and a Method of Research. London:Tavistock.

Leach,E.R.(1976) Culture and Communication:The Logic by which Symbols are Connected. Cambridge:Cambridge University Press.

Leach,E.R.(1982) Social Anthropology. London:Fontana.

Liebkind,K.(1983) Dimensions of identity in multiple group allegiance. In Jacobson-Widding,A.(Ed.) Op cit.

Liebkind,K.(1984) Minority identity and identification processes:a social psychological study. Finnish Society of Sciences and Letters, Commentationes Scientiarum Socialium,22,Helsinki.

McCoy,D.(1986) Identity transition in persons undergoing elective interval sterilisation and vasectomy:an approach based on Identity Structure Analysis. Unpublished D.Phil. thesis. Jordanstown:University of Ulster at Jordanstown.

Marcia,J.(1980) Identity in adolescence. In Adelson, J. (Ed.) Handbook of Adolescent Psychology. New York:Wiley.

Mead,G.H.(1934) Mind, Self and Society:From the Standpoint of a Social Behaviorist. Chicago:Univ. Chicago Press.

Needham,S.(1984) Maternity blues and personal identity development in first-time mothers:an exploratory study. Unpublished research dissertation, Diploma in Clinical Psychology. Leicester:British Psychological Society.

Northover,M.(1987) Bilinguals and linguistic identities. Fifth Nordic Conference on Bilingualism, Copenhagen:Royal Danish School of Education Studies.

Osgood,C.E. and Tannenbaum,P.H.(1955) The principle of congruity in the prediction of attitude change. Psychological Review, 62,42-55.

Ovesen,J.(1983) The construction of ethnic identities:The Nuristani and the Pashai of Eastern Afghanistan. In Jacobson-Widding, A. (Ed.) Op cit.

Redfield,R., Linton,R. and Herskovits,M.J.(1936) Memorandum on the study of acculturation. American Anthropologist,38,149-152.

Rosaldo,M.Z. and Lamphere,L.(Eds.)(1974) Woman, Culture and Society. Stanford:Stanford University Press.

Rosenberg,M.J. and Abelson, R.P.(1960) An analysis of cognitive balancing. In Rosenberg,M.J.,Hovland,C.I.,McGuire,W.J.,Abelson, R.P. and Brehm,J.W. Attitude Organization and Change:An Analysis of Consistency among Attitude Components. New Haven:Yale UP.

Saunders,M.(1975) Individual case study analysis of mothers of ESN children. Unpublished M.Sc.thesis. University of Bradford.

Tajfel,H.(1981) **Human Groups and Social Categories.** Cambridge:
    Cambridge University Press.
Tavris,C. and Offir,C.(1977) **The Longest War: Sex Differences in
    Perspective.** New York:Harcourt Brace Jovanovich.
Van Gennep,A.(1960) **The Rites of Passage.** London:Routledge and Kegan
    Paul.
Wallman,S.(1986) Ethnicity and the boundary process in context. In
    Rex,J.and Mason,D.(Eds.) **Theories of Race and Ethnic Relations.**
    Cambridge University Press.
Weigert,A.J.(1983) IdentityIts emergence within sociological
    psychology. **Symbolic Interaction,**6,183-206.
Weil,S.(1986) The language and ritual of socialisation:Birthday
    parties in a kindergarten context. **Man**(N.S.),21,329-41.
Weinreich,P.(1969) Theoretical and experimental evaluation of
    dissonance processes. Unpublished Ph.D.thesis. London:University
    of London.
Weinreich,P.(1976) The locus of identification conflicts in immigrant
    and indigenous adolescents. **International Congress of
    Transcultural Psychiatry,** Bradford.
Weinreich,P.(1977) Socialization and ethnic identity development.
    Conference on Socialization and Social Influence, **European
    Association for Experimental Social Psychology** and the **Polish
    Academy of Sciences,** Warsaw.
Weinreich,P.(1979a) Cross-ethnic identification and self-rejection in
    a black adolescent. In Verma,G. and Bagley,C.(Eds.) **Race,
    Education and Identity.** London:MacMillan.
Weinreich,P.(1979b) Ethnicity and adolescent identity conflict. In
    Saifullah Khan,V.(Ed.) **Minority Families in Britain.** London:
    MacMillan.
Weinreich,P.(1979c) Sex-role identification, social change and
    cultural conflict. **British Psychological Society (Northern
    Ireland branch) Annual Conference,** Rosapenna.
Weinreich,P.(1980/86) **Manual for Identity Exploration using Personal
    Constructs.** London:Social Science Research Council. Reprint
    London:Economic and Social Research Council.
Weinreich,P.(1982) A conceptual framework for exploring identity
    development:Identity Structure Analysis and IDEX. **10th
    International Congress of the International Association for Child
    and Adolescent Psychiatry and Allied Professions.** Dublin: Trinity
    College, Dublin.
Weinreich,P.(1983a) Emerging from threatened identities:ethnicity and
    gender in redefinitions of threatened identity. In Breakwell, G.
    (Ed.) **Threatended Identities.** Chichester:Wiley.
Weinreich,P.(1983b) Psychodynamics of personal and social identity:
    Theoretical concepts and their measurement in adolescents from
    Belfast sectarian and Bristol minority groups. In Jacobson-
    Widding,A.(Ed.) Op cit.
Weinreich,P.(1985a) Rationality and irrationality in racial and ethnic
    relations:a metatheoretical framework. **Ethnic and Racial Studies,**
    8, 500-515.
Weinreich,P.(1985b) Identity exploration in adolescence. **Inter-
    national Journal of Adolescent Medicine and Health,**1 & 2, 52-71.

Weinreich,P.(1985c) Sectarianism and identity development in Belfast adolescents. Plenary paper to the **20th A.P.S.A. Conference** on IDENTITY AND CULTURE. The Association for the Psychiatric Study of Adolescents. Nottingham:University of Nottingham.

Weinreich,P.(1986a) The operationalization of identity theory in racial and ethnic relations. In Rex,J. and Mason,D.(Eds.) **Theories of Race and Ethnic Relations**. Cambridge UP.

Weinreich,P.(1986b) Identity development in migrant offspring: theory and practice. In Ekstrand,L.H.(Ed.) **Ethnic Minorities and Immigrants in a Cross-Cultural Perspective**. Lisse, Netherlands: Swets & Zeitlinger.

Weinreich,P. and Gault,D.(1984) IDEX-IDIO (Identity Exploration-Idiographic) Computer Program and Userguide. Jordanstown: University of Ulster at Jordanstown.

Weinreich,P.,Harris,P. and Doherty,J.(1985a) Empirical assessment of identity in anorexia and bulimia nervosa. **Journal of Psychiatric Research**,19,297-303.

Weinreich,P.,Wilson,N.,Matthews,D. and Asquith,L.(1985b) **IDEX-NOMO (Identity Exploration-Nomothetic) Computer Program** and **Userguide**. Jordanstown:University of Ulster at Jordanstown.

Weinreich,P.,Kelly,A.J.D., and Maja,C.(1987) Situated identities, conflicts in identification and own group preference:rural and urban youth in South Africa. In Kagitcibasi,C.(Ed.) **Growth and Progress in Cross-Cultural Psychology**. Lisse, Netherlands:Swets & Zeitlinger.

Weinreich,P.,Kelly,A.J.D., and Maja,C.(1988) Black youth in South Africa:situated identities and patterns of ethnic identification. In Canter,D.,Jesuino,C.,Soczka,L. and Stephenson,G.(Eds.) **Environmental Social Psychology**. Kluwer Academic.

ADAPTATION CHANGES IN THE SELF-IMAGE OF SWEDES IN TORONTO

J. Naidoo, A. Bygden & F. Gloade
Wilfrid Laurier University
Waterloo, Canada

In 1972 the Government of Canada adopted a policy of multiculturalism wherein the various cultural groups settling in this country were
encouraged to maintain their ancestral customs, traditions, and language. This policy is based on the belief that the "mosaic" approach
will enrich Canada and all her peoples. In the wake of this new interest in ethno-cultural pluralism, Swedes are rather a "neglected" group.

More attention has been given to the so-called "visible" minorities, characterized by distinct physical, cultural, and religious
differences. Swedish ethnicity and culture are rapidly "disappearing"
as Swedes merge with mainstream Canadians. There is some urgency,
therefore, to tap the cultural resources of this group for historic
posterity.

The present study reviewed the literature and official documents
relevant to Swedish migration, settlement, and contributions to Canada.
It provided preliminary empirical data on the demographic, cultural,
and adaptation experiences of Swedes resident in Southern Ontario,
specifically in Metropolitan Toronto. An exploratory test of respondents' self-imagery relevant to their ethno-cultural identity ranging
from resistance to change to assimilation with mainstream culture was
conducted.

SWEDISH MIGRATION, SETTLEMENT, STATISTICS

An extensive review of the literature yielded a dearth of data on
Swedes in Canada, who today number 78,360* (Statistics Canada, 1984),
resident largely in the Western Provinces, from Manitoba to British
Columbia (Sillanpaa, 1985; Kastrup, n.d.). The province of Ontario has

---

*Most articles estimate the Swedish population at ± 100,000 (Sillanpaa,
1985; Kastrup, n.d.).

12,820 Swedes, the largest concentration in the rest of the country, representing just 0.2% of Ontario's population. Of these 1,960 people (0.09% of Metro Toronto) have settled in Metropolitan Toronto, mostly in the city of Toronto, followed by the boroughs of North York, Scarborough, Etobicoke, East York, and York in that order (Ontario Ethnocultural Population, 1985). At each level of settlement, the proportion of males and females is approximately equal.

Historical Trends. Swedish migration began on a small scale in the early 1870s. The first evidence of Swedish settlers in Canada was in the Red River valley in Manitoba, early in the nineteenth century, at the time Lord Selkirk was engaged in the establishment of a settlement (Selkirk Colony) on the Red River. Among the members of his settlers were five Scandinavians, three of whom were known to be Swedish (Canadian Family Tree, 1967). Until about 1920 most Swedish immigrants came via the United States, primarily Minnesota and North Dakota. In the 1920s arrivals directly from Sweden increased sharply, reaching nearly 12,000. This influx was related to the rapid population growth in Sweden, leading to the rise of a landless agrarian class who consequently sought new opportunities for farming in the New World. According to Kastrup (n.d.) the Canadian census of 1931 showed an all-time high of 34,415 Swedish-born settlers, and a total of 81,000 people of Swedish origin.

The Depression Years (early 1930s) brought a virtual halt to Swedish immigration. Since the 30s, Sweden has developed a large industrial base; hence, Swedish immigration to Canada has been largely on an individual basis, especially since 1945 (Sillanpaa, 1985). The data reflect this state of flux, with people both migrating to Canada and returning to Sweden. Early Swedish immigrants were mainly engaged in farming, logging, fishing, mining, and railroad work (Janssen, 1982; Hardwick, 1978; Howard, 1970); since 1945 they have been business and professional people, and representatives of Swedish export industries.

Pioneer immigrants originated in the Swedish Northland (Norrland), and they tended to settle in areas of Canada where the landscape and climate reminded them of their home districts in Sweden (Kastrup, n.d.).

World War II marked a transition not only in the character of Swedish occupations in Canada, but also in movements of people, languages spoken, and centres of importance. Thus, for example, a certain number of Swedish arrivals after the war settled in Montreal, the English language surplanted Swedish, and, whereas the city of Winnipeg was originally the "capital" for Swedish activities, it is today surpassed by the city of Vancouver.

Of note regarding the importance of the city of Winnipeg in Swedish history was Logan Avenue in that city, virtually a "Swedish Street" with four Swedish churches in the same block, and the founding of Canada Tidningen, "the longest running and most influential Swedish language newspaper in Canada and the establishment of the first Canadian branch of the Vasa Order of America" (Sillanpaa, 1985). Inter-estingly, there has been a recent revival of the Swedish language among younger generations of Swedes. The shift in importance of the two cities pertains to population concentration (10,000 people today in Vancouver), cultural, educational and newspaper activities. Examples include the Swedish Canadian Club of Vancouver, involved in problems of Swedish adaptation and education, and the Bellman Male Chorus, active across North America and the Swea Society, the oldest social club in the region. Best-loved of Swedish festivals is "Lucia Day", December 13, following the longest night of the year. Traditionally on this morning, Lussi, Queen of Light, is said to appear at one's bedside, wearing a garland of green leaves and lighted candles on her head, and singing her song promising the return of the light. The early Church assimilated the pagan tradition, and Lussi was linked with the Italian Saint Lucia (Howard, 1970). A prominent object of the Christmas season is the Christmas Ram (Julbocken), the bringer of gifts. It appears to be a widely used symbol of Swedish culture in books and articles on Sweden.

While many early Swedish immigrants settled in northwestern Ontario as farmers and lumber workers, especially around Kenora, after the second World War, many Swedes settled in Toronto. Major activities include, for example, "Swea" (Swedish cultural group), "Skf" (Swedish ballbearing factory), and "Ikea" (furniture retail outlet). The Swedish community is served by the Swedish Lutheran Church, the Swedish Consulate, and the Swedish Trade Centre.

STUDIES OF SWEDES IN CANADA

The review of the literature yielded "bits and pieces" of data on Swedish customs, traditions, festivals, and foods (The Swedish Commu-nity, 1976; Shopping Basket, 1985) but little of socio-psychological significance concerning Swedes in this country. One study based on informal interviews (Bailyn & Kelman, 1962) with Scandinavian respon-dents offered some viable directions for exploratory hypothesis testing.

Psychologists Lotte Bailyn and Herbert Kelman identify four pat-terns of reactions among Scandinavians to their new American environ-ment. These patterns are derived from two potential outcomes of the adjustment process (change/maintenance in self-image) x two potential foci of adjustment (internal/external anchorage of self-image). The internalization pattern involves changes in self-image based on reorga-nization of internal attributes. Identification describes adoption of new behavior patterns meeting host expectations, while confirmation describes the maintenance of a self-image essentially in its original form. The process of resistance occurs when the self-image is firmly rooted in the ancestral culture with the individual seeking only selec-tive adaptation. The psychological processes involved in image change were not directly operationalized in the Bailyn-Kelman study; rather they were inferred from the interview data.

Given Canada's multicultural character and the scholarly interest in this country's many peoples, the present authors were surprised at the lack of data and paucity of writing on Swedes. It was this concern that challenged the authors to initiate this exploratory study of the adaptation experiences of Swedes in Metro Toronto (Bygden & Naidoo, 1986).

Exploratory Hypothesis. It was predicted that adult Swedish respondents exhibiting high positive scores on two tests of self-imagery (Berger, 1952; Bales & Couch, 1969) would accept the challenge of new host experiences and change with regard to them, either by a process of internalization or identification.

By contrast, respondents exhibiting low scores on these measures would show confirmation or resistance to change, retaining strong in-group feelings and bonding with the ancestral culture.

METHOD

Informed Swedes were located through the Swedish Consulate, the Swedish Trade Centre, and the Swedish-Canadian Chamber of Commerce in Toronto, and from personal University contacts. Detailed pilot telephone interviews were conducted with some 20 informed persons. The Pastor of the only Swedish Church in Toronto and an alumnus of Wilfrid Laurier's Seminary facilitated access to his Swedish congregation. Co-author Bygden visited the congregation, introduced our intent to people, and established good rapport with them.

Items relevant to the adaptation experiences of Swedes in Canada were compiled based on the literature and feedback from informed sources in the Swedish community. Feelings of identity were probed at three levels: in-group cultural, occupational, and out-group relations (mainstream/other minorities). Self-imagery was measured by the 15 self-acceptance items of the Berger Scale (1952) and the 5 individualism factor scales of the Bales & Couch measure (1969). Solid reliability coefficients are reported for both scales (Robinson & Shaver, 1970). To provide wider context for the study, appropriate demographic questions were also included. Most items were closed-ended and/or scaled. 10 selected items of the Crowne & Marlowe (1964) scale were included to probe the tendency to give socially desirable responses.

100 Questionnaires were delivered personally to potential respondents through the kind cooperation of the Swedish Church in Toronto, the Consulate and Trade Centre, the Swedish cultural group, and interested individuals. Questionnaires were self-administered and were mailed to the authors at the Psychology Department, Wilfrid Laurier University, using the provided stamped addressed envelopes.

34% of the questionnaires were returned; some were poorly completed. Although potential respondents showed initial enthusiasm about the project, eliciting the completed questionnaires, even with the assistance of the Swedish Consulate, was problematic. Testing commenced April, 1986 and was brought to closure a few months later. Feedback summary of findings and "thanks" were mailed to all participants and all interested organizations.

RESULTS

Demographic Characteristics. The sample data revealed that most Swedes in Toronto (85.3%) are Swedish born Lutheran (79.4%) in white collar occupations (58.5%), 48.5% Swedish and 33.3% English speaking at home, their citizenship is approximately one third Canadian (35.3%), Swedish (35.3%), or landed immigrant (29.4%). Mostly people with landed immigrant status do not plan on Canadian citizenship (84.6%). English was learned at school in Sweden (79.4%); most respondents did not feel it important to learn French (51.5%); and 55.9% said they practised their religion "very little".

Most respondents originated in the central Uppland-Smäland provinces of Sweden, with 20.6% coming from the city of Stockholm, about the period 1951-1960, as adults (78.1%) on arrival in this country. The sample was basically female (70.0%), married (55.9%) to Swedish (41.7%) and "other" (58.3%) mainly Norwegian spouses, with an average of 1.59 children. 62.5% of the families had just one wage earner, with an average annual income of $30,000 and a predicted future income in 5 years of $40,000. However, 25% of the families grossed an annual income of $60 - 80,000 + with the expectation of $80 - 100,000 + per year in the next 5 years. Only 9.1% were working in Swedish firms in Canada and there was basically no preference for such employment. 42.4% were university educated; 54.6% had either gymnasiet (pre-university) or Kom Vux (adult) education.

Migration and Adjustment. Most Swedes, and the respondents themselves, (35.3%) came to Canada primarily for new opportunities. They were attracted to the country because of its natural resemblance to Sweden (26.5%); some people had visited Canada (17.7%), or had business connections (20.6%) or friends here (17.7%). Initial adjustment problems included inability to communicate with French Canadians (78.1%), geographical distances (48.5%), and loneliness (48.5%). Obtaining jobs, the English language, new currency, and the presence of other races in Canada did not present problems.

Expectations of Children. Most people do not strive to preserve the Swedish language in their children, and 52.6% feel the language will be "lost". 80.0% of the respondents say their children do not attend Swedish school. 57.1% expect that children will practise their religion "very little", nor do people (54.2%) expect their children to marry Swedes. Most important characteristics in children's spouses listed were good education (81.5%), financial security (50.0%), career orientedness (42.3%), white rather than non-white (46.2%), and spiritual/religious (37.0%). High status, Canadian citizenship, European

173

origins in spouses were of negligible importance. 51.8% viewed learning of French for their children as "very important".

Multiculturalism & Intergroup Communication. Mostly, people were neutral to positive (66.6%) about Canadian multiculturalism. Interactions, however, are mainly with white Canadians at work (58.8%), and almost exclusively with either Swedes or white Canadians in home settings (100.0%) or socially. Home invitations for traditional celebrations are extended basically to family (84.4%) or Swedish friends (75.0%). There are few interactions with mainstream Canadians and even less with "visible" minorities on these occasions.

Expressions of Swedish Culture. Most respondents value the retention and annual re-enactment of famed traditional customs surrounding Christmas Eve (88.2%), Lucia Day (57.6%), and Advent and Midsummer (51.5% in each case). Swedish National Day was "moderately important" for most (71.4%). The Epiphany, Surstromming Dag, and Pankaks Torsday were definitely "not important". People were involved in the preparation of special foods and home decorations (69.7%) for main Swedish festivals, participating in Swedish community celebrations (60.6%). Swedish cultural artifacts such as hand blown glass and collector plates (71.9% and 46.9% respectively) are kept in the home.

Feelings re Home/Host Countries. A strong emotional attachment to the ancestral country is exhibited. Thus, 71.4% say "in my heart the country I really love most is Sweden" (14.3% chose Canada), and 48.4% list "Sweden" to the question about the "place I think of as "home" (41.9% list Canada). However, most respondents plan to live in Canada on retirement (66.7%). 58.8% read Swedish newspapers primarily for Swedish news (rather than to keep up Swedish language), 29.4% wished "very much" to be in Sweden during the Olof Palme crisis, and 44.4% think that Swedish citizens in Canada should vote in Swedish elections. However, by contrast, only 28.1% felt involvement in Canadian politics was important. Swedish contributions to Canada were viewed as important (53.2%), and a strong sense of pride is experienced (48.5%) where Swedes have contributed to the host country. Examples include: Hans Lundberg (Airborne geophysical prospecting), Birger Leon (Architect; Associate designer of Maple Leaf Gardens), and Esse W. Ljungh (Theatre/ radio broadcasting) (Kastrup, n.d.).

Tests of Self-Imagery. 65.5% of the respondents exhibited high self-acceptance on the Berger (1952) Scale of this component of self-imagery; 37.5% scored in the medium range. There were no respondents at the low end of the scale. Contrary to expectation only 6.1% showed high individualism on the Bales & Couch (1969) measure of this trait. But, 75.8% were moderate, and just 18.2% low. This last-mentioned finding may reflect the sex composition of the sample.

Test of the Bailyn-Kelman Model (1962). The model predicts that respondents exhibiting high self-image, as measured by appropriate tests, are more likely to accept the challenge of new host experiences and change by a process of <u>internalization</u>. These respondents exhibit confidence in their general adoption of host cultural values. On the other hand, respondents exhibiting low self-image are more likely to show <u>resistance</u> to change to the host culture.

An attempt was made to examine these contentions. The measures of self-imagery utilized were the total scores derived from the 15 items of Berger's Self Acceptance Scale and the 5 items of the Bales & Couch Individualism Scale. Nine items pertaining to Swedish cultural events were used to derive a basic "culture scale". The one-way ANOVA and x^2 tests, computed for scores on the two tests of self-imagery, and scores on the culture test yielded no significant differences. Further testing of the predicted relationship, using the single items of the culture measure and other items in the questionnaire having cultural connotations, yielded a scattering of significant differences. Significant relationships bearing on the exploratory hypotheses, for example, indicated that respondents scoring high on the culture scale (traditional) placed more importance on a spiritual/ religious, high status spouses for their children, read Swedish newspapers, and were more likely to have experienced inadequate job opportunities on arrival in Canada. However, other significant differences bore little stable relevance to the exploratory hypothesis. Overall, respondents do not appear to be rooted in the ancestral culture. Nevertheless, uniformly they value the retention and annual re-enactment of famed traditional customs surrounding, for example, Christmas, Lucia Day, and Harvest festivals.

DISCUSSION

Admittedly, the sample data reported are biased by their derivation from a small number of respondents and volunteers from specific settings. However, they highlight some widely held perceptions about Swedes in this country. These include the oft-repeated comment in the literature that Swedes assimilate easily. Initial enthusiasm about the present study was difficult to sustain. As observed by Runblom in 1982, Swedes exhibit low ethnic consciousness. Loss of language, traditional religion, and ethnic identity through intermarriage appear to be on-going processes. Runblom asserts that the forms of migration to Canada for Swedes weakened inclinations to preserve language, culture, and traditions of their ethnic group. Thus, early migration was male-dominated, people were recruited from several different areas of Sweden, and they were widely dispersed in Canada; hence, homogeneous marriages could not be maintained. Further, their ethnic similarity with mainstream Canadians, coupled with their pre-migratory knowledge of English and relatively high annual incomes, generates a perception of a "low risk" group within the totality of Canada's complex ethno-cultural composition.

Seemingly low-keyed politically, feeling no urgency to become Canadian citizens, markedly in-group, not having experienced problems with job acquisition generally, and basically expressing high self-acceptance and individualism adds to the image of "low risk". Unfortunately, the "low risk" image makes it difficult for researchers to obtain funding for projects studying Swedes. Research assistants, too, feel uncomfortable devoting time to a "low risk", indeed privileged, group, when work relevant to Canada's many "high risk" peoples begs attention. Other multicultural societies are also much more receptive to data on "high risk", usually visible minorities, than they are to data on Swedes whom they do not perceive as threatened. These consequences of the Swedish "low risk" image have recently touched the senior author's experience quite poignantly. Thus, for example, during some months of scholarly interaction in British universities, she found surprising excitement and enthusiasm about research on South Asians, Africans, and refugees in Canada. This interest, however, did not seem to extend to research on Swedes in this country.

The return rate and adequacy of responses to the self-administered questionnaires were disappointing for a literate people, well-versed in English. As with other minorities, personal interviews should elicit more complete data.

Basically, the sample showed high positive self-imagery. Only the rudiments of Swedish culture, such as favorite festivals, seem to linger on. There is a nostalgia for the ancestral country, but this is relatively subdued. Given these findings, the opportune time for testing the Bailyn- Kelman internalization-resistance hypothesis may have passed. At least this sample seemed to be quite assimilated into mainstream Canada. Pursuing the Bailyn-Kelman hypothesis further may prove futile. Most certainly other research on this issue must entail more powerful discriminating measures. A standardized test of integration-assimilation, appropriately modified for Swedish culture, might provide the basis for a more adequate test of this hypothesis.

CONCLUSION

Given the limitations imposed by the nature of the sample utilized in this study, these writers hesitate to make broader statements about Swedes in Southern Ontario. However, observations about their low ethnic consciousness and their perception as a "low risk" minority seem warranted. In a forum, such as the International Association for Cross-Cultural Psychology, it is appropriate that social scientists be alerted to the important need for research on small, less visible, minorities in Canada, such as Swedes, for historic and intrinsic reasons. Further, typically, later generations of ethnic minorities do exhibit a revival of interest in their "roots". Thus, for practical reasons it may be well for Swedes and other concerned persons to register more comprehensively Swedish history, culture, and language for the future.

Acknowledgements. Thanks are expressed to the following individuals for their generous assistance with this project: In Toronto, Mrs. Marlena Hagelstam of the Swedish Consulate, Rev. Tonis Nommik, Pastor of the Swedish Lutheran Congregation, Ms. Lisbeth Jacobson, formerly of the Swedish-Canadian Chamber of Commerce, Mrs. Lena Medin-Russell, President of the Swedish Women's Education Association; and in Kitchener-Waterloo, Ontario, Mr. Victor Constantino and Mrs. Christine Sharma.

REFERENCES

Bailyn, L. & Kelman, H.C. (1962). The effects of a year's experience in America on the self-image of Scandinavians: A preliminary analysis of reactions to a new environment. Journal of Social Issues, 18, 30-40.

Bales, R. & Couch, A. (1969). The value profile: A factor analytic study of value statements. Sociological Inquiry, 39, 3-17.

Berger, E.M. (1952). The relation between expressed acceptance of self and expressed acceptance of others. Journal of Abnormal and Social Psychology, 47, 778-782.

Bygden, A. & Naidoo, J.C. A socio-psychological portrait of Swedes in Toronto. Poster session presented at the meetings of the Canadian Psychological Association, Toronto, June 1986.

Canadian Family Tree (1967). Ottawa: Department of Secretary of State.

Crowne, D. & Marlowe, D. (1964). The approval motive. New York: Wiley.

Hardwick, F.C. (Ed.) (1978). The return of the Vikings: Scandinavians in Canada. (Canadian Culture Series, #7) Canada: Campbell Printing Ltd.

Howard, I. (1970). Vancouver's Svenskar: A history of the Swedish community in Vancouver. Vancouver, British Columbia: Vancouver Historical Society.

Janssen, V.K. (1982). Swedish settlement in Alberta, 1890-1930. The Swedish American Quarterly, 33, #2, 111-123.

Kastrup, A. (n.d.). Swedes in Canada. New York: Swedish Information Service.

Ontario Ethnocultural Population 1981 (1985). Socio-economic characteristics and geographic distributions. Special Report #3. Toronto, Ontario: Ontario Ministry of Citizenship and Culture, Multiculturalism Program.

Robinson, J.P. & Shaver, P.R. (Eds.) (1970). Measures of social psychological attitudes. Ann Arbor, Michigan: Publications Division, Institute for Social Research, University of Michigan.

Runblom, H. (1982). The Swedes in Canada: A study of low ethnic consciousness. The Swedish American Historical Quarterly, 33, #1, 4-20.

Shopping Basket: Foreign flair to giving (1985). The Globe and Mail, December 11, Section E2.

Sillanpaa, L. (1985). Swedes. In The Canadian Encyclopedia. Edmonton, Alberta: Hurtig Publishers.

Statistics Canada (1984). 1981 Census of Canada. Ottawa: Ministry of Supply and Services Canada.

Swedish community at Eriksdale, Manitoba (1976). National Museum of Manitoba, Canadian Centre for Folk Culture Studies, Paper #14.

RETENTION AND ACQUISITION OF NATIONAL SELF-IDENTITY IN POLISH IMMIGRANTS TO CANADA: CRITERIAL AND CORRELATED ATTRIBUTES

Pawel Boski
Wichita State University
Wichita, U.S.A.

For most of us, thinking of oneself in terms of national or ethnic identities is a routine, overlearned activity. Usually it is done as a part of filling out a passport, visa or other application form; or answering similar questions as a foreigner abroad. By contrast to such bureaucratic obviousness, psychological investigations into the issue of national/ethnic identity face considerable conceptual difficulties and there are far from satisfactory solutions at theoretical as well as methodological levels of inquiry.

The purpose of this chapter is to present an approach outlining a social cognitive theory of national self-identity, along with empirical data implementing that theory in a study of identity retention and acquisition among Polish immigrants to Canada.

A SOCIAL-COGNITIVE APPROACH TO NATIONAL SELF-IDENTITY

Tajfel's (1978, 1981) studies on the consequences of social categorization have been milestones in our understanding of stereotyping and intergroup relations. Of particular importance at this point is his distinction between criterial vs correlated attributes of any categorization. According to Tajfel (1981), criterial attributes split the universe into discrete categories or define the boundaries for set inclusion/exclusion, and intersection. Correlated attributes, on the other hand, are dimensional or continuous rather than categorical; they measure certain qualities of all individual exemplars meeting certain criterial attributes.

Tajfel did not formulate any theory based on the two types of attributes, but an impulse once given may be sufficient to influence others. One could think of religions and denominations (Christian/Muslim, Catholic/Protestant); languages (English, Ukrainian) or occupations (fisherman, farmer, professor) as criterial attributes of categorization. Similarly, trait-adjectives that we use to characterize people (bright, responsible, lazy, generous) are examples of correlated attributes. The proposed distinction has important consequences for many social-psychological problems. One of them concerns stereotypes which can be here redefined as correlations, or more often illusorily correlations (Hamilton, 1981), between the two types of attributes, such that the national label is a criterial, while the following trait-adjective becomes a correlated attribute. Hence, when we say 'Turks are aggressive', 'Poles are romantic' or 'Americans are pragmatic', we give classic examples of stereotypic judgments. On the other hand, we shall not consider statements: 'Turks are Muslims' or 'Poles are Catholics' as stereotypical, because their predicates are themselves criterial attributes (and in these cases even the defining ones!).

Tajfel's distinction between the two kinds of attributes leads us straight to the heart of the national identity matter, where the two have been systematically confused. It is here proposed that criterial attributes serve to define ethnic/national entities: "Whom shall we call a Pole, a Canadian?, etc." With the correlated attributes we pose a different question: "What kind of people are Poles, Canadians?, etc." It should be noted, that other authors expressed ideas resembling ours rather closely. Devereux (1975), for instance, made a distinction between ethnic identity as a 'sorting' (classificatory) device (p.48), and ethnic personality as a conceptual scheme, and derived observed behaviors and verbal reports on them (p. 45). Similar intuitions were also recently expressed by Chun (1983) when he wrote: "It is therefore important to separate ethnic identity ('Who am I?') from the characteristics or traits commonly associated with ethnicity ('What am I?'): that is, to distinguish the sense of boundary from what is enclosed by the boundary" (p. 195).

Criterial Attributes and Self-identity. Although the cognitive processes leading to a self-labeling ethnic identity have never been studied, it seems likely that such statements contain and are based mainly on criterial attributes. One reason for that assumption comes from developmental research on gender identity, where boys and girls acquire knowledge or recognition of stable differences making them who they are. The other source of evidence is provided by McGuire's (1984) studies on spontaneous self concept where sharp contextual differences (sex, race, hair color, etc) form the perceptual basis for identity statements. Criterial attributes, because of their visibility and discrete distinctiveness may be informatively more useful to categorize our world. Yet, the examples point to genetic/racial factors which are far from sufficient to form a basis for national identity. We shall propose that it is the cultural system that provides the relevant attributes in this respect.

Usually language and religion are such cultural systems which define national identity with a fairly good accuracy. A prototypical Pole must speak the Polish language (a distinction from billions of other humans who do not) and most likely was born and raised in a Catholic tradition. It is here proposed, however, that the domain of criterial attributes for national identity be defined more broadly, specifically by encompassing Cultural Knowledge Structures and Symbols of Cultural Relevance. Among these elements of cultural store are distinct markers of cultural heritage: historical names, dates, monuments; geographical locations; songs, emblems, pieces of arts and literature. Names such as 'J.Pilsudski' or 'A.Mickiewicz'; dates like 'May 3' or 'November 1'; 'White Eagle' emblem; etc, will be of no meaning or personal relevance to anybody but a Pole (or a researcher on Poland). Such criterial attributes are the key symbols of national identity, and their acquisition is usually a subject of deliberate efforts of school education; they also form what Ichheiser (1946) called a <u>conscious</u> national identity.

With the criterial identity defined in terms of cultural knowledge and symbols, the case is relatively straightforward. What it requires is a "hot" type of knowledge about cultural facts and events of a given nation. It is, in other words, a factual knowledge with a personal quality that makes the facts identified with different from the "cold" knowledge of an expert. But because our criterial identity carries an element of an objective knowledge too, its assessment is direct and does not require any comparison with external models.

<u>Correlated Attributes and Identity by Self-prototype Comparisons</u>. We are moving now to a theoretical elaboration of Tajfelian correlated attributes. These are universal physical/psychological dimensions, that every human being can be measured on. These correlated attributes may significantly vary between social groups but they do not serve as criteria for category membership (e.g. intelligence may be correlated with the level of attained education but there are no social groups that are called "High Intelligent" or "Low Intelligent").

Two questions arise as particularly relevant for the correlated aspect of the national identity problems: one has to do with the content or format of the attributes themselves; the other pertains to the relational nature of self-identity and its measures. As to the content of correlated attributes, one could think of adjective check lists having a research tradition in person perception and national stereotypes. Because of serious weaknesses associated with that methodology (Boski, 1988), it seems more promising to look for inspiration to cross-cultural studies on values. They can be illustrated by the works of Hofstede (1980) and Bond (1987), each based on value surveys in many countries. These studies used factor analytical techniques to extract universal value-dimensions, and to compare profiles or positions of various countries in such multidimensional space. They suggest values as units for comparisons between cultures: universal but of differential importance among various populations. We extend this conclusion by proposing that values and their derivatives be equally appropriate for measuring the correlated aspect of national self-identity.

The relational character of the correlated self-identity demands a broader analysis. Because the attributes are now assumed to be universal, unlike the criterial ones, there must be established some external standard of identity to compare one's self with. Since the case is about a specific type of identity, the standards should bear national names: "Pole", "Canadian", etc. Hence, we are back to the problem of categorization and its criteria. In no other domain are the classical rules of classification into exhaustive and complete sets as unsatisfactory as in human categorization, and nowhere else do the assertions of cognitive psychology intiated by the works of Rosch, fit better. As that author proposed instead, people group natural objects into categories by considering family resemblances among the objects (Rosch, 1976; Rosch & Mervin, 1975; Rosch et al., 1976). Consequently, some exemplars are regarded as better representatives of a category than others because they focus more criterial attributes. Such central specimen the author calls prototypes. On the other hand, we also have some borderline cases which share few family resemblances, and these are called peripherals.

There are clear implications of studies on prototypes for our interests in ethnic/national identity of immigrants. As Cantor & Mischel (1979) and Cantor, Mischel, & Schwartz (1982) have shown, the paradigm established in the Rosch studies on the structure of natural categories and classifications can easily be applied in the field of person perception, yielding basically identical results. As already intimated, national categories seem to be even more fuzzy than those of natural or material objects are. This implies prototypes in the center and members less saturated in family resemblances at the peripheries. Immigrants with their hyphenated identities (eg. Polish-Canadians) are particularly good examples of such border-line cases.

We can conclude at this point that a prototype presents itself as a standard of comparison for establishing the correlated component of national self-identity. With value-statements as the correlated attributes, a possible research scenario on national identity could be conceived of as a task consisting of the following three steps: i) eliciting S's self-description on a set of value-items; ii) using the same set of items to repeat the construction of one or more of S's national prototypes; iii) finding the degree of similarity, (overlap), between Self and that of a national prototype(s): "To what extent am I psychologically similar to someone whom I consider a prototypical Canadian or Pole?" Some convergent theoretical ideas on this issue have been expressed by Aboud (1981), and Markus & Sentis (1982). On methodological grounds, the approach adopted here is very close to Bem's (1983) "template matching" technique, used in his person-in-situation studies.

RESEARCH PROBLEMS

The main problem of the research presented here was to investigate retention and acquisition of criterial and correlated national self-identity among Polish immigrants with different lengths of stay in Canada. More specifically, the interest was in cross-sectional comparisons of Polish and Canadian identities among NEW, OLD, and SECond generation immigrants.

Empirical questions in this study are about the scope of stability and change in identity characteristics over time; and whether or not the processes of retention and acquisition show the same dynamics in criterial and correlated aspects of identity. In answering these questions, as research hypotheses, it should be first observed that the criterial and correlated aspects of identity have different cognitive statuses, and presumably different mechanisms of acquisition. The criterial identity presupposes structured knowledge combined with personal participation (experience), hence it is seen as an outcome of deliberate educational processes (school and/or home). On the other hand, correlated identity conceived as values and value-related traits, is a product of more automatic learning in the socialization process. Consequently, criterial identity should vary with an individual's direct educational exposure and participation in the symbolic environment of any culture. Correlated identity, which does not necessitate such stringent conditions, can be acquired through value transmission in family socialization. Specifically, in a situation of culture change such as immigration, with the length of time spent and a cohort gap equal to one generation, retention of correlated identity should prevail over the retention of criterial identity; acquisition of a new criterial identity should, however, be more complete than acquisition of a new correlated identity. This research hypothesis can be seen schematically tabulated in Table 1.

METHOD

Subjects. Sixty-six individuals participated in the research project; sixty-one satisfactorily completed all parts of the procedure. Most of them were residents of Kingston and Frontenac County of Ontario Province in Canada.

Ss were classified in a 3(GENERATION) x 2(GENDER) design, with at least 10 persons in each category. NEW were the immigrants who arrived to Canada recently, after the 1980/81 crisis and 'Solidarity'

TABLE 1

Critical and Correlated Aspects of National Self-Identity During

the Process of Acculturation: Processes of Retention and Acquisi-

tion (from New Immigrants to Second Generation)

PROCESSES	SELF CRITERIAL	IDENTITY CORRELATED
RETENTION	NEW: HIGH SEC: LOSS	NEW: HIGH SEC: RELATIVELY STABLE
ACQUISITION	NEW: HIGH SEC: HIGH	NEW: LOW SEC: RELATIVELY LOWER

period in Poland. They were in the 30 to 50 age range. OLD were the post-World War II veterans, who arrived to the new country in the late 1940s, after their units had been demobilized in the UK; some were former forced laborers in Germany. All these individuals were born and raised in Poland before World War II; and by the time of the research, they were above 65 years of age for men, or above 60 for women. Finally, the SEC(ond) generation consisted of those individuals who were born from both Polish parents in Canada, and grew up in that country. Between the OLD on the one hand, and NEW and SEC on the other, there was an age difference of one generation.

Materials.

Criterial identity: Symbols of Cultural Relevance. Criterial attributes of national identity were operationalized as symbols of cultural relevance. For the purpose of this study, fifty symbol-words were selected. There were 22 Polish, 19 Canadian, and 9 Japanese/Nigerian control symbols, representing: historical dates; national and religious days; names of politicians, political parties, and newspapers; geographical regions and entities; historical and cultural institutions; foods; sport teams.

A computer program of a lexical decision type was prepared for this material. Symbols were shown in a random order on the screen with the task for S being to decide whether the name appearing on the screen was of "personal relevance", defined and explained to S as a conjunction of 'knowing and feeling' about something or someone; not as a neutral cognition alone. A timer was built into an Apple-2 computer to enable measurement of lexical decision reaction time, for each item.

Correlated identity: Q-Sort value-statements and Q-sort task.
In the absence of validated cultural patterns, we rely on
'commonsensical wisdom' which gives undeniable examples of cultural
differences in people's ways of interpreting, evaluating, and
responding to social situations. The Author's experience with Polish
and Canadian ways of life, and consultations with other 'thoughtful'
Polish immigrants, generated a pool of items for the task of
diagnosing Ss' correlated identity. The list comprised 75 items at
first, that were used in an initial project (see: Berry, Kim, &
Boski, 1988). Based on psychometric criteria, that list was later
reduced for the purpose of the present research to 60 items. Two
examples will serve as illustrations of format and content: "I
can spend long hours on hot political discussions"; "Generally, I
have faith in the honesty of the people and authorities".

As can be seen, items are not simple trait or adjective names but
rather statements of behaviors, or beliefs embedded in values. All
items are correlated in the Tajfelian sense which means that they
could be used for dimensional self/other rating of any adult person
(at least within the two respective cultures).

The 60 statements served as items for the Q-sort task aimed at
obtaining measures of three personality profiles: Self-report, a
Typical Canadian, and a Typical Pole; the last two refered to the
names-labels selected by S as representing prototypes of each
nationality.

National/ethnic prototypes. Ss were asked to decide on Canadian and
Polish national prototypes from brief descriptions of twelve
individuals living in each country. There were equivalent male and
female versions representing possibly all major geographical and
socio/economic/cultural sectors of the two societies. Two cases
should again suffice as examples from these lists: FREDDIE TAYLOR -
Service Manager "Western Star Trucking" Sales & Repairs or VIRGINIA
TAYLOR - Hospital Nurse, Red Deer, Alberta; and ZBIGNIEW STRZELECKI
or LUDMILA STRZELECKA, Design Engineer, Electronic Research Center,
Wroclaw. The thirteenth was the Self category. S's task was to group
the 13 descriptions in piles according to their perceived similarity,
and then to imagine and to pick up the one being "the most
representative example" of a Male (Female) Canadian (Pole).

PROCEDURE

With most Ss the full research procedure took two sessions; the
first one consisted of Q-Sort tasks and was usually arranged at S's
home. The second session consisted of measuring symbols of cultural
relevance which required the use of computer facilities; it was

conducted in the Department of Psychology, at Queen's University. The prototypes and Q-sort statements had equivalent Polish and English versions, and it was up to S's decision to choose between them. The Test of Symbol Relevance had names appear in Polish and English, as their meaning was intimately related to linguistic form. It should be noted that all NEW and OLD Ss decided to take Polish versions of the tests; on the other hand only one SEC generation Ss was able to cope with statements and labels in Polish (and that person was born and raised in UK). This could be seen as an important result in itself, showing that second generation immigrants have lost (if ever acquired) reading skills in the language of their parents, that is one of the criterial attributes of national identity.

RESULTS

Criterial Identity: Effects of generation on CAN, POL Symbol Relevance. Data on SCR (Symbols of Culural Relevance) can be analyzed at two levels: "qualitative", consisting of Yes or No answers; and "quantitative" RT (reaction times) to those responses. Results will be first presented separately and then in a combined way. A comparison of the Yes-answer percentages to symbols of the three country-entities can be seen in Figure 1; it shows large differences between them, $F(2,110)= 312.61$, $p< .001$. This is largely due to marginal recognition and relevance of Jap/Nig symbols, still a contrast between CAN and POL is also significant, $F(1,55)=12.36$, $p<.001$. It demonstrates that the former are, in general, more personally relevant than the latter. Predictably, an interaction between object Country (CAN and POL) and Generation was also found, $F(2,55)= 24.93$, $p<.001$, and indicates stronger attachment to POL symbols by NEW Ss, but stronger relevance of CAN symbols to OLD, and particularly to SEC generation.

Analysis of reaction times to national symbols shows a significant main effect too, $F(2,110)=9.88$ $p<.001$, but different than the one for qualitative answers. Here, RT to POL symbols (M =4.776 sec) are longer than to CAN (M =3.670 sec) and to control JAP/NIG (M =3.918 sec.). Proceeding with the analysis for CAN and POL symbol RTs only, a strong interaction effect with generation categories was found again, $F(2,55)=20.79$, $p<.001$. This shows that while NEW had shorter RT for POL than for CAN, a reverse tendency was found for OLD and SEC Ss. Taken together with the qualitative findings reported in Fig.1, they allow us to say that groups which have higher proportions of Yes answers to a country-related symbols, also respond with shorter reaction times.

The next analysis combines the two levels of response to national symbols. To have this variable expressed in one scale, certain transformations were necessary. It was decided that the transformed scale should run a continuum from a strongly negative

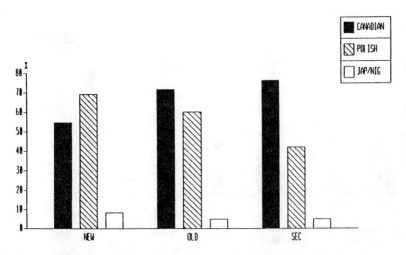

Fig.1 : Personal relevance of Canadian, Polish, and NIG/JAP
cultural symbols for 'New', 'Old', and 'Sec' Generation
Polish immigrants.

(unknown, dissociated) to a strongly positive (known, associated)
pole, with undecisive answers in the middle; or: the shorter the RT,
the stronger (more decisive) the answer. This idea was implemented
in two steps: first the No answers were assigned a " -", and then the
RT-msec. values were transformed into their inverses (1/RT).

Analysis of variance on the transformed scores revealed a strong
Generation Country-object interaction effect, $F(2,55)=28.83$, $p<.001$.
There is a continuous decrease of POL symbol relevance, and even a
more pronounced increase of CAN symbol relevance from NEW, to OLD,
and SEC generation. Hence, the hypothesis about the effect of length
of acculturative contact on the criterial aspect of national identity
has been convincingly confirmed.

Correlated Identity: SELFCAN and SELFPOL in Q-sorts. We can now
examine the overall measures of correlated Self-identity,
operationalized by SELF * CAN prototype, and SELF * POL prototype
correlations (transformed into z-scores); Figure 2 shows these data.
Inspection of Fig.2 shows two important results: SELFPOL identity is
generally higher than SELFCAN between the groups, $F(1,57) = 8.34$,
$p<.01$; but it also has remained consistently stable across generation
and gender categories. For SELFCAN on the other hand, there are

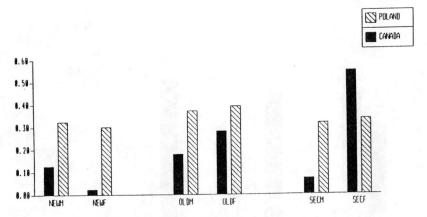

Fig.2 : Canadian and Polish Self-Identities by generation and gender of Polish immigrants.

Generation, Gender, and interaction effects (F/2,57/= 4.37, p<.02), such that Canadian identity is on the rise from NEW F, to OLD F, to SEC F while there has been no such change in the corresponding groups of men. The findings for second generation women are of interest, because it is the only category of Ss with Canadian identity higher than Polish identity. By contrast, SEC men show a very low degree of Canadian identity.

While retention of SELFPOL identity provides clear support for our theoretical reasoning, the gender differences in acquired SELFCAN are as much unexpected as interesting by themselves. We can leave more speculative interpretations for the general discussion and look for possible explanations of these findings in a more detailed analysis of the Q-sort responses, starting with a factor analysis performed on them. Data from all the three object-sortings were subjected to a single factor analysis; a six factor matrix was extracted with Varimax rotation, and with the scree test to decide the number of factors.

The first type of analysis, performed on factor scores, was a comparison of their loadings in the three objects of Q-Sort: Self, Canadian, and Polish prototypes. Figure 3 displays the relevant results. For all but one factor (Workaholic) the differences between the three objects of description are of staggering proportions (all well below p <.001 level). In Materialiam, CAN scores highest,

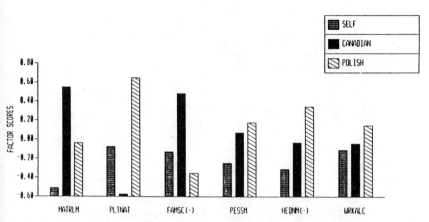

Fig.3 : Q-sort factor scores for Self, and Canadian and Polish
prototypes on six factors.

followed by POL, and SELF lowest; orthogonal comparisons between all
group means are highly significant. For Political Nationalism the
situation is reversed: POL scores highest, CAN lowest, and SELF is
placed in between; all contrasts are again significant. CAN scores
also lowest in Factor 3 which means lack of Family/Social concerns.
Although all the differences between group means in these three
factors are significant, in each case SELF is closer to POL than to
CAN. This tendency is reversed in the next three factors: POL is
rated highest on Pessimism/Past, orientation, on Ahedonism, and on
Workaholism SELF is placed the lowest on these dimensions, and closer
to CAN.

Another observation from that analysis is a tendency for <u>positivity
attributional bias</u> in Self-descriptions: Ss presented themselves as
least Materialistic, moderately Political, Optimistic, and Pleasure
oriented. The next question regarding the Q-Sort factors is to relate
them to the global SELFCAN and SELFPOL identity measures, and to
Gender/Generation effects on these measures. The answers to this
question will be provided in a path analytical format; the SELFCAN
part can be seen in Figure 4. Three sub-variables that account for
75.6% of SELFCAN variance are: CAN Materialism, CAN Family/Social,
and Similarity ratings (interactions) between the two objects in four
factors. In other words, the lower the perception of CAN prototype in
Materialism, the higher that prototype's standing on Family/Social
factor, and (in the third place) the higher the factorial similarity,

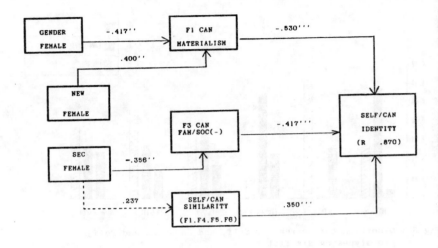

Fig.4 : From generation and gender to Q-sort factors and Selfcan
identity.

the higher S's Canadian identity. What also deserves a special
emphasis, is the absence of SELF scores in this equation: CAN scores
are more important than SELF in determining the SELFCAN identity.

As was reported in Fig. 2, SELFCAN identity was on the rise across
the three cohorts but for females only. We can now see the effects of
gender and cohorts (transformed into dummy variables) on the factors
that account for the global measure of SELFCAN. Their interaction is
clearly seen in Factor 1, where women as a whole perceived CAN
prototype as less materialistic (than men did), but NEW female
immigrants ascribed her higher levels of Materialism. In fact, the
extreme levels in SELFCAN (compared with Fig.2) are reflected in CAN
prototype's standing on Materialism: the lowest scores on the
identity measures among NEW females and SEC males correspond with the
highest scores in CAN Materialism, while the reverse occurs among SEC
females. Among SEC generation women CAN prototype was also found as
less anti-Family/Social oriented than in any other group. All these
micro-analyses shed more light on a distinct status of SEC women's
correlated identity among the other categories of Polish immigrants.

The micro-analysis on SELFPOL identity offers very similar results,
(Figure 5) except for their lower level of predictive accuracy (46.6%

190

of variance accounted for). High level of Materialism, and low
Family/Social orientation inhibit SELFPOL identity this time. The
effects of Generation and Gender categories, and their interactions
on these factors are mutually conflicting, however, and this is
perhaps why no systematic trends in the global scores of SELFPOL were
found. NEW immigrants, for instance, portray POL prototype as more
Materialistic than the two other cohorts do, but not the NEW F. The
latter, on the other hand perceive POL as less Family oriented. SEC
generation, and particularly females, find POL as Family oriented,
but otherwise dissimilar to self.

Throughout this chapter, the criterial and correlated aspects of
national identity have been treated separately. It may be of
interest to ask about the level of their association. This was
measured by the SCR (percentage of Yes answers) correlations with
SELFCAN and SELFPOL indices. Correlation between the two aspects of
self-identity was significant for Canadian, r=.372 p<.01; but not for
Polish identity, r=.142, ns.

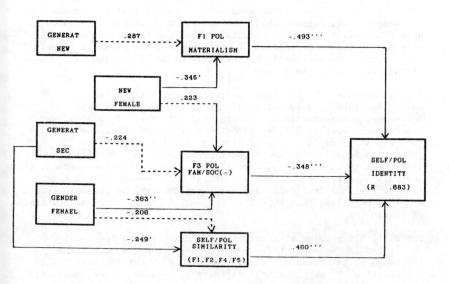

Fig.5 : From generation and gender to Q-sort factors and Selfpol
        identity.

DISCUSSION

The study reported in this paper was based on a theoretical
distinction between criterial and correlated aspects of national
self-identity, and on a hypothesis predicting their differential
processes/outcomes of retention and acquisition. The format of the
study was cross-sectional, with the unit of social time separating
the moment when NEW immigrants came to Canada from the period when
OLD landed (as young adults) and when SEC were born in that country
being equal to one generation of roughly 30 years. The NEW
immigrants, still at the beginning of their acculturation process,
were thus seen as a referent group, against which the processes of
identity retention and acquisition should be gauged.

The findings are basically supportive for the proposed theory: Over
the period of one generation, retention of criterial identity with
Poland suffered high losses, and has been virtually substituted by a
newly acquired identity with Canada; retention of correlated
identity with Poland, on the other hand, showed much stability and
was generally above the level of acquired identity with Canada.
The implications of the criterial - correlated distinction and of
the empirical evidence confirming the hypothesis call for broadening
the scope of discussion. While the two types of person attributes
have a universal domain of application and can be used in any
research on person perception, I shall concentrate on those aspects
which pertain more directly to the study of acculturation,
particularly among immigrants.

For the purpose of this study, criterial attributes were
operationalized as personal knowledge of Symbols of Cultural
Relevance. As hypothesized, retention of this kind of identity was
considerably lost in a life span of one generation. One could add to
this almost a complete loss of reading, writing, and speech
production functions of the parental language. As criterial
self-identity is to a large extent a function of conscious education
and participation in a nation's cultural life, we are on the safe
side to say that immigrants and their children who do not have such
exposure must lose that aspect of national identity with the country
of origin.

The difficult problem with criterial identity is its "personal
aspect", which means that factual knowledge is not a sufficient
(although it is necessary) condition here. With the SCR test in its
present form, it may lower the validity of results, since immigrants
will very likely deny some painful events or symbols of their
countries as 'parts of themselves'. Longer reaction times to Polish
Symbols of Cultural Relevance could result from such ambivalence. A
distinction between the cold factual vs personal knowledge, at the
level of measurement, can be suggested as a methodological

improvement for the future research.

Finally, the present approach to criterial attributes is limited to cultural elements only, the ones which can be retained or acquired in one's life time. Left aside are important inherited or racial criterial attributes such as skin color, hair type, or eye color and shape. With these highly visible attributes the retention of racial (rather than national) criterial identity would have been considerably stronger than in the case of correlated attributes.

Turning to the correlated aspect of identity in this study, one must give attention to some intriguing findings that are difficult to answer at the present time. First, why does the acquisition of Canadian correlated self-identity occur in women but not in men? Or, why do women become more Canadianized than men, even when they start from a significantly lower position? Is it because of their socialization for family roles, rather than a more complex socialization for citizens-of-larger-society? This interpretation would be in line with the results for SEC M counterparts (not different in marital/parental status), who felt much less identified with the self-selected Canadian prototypes. Another element for this group could be their heroic/idealistic identification with Polish fathers (soldiers, war veterans).

As far as the NEW immigrants are concerned, one may speculate that females' low level of SELFCAN identity has to do with differences of gender roles, such that women in Poland are accustomed to be treated, and to carry themselves as Ladies, which is neither ideal nor practiced in North America. Finally, both NEW-women, and SEC-men, who scored lowest in SELFCAN identity, had their Canadian prototypes rated highest in the Materialism factor. Perceived materialism as a hindrance in immigrants'acculturation appears as a counterintuitive finding. It is counterintuitive, in the sense of widespread beliefs that the first generation immigrants in particular, come greedy for material advancement, and they spend their lives to accomplish that goal. One type of explanation would purely be based on self-serving and projective mechanisms. Here, the very low levels of Self-materialism would be seen as a defensive attribution, and high attribution of Materialism to a prototypical Canadian would be indicative of a projective mechanism. That elaborated explanation must be, however, seen as defeated by the fact that SELF and CAN Materialism are positively correlated ($r = +0.40$, $p<.001$) and also by the similar role of Materialism in determining SELFPOL identity. Altogether, Materialism in constructions of other people (social world), is a negative predictor of one's identity, and of positive adjustment.

The general conclusion appears clear, and rich with practical implications: The real or apparent wealth of the new country which seduced so many immigrants, and which is so salient to them after having landed here, has negative consequences for their successful acculturation and healthy psychological adjustment. It happens particularly for those who construe other human beings in these rather dehumanizing terms, or have not been able to see other faces of Canadians.

The findings on correlated national identity also carry some message which is relevant to broader theoretical issues in social cognition. Two results pertinent in this context are: stronger contributions of prototype than of self ratings to SELFCAN and SELFPOL identities; and more pronounced causal and syndromatic effects in SELFCAN than in SELFPOL. We believe that these well docummemented findings converge in what should be called <u>salience</u> and <u>availability</u> mechanisms. Moreover, the findings concerning lesser contributions of self-ratings in identity measurement, contradict a widely accepted view of Self as a "super" reference point in processing social information (Rogers, 1981; Hollyoak & Gordon, 1983; Karylowski, 1988). In our study it is the two national prototypes, and not the self that are the anchor or reference points for self-identity. And our interpretation of this phenomenon is in terms of the prototype's more salient, sharper, even if schematically simplified, contours. Similarly, Canadian prototypes have been part of Canadian day-to-day reality that surrounded our Ss and engaged them. Poland, even if present in their thoughts, feelings, and communications, lacked that quality of immediate sensual, attention grabbing experience (Taylor, & Fiske, 1984, ch.8). "We believe what we see", said Ichheiser (1970), and the present day cognitive social psychologists repeat after him. There are also good reasons to believe that Canadian identity had a simpler cognitive structure: (RT to Canadian symbols had shorter latencies) and perhaps more integrated (association between criterial and correlated components was significant).

Finally and on a critical note again, the method of measuring correlated identity may require some improvements in future research. When selecting a prototype some Ss would ask: "Should it be a typical Pole or an Ideal one?" (Such questions were not asked regarding the Canadian side.) It captures an important intuition, not addressed in the present state of our theory, that there may be ideal, negative and perhaps "average" aspects of an immigrant's identity with the country that he decided to leave. These intuitions have been formalized in Weinreich's theory of identity (Weinreich, Kelly, & Maja, 1987).

FOOTNOTE

I wish to acknowledge the financial and moral support for this
research received from Queen's University, in Kingston, Ontario,
Canada, during my stay there as a visiting professor in 1985/86. I
also wish to extend my thanks to John Berry, who was my sponsor
during that time.

REFERENCES

Aboud, F.E. (1981). Ethnic Self Identity. In: R.C. Gardner, R. Kalin
(Eds.), A Canadian Social Psychology of Ethnic Relations. Toronto:
Methuen.

Bem, D.J. (1983). Toward a response style theory of persons in
situations. In: 1982 Nebraska symposium on motivation:
Personality - Current theory and research. Lincoln: University of
Nebraska Press.

Berry, J.W., Kim, U., & Boski, P. (1988). Acculturation and
psychological adaptation. In Y.Y.Kim, & W.B. Gudykunst (Eds.),
Current studies in cross-cultural adaptation, vol. 11, Newbury
Park: Sage.

Bond, M. (1987). Chinese values and the search for culture free
dimensions of culture. Journal of Cross-Cultural Psychology, 18,
143-164.

Boski, P. (1988). Cross-cultural studies on person perception:
Effects of in-group/out-group membership and ethnic schemata.
Journal of Cross-Cultural Psychology, 19.

Cantor, N., & Mischel, W. (1979). Prototypes in person perception.
In L.Berkowitz (Ed.), Advances in experimental social psychology,
vol.12, N.Y.: Academic Press.

Cantor, N., Mischel, W., & Schwartz, J. (1982). Social knowledge:
Structure, content, use, and abuse. In A.H. Hasdorf, A.M. Isen
(Eds.), Cognitive social psychology, NY: Elsevier/North-Holland.

Chun, Ki-Taek (1983). Ethnicity and ethnic identity: Taming the
untamed. In T.S. Sarbin & K.E. Scheibe (Eds.), Studies in social
identity, NY: Praeger.

Devereux, G. (1975). Ethnic identity: Its logical foundations and
its logical dysfunctions. In: G. DeVos, & L. Romanucci-Ross
(Eds.), Ethnic identity: Cultural continuities and change. Palo
Alto: Mayfield.

Hamilton, G. (1981). Cognitive processes in stereotyping and intergroup behavior, Hillsdale: Erlbaum.

Hofstede, G.H. (1980). Culture's consequences: International differences in work-related values. Beverly Hills: Sage.

Hollyoak, K.J., & Gordon, P.C. (1988). Social reference points. Journal of Personality and Social Psychology, 44, 881-887.

Ichheiser, G. (1946). Diagnosis of anti-semitism: Two essays. Sociometry Monographs, no.8, NY: Beacon House.

Ichheiser, G. (1970). Appearances and realities. San Francisco: Jossey Bass.

Isajiw, W.W. (1974). Definitions of ethnicity. Ethnicity, 1, 111-124.

Karylowski, J. (1988). Social reference points and accessibility of trait-related information. (Paper presented during the 96th Annual Convention of APA, Atlanta).

McGuire, W.J. (1984). Search for the self: Going beyond the self-esteem and the reactive self. In R.A. Zucker, J. Aronoff, & A.I. Rabin (Eds.), Personality and the prediction of behavior. Orlando: Academic Press.

Markus, H., & Sentis, K. (1982). The self in social information processing. In: J. Suls (Ed.), Psychological perspectives on the self, vol. 1. Hillsdale: Erlbaum.

Rogers, T.B. (1981). A model of the self as an aspect of the human information processing system. In N. Cantor, & J.F. Kihlstrom (Eds.), Personality, cognition, and social information, Hillsdale: Erlbaum.

Rosch, E. (1976). Classification of real-world objects: Origins and representations in cognition. In: P.N. Johnson-Laird & P.C. Wason (Eds.), Thinking. Cambridge: Cambridge University Press, 1985.

Rosch, E., & Mervis C.B. (1975). Family resemblances: Studies in the internal structure of categories. Cognitive Psychology, 7, 573-605.

Rosch, E., Mervis, C.B., Gray, W.D., Johnson, D.M., & Boyes-Braem, P. (1976). Basic objects in natural categories. Cognitive Psychology, 8, 382-439.

Scheibe, K.E. (1983). The psychology of national identity. In T.R. Sarbin & K.E. Scheibe (Eds.), Studies in social identity. NY: Praeger.

Tajfel, H. (1978). Social categorization, Social identity, and Social comparison. In: H. Tajfel (Ed.), Differentiation between social groups. London: Academic Press.

Tajfel, H. (1981). Social stereotypes and social groups. In: J.C. Turner, & H. Giles, Intergroup behavior. Oxford: Basil Blackwell.

Taylor, S.E., & Fiske, S.T. (1984). Social Cognition. Boston: Addison-Wesley.

Weinreich, P., Kelly, C. & Maja, C. (1987). Situated identities, conflicts in identification and own group preference: Rural and urban youth in South Africa. In C. Kagitcibasi (Ed.), Growth and progress in cross-cultural psychology. Lisse: Swets & Zeitlinger.

THE EFFECTS OF A WHITE OR INDIAN MODEL UPON WHITE CHILDREN'S RACIAL AWARENESS

R.C. Annis, B. Corenblum & C. Woesting
Brandon University
Brandon, Canada

When White children respond to race related questions they accurately apply racial labels to their own group and other-group members, accurately identify pictures which look most like themselves and have strong preferences for pictures of children of their own race (Aboud and Skerry, 1984; Corenblum and Annis, 1987). Canadian Indian children, however, respond very differently to these kinds of race related questions. Indian children, living on an Indian Reserve or in an urban setting, demonstrate less accurate racial labelling, more cross-racial self-identifications, and exhibit other-group preferences (Annis and Corenblum, 1986; Corenblum and Annis, 1987; and Hunsberger, 1978). When Indian children were presented with dolls or pictures of White and Indian children they were less accurate than White age peers in labelling which stimulus figure looked like an Indian child, were less likely to accurately identify the figure which looked most like themselves and were much less likely to demonstrate preferences for children of their own race. Age related changes in Indian children's racial labelling, self-identification, and preferences have also been explored, and although data in this area is inconclusive, it appears that while labelling accuracy increases with age, such changes are not necessarily accompanied by increases in self-identification accuracy or own-group preferences (Aboud, 1980; Blue, Corenblum and Annis, 1987). One conclusion from these findings is that while young Indian children know and can correctly apply the label "White" and "Indian" to others they do not yet apply these labels to themselves. It may be that for Indian children the perception of racial differences precedes the incorporation of those differences into the self-concept.

In the present study the development of young children's awareness of racial labelling, preferences and self-identification are examined. In addition, the stability of children's knowledge about race and race-related constructs are also explored. Although Aboud and Skerry (1984) suggest that minority group children acquire the race construct later than do majority group children, this does not mean

that even for White kindergarten children race constructs are firmly
established. Aboud (1980) demonstrated that when young children
dressed in the clothing of other ethnic groups this altered their
answers concerning perceptions of their own racial identity. This
suggests that between the ages of 4 and 5, children have an
incomplete understanding of race and race-related constructs and are
unable to maintain race constancy when racial stimuli are
transformed. The present investigation further explored this issue
by asking young White children to view a video tape of a White or
Indian child (the model) answering racial labelling, identification
and preference questions and to indicate whether they agree with the
model's choices. The extent to which children would agree with the
model, particularly when the model made errors on racial labelling
and identification questions or expressed other-group preferences was
examined. In this way the study was designed to test whether the
frequency of agreement with the model would vary by the type of
question posed and by the race of the model. We anticipated that
subjects would be more likely to correct a model when the model made
errors on questions that reflect a domain that subjects know well;
and subjects would correct an Indian more frequently than a White
model.

METHOD

Subjects. Forty-five White children (19 females) from kindergarten
and pre-school classes participated. The mean age of the sample was
5 years 3 months (SD=6.7 months).

Procedure. Subjects were tested individually by a White female
experimenter. Subjects were told that they would be asked questions
about some pictures and they were to respond by pointing to the
picture that best reflected their answer.

The stimuli consisted of three groups of drawings: the first group
was composed of water colour drawings of white and brown cups and
rabbits. Since these drawings were used only to familiarize subjects
with the general nature of the task, they will not be discussed
further. The second group were line drawings of four houses varying
in height, four balls varying in size, three glasses varying in
fullness, three lines differing in length and three lady bugs with
different numbers of dots on their backs. The final group consisted
of life-like water colour drawings of a White boy, a White girl, an
Indian boy and an Indian girl. Except for skin colour and other
racial features, these head and shoulder pictures were similar. A
list of all questions posed to subjects is presented in Table 1. The
set of ten object questions was presented first. For each question
the experimenter placed the appropriate line drawing in front of the
child and, for example, asked, "Point to the glass that is empty."
Subjects were then presented with pictures of White and Indian
children and asked questions tapping racial self-identification
(questions 11 to 14), racial labelling (questions 15 to 18), and
racial preferences (questions 19 to 22). These questions were
presented in a fixed random order.

TABLE 1

QUESTIONS ASKED TO THE SUBJECT AND THE MODEL

QUESTION TYPE

Object Questions.

    1.   Point to the glass that is empty.
 *2.   Point to the ball that is biggest.
    3.   Point to the house that is smallest.
 *4.   Point to the ball that is smallest.
    5.   Point to the house that is tallest.
 *6.   Point to the line that is longest.
    7.   Point to the bug that has most dots.
 *8.   Point to the line that is shortest.
    9.   Point to the bug that has fewest dots.
*10.   Point to the glass that is fullest.

Self-Identification Questions.

**11.   Which one would your friend say looks most like you?
**12.   Which one would your mother say looks most like you?
  13.   Point to the child who looks most like you.
  14.   Which one is most like the one you would see if you looked in a mirror?

Racial Labelling Questions.

 *15.   Point to the child who is a White girl.
  16.   Point to the child who is an Indian girl.
**17.   Point to the child who is an Indian boy.
  18.   Point to the child who is a White boy.

Racial Preference Questions.

  19.   Point to the one who gets into trouble.
  20.   Point to the child who is nice.
  21.   Point to the child who is friendly.
  22.   Point to the one who is bad.

*Model was incorrect when responding to these questions.
**On these questions the model responded by pointing to a picture that was of the same sex but different race from themselves. On all other identification, labelling, and preference questions, models responded by pointing to pictures that were of the same race and sex as themselves.

Subjects were randomly assigned to one of two task orders. In the first order, approximately one-half of the subjects responded to the questions, and then saw a video-tape of a six-year-old child answer the same questions. In the second order, subjects observed and responded to the model's performance and then answered the questions by themselves.

In both task orders all subjects saw a model that was the same sex as themselves, but half of the subjects observed an Indian model while the other half observed a White model. To control experimenter effects, the same female experimenter administered the questions to all subjects as well as to the models.

The model was shown on the top third of the screen with the drawings of the stimulus pictures displayed beneath. In response to each question a black pointer could be seen indicating the model's answer. These "answers" were pre-determined as indicated in Table 1, and were filmed independently of the model's actual choices. The models were incorrect on half of the object questions and on half of the racial labelling and self-identification questions the model pointed to a picture of a child whose race differed from that of the model. In answer to the preference questions models always pointed to pictures that were of the same race as themselves.

After each of the model's responses subjects were asked if they agreed with the model's choice; if subjects disagreed, they were asked to indicate which picture the model should have chosen.

RESULTS

Analysis of Object Questions. A 2(subject sex) x 2(task order) x age analysis of variance on subject responses to the the object questions showed no significant main effects or interactions. Overall, subjects were highly accurate (88%) on these questions. Subject responses to the model's answers to these questions were analyzed in a 2(model race) x 2(subject sex) x 2(task order) x age x 2(questions: model correct-model incorrect) analysis of variance with repeated measures on the last factor. The analysis revealed no significant main effects or interactions. When the model was correct, 89% of subjects agreed that the model answered correctly; when the model was incorrect 91% of subjects so stated, and subsequently indicated the correct response.

Analysis of Racial Labelling Questions. Responses to these questions were scored so that responses would reflect selections indicating that subjects were correct in terms of both race and sex (scored 3), correct race but wrong sex (scored 2), correct sex but wrong race (scored 1) or incorrect on both (scored 0). (This scoring procedure is also used in all subsequent analyses). A 2(subject sex) x 2(task order) x age multivariate analysis of variance (MANOVA) on the four labelling questions revealed no significant main effects or interactions. Post hoc analysis indicated that 82% of subjects correctly labelled the four water colour drawings. These findings indicate that children were able to correctly apply racial labels, and that the stimulus pictures corresponded to the childrens´ conception of White and Indian children.

A 2(subject sex) x 2(model race) x 2(task order) x age x 2(correct label-incorrect label) MANOVA of subject responses to the models´ answers revealed a significant age effect $F(4,33)=5.48$, p=.002. Older children were more likely than younger children to point out and correct the model´s error. Overall, however, subjects maintained a high level of accuracy, 80%, in labelling these pictures and did so regardless of whether they viewed a model who responded correctly or incorrectly to these questions.

Analysis of Self-Identification Questions. Responses to these questions were scored as above for correctness of race and sex and entered into a 2(subject sex) x 2(task order) x age MANOVA. When the subjects answered the questions by themselves the analysis revealed no significant main effects or interactions. Subjects were highly accurate on this task, 80% selected pictures that were of the same race as themselves. These results are comparable to those reported by Corenblum and Annis (1987) who found that 75% of White kindergarten children made same race choices in response to similar self-identification questions.

Subject responses to the model´s self-identification choices were also scored as above and entered into a 2(subject sex) x 2(model race) x 2(task order) x age x 2(model response: own race-other race identifications) MANOVA with repeated measures on the last factor. The analysis revealed a marginally significant model race x questions interaction, $F(1,29)=3.59$, p=.06. Univariate analysis indicated that when White models made correct responses, i.e. selected pictures of White children as looking most like themselves, subjects were more likely to agree with such choices (m=2.36) than when Indian models made correct responses to these questions (m=1.60). There were no significant differences when models answered incorrectly.

Analysis of Preference Questions. Responses to the racial preference questions were scored as above and entered into a 2(subject sex) x 2 (task order) x age MANOVA. The analysis indicated no significant main effects or interactions. Examination of the data revealed, however, that this result was due to a white bias present in subjects´ preferences. Subjects were more likely to attribute positive traits to pictures of White children (63%) but to attribute negative traits to pictures of Indian children (63%). Specifically, subjects rated pictures of Whites as friendly and nice (z = 2.38, 1.36; p = .01, .08) and rated Indians as bad and getting into trouble (z = 2.73, 1.06; p = .003, .14).

Responses to the model´s preference choices were scored as before and entered into a subject sex x model race x task order x age x questions MANOVA with repeated measures on the last factor. The analysis indicated no significant main effects or interactions. However, when responses to preference questions were scored for the percentage of subjects who agreed with the model's choices in terms of race alone, both model race and the evaluative nature of the questions influenced subject responses. As can be seen in Table 2, subjects were more likely to agree with the White models' attributions of positive traits to pictures of White children than to agree with Indian models' attributions of the same traits to pictures of Indian children (z = 3.94, p = .001). On the other hand, subjects were more likely to agree with the Indian model's attributions of negative traits to pictures of Indian children than with White model's attributions of the same traits to pictures of White children (z = 1.94, p = .03).

TABLE 2

SUBJECT'S AGREEMENT WITH MODEL'S
PREFERENCE CHOICES BY RACE ALONE (%)

Model Race	Question Type	
	Positive	Negative
White (n=21)	88	62
Indian (n=24)	53	80

In order to further examine the influence of a model upon subjects' racial preferences, comparisons were made between responses subjects gave in the model test condition with those given when they did the task by themselves. The analysis showed that when White models attributed positive or negative adjectives to pictures of White children subjects changed their responses in the direction indicated by the model (z = 2.94, p = .001; z = 2.00, p = .02 respectively). The analysis also indicated that when Indian models attributed positive attributes to pictures of Indian children subject responses were not significantly influenced by the model's choices (z = 1.25, p = .11), but they were significantly altered in the direction indicated by the model when Indian models attributed negative attributes to pictures of Indian children (z = 1.87, p = .03). These results indicate that White subjects were influenced by the responses given by White models, but they were influenced by Indian models only when that model said negative things about Indians.

DISCUSSION

In the present study White children answered questions about race by responding to racial labelling, identification and preference questions. In addition, the extent of their agreement with a White or Indian model's answers to the same questions were recorded. This procedure allowed an assessment of the influence of a model and of the race of the model upon race-related questions. Such comparisons permit an examination of the stability of children's use of race concepts.

Corenblum and Annis (1987) found that by age five most White children
have acquired an understanding of racial concepts and use them to
categorize both self and others. The results of the present study
confirmed these earlier findings. When subjects answered the
questions by themselves, they showed own-group preferences and
other-group rejection, chose pictures of White children as looking
most like themselves, and applied appropriate racial labels to
pictures of White and Indian children.

When subjects saw a model answer questions about racial identity and
preference, results indicated that the model's presence influenced
their responses. Subjects were more likely to agree with White
models who correctly chose pictures of White children as looking most
like themselves than with Indian models who gave correct responses.
White models also had a greater influence in swaying subject
responses on the preference questions. When White models attributed
positive or negative attributes to pictures of White children
subjects agreed with those attributions, but they agreed with the
Indian models attributions only when that model attributed negative
traits to Indian children. It should be noted that the lack of a
significant change in subject responses when Indian models attributed
positive traits to pictures of Indian children cannot be explained by
a general reluctance to correct a model whose race differs from that
of the subject, nor can it be attributed to the idea that race
constructs were not firmly established. In this study subjects
readily and accurately agreed with or corrected both White and Indian
models when these models responded to both the object and racial
labelling questions. However, on questions on which there is
response uncertainty, children are influenced by the presence of a
model, particularly when that model is White.

Bandura (1977) points out that the degree of similarity between a
model and an observer and the amount of power or control the model is
perceived to have over desirable resources determines how influential
the model will be upon the observer's subsequent behavior. In this
study a majority of subjects showed a strong White bias when they
responded to preference questions by themselves. Such responses
imply that White models are perceived to have access, directly or
indirectly, to desirable outcomes. According to social learning
theory, subjects should more readily attend and respond to White than
Indian models. Some support for these ideas was found, even to the
extent that subjects were willing to ascribe negative attributes to
pictures of White children when White models did so.

In this study both the experimenter and the subjects were White.
This leads to questions about the influence of experimenter race as
well as questions about the nature of responses of Indian children
when exposed to White and Indian models. If similarity between model
and observer is an important variable in influencing subject
responses then Indian children should be more influenced by Indian
than White models. On the other hand, if perceived control is an
important variable, then White rather than Indian models should be
influential for both White and Indian children. This outcome is also

predicted, but for different reasons, by the light colour bias hypothesis (Williams and Morland, 1976), Clark and Clark's (1939) escape hypothesis, and construct accessibility theory (Higgins and King, 1981).

Corenblum and Annis (1987), Annis and Corenblum (1986), Porter (1971), and Trent (1964), have shown that experimenter race, test language, age and social context influence children's thinking about race. These studies highlight the importance of contextual variables. Much of this research, however, has been confined to static test conditions. The present study reminds us that the concept of race arises out of a social context, and for these reasons, it is important that future studies attend to the interactive social situation in which race concepts are used.

NOTE.

1. Support for this research was provided by a Social Sciences and Humanities Research Council grant 410-88-0764 and by a Brandon University Research Grant. We would like to thank Cliff Anderson for his comments on a previous draft of the manuscript.

REFERENCES

Aboud, F. (1980). A test of ethnocentrism with young children. Canadian Journal of Behavioural Science, 12, 195-209.

Aboud, F. & Skerry, S. (1984). The development of ethnic attitudes: A critical review. Journal of Cross-Cultural Psychology, 15, 3-34.

Annis, R.C. & Corenblum, B. (1986). Effect of test language and experimenter race on Canadian Indian children's racial and self-identity. Journal of Social Psychology, 126, 761-773.

Bandura, A. (1977). Social learning theory. N.J. Prentice-Hall.

Clark, K.B. & Clark, M.P. (1939). The development of the consciousness of self and the emergence of racial identity in Negro preschool children. Journal of Social Psychology, 10, 591-599.

Blue, A., Corenblum, B. & Annis, R.C. (1987). Developmental trends in racial preference and identification in northern Native Canadian children. In C. Kagitcibasi (Ed.) Growth and progress in cross-cultural psychology, Lisse, Holland, Swets and Zeitlinger.

Corenblum, B. & Annis, R.C. (1987). Racial identity and preference in Native and White Canadian children. Canadian Journal of Behavioural Science, 19, 254-265.

Higgins, E.T. & King, G. (1981). Accessibility of social constructs: Information processing consequences of individual and contextual variability. In N. Cantor and J. Kihlstrom (Eds.) Personality, cognition and social interaction. Hillsdale, NJ: Erlbaum.

Hunsberger, B. (1978). Racial awareness and preference of White and Indian Canadian children. Canadian Journal of Behavioural Science, 12, 195-209.

Porter, J.D.R. (1971). Black child, white child: The development of racial attitudes. Cambridge, MA: Harvard University.

Trent, R. (1964). The color of the investigator as a variable in experimental research with Negro subjects. Journal of Social Psychology, 40, 280-284.

Williams, J.E. & Morland, J.K. (1976). Race, color and the young child. Chapel Hill: University of North Carolina Press.

BILINGUALS OR "DUAL LINGUISTIC IDENTITIES?"

Mehroo Northover
University of Ulster at Jordanstown
Newtownabbey
Northern Ireland

ETHNIC IDENTITY AND LANGUAGE

Rightly or wrongly, there is an emotive conviction which is widely
prevalent that those individuals who grow up to speak a language
other than their 'first language' or 'mother tongue' are deprived
of the full enjoyment of their personal identity. In the case of
bilinguals, by extension of this commonly held belief, the problem
which is often posed is that each language binds the user to a
particular set of cultural beliefs and values associated with that
language and that each of a bilingual's languages is the mediator
between two differing cultural identities within one and the same
person. One experiment reported by Ervin-Tripp (1964) involving
French/American bilinguals came to this conclusion.

In 1954, she had posited that the development of a child's primary
identifications with parents is mediated through a particular
language and becomes encoded within that language. In this view,
language is the chief mediator whereby a child's parents and other
significant people act as the agents of society, passing on its
values and introducing to the child an awareness of the general or
corporate morality.

It is apparent though, that even prior to the development of
language, the child must be aware of non-verbal behaviour, the
rituals, the music, and sounds of the family circle into which he
or she is born. These are also symbolic of the cultural specifics
of a family and of the circle of friends, the neighbourhood, or
religious group to which the child belongs. The development of
language may overtake these symbols in the degree of significance
it holds for a person, but it never obliterates them. At the same

time, language becomes a powerful symbol of primary and later secondary identifications for a person. A principle can now be stated that:

Children develop their primary identifications with their parents who constitute their positsive role models. Some mediating symbols of the affective ties and dependency/power relations between children and parents are non-verbal language, rites of passage, rituals, emblems, folk-lore and language.

In the case of a bilingual, subsequent identifications in life with members of a different culture may be encoded in a second language, thus each language is symbolic of its respective culture. For most children of ethnic minorities, it is in the course of secondary socialisation at school that they form secondary identifications with teachers, peers and others of the indigenous culture in a second language.

A statement of this principle is:

Bilingual dually enculturated children form part identifications with new role models which are encoded in the second language associated with secondary socialisation and the development of intellectual skills.

For dually enculturated bilinguals, their first language is the prime symbol of identifications with agents such as parents, and of the cultural values they represent as role models. Subsequent identifications with role models such as teachers, if associated with another language, are symbolised by the second language. The symbolism of language therefore triggers changes of identification with role models. The stereotypical expectation of such changes is that each language context brings about a reversion to the cultural values of the ethnic group associated with the language (cf. Ervin-Tripp, 1964). Weinreich (1979c), on the other hand, reports the converse in the case of an Asian woman in Britain who showed increased identification with English people while having decreasing identification with Pakistani people in the Urdu language which was her mother tongue.

To pursue an investigation of identity structure across languages, it is necessary to be more specific as to how the processes of identification interact with the use of language. Consequently, it becomes mandatory to operate within the framework of a broader theory of identity structure and to develop empirically-grounded theories relating to language and ethnic identity. A further requirement is to have a means of measuring identity changes within individuals and across languages.

The theory of Identity Structure Analysis (ISA) (Weinreich, 1969,

1979c, 1980, 1983a) provides such a framework, which is a part synthesis of key concepts of Erikson's psychodynamic theory of identity development (1959, 1968), Kelly's personal construct theory (1955), cognitive-affective consistency theory (Festinger, 1957; Weinreich, 1969), and perspectives from the symbolic interactionists.

This conceptualisation gives rise to an individually-tailored identity instrument whereby an individual can rate people significant to self against a series of bipolar constructs. The value system of the individual can then be expressed in terms of the structural pressure within the person that maintains the constituent constructs of one's construal system. High structural pressure on a construct denotes that it is used by an individual in a stable and consistent manner to evaluate self and others. Low structural pressure, on the other hand, indicates that the construct is being used in an evaluatively inconsistent or ambivalent manner.

Disposing of an ambiguity in the psychodynamic tradition, ISA differentiates identification into two main types. The first type is identification with role models, consisting of idealistic-identification with positive role models and contra-identification with negative ones, which are the source of a person's value system. The second main category of identification is empathetic identification which refers to the degree to which an individual shares both the good and bad qualities which he perceives in others. From the basic distinction between the two main types arises the concept of conflicted identification, which refers to the individual's simultaneous empathetic and contra-identification with another. In terms of one's current self-image, the extent of a person's identification conflict with another is conceptualised as a "multiplicative function of his current and contra-identification with that other" (Weinreich, 1980). These are some of the indices of identifications which provide measures of modifications of identity taking place within an individual and employed in the present paper.

Another feature of ISA is the incorporation of those strands of symbolic interactionism which provides for a metaperspective of self and a self-view when situated in the social context, i.e., 'role-making' and 'role-taking' (Hewitt, 1976:81), which is dealt with in some detail in the following section.

SITUATED IDENTITIES AND BILINGUALS

It was the symbolic interactionists who provided a further insight into the importance of "the situation" in an interaction, by drawing our attention to the characteristic of people to modify their behaviour in the course of social interaction by both taking

the role of the other and by making a role for self. Alexander and
Wiley (1981:273) described conduct as 'situated activity' "when it
is anchored outside the self and constrained by presumed
monitoring.... it does not have to be actual monitoring, merely
presumed or potential".

While this concept sheds useful light on changes and shifts in a
person's conduct or language behaviour in particular situations,
some consider this view of self-concept to be too chameleon-like to
be realistic, and a view which fails to express the nature of
identity as an evolving process with continuity over time.
Weinreich (1987) expresses this objection and defines one's
identity when situated in a specific social context as "that part
of the totality of one's self construal in which how one construes
oneself in the situated present expresses the continuity between
how one construes oneself as one was in the past and how one
construes oneself as one aspires to be in the future".

Synthesising the concept of the situated identity with that of
conflicted identification with another, one may provide a rationale
of a psychological nature for the variations of speech depicted by
linguists. A person's role model identifications or empathetic
identifications, or both, are modified in the presence of another.
In addition, for dually enculturated bilinguals, each of their
languages is symbolic to some degree of the identifications with
significant people associated respectively with each language and
culture. Thus either or both language and social context can give
rise to increased conflicted identifications. As a result, a
bilingual person may try to minimise such conflicted
identifications by choosing whenever feasible to speak in one or
other language.

The study to be reported here investigates the relationship between
a bilingual person's identity in situated contexts and the language
of interaction.

METHODOLOGY

Fifty-two young British Asians (29 females and 23 males), aged
between 14 and 18 years, communicatively competent and literate in
Gujarati and English, cooperated in the study which was carried out
using the ISA instruments one in Gujarati and the other in English
designed for this study. The instruments were presented at
intervals of approximately three weeks' duration. A group of 27
female and 20 male indigenous monolinguals of comparable age and
education were also presented with an identity instrument once only
in the English language. By this means it was possible to compare
the bilinguals' identity measures in the two languages and to
compare these measures against identifications of a 'comparison'
indigenous sample.

The concepts of ISA have been operationalised by means of algebraic formulae. Raw data for obtaining indices of identity structure as defined by Weinreich (1980) can be obtained by using a tailor-made identity instrument. It consists of a series of bipolar constructs which are used to rate facets of the self-image and a selection of people significant to the respondents. Both the constructs and entities to be rated were elicited through two interviews in Gujarati and English, respectively, the final selection of constructs reflecting the value systems of the respondents in both languages. Some of the constructs as elicited referred to specific ethnic values such as 'parents should select marriage partner'. Others were directed at 'traditional' values such as 'only women should do housework'. A third set of constructs were directed toward personal attributes such as 'feels confident'. Since the anchoring of the value system in ISA derives from the respondent's own ideal self-image, it facilitates the comparison of identifications with entities formed by the bilinguals in each of their languages. Other mandatory entities in the instrument are current and past self-image. For the purpose of capturing situated self, the entities self with Gujaratis and self with the English were also included. People selected for inclusion in the instrument were those considered significant or influential by the respondents, such as parents, siblings, teachers, a religious person, and others. Groups such as Gujaratis, English people, and Afro-Caribbeans were also included.

Raw data collected from each instrument, one in Gujarati, the other in English, was processed by means of the computer program IDEX-IDIO which provided an idiographic profile of each bilingual in each language. At a second stage, the individual profiles in each language were pooled and separately collated within each language, by means of a second computer program, IDEX-NOMO, which collates indices of identifications across individuals.

RESULTS AND DISCUSSION

Orientations. During early stages of the analysis of data, it became clear that the bilinguals did not have a homogeneous value system. Two distinct orientations emerged among both males and females. This was on the basis of the crucial construct, 'feels English/feels different from English people'. Further differences were also found in the value systems of the two orientations. One subgroup consisted of females who preferred the polarity 'feels different from English people' in both Gujarati and English languages (GL and EL), who are hereafter called 'Indo-oriented'.

Due to the constraints of space, discussion in the rest of this paper will focus on only a few of the findings concerning Indo-oriented girls. It will concern changes in identity resulting from

Table 1 SITUATED IDENTITIES: INDO-ORIENTED females: natural
and situated selves, in Gujarati and English languages. CURRENT
EMPATHETIC IDENTIFICATION with selected target entities.
(Scale=0.00 to 1.00)
ANOVA: Factor (i) Language (2 levels); (ii) Situated Selves
(3 levels)

Main effect: (i) Language

Target Ent.	GL	EL	F ratio	df	p
Mother	0.71	0.77	5.2440	1,59	<0.01
Father	0.73	0.79			
Gujaratis	0.71	0.83	8.7987	1,59	<0.01

Main effect: (ii) Situated identities

Target Entities	Natural Self	Withi Gujarati	With the English	F ratio	df	p
Mother	0.78	0.79	0.65	10.9966	2,59	<0.01
Father	0.80	0.82	0.66	8.9242	2,53	<0.01
Gujaratis	0.78	0.86	0.67	7.2958	2,59	<0.01

Table 2 SITUATED IDENTITIES: INDO-ORIENTED females:
CONFLICTS IN IDENTIFICATION with selected target entities.
ANOVA: Factor (i) Language (2 levels); Factor (ii) Situated
Selves (3 levels).

Main effect: (i) Language

Target Ent.	GL	EL	F ratio	df	p
Mother	0.34	0.30			
Father	0.32	0.27	4.3982	1,53	<0.05
Gujaratis	0.39	0.25	13.3266	1,59	<0.01

Main effect: (ii) Situated selves.

No main effect.

NOTE: In the tables, degrees of freedom (df) vary because not all
the target entities designated for evaluation were relevant for all
the females in the group. Only statistically significant results
are presented in detail.

a 'situated self' which take place first in each language respectively, then the changes between the two language contexts.

Resolution of Conflicted Identifications and Ethnic Identity. When empathetic and contra-identification with a person are simultaneously high, conflicted identification with that person is also high. One way to resolve such conflicts is by "inducing a re-evaluation of self in relation to the others within the limitations of one's currently existing value system" (Weinreich, 1983a;153). Further, Weinreich (1983a) states that the "specific nature of ethnic redefinitions depend on the avenues open to individuals given their patterns of identification with significant others".

Therefore, the underlying orientation of the Indo-oriented group should cause shifts in their empathetic identifications towards their own group, particularly in the Gujarati language and when with Gujarati people and simultaneously low contra-identification with them. A further strategy they might be expected to adopt would be to decrease their empathetic identification with English people.

As the operationalisation of ISA concepts enables the measurement of empathetic and conflicted identifications based in a person's situated self, i.e., in some particular social context, the following results compare the empathetic identifications of Indo-oriented girls in their 'natural self' with their alternative self-images, i.e., when they are with Gujarati people and when situated with the English. 'Natural self' hereafter refers to a person's current self-image as apart from one's image of self in a social context.

Below is a comparison of the empathetic and conflicted identifications of Indo-oriented girls with selected targets, between their two languages, situated in their natural and social selves, in order to focus on the effect of language context on these two indices.

There are significant differences in the current empathetic identification of these females with significant others in using their two languages as Table 1 shows. Focussing on the effect of language first, the table shows that the empathetic identification of the girls with their mother and Gujarati people is significantly greater in the English language than in the primary language.

Table 2 shows that when "situated with Gujarati people", the girls' empathetic identifications with their parents and other Gujaratis decreases significantly than when "situated with English people". This result runs counter to our expectations. It is inconsistent with general beliefs about the mother tongue being the language most likely to bring about a fulfilment of one's ethnic identity. It is not, however, inconsistent if one places the concept of the

213

situated self within the general meta-theoretical framework of ISA.

A person who is either actually in the presence of another or simply imagines an interaction with another negotiates a role for self in the light of the other's perception of oneself, assuming a temporary self-image. The changes in current empathetic and conflicted identifications. of these females are temporary responses spontaneously arising from a particular social context. Nevertheless, temporary changes of persona are rooted in ongoing identification processes with persons or groups who are strong influences on oneself. Conflicts with family and own group are the result of ongoing contra-identifications with them in respect to certain ethnic values with which they disagree, and which become sharpened in the Gujarati language which is symbolic of these values.

One cause of conflicted identification for females is gender-related. There is very little research reported on the socialisation of boys and girls within Asian cultures. Ghuman and Gallop (1981:131) make a valuable distinction between Hindu and Muslim parents' attitudes towards co-education, the latter being less in favour of this than the Hindus. Ekstrand and Ekstrand (1985) report that in India parents have no great expectations of female children. Parents also believe that whether girls' have careers or not is largely dependent upon decisions taken by their husbands and fathers-in-law. Asian British girls also have far greater restrictions placed on their social lives than their indigenous counterparts, and are well aware of the freedom enjoyed by indigenous females.

Thus the Gujarati language sharpens their sensitivity to contra-identifications with their family and own group. Many of these are gender related, and while the girls may wish to increase empathetic identification with their own group, there are bound to be areas of disagreement with parents and group elders.
An empirically grounded statement can now be made:

Issues of gender role in dually enculturated bilinguals arouse conflicted identifications with role models which will be intensified by the symbolism of the language associated with such conflicts.

CONCLUSION

Throughout an interaction, language is a symbol of identifications for dually enculturated bilinguals, but such symbolism is not impervious to the situation of self in a particular social context. For these bilinguals, it is possible to "monitor their own conduct" while they are in the actual presence of other Gujarati people, in the light of English people's perception of them. The monitoring occurs both in the Gujarati and in English language context.

Similarly, while with English people, the approval of their own ethnic group may be ever present in their minds. Therefore language and social context are never entirely separable for bilinguals who are in contact with two cultural communities within the same society. Modifications of a bilingual's identifications take place in both linguistic and social contexts.

REFERENCES

Alexander, C. N. & Wiley, M. G. (1981) Situated activity and identity formation. In (Eds) Rosenberg, M. & Turner, R. Social Psychology: Sociological Perspectives. New York: Basic Books Inc.

Ekstrand, G. & Ekstrand, L. H. (1985) Patterns of socialization in different cultures: the cases of India and Sweden. In (Ed) Diaz-Guerrero, R. Cross-Cultural and Natural Studies in Social Psychology, Vol. 2, Amsterdam: North-Holland.

Erikson, E. H. (1968) Identity: Youth and Crisis. New York: Norton.

Ervin-Tripp, S. (1954) Identification and Bilingualism. In Ervin-Tripp, S. (1973) Language Acquisition and Communicative Choice. Stanford: Stanford University Press.

Ervin-Tripp, S. (1964) Language and TAT content in bilinguals. ibid.

Festinger, L. (1957) A Theory of Cognitive Dissonance. Evanston: Row, Peterson.

Ghuman, P. A. S. & Gallop, R. (1981) Educational attitudes of Bengali families in Cardiff. Journal of Multilingual and Multicultural Development, 2, 2, 127-144.

Hewitt, J. P. (1976) Self and Society: a symbolic interactionist social psychology. Boston: Allyn & Bacon.

Kelly, G. A. (1955) The Psychology of Personal Constructs. New York: Norton.

Mead, G. H. (1934) Mind, Self and Society: from the standpoint of a social behaviorist. Chicago: University of Chicago Press.

Weinreich, P. (1969) Theoretical and experimental evaluation of dissonance processes. Unpublished PhD thesis. London: University of London.

Weinreich, P. (1979c) Sex-role identification, social change and cultural conflict. The British Psychological Society (N Ireland branch) Annual Conference, Rosapenna.

Weinreich, P. (1980) <u>Manual for Identity Exploration using Personal Constructs</u>. London: Social Science Research Council.

Weinreich, P. (1983a) Emerging from threatened identities: ethnicity and gender in redefinitions of threatened identity. In Breakwell, G. (Ed) <u>Threatened Identities</u>. Chichester: Wiley.

Part IV

PSYCHOLOGICAL ASSESSMENT

ASSESSMENT AND SPECIAL EDUCATION OF MINORITY AND IMMIGRANT CHILDREN IN THE UNITED STATES: ISSUES AND DEVELOPMENTS

Reginald L. Jones
University of California,
Berkeley, U.S.A.

Juliette M. Jones
Hampton University
U.S.A.

In this chapter we present a brief overview of the assessment and special education of minority and immigrant children in the United States. We give particular attention to the issues of identification, assessment and special education placement and to programs and practices designed to deal with the problems identified. Given limited space, the discussion, of necessity, will be limited.

We deal specifically with two problems. The first is the documented overrepresentation of minority group children in classes for the mentally retarded, emotionally disturbed, and learning disabled. The second problem is the increasing numbers of immigrant and minority children enrolling in American schools who require special education services. We believe the problems of assessing and placing immigrant children in special programs and the problems of assessing and placing minority group children in special education programs are closely related.

OVERREPRESENTATION OF MINORITIES IN SPECIAL EDUCATION

We first address the issue of minority group overrepresentation in special education programs in the United States. We ask: what is the extent of disproportion in classes for the educable mentally retarded (EMR) (the group of most concern in the disproportion issue)? We next address hypothesized causes of the disproportion. Finally, we ask if disproportion is problematic or symptomatic? The discussion following is drawn from the report of the ad hoc Panel on Selection and Placement of Students in Programs for the Mentally Retarded. (See Committee on Child Development Research and Public Policy, 1981). The report was prepared for the Office of Civil Rights (OCR) which was concerned with the possible overrepresentation of minority group children in special education classes, especially in classes for the educable mentally retarded. The following discussion is taken directly from the Committee's report. The senior author of the present paper was a member of the panel which developed the report.

The Extent of Disproportion in Classes for the Educable Mentally Retarded (EMR) in American Public Schools. As a first step in its investigation, the Panel sought to describe the magnitude of disproportion in EMR programs by race/ethnicity and gender, and the demographic conditions under which larger or smaller disproportions arise. The survey data collected biannually by the Office of Civil Rights were used for this purpose. In particular, the 1978 survey sampled 6,040 school districts containing 54,082 schools, or about one-third of the districts in the nation. Questionnaires were sent to all district offices and to each school requesting counts of the total number of students enrolled, the number of pupils enrolled in special education programs, and additional global characteristics of the student population. All student counts were classified by racial/ethnic identity and some by gender. Both sex and race classifications were required (but not sex-by-race crosscounts) for students in special education programs for educable mentally retarded, trainable mentally retarded, seriously emotionally disturbed, specific learning disability, and speech impaired children.

For purposes of correlating the degree of disproportion with other school - related characteristics, a "log-odds index" of disproportion was calculated for each special education category. The index is positive whenever the odds of minorities being assigned to a special program are higher than the odds for whites; it is zero if the odds for minorities and whites are equal and is negative if the odds of minorities being assigned to special education classes are lower than the odds for whites. The log-odds index is a linear contrast of the logarithms of the two "odds," has a distribution in the population of school districts that closely approximates the normal, and thus is particularly appropriate for analysis by normal-theory methods, e.g., Pearson correlations or analysis of variance. Unfortunately, it is not simple to interpret since it is unbounded, i.e., it can vary from - to +, depending upon the magnitude of the disproportion. However, for interpretive purposes the log-odds index can be transformed to a correlation-like measure, Yule's Q-statistic, which is limited to values between -1 and +1. For EMR programs, the correlation of race/ethnicity (minority vs. non-minority) with placement (EMR vs. none) is approximately + .42.

Despite the fact that a race/ethnicity EMR disproportion appears to be a national phenomenon--the average percentage of minority students in EMR classes exceeds the average percentage of whites in every state except four--massive regional variation in minority disproportionality is evident in the survey data. The average disproportion in southern states is consistently and notable high. In the south, the correlation (Q) between race/ethnicity and EMR placement associated with the median disproportion is .63. Although substantially lower than in the south, relatively high minority disproportion also pervades the data for the border states; the correlation corresponding to the median disproportion value is .32. On the other hand, minority disproportion does not appear as a general problem in the northeast or the midwest where the corresponding correlation in each region is .03. Minority disproportion in the west is also relatively low; the correlation between race/ethnicity and EMR placement is .17.

The panel found the average level of racial disproportion in EMR programs is smallest for districts with 1,000 to 3,000 students. It is somewhat higher for districts with fewer than 1,000 students, higher for districts in the 3,000 to 10,000-student range, and is highest for districts with over 30,000 students.

Each minority group identified in the survey (American Indian or Alaskan Native; Asian or Pacific Islander; Hispanic; or Black) is characterized by some idiosyncratic discrepancies from the total minority group results. For example, students of Asian/Pacific Island origins are typically assigned to special education programs at rates that are considerably below those for whites. However, in small districts in several western states positive disproportions are found that might reflect relatively high incidence of recent immigrations. Verification of this hypothesis was not possible within the survey data. Although there was a tendency for American Indiana/Alaskan Native students to be assigned more frequently than white students to EMR programs, the panel concluded that the OCR survey may not provide an adequate data base for evaluating the extent of disproportion since relatively large number of American Indians are enrolled in schools or programs outside of those sampled by OCR.

Despite the fact that the nationwide summary statistics indicate that the proportion of Hispanic pupils enrolled in EMR classes is slightly below those for whites, the reverse situation obtains in 26 or 31 states reporting ten percent or more total minority enrollment. Unlike disproportion for all minorities combined, or for blacks in particular, the small Hispanic-white difference for the nation as a whole is an average of many sizeable positive and negative disproportions. Correlates of this phenomenon, include the districts' racial composition and the availability of bilingual education.

Unlike disproportion by race/ethnicity, the panel found that overrepresentation of males in EMR programs is relatively uniform across geographic regions.

Potential Causes of Disproportion in EMR Programs. While the

magnitude of the minority/white and male/female disproportion in EMR
lacement rates and the systematic variation in EMR disproportionality
as a function of geographic region and demographic characteristics
were clearly documented, the panel expressed the view that factors
that account for this disproportion are less easily analyzed. The
multiplicity of potential causes/explanations of disproportionate
placement rates were categorized under six main rubrics.

Legal And Administrative Requirements. Federal, state and local
legal and administrative requirements establish a network of
incentives and constraints within which special education programs
operate. Definitions of particular diagnostic categories, policies
adopted that establish a particular referral and evaluation system,
and policies concerning the funding of special education programs
affect which children are referred for special education, how they
are evaluated and placed, and the types of services that are
available in special education programs. Some of these factors may
contribute to disproportionate placement of minorities in EMR
programs. For example, funding schemes that directly tie the number
of dollars made available to a special education program to the
number of children in that program may encourage overcounting, and
minority children may be particularly vulnerable to inclusion in
expanded special education programs.

Characteristics of the Students. A variety of causes for
disproportionate placement have been proposed that focus directly on
characteristics of the student. Students may experience difficulty
in school because of undiagnosed or untreated medical and physical
problems, because of difficulties in cognitive information-
processing, comprehension, reasoning or judgment; because of
emotional or behavior disorders or motivational disturbances such as
anxiety that disrupt or block effective leaning; because of the
absence of adaptive skills and behaviors that are needed to survive
in school, and because of limited learning potential. Learning
deficiencies that emerge in the early grades, unless corrected, may
persist in later years and become barriers to future achievement.

Characteristics of the Instruction Received. An almost uniform
feature of the selection process for EMR placement is that it begins
with an observation of weak academic performance. Poor performance
may be accompanied by other behaviors such as disruptive classroom
behavior, but referral for EMR placement seldom occurs in the absence
of weak academic performance. To the extent that a greater
proportion of minority children are below accepted norms on
achievement measures used in particular schools, they will be
overrepresented in the pool of "potential" special education
children.

While academic failure is often attributed to characteristics of the learners, current achievement also reflects the child's opportunity to learn in school. If such opportunities have been lacking, or if the quality of instruction offered varies across subgroups of the school-age population, then school failure and subsequent EMR referral and placement may represent a lack of exposure to quality instruction for minority children.

Possible Biases in the Assessment Process. Measures employed in classification procedures for EMR placement may not yield valid assessments of the cognitive skills for particular minority or disadvantaged groups. Much of the controversy has centered on the IQ test, a primary instrument in the determination of eligibility for placement in EMR programs. Critics charge that IQ tests underestimate the skills and potential of minority children--that the items do not tap the same underlying construct for minority groups as for white middle-class children, that particular items are insensitive to minority cultures, that differences exist in the predictive validity of the test for different groups. Futhermore, the test-taking situation may artificially depress the scores of minority children compared to those of whites. This position emphasizes the fundamental mismatch between the language and culture reflected in IQ tests and those of various minority groups. This mismatch could produce inferior functioning on IQ tests by minorities, which in turn has profound implications for later educational experiences, including an increased likelihood of EMR placement.

Characteristics of Home and Family Environments. Hypothesized relationships between parents' socioeconomic status and children's school performance have led to the investigation of variations in home environments and child-rearing styles as possible causes of low achievement among minority and disadvantaged children. For example, many of the intervention efforts of the 1960's aimed at improving the achievement of minority children were premised on the belief that minority parents did not inculcate in their children the necessary motivation, skills and competencies for later success in school. Proposed differences in home environments include the extent to which motivational support is provided for cognitive achievement, and the extent to which parents and others encourage verbal development and provide appropriate verbal models. Families may also differ dramatically in the degree to which children are encouraged or required to practice the use of complex systems of verbal symbols. Some speculate that the lack of such practice may be related both to the underdevelopment of cognitive skills and to an increased likelihood of EMR placement.

Characteristics of the Broader Historical and Cultural Contexts. As noted above, many of the proposed causes of disproportionate EMR placement are attributed to the student directly and so it is not surprising that to date, studies of mental retardation have generally emphasized individual factors. The problem of disproportion can also be viewed in a broader sociocultural context--not just the sociocultural influences on individual students of their familial and street cultures but a pervasive collective influence of minority status within a dominant majority culture. On one hand, discontinuities arise from the child's experiences as mediated by the family and home environment, especially when children from various subgroups are confronted with the curriculum and value structures of the public schools, which are primarily based on the culture and traditions of the Anglo-American mainstream. On another level, however, discontinuities also arise from the collective historical confrontation and conflict between minority cultures and the dominant culture. The long-term denial of equal opportunity, status, and rewards for minorities has led to the development of coping mechanisms and survival strategies in response to this collective experience. At each level, possible societal causes of educability problems for minority children may be identified that in turn contribute to disproportionate EMR placement rates. An example of this perspective particularly as it pertains to experiences and perceptions of the connection between education and occupational success and to differences between immigrant and indigenous minority groups appears in Ogbu (1978, 1981).

DISPROPORTION: PROBLEMATIC OR SYMPTOMATIC?

The Panel agreed that disproportion undoubtedly reflects all of these causes--singly and in combination--in some school districts, some of the time. However, it became apparent that even if the multiplex causes of EMR disproportion could be identified and disentangled, it is unlikely that remedies could be easily or effectively implemented.

Rather than inquiring about the causes of disproportion and how to remedy the problem of disproportion in special education and in EMR classes in particular, the Panel believed that a different and more constructive perspective is obtained by asking, "Under what circumstances does disproportion constitute a problem?" While remedies to disproportion per se are based on an assumption that the inequalities in themselves constitute an inequity, the educational and social conditions under which that assumption is true need to be examined explicitly. Three aspects of the regular and special education programs and placements procedures are most salient in this regard: Disproportion is a problem (1) if children are invalidly placed in programs for mentally retarded students, (2) if they are unduly exposed to the likelihood of such placement by virtue of having received poor quality regular instruction, or (3) if the quality and academic relevance of the special instruction programs block educational progress, including a decrease in the likelihood of students' return to the regular classroom.

<u>Disproportion is a problem if children are invalidly placed in</u>
<u>programs for the mentally retarded</u>. If children are systematically
misdiagnosed or assigned to EMR classes when other settings would be
more beneficial, then the assessment system for special education is
of questionable validity, either for students in general or for
particular subgroups that are over-identified. On the other hand, if
the assessment system results in disproportion for particular
subgroups, the assessments may still be successfully defended if
their educational utility and relevance can be demonstrated. Failing
that, the procedures should be changed to improve their validity and
to lead more directly to appropriate and demonstrable effective
educational practices. From this perspective, the Panel's primary
concern is with the validity of the assessment system and its
implications for educational practice rather than on the resulting
adverse disproportionality as such.

Federal regulations require that mental retardation be defined as
"significantly subaverage general intellectual functioning existing
concurrently with deficits in adaptive behavior and manifested during
the developmental period which adversely affects a child's
educational performance." These guidelines are often implemented by
testing a child's IQ and sometimes applying "adaptive behavior
scales" as well, as part of an extensive evaluation that may lead to
EMR classification. The assessment procedure affords numerous
opportunities for errors of misclassification to occur.

First, educable mental retardation is operational in different ways
at different times in different localities. Since the meaning of the
placement category is both variable and vague, it is not surprising
that slippage occurs in implementation. The category of educable
mental retardation is at least in part a function of the social and
educational demands on an individual as well as a characteristic of
the person. This allows a wide variety of measurement practices to
be employed in the schools. School districts are relatively free to
choose the tests to be used in assessing children for special
placement. For example, adaptive behavior ratings--sometimes
focusing on achievement-related behaviors and other times not--play a
variety of different roles in special education assessment (Mercer,
1973). In addition, IQ cutoffs scores vary from district to
district, and different cutoff scores may result in different
proportions of students being classified as EMR; a regular student in
one district may be classified as mentally retarded in another. At
the same time, the resulting category of EMR children is far from
homogeneous. A variety of different functional needs are subsumed
under this single diagnostic label.

Moreover, the measures used to classify students as mentally retarded
may not yield valid assessments of cognitive functioning or of

adaptive behavior for particular groups of children, and hence may
not be valid for the placements that result. Individually
administered IQ tests are a major instrument used in the ultimate
classification of referred students. The ability of IQ tests to
predict a variety of school achievements makes such tests appealing,
and their high reliability gives the user confidence in the results.
However, if the response styles or levels of motivation and effort of
minority students are different from those of white students, then
their final score may not reflect the same mental processes as for
white students. Of course, IQ tests administered entirely in English
to students for whom English is not their native language are clearly
inappropriate measures of intelligence. Because of these and a host
of other disruptive factors, there is no direct way to infer
incompetence from incorrectly answered test items. Thus failure to
perform correctly on IQ tests does not necessarily imply inability to
perform specific school-related tasks. In addition, IQ tests do not
provide the kinds of information needed to design an individualized
curriculum for a child in academic difficulty. In particular, IQ
tests do not identify the content and skill areas in which the child
needs further assistance, nor do they lead to the choice of a
specific mode and pace of instruction likely to be most effective.
Assessments that stress a child's functional educational need would
be more appropriate.

Futhermore, despite federal law and regulations, imprecision and
looseness in the referral, assessment, and placement systems may
allow personal bias to affect placement decisions. After all,
referral is a discretionary matter resting largely in the hands of
the classroom teacher. If the teacher is distracted by the higher
activity level of boys or feels uncomfortable in the presence of
minority students, then those groups may be more likely to be
referred for possible special placement. Similarly, the choice of
assessment instruments and their interpretation leaves much to the
discretion of the school psychologist. In some districts, the lack
of firm statewide or districtwide criteria for EMR placement, or the
use of very lenient criteria that leave decisions to local discretion
permits a wide range of extraneous factors to affect placement
decisions.

Disproportion is a problem if children are unduly exposed to the
likelihood of EMR placement by being in schools or classes with poor
quality regular instruction. Students are referred for special
education assessment primarily after they have experienced academic
failure. However, children whose regular classroom instruction is
poor may experience failure at a higher rate than they would if the
quality of instruction were better. Since assessment instruments
typically measure the outcomes of learning rather than learning
processes, there is a danger that the child who has not learned from
poor instruction will be judged unable to learn from any instruction.

The panel asked these question: Would fewer minority students be classified as mentally retarded if they were exposed to the highest quality instructional practices? Can learning potential be validly inferred when the quality of instruction is poor or when opportunities to learn are limited?

<u>Disproportion is a problem if the quality and academic relevance of instruction in special classes block educational progress, including a decrease in the likelihood of returning to the regular classroom</u>. There has been longstanding debate over the advantages and disadvantages of separate classes for children diagnosed as EMR. Proponents point to the advantages of smaller classes and more individualized instruction for EMR students. Critics argue that expectations for children classified as EMR are low and charge that the EMR curriculum--based on the assumption that educable mental retardation is a permanent and unremediable disability--is not designed to help students learn the skills necessary to return to the regular instructional setting. Indeed, early concepts of mental retardation were explicit on this issue; Doll (1941) included both "constitutional origin" and "essentially incurable" among the necessary components of the definition of mental deficiency. However, by the early 1960's the belief that intelligence is predetermined and fixed by genetic endowment was replaced by the understanding that intelligence is not fixed at birth, that it can be modified through environmental manipulation, and that it partially reflects learned skills and behaviors (Hunt, 1961; Kirk; 1958). Thus, a reasonable goal for programs for EMR students, especially those serving children in the elementary school grades, may be to prepare students to reenter the regular instructional program.

The question as to what constitutes quality instruction for students in special programs is complex, both because there are a variety of outcomes to consider (including the positive and negative effects on the special group, the positive and negative effects on the regular students, and the consequences for the regular classroom teacher) and also because EMR programs frequently serve children with a wide mix of functional needs (including diverse combinations of cognitive disabilities and adaptive behavior problems). Research on the efficacy of EMR classes has generally focused on the effects of particular settings--mainstreamed regular classes or separate special education classes--rather than on characteristics of effective instruction. Given that children in EMR programs have functional educational needs that are pressing and real, improved educational practices will depend on the appropriate match between instruction and each child's individual needs.

A significant question also arises as to the mechanism by which special instruction may best be provided. In particular, to what extent must children be classified and labelled according to a

generic class of deficiencies in order to receive special education
services? Diagnostic categories such as educable mentally retarded
seem to be more an administrative convenience than an educational
necessity, allowing schools to count the number of children in this
and other special programs in accord with federal agency
requirements. Though such labels are presumed to initiate a process
of individual diagnosis and planning, there are doubts that this
individualization challenges the students or provides for their
unique functional needs. If categorical labels are required for
administrative purposes, they could be chosen to reflect the services
provided rather than the deficiencies of the child, thereby helping
to reduce the negative impact of stigmatizing diagnostic labels.

IMMIGRANT GROUPS AND SPECIAL EDUCATION

The United States is witnessing an increasingly large number of
immigrant children who enroll in the public schools each year. These
children come from many countries and therefore bring with them many
language backgrounds. For example, in the 1984-85 school year,
students from some 81 countries enrolled in the San Francisco public
schools. Children whose home language is other than English were
found to constitute 47.5% of the school population (30,042 out of
63,215). The growth of non and limited -English proficient students
in San Francisco has been phenomenal--single year enrollments have
increased from 7,844 in 1979-80 to 18,669 in 1984-85.

In the state of California as a whole there were 487,835 limited
proficient enrollments. The largest groups were Spanish, Vietnamese,
Cantonese, Korean and Philipino.

In the Dallas (Texas) Unified School district 55 language groups are
represented. Altogether in 1984-85, 16,416 students were identified
as limited English proficient in the Dallas schools.

Some immigrant students will be handicapped and hence will be
candidates for special education services. Unfortunately, data on
the numbers of immigrant children in special education programs seem
to be unavailable. No such data are available for Dallas, for San
Francisco, or for the State of California as a whole. We did learn
that students in New York City education programs come from
more than 50 countries, but the numbers identified as mentally
retarded, learning disabled, blind, emotionally disturbed or deaf by
country of origin, for example, are unknown.

Whatever their classification, the impact of language must be
separated from other possible factors that influence assessment and
diagnosis. Also, appropriate curriculum materials should be
available. In the areas of language disorders, for example, a tough
diagnostic problem is to differentiate difficulty in learning a

228

second language from a language disorder. In the area of
intellectual assessment the appropriateness of tests of intelligence
for groups on which the test were not standardized is at issue. For
students from many countries, questions about emotional disturbance
require that cultural patterns and practices unique to the students
country of origin be taken into account.

In the sections following we briefly address several programs and
issues related to the assessment and placement of immigrant children
in special education programs.

Assessment. Assessing immigrant children for possible handicapping
conditions poses problems which are of major concern to educators.
In many cases the assessment tools used are inappropriate for these
children, especially in instances in which the child's primary
language is not English.

School systems around the United States have been implementing
various techniques for identifying, assessing, placing and evaluating
their immigrant children with special needs. The Brockton Public
School System in Massachusetts, for example, has developed the
Brockton Battery, a collection of four independent instruments
designed to assess special education minority students (Sennett,
1981). The battery consists of the Boehm Test of Basic Concepts and
the Beery Test of Visual Motor Integration which are used in
understanding whether or not the child understands the primary
concepts of test taking; tests of language abilities; tests of
language development; tests of reading abilities, tests of learning
rate and method, and the adaptive behavior scales.

In California, some of the factors included during the identification
process are the students language of instruction based on assessment
of reading, writing, speaking, and comprehension; the level of
difficulty of the materials; and the use of a support system to allow
the student to move from the special education program into the
bilingual and other regular programs.

A program in California designed to assess bilingual children for
giftedness uses a multiple assessment procedure which includes
questionnaires, parent conferences, teacher evaluations, and peer
information. The program stressed both the need to observe the
"problem child" for giftedness and the importance of testing
bilingual students in their primary language.

A group of Minnesota scholars has developed a procedure for testing
which involves the development of local norms for subsets of
immigrant children. The norms are based on short tests of reading,
arithmetic, spelling, etc. The students tested have similar language
and experiential backgrounds--i.e., exposure to English, length of

time in the United States, etc. The information acquired from administration of the tests to these specified subsets of immigrants provides baseline data for identifying deviance in achievement and in monitoring the student's progress.

The Los Angeles school system has developed an innovative program for assessing potentially gifted immigrant and minority children based on extensive observations and teacher ratings and exposure to a special class setting in which the child is taught and observed by an experienced teacher of the gifted. In consultation with other specialists the teacher makes a determination of whether the child should receive placement in a regular classroom for gifted youngsters. The Los Angeles procedures and others such as behavioral assessment, Piagetian assessment and learning potential assessment, among others, have been recently described in a volume by Jones (1985) which has as its purpose the identification of innovative procedures for assessing immigrant and minority group children for possible special education placement.

Programs. Various school districts and government agencies have funded and piloted programs to address the needs of the bilingual exceptional child.

In New York City, a variety of programs have been developed for Hispanics and Haitians. The Bilingual program for the physically handicapped (Sanua, 1975) was designed with an emphasis on improving students self-understanding and self-image through demonstrating the worth and value of the students' native language. The program has four components: instructional, curricular and materials development, teacher training and parental involvement

A second program designed in New York City for the bilingual exceptional child was Project Kanpe (Keane, 1983). Project Kanpe was designed as a bilingual program to help older talented Haitian students acquire English language proficiency while developing their academic skills. However, the project was not able to serve its targeted group because the students were in need of basic skills and remediation.

The Bilingual Program for Children in Bilingual Classes for Retarded Mental Development (BCRMD) (Sirota, 1976) was designed to provide equal education for non-English speaking students through activities that maximize native language proficiency while developing competence in English. The program also seeks to train bilingual teachers and develop bilingual-bicultural curriculum.

Project Trabajo and the Individualized Bilingual Education for Children with Retarded Mental Development (NYC Board of Education, 1981) are two New York based programs designed to provide supplementary and instructional support for 150 mildly and moderately mentally retarded Limited English Proficient (LEP) students. Both programs work jointly and cooperatively while encouraging staff development, curriculum and materials development, and parental involvement. Project Trabajo is designed to serve intermediate junior and senior high school students.

A sixth program, the Bronx Multidiscipline Special Education Bilingual Program (NYC Board of Education, 1982) is designed to supplement the basic education programs for handicapped LEP students in the Bronx vicinity. In 1980-81 the program provided 132 Hispanic handicapped students direct individualized instruction, resource assistance, staff development and parent training through greater involvement.

Outside of New York State a number of programs have been designed to facilitate the needs of bilingual exceptional children. For example, in New Mexico, the Responsive Environmental Program for Spanish American Children (REPSAC) was established. This program serves as an intervention program for 3-5 year old high risk Spanish American Children.

Another program, the Ability Development Project (Askins, 1975) was designed to both identify 4 year old Mexican American children with learning disabilities and to develop appropriate curriculum materials for the. Some of the results of the project include development of Spanish/English language preference screening, observational checklists for referral, criterion referenced tests, supplementary activities, and a manual on working with parents with handicapped children.

Encendiendo Una Llama, Harford Connecticut's Bilingual Program for the Gifted and Talented, serves 173 LEP students grades 3-6 (Roby, 1982). The program's goals are to develop English and Spanish language skills, high level thinking skills, and creativity.

Issues. Identifying, assessing and placing immigrant and minority children is a problem of growing concern in the United States. The issues surrounding these problems are multiple. They include inadequate systems for identification and placement, lack of adequate assessment instruments, lack of training in identification and referral, confusing definitions and criteria, teacher insensitivity to the needs of the children, educators' biased perceptions of the culturally diverse, children's perceptions of the education system, and an inadequacy or nonexistence of programs to meet the needs of the students.

There exists a general understanding that bilingual/multicultural children are overrepresented in special education classes in comparison to their percentage of the total population. Not only are immigrant and minority groups overrepresented with regard to special education placement but they also are underrepresented with regard to special education services. A national survey revealed that only 31 to 32 percent of the districts receiving special government funds had or were planning special education programs which were to be operational in two years, and those programs served only 17 of the approximately 80 language groups served by regular bilingual programs.

As the issues that surround the problems are multiple, the solutions to these problems are multiple as well; many alternatives have been developed and piloted. They include making a variety of options of service available, giving priority to children with less severe handicaps, increasing the number of training facilities for bilingual special educators, adapting the materials to meet the needs of the students, developing more appropriate assessment tools, and increasing parent involvement.

Finally, we note that the problems in the United States are not dissimilar from those in Canada and probably many other countries. Samuda (1982) studied the intake and review process for new students (placement, testing, counseling and special programs) by interviewing 245 schools and 34 school boards in Ontario, Canada. His findings indicated problems in assessment, inadequate counseling, and a need for systematic planning. Among his 14 recommendations were the need for immediate initiation of a planning structure, inclusion of an acceptable multicultural education program in provincial teacher training establishments, and counselor inservice in multicultural education.

REFERENCES

Askins, B.E. (1975). Responsive environment program for Spanish American children (REPSAC): Fourth year evaluation study. Final evaluation report, 1974-75. Unpublished study, Clovis, New Mexico Public Schools. 57pp.

Committee on Child Development Research and Public Policy. (1981). Final report of the panel on selection and placement in programs for the mentally retarded. Washington: Assembly of Behavioral and Social Sciences, National Research Council, National Academy of Sciences.

Doll, E.A. (1941). The essentials of an inclusive concept of mental deficiency. American Journal of Mental Deficiency, 46, 214-219.

Hunt, J. McV. (1961). Intelligence and Experience. New York: The Ronald Press Co.

Jones, R.L. (Editor). (1985). Non-discriminatory (high validity) assessment of minority group children: A Casebook. Unpublished manuscript.

Keane, D.N. (1983). Project Kanpe, 1981-82. O.E.E. evaluation report. Unpublished study, NYC Board of Education. 43pp.

Kirk, S.A. (1958). Early Education of the Mentally Retarded. Urbana: University of Illinois Press.

Mercer, J. (1973)., Labeling the Mentally Retarded: Clinical and Social System Perspectives on Mental Retardation. Berkeley: University of California Press.

NYC Board of Education, Brooklyn N.Y. Office of Educational Evaluation. (1981). Project TRABAJO and individualized bilingual education for children with retarded mental development ESEA Title VII and chapter 720 annual evaluation report, 1980-81. NYC Board of Education. 45pp.

Ogbu, J.U. (1978). Minority Education and Caste: The American System in Cross-Cultural Perspective. New York: Academic Press.

Ogbu, J.U. (1981). Schooling in the Ghetto: An Ecological Perspective on Community and Home Influences. Paper prepared for NIE Conference on Follow Through, Philadelphia.

Roby, W. (1982). 1981-82 project evaluation for Encendiendo Una Llama: A program for bilingual gifted and talented students. Hartford (CT) Public Schools. 28p.

Samuda, R.J. (1982). Placing immigrant students in the Ontario school system. B.C. Journal of Special Education, 249-262.

Sanua, V.D. (1975). Bilingual program for physically handicapped children: School year, 1974-75. Unpublished paper, NYC Board of Education. 33pp.

Sennett, K.H. (1981). Special needs assessments for linguistic minority students in the Brocton (Mass) Public School System. Paper presented at the Council for Exceptional Children Conference on the Exceptional Bilingual Child, New Orleans.

Sirota, N. (1976). Bilingual program for children in CRMD classes, school year, 1975-76. Unpublished paper, NYC Board of Education. 33pp.

PSYCHOMETRIC ABUSE IN ASSESSING MINORITY STUDENTS: A CANADIAN PERSPECTIVE

Ronald J. Samuda
Queen's University
Kingston, Canada

Psychometric abuse in assessing minority students occurs as a consequence of the selection, use, and administration of standardized tests. The most poignant aspect is in the interpretation of test scores to justify the labelling and consequent streaming of ethnic minority students into minimally stimulating curriculum programs. But, more importantly, this chapter focuses on the fallacies in the theory and practice of the testing of aptitudes, mental ability, and learning potential of students who are culturally or socioeconomically different from the dominant Angloceltic society. In other words, this chapter examines some of the ways in which psychometry can be counterproductive in a multicultural milieu by promulgating institutional and structural racism in the schools and, thus, retarding social justice in the society at large.

THE SIGNIFICANCE OF PSYCHOMETRY

There are those who would define the psychometric enterprise in technical terms. However, when regarded in the broader context, psychological testing becomes much more than merely an technical issue. It is, in fact, a fundamental part of the social, political and economic fabric of our society. For, standardized assessment has been the very cornerstone of our immigration policy and a vital factor in the determination of the ethnic and cultural composition of North America. It has seriously influenced the curricular organization of schools. In fact, the tenets of the genetic interpretations based on test results have been explicitly taught in what used to be called the "normal schools" and teachers' colleges of Canadian systems of education.

Despite the more recent anti-testing revolt and the numerous articles, books, lawsuits and policy statements condemning the indiscriminate and unfair consequences of psychometry, especially when used to label and place ethnic minority immigrants in the schools, there is still a serious lag in the implementation of new policies. Meanwhile, research into conditions in the schools of Ontario has demonstrated that many teachers still cling to concepts and attitudes that are counterproductive in the promulgation of effective teaching methods and in the enhancement of the ideals of multiculturalism.

To examine the significance and truth of the above statements, let us look at the etiology of the testing movement and the effects on immigration policy, school organization, and the education of minorities. Reviews of the pioneering endeavors of such luminaries as Galton, Goddard, Terman, and Cattell leave no doubt that standardized test results were interpretated as reflecting inherent genetic endowment. Such distinguished leaders as Yerkes and Brigham used the results of the Army Alpha and Army Beta to persuade the U.S. government that certain non-European immigrant groups should be restricted in order to "protect the U.S. genetic pool from an insidious decline" (Cummins, 1984, p.66). While it is true that recent court rulings in the United States and the establishment of policy decisions resulting from them have largely curtailed the indiscriminate abuses of tests, there still remains a reactionary residue of resistance in the attitudes of some practising teachers.

The concepts underlying the interpretation of test scores originated in Great Britain and the United States; yet, they were imported directly (often without any allowance for local or regional differences) for use in Canadian Schools. Canadian teachers read the same books as their British and American colleagues and are influenced by the same perspectives. Psychometry is, in fact, largely a product of middle-class Euro-American culture and the tests themselves reflect the Euro-American experience and are normed extensively on middle-class Euro-American children.

Despite the drive for Canadian distinctiveness, the paraphernalia of standardized tests, and the homogenous grouping that follows from the interpretation of their results, were imported lock, stock and barrel from the United States. Indeed, the same discriminatory consequences in immigration practices were similarly applied in Canada to encourage the entry of British and North-Western European stock while systematically excluding non-Europeans and those people from Southern and Eastern Europe.

The massive influx of immigrants into Canada in the late fifties and early sixties resulted from a change in immigration policies and the lifting of discriminatory restrictions in 1962. That event signalled a landmark in Canadian history that would have very telling industrial, economic, social and political consequences. It represented a change of unparalleled dimensions that determined the shape and character of things to come in Canadian society and especially in the demographic composition of schools of major urban centres like Vancouver, Edmonton, Calgary, Toronto, Montreal and Halifax.

To illustrate the trends, we might do well to examine some of the statistical sources. From a mere handful of privileged South Asians and West Indians arriving in Canada in the two decades following the Second World War, the numbers rose to almost 100,000 by 1977 from Jamaica and Trinidad alone (55,167 and 36,968). Similarly, nonwhite immigrants from Asia and Africa arrived in unprecedented numbers of 271,598 and 54,485 respectively (Samuda and Crawford, 1980).

For a decade and a half, multiculturalism has been in effect as a federal Canadian policy and has been accepted by the governments of most of the provinces. It aims at preserving human rights, developing a distinctive Canadian identity based on the principle of cultural diversity, the reinforcement of Canadian unity and, most important, the greater participation of all Canadian citizens as free and equal partners in a society that promotes unity in diversity.

CHANGES IN SCHOOL POLICY

What are the educational implications of the federal policy of multiculturalism? How have the provincial systems of education responded to the goals of multiculturalism and the reality of a changing school population? How have local education authorities altered their policies to ensure the concomitant changes in practice at the level of the school and in the basic unit of the classroom? And, most important of all, what provisions have been made to change the training of teachers in the faculties of education and to address the outmoded attitudes or practising teachers through adequate and sustained in-service professional development?

Those are some of the questions we attempted to address in a study conducted in Ontario school boards throughout 1978 and 1979. That study was reported in 1980 and documented the responses by teachers, administrators, and counsellors in the testing, assessment, placement and counselling of ethnic minorities (Samuda and Crawford, 1980).

What we found gives all of us as educators cause to be concerned. For, there exists a wide disparity between policy and the implementation of effective practice. That is not to play down or deny the major changes that have taken place over the past ten years especially. Within the U.S. context, court cases have inspired the landmark legislation which guarantees to all handicapped children the right to a full public education, to an individualized education program, to due process and to the least segregated environment. But more importantly, it proscribes the use of culturally discriminatory assessment and advocates a system of relevant and multi-dimensional assessment (Figueroa, 1980:p.150). Such legislative acts have

drastically altered the process and shape of psychometry in the
United States and especially in the effects on ethnic minorities.
Questions have been raised about the appropriateness of the WISC-R IQ
test for minority students of Black, Mexican and Puerto Rican
backgrounds.

In the Canadian context, there have been serious attempts to respond
to the cultural and linguistic diversity in the schools of
Metropolitan Toronto where more than 50 percent come from homes where
a language other then English is the norm. In Vancouver, the
comparable figure is 40 percent (Young, 1982). As early as 1970, the
Dante society (an Italian-Canadian cultural organization) confronted
the educational establishment about the disproportionate numbers of
immigrant students in vocational rather than academic programs. They
criticized the school for the use of culturally and linguistically
biased assessment procedures.

The effect on many school boards was the formulation of the policy of
delaying educational testing until the immigrant child had two years
of acculturation in Canada. And further legislation at the
provincial level was probably influenced by the U.S. legislation and
the lobbying by many community and parental groups leading to the
passage legislation in Ontario in December 1980. This piece of
legislation mandates that school boards will identify all exceptional
students (e.g. learning disabled, gifted) and devise and establish
programs suited to their needs and abilities. Moreover, decisions
for individual students must be based not only on initial screening
tests but also on a more detailed assessment by a psycho-educational
consultant to advise the Identification, Placement and Review
Committee.

These are laudatory developments in the recognition of the cultural
diversity of students in our schools and the need to change the
system to meet student needs. But these legislative measures cannot
succeed without a concomitant program of training and retraining for
teachers. As the responses to our Ontario research indicate,
teachers are beset by the difficulties of assessing ethnic minority
students, particularly in the age groups between 11-15 years of age.
The expressed concerns include: What is the best way to determine
the students' level of functioning? Should we pay more attention to
their social development or their academic development? How do we
distinguish a language problem from a learning problem? How do we
know that a particular assessment is accurate?

For those respondents who work with minority students in areas of
high ethnic and cultural concentration, assessment difficulties are
compounded by the fact that the immigrant student often does not
possess documents that contain meaningful information about his
previous school experience. Confronted with a large number of

students from a wide range of ethnic backgrounds, it is not easy to bridge the gap between the expectation of Canadian schools and the experience of immigrant students. Thus, the disjuncture between what the school expects and what the immigrant student presents is often referred to by teachers and counsellors as a problem in assessment. In an attempt to find solutions to this problem, it may be helpful to break down this disjuncture into the following areas of difficulty: diagnostic assessment; the students' background information; the students' home language as it relates to the language used in the school; and the students' learning style and adjustment in school

In terms of the first area, diagnostic assessment, significant differences between the student and the population on which the norms for the test were based render such tests invalid for measuring his or her academic level and potential (Samuda, 1975). This situation necessitates finding alternative methods for assessing the ability of students from ethnic minority backgrounds. When neither adequate research facilities nor resource people familiar with the problems of cross-cultural testing are available within a school board, assessment and placement is likely to become a contentious issue between immigrant communities and local schools. The situation is further complicated when students have incomplete academic records or none at all since it leaves the school administration without a tool upon which it can place great reliance. The training of the teachers also often leave them ill-equipped to operate effectively in a cross-cultural context, even where language is not a barrier. Thus, few can, without considerable difficulty, draw from their students the pertinent information upon which an accurate assessment can be based. This, then, constitutes the second area of concern.

The third problem area of language is perhaps the most significant since it critically affects various aspects of the assessment process. It presents, for example, an obvious constraint on the use of standardized tests with students whose first language is not English. It also presents a serious barrier to communication between student and teacher.

Problems related to the fourth area, learning style and personal adjustment, are very much rooted in the student's home culture and the quality of his initial interaction with peers and adults in the society at large. As Berry (1976) amply demonstrates, culture can have an enormous impact upon an individual's cognitive style. Thus, qualitative differences between a student's learning style and the mode of instruction in the school can heighten his or her feelings of disorientation and consequently impair academic performance. Learning styles which may have been appropriate in a home culture may prove to be inapplicable in a new school environment (Das, 1973).

When one considers the scope of the changes which the student faces in the community outside the classroom, the range of subtle behavioural contaminants which increase the difficulty of making a fair assessment becomes clear. Danzinger (1971) observed, for example, that among the Italian immigrant students he studied, there was a significant correlation between low motivation to achieve academically and low levels of self-esteem. Others have found similar connections between adjustment problems experienced by West Indian students and the problems they experienced with their work in school.

Certain general impressions gained from these studies merit some elaboration at this point. First, it is apparent that few boards have well-articulated policies with respect to the reception, assessment and placement of ethnic minority students. Those few are confined to jurisdictions in Metropolitan Toronto. (It should be noted that the data for the study was drawn from board documents as well as interviews.) Second, there appears to be little recognition of special educational needs among minority group students, except for English as a Second Language (ESL) programs. Third, ESL programs are often lumped together with other special education programs with which they are not compatible, such as services for the learning-handicapped. This might mean that the differences of culture exhibited by immigrant students are perceived by administrators as learning handicaps. Fourth, the level of ethnic concentration appears to be the most critical factor bringing about change in individual school systems.

Yet another significant finding is the little importance and attention given to counselling. The fact is that the guidance enterprise seems obscured as school officials reported on their procedures of receiving and placing new immigrant students. An analysis of the contents of 128 interviews on the matter revealed that only one of the total made a specific reference to the involvement of guidance and counselling. There seems to be no procedural protocol for guidance teachers and counsellors to participate directly in student assessment and placement. Only in some Metropolitan Toronto schools with heavy ethnic concentrations was the involvement of guidance personnel required in the assessment and placement processes. However, there were sometimes marked discrepancies between the responses given by board officials and those of school principals, indicating a gap between board policy and school practice. This phenomenon seemed more evident in large city school systems. It would seem that the entire guidance enterprise would have to exert itself more diligently if it is to help ethnic minority students to adapt to Canadian schools.

If the problems of assessment and placement outlined earlier in this chapter are to be satisfactorily resolved, schools must move from a mere reactive stance to multiculturalism to one of positive commitment. Before this can occur, teachers and administrators must receive the kind of preparation that will enable them to become effective agents for change. In the first place, teachers and administrators need to have a clearer understanding of the basic intent of the multicultural policy and what it means in terms of educational policy and practice. While published policy statements and some curriculum guidelines are available, it seems that much more discussion and exploration of the concepts are needed than is currently taking place.

Current efforts towards in-service education need to be further developed and expanded. Fortunately, there is increasing recognition of the need for system sensitization. The nature of this sensitization has already been given serious thought by a number of educators (Mallea and Young, 1978). One must emphasize, however, that teacher involvement should be universal rather than selective. "To argue that teachers who have certain specializations, or who intend to teach in certain areas, will never interact with children from a variety of cultural backgrounds, is to miss the point; teachers need to prepare themselves and their students for life in a multiethnic, multiracial society" (Mallea and Young, 1978).

It was very clear, in the school-board survey, that many principals held the view that to recognize openly the ethnic mixture a school is tantamount to discrimination (Samuda and Crawford, 1980). Yet how can the school begin to attend to the special or differential needs of its students if the fact of cultural difference is not acknowledged? The paradox of a multicultural school population is that, in some situations, it is necessary to treat students differently in order to ensure the equality of education.

The real problem lies in the difficulty of matching instruction to the results of assessment, and without that link, the whole psychometric enterprise becomes futile. Reschly (1980) speculates that the problem in discussions of non-biased assessment stems from a focus on the wrong problems and questions. The major concern in non-biased assessment has been with the assessment of ethnic minorities. However, a more significant issue to address is whether we can ensure educational experiences that maximize competencies and opportunities for ethnic minority students. Bias in tests, or bias in assessment generally, should be evaluated according to outcomes for individuals:

> The concern for outcomes for individuals directs our efforts toward ensuring that assessment activities yield information useful for educational and psychological interventions and toward the effectiveness of these interventions (Reschly, 1980, p.1).

Assessment which leads to improvement in instructional practices should be undertaken whenever possible, but such a view should not be used to denigrate activities which have as their goal determining appropriate classification or educational placement. It is unlikely that any single test or assessment system will meet the needs of all of the educational problems of any given child. We can (and should) expect that a number of complementary assessment procedures will often be required to determine what is appropriate for any given child. But, more importantly, the thrust towards more adequate and innovative techniques and assessment procedures should incorporate the most recent work of Feuerstein, (1979) and Vygotsky (1978). Such methods and procedures are sorely needed in order to determine what educational programming is appropriate for the child -- especially for those who are different by virtue of culture or socioeconomic circumstances.

REFERENCES

Berry, J.W. (1976). Human ecology and cognitive style: Comparative studies in cultural and psychological adaptation. London: Sage.

Cummins, J. (1984). Bilingualism and special education: Issues in assessment and pedagogy. Clevedon, England: Multilingual Matters.

Das, J.P. (1973). Cultural deprivation and cognitive competence. In N. Ellis (Ed.), International review of research in mental retardation. New York: Academic Press.

Deosoran, R. (1976). The 1975 every student survey: program placement related to selected countries of birth and selected language. Toronto: Toronto Board of Education Research Department.

Deosoran, R., Wright, E. and Kane, T. (1976). The 1975 every student survey: Students' background and its relationship to program placement. Toronto Board of Education Research Department.

Jones R. (Ed.) (1985). Non-discriminatory (high validity) assessment of minority group children: A casebook. Berkeley: University of California Press.

Mallea, J. and Young, H. (1980). Teacher education for a multicultural society. Paper presented at a symposium on international education on community development. Toronto: Faculty of Education, University of Toronto.

Feuerstein, R. (1979). The dynamic assessment of retarded performers. Baltimore: University Park Press.

Oakland, T. (Ed.) (1977). Psychological and educational assessment of minority children. New York: Brunner/Mazel.

Pascual-Leone, J. (1987). Dynamic mental processes and the assessment of culturally-diverse children. Paper presented to the Ontario Ministry of Education Committee for Student Assessment, Programme Placement for Equal Education Opportunity. Toronto: York University.

Reschly, D. (1980). Unbiased assessment. Des Moines, Iowa: State of Iowa Department of Public Instruction.

Reynolds, C. & Brown, R. (1982). Perspectives on bias in mental testing. New York: Plenum.

Reynolds, C. Gutkin, T. (Eds.) (1982). The Handbook of School Psychology. New York: Wiley.

Samuda, R. (1975). Psychological testing of American minorities. New York: Harper and Row.

Samuda, R., Berry, J. and Laferrière, M. (Eds.) (1984). Multiculturalism in Canada: Social and educational implications. Toronto: Allyn and Bacon.

Samuda, R. and Crawford, D. (1980). Testing, assessment, counselling and placement of ethnic minority students: Current methods in Ontario. Toronto: Ministry of Education.

Samuda, R. and Kong, S. (Eds.) (1986). Multicultural education: Programmes and methods. Kingston/Toronto: ISSP.

Samuda, R., Kong, S. and Ijaz, A. (1988). Assessment and placement of minority students in Canadian schools. Kingston/Toronto: ISSP

Samuda, R. and Wolfgang, A. (Eds.) (1985). Intercultural counselling and assessment: Global dimensions. Toronto: Hogrefe.

Sattler, J.M. (1973). Intelligence testing of ethnic minority group and culturally disadvantaged children. In N. Mann and D. Sabatino (Eds.), The first review of special education, Volume 2. Philadelphia: The JST Press.

Vygotsky, L.S. (1978). Mind in society: The development of higher psychological processes. Cambridge, Mass.: Harvard University Press.

Ysseldyke, J. & Algozinne, B. (1982). Critical issues in special and remedial education. Boston: Houghton Mifflin.

INNOVATIONS IN THE ASSESSMENT OF MINORITIES: DYNAMIC APPROACHES

John Lewis
Brandon University
Brandon, Canada

Deliverers of psychological services have the difficult task of recon- ciling the unique and general elements that transect cultural lines. One area that has been neglected in this aspect is cross-cultural assessment. The literature is replete with criticisms of psycho- metric assessment in a cross-cultural setting (Sundberg & Gonzales, 1981). Bias in the content of instruments and the procedures of ex- aminers has been documented (Samuda, 1975, 1986). Inadequacies in the interpretation of psychological tests with the culturally different have been explored (Feuerstein & Hoffman, 1982, Jones, 1985). In spite of the flaws in the use of psychometric evaluation, Samuda (1975) called for an expansion and elaboration of testing rather than an abolition of assessment. The quality of the instruments and the degree of sensitivity and care in their use are of paramount concern. The area of particular concern is ability testing. This paper is concerned with the examination of new instruments and procedures for assessing minority children in the schools.

The main concern, at this point, is the assessment of minorities; how- ever the theoretical issue of a concept of intelligence needs brief treatment to facilitate the argument of innovative approaches to testing. Carroll (1983), Detterman & Sternberg (1982), and Sternberg (1977) state that tests are inadequate if they are based on single or multiple factors of intelligence. Furthermore, tests that utilize a "g" factor as the main concept for intelligence ignore between and within group differences and intra-individual differences. Studies using factor analysis in intelligence serve very little purpose in the diagnosis and prescription of educational problems. A corollary issue is the realization that test scores reflect a present level of functioning and as such are descriptive. They do not indicate the why or how of performance. What psychometric instruments suggest is the amount and type of learning that has previously occurred. Thirdly, the cognitive structure of an individual is fluid and dynamic. Tests of cognitive ability which are based on static measures of "g" do not account for the fluidity of intelligence; as such, there is a need to evaluate instruments of cognitive ability which concern themselves with the process of ability rather than the product; it is the accumulation of experiences and the nature of this acquisition which will affect product-type assessment.

The theory of intelligence addressing these concerns is Cattell's notion of fluid and crystallized intelligence. Fluid intelligence can be considered as a basic capacity to adopt to new situations (Cattell, 1971). It also represents the inherent capacity for learning and problem solving independent of either education or cultural experience. Fluid intelligence is trans-situational and thus can be generalized across subject areas. Crystallized intelligence is the direct result of the person's interactions between fluid ability and culture. This occurs through the interaction of the individual with a formal system of education. It, therefore, reflects the existing organization of conceptual knowledge. Crystallized ability illustrates the developed processes in the cognitive system as they are seen on the static measures of achievement and ability tests.

Fluid ability represents flexible adaption to novel situations and encompasses a plethora of inductive skills. The attractiveness of Cattell's construct appears, at least on the surface, to resolve the dilemma of achievement versus aptitude. Fluid ability suggests a more dynamic, active system still open to discovering hidden potential not captured on static measures. Cognitive ability can be increased or improved. Crystallized intelligence exemplifies what can be quantified as reflected by developed abilities. With these considerations in mind, the following criteria are necessary to redefine intelligence.

1. The mind is an active agent.
2. Intelligence is responsive to instruction.
3. Intelligence involves the anticipation of novelty situations.
4. Intelligence includes planning behavior.
5. Intelligence is flexible.
6. Intelligence addresses executive processing skills.

These characteristics represent the basic assumptions for assessment, for choosing instruments, and planning interventions.

Traditional cognitive testing could be referred to as "static" in that it does not assess the degree to which instruction will modify an individual's test performance. Static appraisal techniques have been criticized in the literature most notably by Haywood, Filler, Shipman and Chatelanat (1975) who have worked with intellectually retarded clients. Budoff (1973) and Feuerstein (1979) have criticized such techniques when dealing with culturally different minority groups. Mercer (1979) in the SOMPA manual has gone to great lengths to point out the deficiencies of such an approach in dealing with culturally different children. With these criticisms in mind, it seems logical to explore alternative approaches to static assessment. Some of these alternatives which have been suggested are:

(1) Develop new tests that are culture free (2) develop culture fair tests, (3) use a common culture approach such as perceptual tasks, (4) develop culture specific tests, (5) modify existing tests and re-norm, (6) change the administrative procedures of existing assessment devices, (7) use a test - train - test format, and (8) develop plural-istic norms.

Jane Mercer developed the System of Multipluralistic Assessment (S.O.M.P.A.) as a comprehensive battery of tests to assess children multi-dimensionally. Mercer's (1979) purpose was to (1) reduce label-ling of non-Anglo children as mentally retarded and low functioning; (2) to provide more socio-cultural information as a linkage component of learning potential; and (3) to identify educational needs of min-ority children.

The S.O.M.P.A. was designed to produce an estimate of learning poten-tial by using norms that are socio-culturally and ethnically approp-riate. It was also designed to introduce multiplicity into the test-ing process; that is, by investigating cognitive, perceptual, and adaptive responses, a more complex analysis of the child's function could be facilitated. These general objectives of the test are the S.O.M.P.A.'s main strengths. The test has been standardized on Black, White, and Hispanic populations in an attempt to remove inappropriate culture bias in test interpretation.

In addition to the modified norms, Mercer has introduced the concept of using three assessment models to provide a more comprehensive view of the child's functioning - medical, social systems, and pluralistic. These approaches provide several advantages: (1) the parent is used as a significant helper in the assessment, (2) physical and perceptual abilities are examined, (3) significant background health information about the child is obtained, (4) a view of the child's functioning in social settings outside of school is acquired, (5) measure of the child's adaptive behavior is secured, and (6) the wide range of variables examined provide clues to effective intervention strategies.

The strengths of the S.O.M.P.A. system must, however, be considered in light of some weaknesses. The first weakness in the approach is that only three ethnic groups have been used. Coupled with this is the fact that the standardization sample is primarily California-based and lacks extensive geographical norms. A second flaw is in the Spanish language version; a more tightly constructed translation is necessary. A third weakness lies in the lack of precise predictability of the ELP score. A more carefully analyzed interpretation of ELP scores is necessary. The last limitation is the concern with the "utility" of scores - at present, no effective strategies have been formulated for educators.

Dynamic Assessment. Dynamic assessment has its origin in Vygotsky's concept of the "Zone of Proximal Development" (Vygotsky, 1978). This Zone is developmental in nature and is defined as:

the distance between the actual developmental level as determined
by independent problem solving and the level of potential development as determined through problem solving under adult guidance
or in collaboration with more capable peers (Vygotsky, 1978).

Vygotsky therefore stated that an essential feature of learning is
that it stimulates the process of internal development that only operates when a person interacts with people around him through the process of peer cooperation. Once these processes become established,
they then become integrated in the cognitive developmental achievement
of a person.

Vygotsky realized that standardized instruments do not capture potential, but product. He recognized that IQ scores supply minimal information on either cognitive functions or processes. The opposite of
traditional psychometric methods is to assess an individual's level of
potential development and not his actual development. This method
employed by Vygotsky is a test-teach-test format using items from conventional IQ tests. After completing the item, the individual is trained how to answer questions of the type given. This training continues
until competency is achieved on the incorrect items.

What is tabulated are the number of prompts needed to solve the task.
The degree or number of prompts equals the width or band of potential.
Having achieved competence, a task similar to the original is introduced. The amount of transfer can be assessed by the number of cues
used on this additional task. Transfer and flexibility in recognizing
similarity of components across tasks become the key outcome measure.
If transfer is successful, the students' potential for learning is
high. A general notion of a student's ability to profit from intervention, the speed of learning new material, and subsequent transfer
across domains and tasks are the chief benefits of this methodology.
Specifically, if the width of the zone is wide then the number of
prompts or cues needed for transfer would be low. An example of reduced or low potential occurs when the transfer task has many components of similarity and the number of prompts remains equal to more than
the original task. It is imperative, then, that the clinician must
have a comprehensive picture of the initial and transfer tasks in order
to design appropriate training strategies. Therefore, if cognitive
potentiality is dormant, its discovery is facilitated under the tutelage
of the significant other. Specific examples can be discovered of fluid
intelligence and crystallized under instruction during the testing
session itself. Instructional testing situations are likely to provide
evidence of problem-solving skills that remain undeveloped and un-
discovered by conventional testing practices.

It is because of the limitations imposed by traditional static measurement approaches that Budoff and Feuerstein have employed a test-train-
test model as part of a dynamic assessment approach. We turn now to
an examination of both methodologies.

Budoff. The Budoff method of assessment consists of presenting the examinee with either a familiar or novel task; this presentation is somewhat like the administration of a pre-test in psychological experiments or scholastic achievement measurement. This task provides a base-line measure which can be compared to subsequent performance on the task. The examiner, then, functions as a tester/teacher in the second phase of assessment. This phase of assessment is used by the tester to teach the underlying rules of thought and logic which form the substructure of items on the pre-test; the examiner can either deal with general reasoning principles such as induction and deduction methods, or he can teach basic concepts. He can, thus, train using content and/or process as the main focus. The examiner finishes this phase of testing and then re-introduces the original task. This task has been changed however, in that the task is hierarchically organized in such a way as to have the task requirements graded on a continuum from easy to difficult. The examinee is then asked to perform the tasks starting with the easiest and moving in progression to the most difficult; this methodology enables the examiner to ascertain the effectiveness of training on two levels: (1) did the examinee improve his performance? and (2) by how much? It also allows for some assessment of the generalization of the training to a more difficult task. It provides the examiner a clearer understanding of the potential of the client or how much time and energy needs to be invested to ascertain progression in the examinee's performance. It also provides neuro-linguistic programming information, as to the preferred modality of cognitive transmission, most successful in producing gains in the examinee's performance; these modalities include visual, auditory, and kinesthetic approaches to cognitive awareness.

The test-train-test paradigm can incorporate a singular task or a multi-task assessment approach. Multiple test approaches employ a battery of tests using the test-train-test model. Feuerstein's (1979) approach has been to assess children using a multiple test battery. Budoff, on the other hand, has tended to concentrate on assessment using the singular task approach. Budoff felt that children should be tested using a non-verbal reasoning task; he felt that through this relatively culture-free exercise children could be given the opportunity to gain cognitive experience through the training of the examiner, which would, subsequently, improve their cognitive ability scores. To this end Budoff employs two specific non-verbal tests - the Kohs Block Designs Test (1920) and the Ravens Coloured Progressive Matrices (1965), the latter of which was modified by Feuerstein and his associates. The non-verbal tasks used were specifically chosen to offset situational factors in the assessment process, that is, the effects of failure in school, cultural factors, and language deficiencies.

Several studies (Budoff 1973,1974) have been completed using Budoff's methodology and these have demonstrated the usefulness and effectiveness of the test-train-test model. This method has also spawned a similar approach in the Soviet Union. Wozniak (1975) described an approach in which the child is required to perform a task independently; the examiner then acts as a tutor, and the child is asked to perform the task again under his tutelage. Finally the child is asked to perform the same task independently. The procedure is similar to Budoff's approach in that the test-train-test model is used; however Budoff uses psychometric normative devices (Kohs Block Test and Ravens Progressive Matrices) to evaluate post-test performance while the Soviet approach uses no "normative" evaluation procedures. The second major difference lies in Budoff's insistence on non-verbal instruments. This restriction does not apply in the Soviet methodology.

Feuerstein. Feuerstein (1979), like Budoff, uses a test-train-test model; however, the training is different than that of Budoff. The stress during training is on the "relationship" between examiner and examinee. In this method the client is constantly encouraged to interact with the examiner to optimize and maximize the potential for cognitive understanding. Hence, Feuerstein's approach is one in which both client and psychologist are involved in an active modificational system; the basic assumption is that a child or adult who is culturally deprived or deprived of his/her own culture has a much higher potential than he is able to demonstrate through conventional assessment devices.

Feuerstein tried to assess intelligence and cognitive potential (as opposed to current functioning levels) and concluded that standardized tests were not adequate. He felt that inadequate assessments were occurring because the instruments used were "static"; that is, they measured manifest levels of function; these tasks were done poorly by culturally different clients. The instruments only tended to confirm the opinions of the dominant culture that culturally different clients (either ethnically different or varied in terms of cultural deprivation) would score poorly on the tests. Feuerstein felt that a "dynamic" approach should be used to examine the underlying cognitive functions and deficiencies.

Feuerstein's concern has been to understand and remedy a syndrome that he has referred to as cultural deprivation. By that term he means not that an individual from a particular culture is deprived, but rather that the individual himself is deprived of his/her culture, whatever that culture is. It might be delineated along racial, religious, or socioeconomic lines. Feuerstein feels that this deprivation leads to low or reduced modifiability; it reduces the client's ability to learn or change. In essence this condition leads to low cognitive performance on tests. Unlike cultural difference, which can be marked by failure in areas of knowledge restricted to the dominant culture, cultural deprivation can be characterized by manifestations of reduced motivation and ability to learn or change in testing situations, even when the examination milieu is reasonably favourable.

Feuerstein believes that cognitive modifiability can occur when a mediated learning experience (M.L.E.) is present; M.L.E. is a situation in which a mediator interposes himself between the person and the environment and acts as an interpreter to experiences and perceptions of the world. M.L.E., therefore, is not merely a social interaction, but rather an encounter during which information is mediated; in fact, meaning is transmitted to the client. Typically mother-child interactions are replete with examples of mediated learning; the mother selectively accepts and rejects certain stimuli to present to the child. She, in fact, frames, filters, schedules, and sequences events in the environment when she interacts with the child. In this way the mother and other caregivers mediate temporal, spatial, and causal relationships. This type of mediated experience, then, not only links the child to his cultural past, but also builds the foundation for cognitive structural growth.

It seems that the need to impose order on the environment and formulate cognitive schema to do this can most readily be achieved from one's own culture; this cultural transmission is most likely the way that will provide the methodology by which to understand and interpret the world. It is far more likely that environmental or individual sources will provide adequate transmission of meaning. Mediated learning experience in its widest meaning therefore could be considered the psychological component of cultural transmission.

Different cultures might be said to provide a structure within which the organization, interpretation, and understanding of events can occur through exposure and experience. An understanding and a link to past cultural events and, consequently, a projection and anticipation of future cultural events could be thought of as a form of cultural imperative that enables the individual to be cognitively flexible, and adaptable. Individuals might also project future experiences in their culture by developing relational processes that connect past, present, and future. Language plays a very important part in the process; it is, however, not essential in the transmission of culture. M.L.E. may be given through modalities other than language. M.L.E. is an intentional interpretation to the client of the experienced world. The level of language facility according to Feuerstein does not determine the effectiveness of M.L.E. Mediated Learning Experience, to Feuerstein, therefore, may be viewed as the transmission of universal cognitive structure by the initiated members of society to the uninitiated members it is the acquisition of new structures that enables individuals to become adaptable, flexible, and consequently modifable. This theory, then has practical implications for assessment.

There is a large difference in the basic nature and intent of the goals and methods of intervention. Feuerstein's approach has been one in which both client and counsellor are involved in an active modificational system; the basic assumption is that a child or adult who is culturally deprived has a much higher potential than he is able to demonstrate through conventional standardized assessment devices.

Many of the attempts to change current standardized tests are riddled with problems. Standard psychometric tests fail to distinguish between the concepts "culturally different" and "culturally deprived". It is essential to differentiate between these two groups so that increased understanding can lead to effective strategies of change. Although poor functioning is "observable" in culturally different clients who are continually confronted with expectations and tasks that are unfamiliar from their own frame of reference, there is an optimism that through strong cultural affiliations they will have been exposed to their cultural tradition which in turn can provide a strong psychological or cognitive foundation with which they can effectively deal with elements of the dominant culture. In essence, their own culture has made them able to successfully acquire differing cultural elements that will allow them greater opportunities or accessibility within the dominant culture. The culturally deprived individual, however, has become alienated from his own culture. This alienation may have been caused by any number of single or interactive factors (sociological, economic, geopolitical, psychological, physical, or cultural) affecting the group. Feuerstein and Hoffman (1982) believe that alienation is reflected in "a disruptive of inter-generational transmission and mediational processes". Thus, cultural deprivation refers to an <u>intrinsic</u> criterion of the specific culture, that is, the absence of intergenerational transmission - a process which is inherent in most cultures. The concept differs from traditional definitions of culturally deprived which refers to the <u>extrinsic</u> criterion by which the culture of certain ethnic minority sub-groups are viewed as depriving the members and thus affecting their capabilities in a cognitive sense.

Cultural deprivation may significantly affect the individual's adaptive capabilities. The problems of cognitive functioning and consequently its assessment must be approached differently for cultural deprivation than cultural difference. Feuerstein, as stated previously, has developed a form of "dynamic" testing designed to deal with cultural deprivation. Such a dynamic approach to testing requires that goals in the psychometric process be delineated. The following goals were defined:

1. To assess the modifiability of the individual when he is confronted with conditions aiming to produce a change in him.
2. To assess the extent of the examinee's modifiability in terms of levels of functioning made accessible to him by this process of modification, and the significance of the levels attained by him in the hierarchy of cognitive operations. (Here the question is to what extent the achieved modification is limited to the area of perceptual or other types of elementary functioning, or whether change enables the examinee to accede to other higher mental processes, such as abstract thinking or logical operations).
3. To determine the significance of the modification achieved in a given area for other general areas of functioning. (To what extent are the patterns of functioning acquired in the assessment-training process applied in areas other than that of training?)
4. To search for preferential modalities of the individual, which represent areas of relative strengths and weaknesses both in terms of his existent inventory of responses and in terms of preferential strategies for affecting the desired modification in the most efficient and economical way. (Feuerstein, 1979)

Dynamic assessment is carried out during an attempt to change the client's cognitive performance, and it represents an effort to, roughly, qualitatively assess the amount of investment of the psychologist or educator needed to produce significant changes in the cognitive performance of the client; it also is designed to predict the level of change potential in the client. To facilitate this end, normal testing procedures have been changed in four specific ways:

1. The examiner, instead of being a neutral, standard questioner, has to be a responsive, excited, individualized teacher-trainer. Regular static testing sessions permit limited flexibility in this area.
2. The test instruments must be changed. Ideally the instruments will be clear and well-sequenced; they will permit ready assessment of current functioning and the relative ease of change in problem solving processes and relational thinking.
3. The assessment must focus on process rather than product. How many correct responses should be de-emphasized; the change in problem-solving skills should be emphasized.
4. Especially excellent responses reflecting process and product should be viewed as extremely salient factors in potential.

These four departures from standard procedure are incorporated in a test-train-test sequence. Assessment is initiated to determine the individual's strengths in processing information. The process is fluid and highly interactive between examiner and examinee. The strengths of this approach are many.

1. The assessment is dynamic.
2. The encounter between the tester and testee is active and intense.
3. The examiner is a responsive teacher-trainer with a great deal of flexibility.
4. The assessment focuses on process not product.
5. The level of potential or modifiability of the client is assessed.
6. Intervention strategies are revealed.

There are some weaknesses in the L.P.A.D. assessment procedure. The first concern is centered around the measurement of modifiability; even though the L.P.A.D. is concerned with process, there is still a tendency to measure cognitive gain on standardized measures. The second weakness is centered upon the complex nature of the instruments; furthermore each tester can approach assessment in his/her own way, thus reducing the reliability of the instruments. These points, however, do not detract from the overall significance of this approach in the testing of minority clients.

Kaufman's A-B-C. One further approach to testing needs mention at this time. The Kaufman Assessment Battery for Children (K-ABC, 1983) is a test of intelligence and achievement which is administered individually; it is standardized on a nationwide sample of both exceptional and normal students between two and a half and twelve and a half years of age. Intellectual functioning is measured in four broad categories: Sequential

Processing, Simultaneous Processing, Mental Composite Processing (combination of the previous two scores) and Achievement. The manual includes norms which reflect socio-cultural factors and can be used when children from different ethnic backgrounds are assessed. A non-verbal scale is included to test children with language problems, both language disorders and language differences. The scales of processing directly reflect the concern of Kaufman with the need to assess "fluid intelligence". The achievement scores are used as a measure of crystallized ability, in that achievement through content are measured.

The concept of sequential and simultaneous processing finds its theoretical antecedents in the neurophysiological concepts of Luria (1966) which examine the differential functions of the left and right brain hemisphere and the localization of differential function in the brain.

The K-ABC utilizes the concept of sequential process which finds its description in Luria (1966) who describes tasks such as the habitualization of skills, rote memory tasks, and narration. Simultaneous processing deals with spatial organization and finds its expression in linguistic process tasks, comparison and contrast, and spatial tasks. The recent use of the K-ABC has extended into the schools of Canada. It remains to be seen, through the accumulation of empirical data, whether or not the test will provide effective testing for minority students.

The issues involved in cross-cultural assessment are complex and numerous; the need to understand cultural variation, the role of culture in test performance, the mesh between concepts of difference and deficit, coupled with the need to examine the concept of potential, and the emphasis within group variation in response to between group assessments, are just a few of the salient concerns in multicultural testing. The focus of this discussion has been the contention that the "potential" for being changed by learning should be the key concern of intellectual assessment. It is felt that this potential ability can only be measured by a process that is active, intentional, and involving; it cannot be discovered through a static evaluation of an individual's abilities.

It might be stated that a dynamic assessment of cognitive functioning can have implications in the areas of social and cultural betterment. In one sense a clearer understanding of terms such as intelligence and capacity might evolve. Secondly, a better understanding of differences which are culturally-based might emerge. Cross-cultural studies which use static assessment devices to describe differences between ethnically or culturally different clients might benefit from a dynamic approach which could add more relevant information to the study. In light of rapid technological and social change in many cultural settings, it seems that an active process of appraisal would be beneficial. Finally and probably most important, dynamic assessment provides an immediate approach to help in understanding individuals; crucial educational and vocational decisions are made about individuals without an accurate appraisal of modifiability potential. These decisions can affect the career and personal development of individuals. More vital information is obtained through dynamic assessment than through static methods.

Techniques of dynamic assessment have been used to re-affirm that cultural diversity exists, and that within cultural groups, there is in fact internal diversities that need to be dealt with in a non-culturally-encapulated way. There is a great deal of hope that the techniques of dynamic assessment will be refined and modified to enable counsellors, educators, and psychologists to better understand and help their clients.

Sundberg and Gonzales (1981), in their excellent review of cross-cultural assessment, point out that what is needed in thie area is an understanding of the underlying bases of learning; they feel that an understanding of information-processing variables present in the client and their constant sensory underpinnings can shed light on therapeutic outcomes. They point out that the dynamic approaches seem to proceed towards the clarification of the needs of ethnic minority and other cultural groups. It is hoped that dynamic testing will receive consideration in the literature in order to better serve culturally different groups and individuals.

REFERENCES

Budoff, M. (1973). Learning potential and educability among the educable mentally retarded. Progress report grant No. OE6-0-8-08056-4597. National Institute of Education, H.E.W. Cambridge, Mass.: Research Institute for Educational Problems.

Budoff, M. (1974) Learning potential and educability among the educable mentally retarded. (Rep. No. 312312). Cambridge, Mass.: Research Institute for Educational Problems, (Cambridge Mental Health Association.)

Carroll, J. (1983) Studying individual differences in cognitive abilities. Through and beyond factor analysis. In R. Dillion, & R. Schmeck (Eds.), Individual differences in cognition VI. New York: Academic Press.

Cattell, R.B. (1971). Abilities: their structure, growth and action. Boston: Houghton Mifflin.

Detterman, & Sternberg (1982). How and how much can intelligence be increased. Norword, NY: Ablex Publishing.

Feuerstein, R. (1979). The dynamic assessment of retarded performers. Baltimore: University Park Press.

Feuerstein, R. & Hoffman (1982). Intergenerational conflict of rights: Cultural imposition and self realization. Unpublished manuscript.

Haywood, H., Filler, J., Shipman, M. & Chatelanat, G. (1975).
Behavioural Assessment in Mental Retardation. In P. Reynolds (Ed.),
Advances in psychological assessment (Vol. 3). San Francisco:
Jossey Bass.

Jones, R. (Ed.). (1985). Nondiscriminatory (high validity) assessment
of minority group children: A casebook. Berkeley: University of
California.

Kaufman, A. & Kaufman, N. (1983) The Kaufman assessment battery for
children. Circle Pines, MN: American Guidance Service.

Kohs, F. (1920). Block Design Test. Journal of Experimental Psychology, 3, 357-76.

Luria, A.R. (1966). Human brain and psychological processes. New
York: Harper and Row.

Mercer, J. (1979). SOMPA technical manual. New York: Psychological
Corporation.

Raven, J. (1965). Guide to using the coloured matrices sets A AB B.
London: H.K. Lewis.

Samuda, R.J. (1975). The psychological testing of American
minorities. New York: Harper and Row.

Samuda R.J. (1986). The role of psychometry in multicultural
education: Implications and consequences. In R.J. Samuda, & S.L.
Kong (Eds.), Multicultural education: Programmes and methods
(47-57), Intercultural Social Sciences Pub. Inc.

Sternberg, R.J. (1977). Intelligence, information processing and
analogical reasoning: The componential analysis of human abilities.
New Jersey: Lawrence Erlbaum Associates.

Sundberg, N., & Gonzales, L. (1981) Cross cultural and cross ethnic
assessment overview and issues. In P. McReynolds (ed.), Advances
in Psychological Assessment (Vol. 5). San Francisco: Jossey Bass
Inc.

Vygotsky, L. (1978). Mind in society. The development of higher
psychological processes. Cambridge: Harvard University Press.

Wozniak, R. (1975). A dialectical paradigm for psychological research:
Implications drawn from the history of psychology in the Soviet
Union. Human Development 18 (1-2), 18-34.

ASSESSMENTS OF LEARNING POTENTIAL WILL INCLUDE BOTH COGNITIVE SKILLS AND MOTIVATIONAL FACTORS

Peter J. Gamlin
The Ontario Institute for Studies in Education
Toronto, Canada

INTRODUCTION

In this paper I make the point that it is by understanding what is common across cultures that we begin to understand the uniquely stressed aspects of particular cultures. As I see it, we need theories that interpret the individual case against the "bigger picture" provided by more general (and perhaps universal) principles of learning and motivation.

One could argue that individual cultures are each special cases. On this view, however, one would need different theories of learning and motivation to account for school performance that was culture specific and, as well, we would need to design quite different procedures for determining students' potential to learn. The evidence, it seems to me, suggests otherwise. Performance at school and on tests of learning potential are better explained by recourse to more general (and I would argue universal) theories of learning and motivation (see Gamlin, 1985). As I see it, when we consider intercultural differences we are considering differences not in kind but in relative strength. This is what I mean by potential. And just as an individual may have certain strengths or potentials so must the culture. And just as the individual has the potential to change, likewise is the culture modified. I would like to turn now to a very general consideration of learning and motivation to make these ideas clearer.[1]

Learning, Motivation, and the Modifiability of Potential. A growing
research literature has begun to document the relationship between
individuals' attitudes about learning and their decisions as to whether
or not they will choose to practice and use their learning skills.
Attitudes about learning will determine what individuals get out of
learning environments. Necessarily these attitudes will determine what
an individual will do in an assessment situation where the objective is
one of describing that individual's potential to learn.

As I see it as we move into the 21st century, psychologists and
educators will increasingly want to consider the relationship between
attitudes and learning in their attempt to describe an individual's
potential to learn. The focus here is on what the individual thinks
about learning and the kinds of attitudes that come out of this. In
this paper I shall outline what educational psychologists currently
understand about the relationship between attitudes and learning but
first I shall suggest one additional trend in the assessment of
learning potential that I see continuing past the year 2000.

From this latter perspective, I see increasing pressure on educational
diagnosticians to understand learning potential with respect to its
plasticity or modifiability. Current "achievement" will not be
perceived as an end in itself but rather as a "clue" for going on.
Given this trend, the need for "coaching" becomes an important aspect
of learning environments and assessment situations. Teachers will
understand that the potential to learn is not a "fixed" potential but
rather that the potential to learn is "malleable," modifiable and

---

[1]I make these remarks fully cognizant of ecocultural approaches (of
the kind pioneered by the Whitings, e.g., Whiting, 1980) to the study
of socialization. Ecocultural variables unquestionably impact upon
such things as schooling. As colleagues in the Laboratory of
Comparative Human Cognition put it, "On the one hand, it is important
for participation· in modern industrialized societies that children be
taught the practices of schooling as they relate to the needs of adult
life. On the other hand, when people perform poorly in school
contexts, one should not be tricked into thinking that all their home
culture provided them with was a weaker mind" (Laboratory of
Comparative Human Cog., 1986, p. 1054). As I see it, while ecocultural
approaches may account for variation in performance, still left to
explain is how under the appropriate circumstances and with an
appropriate experience base people are able to come to a common
understanding about the way things are -- this in spite of the fact
that they may concurrently realize that had they been wearing a
"different hat" (had they been influenced by a different set of
ecocultural variables) they could conceivably have come to a quite
different understanding of things.

incremental. These notions were given some prominence early on by
Vygotsky (1978, 1986) and have been subsequently popularized by Rubin
Feuerstein (Feuerstein, 1980), Ann Brown (see Brown & Ferrara, 1985)
and others (e.g., Campione, Brown, & Bryant, 1984). My own work
continues in this tradition.

ATTITUDES AND LEARNING: ATTRIBUTIONS

I describe the relationship between attitudes and learning using an
attributional framework. In a word, attributions are the explanations
individuals give for causal events including having succeeded or
failed. These explanations are "naive" in that they are the "common-
sense" kinds of explanations "people on the street" offer to explain
why things have come about in the way that they have. Fritz Heider was
responsible for introducing the basic tenants of the attributional
framework in a very influential book in 1958 (Heider, 1958).

Motive. First, according to attributional theory, we must have a
motive. As one example, we are motivated sometimes because we fear
failure. Will I be able to keep up with the others? On the other
hand, we sometimes do things because we desire something challenging.
Do I want to learn something new?

Can I Succeed. Second, we have the question of belief in our ability
to succeed. Do I have what it takes to succeed?

Do I Want to Succeed. Third is the question of value - is this
something I really want to do?

What Will It Take. Fourth, if I want it, will I need to acquire new
skills or do I already know enough or have the requisite skills? Do I
have the courage? What sorts of goals must I set for myself?

Answers to these questions will always turn around how one appraises
oneself and the situation. For example, do I think I am "smart" -- in
that situation? Will I look smart in that situation? Is that task so
easy it is an insult to my intelligence? Will I have to work really
hard to succeed on that task? If I tackle that task, will my
inadequacies show? Should I ask for help -- now?

We say individuals have good mental health if they are able to make
"realistic" and "conscious" appraisals of themselves and the situation.
I find this attributional framework very helpful for understanding
attitudes/beliefs about learning. Dweck (1986) works from a similar
framework. She has identified two basic types of learners -- those who
believe that ability is "fixed" and those who believe that ability can
change - that is is malleable. The former type of learner - the
"fixed-ability" learner, goes into situations concerned about what

others will say. The "fixed-ability" learner wants an "A" because it is a standard whereby one's performance can be compared to and by others. The "fixed-ability" learner puts an emphasis on achievement, relative to others. "Fixed-ability" learners believe that high levels of achievement are so desirable that learning tasks are chosen to guarantee a successful outcome. They will choose tasks that may conceal their ability to protect it from negative evaluation. Above all, the "fixed-ability" learner has a view of his or her ability that is dependent on the evaluation and approval of others.

On the other hand, the learner who believes that ability can be changed, that it is malleable, adopts "learning goals" whereby learning becomes an end in itself. The main effort of children with a learning goal is to understand or master something new. Children with a learning goal persist in the face of obstacles even when they believe their ability is low; "... with a learning goal, children are willing to risk displays of ignorance in order to acquire skills and knowledge. Instead of calculating their exact ability level and how it will be judged, they can think more about the value of the skill to be developed or their interest in the task to be undertaken" (Dweck, 1986, p. 1042). In my work I have described these children as striving for a "personal best," enabling them to take pride in their accomplishments (Gamlin, 1988; Gamlin & Fleming, 1985) "Malleable-ability" learners are able to set "realistic" goals for themselves because they have a great sense of their own limits and horizons.

Bill Blatz (1944, 1966) who founded the Institute of Child Study at the University of Toronto said some very similar things back in the thirties and forties. He described learners who were "immaturely dependent" (on others) and learners who were relatively independent (of others). Blatz suggested that the "immaturely dependent" learner had had a less secure relationship with significant others early on compared to the "independently secure" learner. Because the more independently secure learner was less dependent on others for decision making, this type of learner was more able to accept the consequences of his or her behavior. On this view, the "independently secure" learner had more control over what was learned and how it was learned. Above all, this individual would "consciously" interact with his or her environment with a rather full understanding of the causes that have led to different results in their personal domain. These individuals are therefore able to effect changes that are adaptive not only for themselves but more generally for society as a whole. The "immaturely dependent" learner, on the other hand, relies on what Blatz called "deputy agents" (sometimes parents) to assume responsibility for decision making. Learning is what others want you to learn. Learning is also not very exciting since it is not self-directed nor is it oriented to personal accomplishment. This individual does not learn how to learn because the emphasis is put on rote learning or perhaps learning up to a standard; getting an "A" is the single most important reason for learning. Given the profile just described, perhaps it is not surprising to learn that the "immaturely dependent" learner is least likely to adapt to, or cope with rapidly changing situations or problem types.

You will notice that both Dweck and Blatz provide very similar descriptions of individuals who have learning as their primary goal. Dweck suggests that the individual's orientation towards learning is determined by his or her beliefs about "intelligence." The individual who believes that intelligence is malleable also believes that learning is incremental -- that one will never, if you will, achieve the final answer on anything. Blatz suggested that his "independently secure" learner was just that -- secure enough to be what he called "maturely" independent; able to accept the consequences of his or her actions and "responsibly" so, by taking into account the values and goals (the equally independent actions) of significant others. Furthermore, Blatz suggested that his "maturely" independent learner would conclude that learning is never finished in that "learning exposes the need for further learning." It is tempting to suggest, as I have done, (Gamlin, 1988) that the development of human security must antedate the beliefs one develops about one's ability. Present work in attachment theory (see Bretherton & Waters, 1985) would tend to support this suggestion. In any case, researchers in these areas have achieved a considerable consensus as to how to characterize the process of optimal learning and conversely there is much agreement as to the characteristics that best describe the optimal learner. The one concept that seems to provide a reasonable "fit" across the various extant theories is that of modifiability. The extent to which we are willing to modify our behavior, act as a change agent, is probably a good indicator of how responsive we will be in new learning situations. In this sense, then, our attitudes about ourselves as learners will determine the extent to which we are willing to profit from instruction. I shall make this point clearer in a brief consideration of Vygotsky's work.

VYGOTSKY AND THE ZONE OF PROXIMAL DEVELOPMENT

Vygotsky wrote a book in the early thirties (1934/1978) and in it one of the significant observations he made was that a child's development or potential for development cannot be seen only on the basis of what the child can already achieve without help. He made this point in the following way. He asked his reader to consider two children who are both ten years old chronologically but only eight years old in terms of mental development. He suggests that these children are able to deal with tasks "up to the degree of difficulty that has been standardized for the eight year old level." But he goes on to question whether these children have the same potential to learn. Suppose he says that we in some way or another help these children understand the nature of the problems they could not solve. Suppose furthermore that with instruction, one of these children can go on to solve problems at the twelve year old level while the other can succeed at the nine year old level. For Vygotsky, this result means that they are not mentally the same age and consequently that what they are able to understand will not be the same. Vygotsky goes on to make this often quoted assertion.... "This difference between twelve and eight, or between

nine and eight, is what we call the zone of proximal development. It
is the distance between the actual development as determined by
independent problem solving and the level of potential development as
determined through problem solving under adult guidance or in
collaboration with more capable peers" (Vygotsky, 1934/1978, pp.
85-86). And again from Vygotsky (1962, p. 103), "the discrepancy
between a child's actual mental age and the level he reaches in solving
problems with assistance indicates the zone of his proximal
development; in our example, this zone is four for the first child and
one for the second. Can we truly say that their mental development is
the same? Experience has shown that the child with the larger zone of
proximal development will do much better in school. This measure gives
a more helpful clue than mental age does to the dynamics of
intellectual progress."

For Vygotsky then, a narrow zone would indicate that the child will not
advance much beyond his or her initial, unaided demonstration of
competence across many areas of school activities. In contrast, a wide
zone would indicate that the child is likely able to advance beyond
current levels of performance across these same school activities.
Therefore, as suggested by Campione et al. (1984), the zone of proximal
development provides information about readiness, since it
characterizes cognitive development prospectively. On the other hand,
the information provided by static measures focuses on actual levels of
development and characterizes mental development retrospectively. It
is this notion of the zone of proximal development as an "individual
difference metric" that has directed the research of Campione et al.
(1984) and Brown & Ferrara (1985).

In a recent chapter (Gamlin, 1988), I have made some suggestions as to
how the individual is able to make use of "knowledgeable others" --
that is to go beyond his or her present achievement with help. I
describe the thinking the individual uses as he or she moves from the
given (old experience) to the new, taking advantage of the instruction
("scaffolding") provided by others. I suggest that these thinking
skills are common across cultures. In this paper, I introduce the
issue of modifiability in a different way by focussing on the learner's
attitudes and beliefs. In my view, an individual's movement in the
zone of proximal development is determined in large part by the
attitudes the individual brings to the learning or assessment
situation. And again, in my view, these attitudes will determine in
large measure the extent to which the individual is "ready" to profit
from instruction. If, for example, the individual believes he or she
does not have the ability (can't) and doesn't value the exercise (why
bother) then that individual will not perform to his or her potential;
will not show much movement in the zone of proximal development no
matter what help is offered by a tutor. On the other hand, should the
individual have an attitude about learning that is incremental where
the emphasis is put on accepting challenges and giving new situations,
a real try (when the going gets tough, the tough get going) then a more
accurate picture of that particular individual's potential to learn

will be derived (we will observe more movement in the "Zone"). And following Blatz, we will come to a better understanding of that individual with respect to his or her feelings of security. Does that individual act in an independent and maturely responsible fashion? Does that individual value learning because it leads to new learning? Is that individual striving for a personal best?

Following on Dweck's (1986) analysis, the educational implications for students with performance as opposed to learning goals is staggering. Research demonstrates that those with performance goals, those who believe their ability is fixed, will resist pursuing challenges because they must believe that their ability is high before they will seek a challenging task. Furthermore, they are more likely to attribute errors or failures to a lack of ability and in turn to predict continued failure, which typically results in a defensive withdrawal of effort. In contrast, students with learning goals are more likely to see obstacles as a prompt to increase their effort or to improve their strategies, which tends to result in improved performance. Consequently, with respect to satisfaction with outcomes, the emphasis is on ability versus effort: children with performance goals base their assessment of satisfaction on the ability they believe they have demonstrated; children with learning goals base their assessment on the effort they have applied. Citing the work of Ames, Ames, & Felker (1977), Dweck (1986) notes that children with learning goals possess an autonomous reward structure based on the amount of effort they have exerted, whereas children with performance goals base their feelings of pride within a competitive reward structure. Performance-goal children are likely to perceive high effort with little satisfaction as it is perceived as being indicative of low ability.

On this account, one can understand why performance-goal children might develop a view of intelligence that is fixed and global and, furthermore, why they would view any help they were given to facilitate movement in the zone of proximal development as indicative of their lack of ability. Consequently, one would expect that these children would show little movement in the zone and would feel badly about the experience. Indeed the emphasis on performance and achievement would tend to neutralize any intrinsic interest the task had to offer.

This is not a pretty picture. One is reminded of the "learned helplessness" literature. According to learned helplessness theory (see Alloy, Abramson, Peterson, & Seligman, 1984), "learned helplessness" is displayed when people regard their actions or responses as futile or irrelevant to subsequent outcomes (see Diener & Dweck, 1980). If failure is attributed to global causes then helplessness will generalize widely across situations. Furthermore, if failure is attributed to stable and uncontrollable factors (i.e., invariant factors such as ability) performance decrements will ensue. In a word I am suggesting that performance oriented children, those children who believe that ability is fixed, are ripe for feelings of depression and helplessness (see Forsterling, 1986). On this view, there most certainly are a group of learners who have attitudes about learning that are at odds with being able to profit from instruction. They do not easily modify their behavior in new learning situations. As I see it, these various attitudes about learning and consequently the way people feel about learning something new can be found universally across cultures.

THE NATIVE INDIAN CULTURE AND CONCLUDING REMARKS

In this paper I have described how motivation and attitudes about learning will decide what is learned, how it is learned and with what degree of enthusiasm it is learned. I have suggested a very general (and I believe universal) framework to account for this phenomenon. Above all, I have stressed the notion of modifiability and individuals acting as change agents to achieve flexibility in their adaptations as they attempt to successfully engage their environments.

I want now to give these ideas greater clarity in the context of cultural issues by considering traditional Native Indian conceptions about learning. My understanding (see More, 1986, May) is that in the teaching situation the Watch-then-Do oreintation requires that one does not "teach" a child to learn. This kind of intervention "would risk forever destroying the child's ability to observe and learn from his own motives. The child is encouraged only to seek out knowledge of human experience and skills by being present in practice or their telling. Children were allowed to explore and be independent as soon as they were able. Often misbehavior was ignored so that the child would learn the natural consequences of misbehavior and learn to be in charge of his or her own behavior" (Scollon & Scollon, 1983, p. 101). Non-verbal communication "was much more important than in contemporary Western society. Eye contact and quiet calmness were important methods of discipline and communication. Children were not tested or questioned after a learning situation -- they were expected to self test" (see More, 1986, May, p. 9).

Notice in this account the similarities between the Blatzian conceptions of the independently secure learner and the child rearing practices of the traditional Native Indian culture. The emphasis is placed on the child learning how to accept the consequences of his or her behavior in a secure learning environment and in the case of the Native Indian culture, this occurred in the extended family where grandparents and other elders were responsible for setting up "opportunities" for the child to learn. In this kind of environment, one can see the possibility for the child to acquire the kinds of learning goals Dweck describes; learning for the sake of learning and aspiring to ones personal best. Attributions to account for successful performance in this tradition are always personal and behavior is always responsible.

These comments are directed to pointing out the similarities in conceptions between general theories of motivation and learning and the traditional Native Indian culture. I have done this to highlight the "strengths" of traditional Native Indian child rearing practices to show that these are differences not of kind but of emphasis. Furthermore, I wanted to point out that these "differences" are highly valued in contemporary Western society.

Finally, in this paper I have not considered the cognitive skills issue, and with respect to the Native Indian culture, the thinking so predominant in a learning style we have come to call global or holistic, a learning style that I believe is deeply rooted in the development of symbolic competence (see Gamlin, 1988). Again, the differences here seem to be ones of emphasis not of kind. In traditional Native Indian cultures, legends and stories were the primary method of learning values and attitudes. "The legends and stories had very deep meanings, and involved very intricate relationships.... the use of symbolism, anthropomorphism... animism... and metaphors was an extremely effective method of teaching very deep and complex concepts. These methods allowed the learner to understand at his or her level of cognitive and emotional development. When the learner came back to the story or legend a few years later, it had an even deeper meaning..." (see More, 1986, p. 8).

In my work I have described the development of symbolic competence using a general (and I believe universal) theoretical approach (see Gamlin, 1985, 1988; Gamlin & Fleming, 1985, Chapter 6). I would argue that the development of symbolic competence is one of the "strengths" of traditional Native Indian child rearing practices, a "difference" not of kind but of emphasis. And again, I would suggest that these "differences" are highly valued in contemporary Western society. As I see it, the development of symbolic competence offers the most potential for modifiability. The use of metaphor, for example, makes it possible to transfer knowledge from one conceptual domain to another and, in addition, provides a vehicle whereby existing knowledge may be reorganized and in some cases radically restructured (see Vosniadou & Brewer, 1987). Of course, attitudinal factors such as "learned helplessness" may interfere in the use of this kind of potential.

I will go back to my opening comments to suggest that it is by understanding what is common across cultures that we begin to understand the uniquely stressed aspects of particular cultures. We achieve harmony in this strategy as we learn how to celebrate difference.

REFERENCES

Alloy, L. B., Abramson, L. Y., Peterson, C., & Seligman, M. E. (1984). Attributional style and the generality of learned helplessness. Journal of Personality and Social Psychology, 46(3), 681-687.

Blatz, W. E. (1944). Understanding the young child. Toronto: Clarke, Irwin.

Blatz, W. E. (1966). Human security: Some reflections. Toronto: University of Toronto Press.

Bretherton, I., & Waters, E. (Eds.). (1985). Growing points of attachment theory and research. Monographs of the Society for Research in Child Development, 50. (1-2, Serial No. 209).

Brown, A. L., & Ferrara, R. A. (1985). Diagnosing zones of proximal development. In J. V. Wertsch (Ed.), Culture, communication and cognition: Vygotskian perspectives. New York: Cambridge University Press.

Campione, J. C., Brown, A. L., & Bryant, N. R. (1984). The zone of proximal development: Implications for individual differences and learning. In B. Rogoff & J. V. Wertsch (Eds.), Children's learning in the "zone of proximal development." San Francisco: Jossey-Bass.

Diener, I. I., & Dweck, C. S. (1980). An analysis of learned helplessness: II. The processing of success. Journal of Personality and Social Psychology, 39(5), 940-952.

Dweck, C. S. (1986). Motivational processes affecting learning. American Psychologist, 41(10), 1040-1048.

Feuerstein, R. (1980). Instrumental enrichment: An intervention program for cognitive modifiability. Baltimore: University Park Press.

Forsterling, F. (1986). Attributional conceptions in clinical psychology. American Psychologist, 41(3), 275-285.

Gamlin, P. J. (1985). Cognitive strategies in cognitive assessments: An intercultural perspective. In R. J. Samuda & A. Wolfgang (Eds.), Intercultural counselling and assessment: A global perspective. Toronto: Hogrefe.

Gamlin, P. J. (1988). Blatz, Vygotsky, and attributional conceptions: Implications for security theory. In R. Volpe, E. Flint, & R. D. fleming (Eds.), Consciousness and consequences: A festschrift for William E. Blatz. University of Toronto Press.

Gamlin, P. J., & Fleming, D. R. (1985). Responding to individual needs: A guide for teachers. Toronto: Hogrefe.

Heider, F. (1985). The psychology of interpersonal relations. New York: Wiley.

Laboratory of Comparative Human Cog. (1986). Contributions of cross-cultural research to educational practice. American Psychologist, 41(10), 1049-1058.

More, A. J. (1986, May). Progress report review of research on Native learning styles: For executive meeting Mohokit Indian education research association. London, Ontario, Canada.

Vosniadou, S., & Brewer, W. F. (1987). Knowledge restructuring in development: A theoretical review. Review of Educational Research, 57(1), 51-67.

Vygotsky, L. (1962). Thought and language. Cambridge, MA: MIT Press. (Original work published in 1934).

Vygotsky, L. (1978). Mind in society: The development of higher psychological processes. Cambridge, MA: MIT Press. (Original work published in 1934).

Vygotsky, L. (1986). Thought and language (A. Kozulin, Trans.). Cambridge, MA: MIT Press. (Original work published in 1934).

Whiting, B. B. (1980). Culture and social behavior. Ethos, 8, 95-116.

HOFSTEDE'S CULTURE DIMENSIONS AND ROKEACH'S VALUES: HOW RELIABLE IS THE RELATIONSHIP?

Barbara B. Ellis
University of Connecticut
Storrs, U.S.A.

INTRODUCTION

In his book Culture's Consequences, Hofstede has presented a taxonomy of four dimensions of culture based on data from a large scale cross-national study involving over 40 countries. Subjects, primarily employees of a multinational business organization, responded to a paper-and-pencil survey of work-related values. An ecological factor analysis of country mean responses revealed four factors:

1. Power Distance - Power Distance refers to "the extent to which a society accepts the fact that power in institutions and organizations is distributed unequally" (Hofstede, 1980b, p. 45).

2. Uncertainty Avoidance - Uncertainty Avoidance refers to "the extent to which a society feels threatened by uncertain and ambiguous situations and tries to avoid these situations by providing greater stability, establishing more formal rules, not tolerating deviant ideas and behaviors, and believing in absolute truths and the attainment of expertise" (Hofstede, 1980b, p. 45).

3. Individualism / Collectivism - The Individualism / Collectivism dimension refers to the value a society places upon the "I" versus the "we", or the degree of inter-dependence among individuals within a particular society (Hofstede & Bond, 1984).

4. Masculinity / Femininity - The Masculinity dimension refers the extent to which a society values traditionally male qualities i.e., "assertiveness, the acquisition money and things", versus the value placed on those things associated with femininity, i.e., "caring for others, the quality of life or people" (Hofstede, 1980b, p. 46).

Hofstede and others have validated these four cultural dimensions by
demonstrating their correlation with other survey instruments
administered in numerous countries. Hofstede and Bond (1984)
demonstrated the ecological correlation between Hofstede's dimensions
and Rokeach's Value Survey (Rokeach, 1973) in a group of six countries
(Australia, Hong Kong, India, Japan, New Zealand, and Taiwan).
Rokeach's Value Survey (1973) consists of 18 "terminal" and 18
"instrumental" values. "Terminal" values are those beliefs that are
related to final end-states such as "a world at peace" or "salvation".
"Instrumental" values are those beliefs related to modes of conduct
such as "honest" or "obedient". Subjects must rank each list of 18
values according to their importance as guiding principles in life.

Hofstede and Bond (1984) have identified the values in Rokeach's
survey which were shown to be related to Hofstede's dimensions of
culture on the basis of an ecological factor analysis of mean country
scores from Asian and Pacific countries. The relationships at the
aggregate level are as follows:

   1. High Power Distance was associated with high value for
   "salvation", "courageous", "capable", "social recognition",
   and "imaginative".

   2. High Femininity was associated with high value for
   "independent", "self-controlled", "inner harmony", "social
   justice", and "self-respect".

   3. High Uncertainty Avoidance was associated with high value
   for "cheerful", "polite", "obedient", "happiness", and "a
   comfortable life"

   4. High Individualism was associated with high values of "an
   exciting life" and "a world of beauty".

The present study entails a shift in the level of analysis from that
used by Hofstede. The analysis was done within rather than across
countries. It is, of course, clear that the same relationships that
exist at the aggregate level do not necessarily exist at the
individual level. However, from the standpoint of generalizability,
it would be desirable to determine whether the same relationships
exist at both levels. Therefore, predictions within countries were
made on the basis of Hofstede and Bond's transnational ecological
findings.

Germany and America were the two national cultures examined in the
present study. Predictions regarding Rokeach value rankings were made
on the basis of Germans' and Americans' standings on Hofstede's
cultural dimensions.

Hofstede (1980) has reported that American and German country scores differ most on the dimensions of Uncertainty Avoidance and Individualism. Germany scored higher than America on Uncertainty Avoidance, and America scored higher than Germany on Individualism. There was relatively little difference between Germany and America on Power Distance and Masculinity.

In keeping with the Hofstede and Bond (1984) results, the following predictions were made:

1. Germans, being higher on Uncertainty Avoidance, would rank the Rokeach values "polite", "obedient", and "a comfortable life" higher than Americans. (Note: The values "cheerful" and "happiness" tested in the Hofstede and Bond (1984) study were taken from an earlier version of Rokeach's Value Survey and could not be tested in the present study which employed the most recent version of this survey.)

2. Americans, being higher on Individualism, would rank "an exciting life" and "a world of beauty" higher than Germans.

• METHOD

Procedure. The most recent version of Rokeach's Value Survey, Form G, was translated into German. A German translation of an earlier version of the survey, Form E, (Morris, 1975) served as a starting point for the translation. The two forms differ with respect to one "terminal" value and one "instrumental" value. The "terminal" value "happiness" is replaced by "health", and the "instrumental" value "cheerful" is replaced by "loyal". The new values were translated into German by a bilingual, native-speaking German and back-translated into English by a bilingual, native-speaking American. Differences were reconciled collaboratively.

The German version of Rokeach's Value Survey was administered to a sample of 39 male and female German subjects, most of whom were college students. The English version was administered to 56 male and female American college students.

Analysis. Mean ranks for German and American subjects were determined and t-tests were used to test the differences between the means. Composite ranks were assigned to each value, i.e., the rank order of the mean scores, and the Pearson rank order correlation coefficients were calculated.

RESULTS

The mean and standard deviations of the rankings of the 18 "terminal"
values are presented in Table 1. Overall there was significant
agreement between Americans and Germans in their rankings of the
"terminal" values. The rank order correlation of composite ranks was
.77 (p <.01). However, when considered individually, Americans' and
Germans' rankings differed significantly on seven "terminal" values.
Americans ranked the values "a comfortable life", "family security"
and "salvation" significantly higher than Germans. German subjects
ranked "a world at peace", "a world of beauty", "health", and "wisdom"
significantly higher than American subjects.

The means and standard deviations of the rankings of the 18
"instrumental" values are presented in Table 2. Again, there was
significant overall agreement between the American and German
composite ranks of "instrumental" values. The rank order correlation
was .81 (p <.01). Nevertheless, when considered individually,
Americans' and Germans' rankings differed significantly on seven of
the 18 "instrumental" values. Americans ranked the values "ambitious",
"obedient", and "self-controlled" significantly higher than Germans.
The values "courageous", "imaginative", "intellectual", and "logical"
were ranked significantly higher by Germans than by Americans.

Predictions regarding differences in Americans' and Germans' rankings
for Rokeach Values on the basis of the relative standing of the two
national groups on the Uncertainty Avoidance and Individualism
dimensions were not borne out by the data. Because Germans scored
higher on Uncertainty Avoidance than Americans, it was predicted that
they would rank the values "polite", "obedient", and "a comfortable
life" higher than Americans. The difference between Americans' and
Germans' rankings of the value "polite" were not significant, and in
the case of "obedient" and "a comfortable life", Americans ranked
these values significantly higher than Germans, contrary to
expectations.

Similarly, the data did not support the second hypothesis, that
Americans, who scored higher on Individualism than Germans, would rank
the values "an exciting life" and "a world of beauty" higher than
Germans. In the present study, Americans and Germans did not differ
in their rankings of "an exciting life", and Germans ranked the value
"a world of beauty" higher than Americans.

Table 1

Mean Rankings of 18 Terminal Values for Americans and Germans

		Americans	Germans
A COMFORTABLE LIFE	****	9.70 (4.5)	13.35 (3.7)
AN EXCITING LIFE		10.11 (4.4)	9.05 (4.7)
A SENSE OF ACCOMPLISHMENT		7.25 (3.8)	7.37 (4.7)
A WORLD AT PEACE	****	10.81 (5.1)	6.68 (4.7)
A WORLD OF BEAUTY	*	14.19 (3.3)	12.16 (4.2)
EQUALITY		11.08 (4.2)	11.54 (4.5)
FAMILY SECURITY	****	6.36 (4.5)	10.00 (4.1)
FREEDOM		7.17 (4.2)	6.79 (4.4)
HEALTH	*	5.89 (4.4)	4.05 (3.5)
INNER HARMONY		6.45 (4.9)	8.42 (5.0)
MATURE LOVE		7.49 (4.1)	7.63 (4.5)
NATIONAL SECURITY		15.04 (3.6)	13.49 (3.8)
PLEASURE		10.87 (3.9)	10.53 (3.9)
SALVATION	*	14.32 (5.2)	16.26 (4.0)
SELF RESPECT		5.38 (3.7)	4.68 (2.9)
SOCIAL RECOGNITION		12.98 (3.9)	11.27 (4.3)
TRUE FRIENDSHIP		7.06 (3.8)	7.46 (3.9)
WISDOM	*	8.77 (4.5)	6.87 (3.9)

* $p < .05$
** $p < .01$
*** $p < .001$
**** $p < .0001$
Note: Numbers in parentheses are standard deviations.

Table 2

Mean Rankings of 18 Instrumental Values for Americans and Germans

		Americans	Germans
AMBITIOUS	****	8.58 (4.5)	13.21 (4.3)
BROADMINDED		6.73 (4.6)	5.84 (3.9)
CAPABLE		9.73 (4.3)	10.45 (3.5)
CLEAN		14.65 (4.1)	15.50 (3.1)
COURAGEOUS	****	11.71 (4.4)	8.03 (3.7)
FORGIVING		9.29 (4.1)	9.29 (4.2)
HELPFUL		9.00 (4.5)	9.26 (4.2)
HONEST		4.60 (3.6)	5.29 (4.7)
IMAGINATIVE	***	10.02 (4.7)	7.50 (3.6)
INDEPENDENT		7.55 (4.9)	8.13 (4.0)
INTELLECTUAL	*	8.76 (4.7)	6.89 (3.9)
LOGICAL	*	11.51 (4.1)	9.55 (4.7)
LOVING		6.05 (4.7)	4.47 (4.3)
LOYAL		8.07 (5.2)	7.36 (3.9)
OBEDIENT	****	15.31 (2.9)	17.13 (1.3)
POLITE		12.44 (3.9)	13.53 (3.1)
RESPONSIBLE		5.87 (3.9)	6.11 (4.2)
SELF-CONTROLLED	*	11.18 (5.0)	13.11 (3.5)

*	$p < .05$
**	$p < .01$
***	$p < .001$
****	$p < .0001$

Note: Numbers in parentheses are standard deviations.

DISCUSSION

With respect to the primary purpose of the present study, that is to examine the replicability of the relationship between Hofstede's culture dimensions and Rokeach's Value Survey, the results were not positive. None of the predictions made on the basis of the Hofstede and Bond study regarding American and German rankings of five Rokeach Values were supported by the present data.

There are a number of possible explanations for these negative findings. First of all, the fact that the samples were relatively small and that the German sample differed slightly in composition from the American sample may have influenced the results.

Another possible explanation for the unsuccessful prediction of value rankings is that the national cultures examined in the present study lie outside the cluster of national cultures examined in the Hofstede and Bond study. The national groups examined in the latter study were Asian and Pacific countries. It may be too much to expect that factors generated on the basis of data from these groups would be useful in making predictions for Western cultures such as America and Germany. A test of this explanation would be an ecological factor analysis, i.e., a factor analysis of country mean scores, of Rokeach's values and the subsequent examination of the relationship of these factors to Hofstede's dimensions using Western countries.

Finally, these unexpected results may have been due to the fact that the factor analysis was at the individual rather than at the ecological level. As Hofstede has pointed out, just because two variables correlate at the aggregate level does not necessarily mean that they will correlate at the individual level. It is possible that within a country, variables X and Y may be correlated in the opposite direction from which they are correlated across countries at the aggregate level, or they may not be correlated at all.

Indeed, Hofstede and Spangenberg (1987) have noted this lack of transference from one level to the other. They pointed out that the concept of Individualism operationalized at the aggregate level could not be used to measure this construct at either the occupational or organizational level. On the other hand, there was some support for the Masculinity/ Femininity dimension at the occupational and the organizational level of analysis. Hofstede and Spangenberg (1987) indicated that the Individualism/Collectivism and Uncertainty Avoidance dimensions may be most sensitive to the shift in level of analysis and, therefore, probably require different operationalization at different levels of analysis. The authors proposed that the Power

Distance and Masculinity/Femininity dimensions can probably be measured in the same way at different levels with the exception of the individual person (Hofstede & Spangenberg, 1987, p. 121). A study by Bosland (1985) indicated that none of Hofstede's culture dimensions could be replicated in a factor analysis of the Value Survey Module at the individual level.

How reasonable is it to expect that findings at the ecological level will survive the shift to other levels of analysis? Ecological analysis is certainly useful and informative for cross-cultural research. Indeed, it may be the only logical starting point for cross-cultural research. However, many researchers also want to gain understanding of the differences and similarities among variables measured across individuals within national cultures. For example, it is important to know that mean country scores on Rokeach's values "an exciting life" and "a world of beauty" are related to Individualism scores across ten Asian and Pacific national cultures. However, it would also be useful to know whether and how these two values are related to Individualism within those national groups. The degree to which findings at the aggregate level can be expected to be replicated at other levels of analysis, including the individual level, is a question for empirical evaluation.

On the more positive side, the present study reveals some interesting results with respect to the differences and similarities between Americans and Germans with respect to Rokeach's Values. When values are examined individually, there are significant differences between Americans' and Germans' mean rankings for 7 out of 18 "terminal" values and for 7 out of 18 "instrumental" values. Americans tend to place higher value on those end states and modes of conduct that can be termed "task-oriented" or "pragmatic", for example "a comfortable life", "family security", "ambitious", "obedient", and "self-controlled". The only value that does not readily fit this categorization is "salvation". Germans, on the other hand, tend to place significantly higher value on those end states and modes of conduct that can be termed "idealistic", for example "a world at peace", "a world of beauty", "wisdom", "courageous", "imaginative", and "intellectual". Only two values, "health" and "logical", do not fit this pattern.

It is interesting to note the degree of agreement in ranking the "terminal" and "instrumental" values within each group. For Americans and Germans the smallest standard deviations (i.e., the greatest agreement) was shown for the value "obedient". Both Americans and Germans rank "obedient" as being least important as a guiding principle in their lives. Intuitively this result seems to fit the high Individualism score for Americans (highest of the 40 countries measured by Hofstede). However, this result is counter intuitive in the case of Germans. Logically one would expect that Germans, who are higher on the Collectivism end of the dimension, would place a higher value on "obedience" relative to Americans. One may speculate that low value placed on "obedience" by German college students may be a reaction to the negative implications of being an obedient member of German society during World War II. A test of this hypothesis would be a comparison of the rankings of Rokeach's Values given by German college students with those given by older Germans.

Finally, the results of the present study indicate that overall there is significant agreement between Americans and Germans in their rankings of Rokeach's "terminal" and "instrumental" values. The rank order correlations for both surveys were .77 and .81 respectively. In spite of the fact that Americans and Germans differ in some specific values, there is an impressively high level of agreement between the two national groups in terms of their overall pattern of values. These results provide insight and encouragement for those who seek to foster and improve relations between the citizens of America and Germany.

REFERENCES

Bosland, N. (1985). The (ab)use of the values survey module as a test of individual personality. Working Paper 85-1, Arnhem, Netherlands: Institute for Research on Intercultural Cooperation.

Hofstede, G. (1980a). Culture's consequences: International differences in work-related values. Beverly Hills, CA: Sage.

Hofstede, G. (1980b). Motivation, leadership, and organization: Do American theories apply abroad? Organizational Dynamics, Summer, 42-63.

Hofstede, G. (1982). Values survey module. Arnhem, Netherlands: Institute for Research on Intercultural Cooperation.

Hofstede, G., & Bond, M. H. (1984). Cultural dimensions: An independent validation using Rokeach's Value Survey. Journal of Cross-cultural Psychology, 15, 417-433.

Hofstede, G., & Spangenberg, J. (1987). Measuring individualism and collectivism at occupational and organizational levels. In C. Kagitcibasi (Ed.), Growth and progress in cross-cultural psychology (pp. 113-129). Lisse: Swets & Zeitlinger B. V.

Morris, C. A. (1975). Zeichen, Wert, Aesthetik. Frankfurt/M.: Suhrkamp.

Rokeach, M. (1973). Nature of human values. New York: The Free Press.

THE WISC-R IN A NATIVE APPLICATION: INTERNAL AND EXTERNAL ANALYSIS

Roland D. Chrisjohn
University of Guelph
Guelph, Canada

Shelagh M.J. Towson
University of Windsor
Windsor, Canada

Deborah F. Pace
Utah State University
Logan, U.S.A.

Michael Peters
University of Guelph
Guelph, Canada

INTRODUCTION

In the summer of 1985 we were approached by the Band Council of the Kainai of southern Alberta to help identify children in need of special education services, as well as to undertake a general survey of the status of reserve-based education. We made a special effort to avoid practices of which we had been critical (Chrisjohn and Lanigan, 1986), and initiated a process of assessment, data gathering, and analysis we hoped would be more valid and useful than typical research with Indian nations. This report is one in a series describing this project (Chrisjohn, Towson, Goodstriker, Pace, and Peters, 1986; Chrisjohn, Towson, and Peters, 1988), and will deal specifically with our use and analysis of the Revised Wechsler Intelligence Scale for Children (WISC-R; Wechsler, 1974).

The decision to use the WISC-R was based on its popularity, its extensive literature (much of it bearing on the assessment of Indian children; McShane and Plas, 1984), and the range of tasks of potential relevance to educational evaluation of children. Unlike any of the previous applications we have found, we took seriously Irvine's (1985; Irvine and Sanders, 1972) warning that one cannot assume that a test measures the same "thing" in disparate groups, and instituted a number of modifications in keeping with his suggestions for increasing the comparability of tests across cultures. First, the item content was changed to reflect Canadian rather than American life. These changes are common in the use of the Wechsler series by Canadian psychologists (e.g., Crawford and Boer, 1985). Second, community members were asked for their input concerning possible problems in tests and procedures. Their ideas were noted and incorporated as far as possible into test administration and project operation. Third, members of the community were trained to administer the test under the supervision of qualified psychologists. This feature was crucial, in that Kainai testers would be more sensitive to language and cultural issues than testers from outside the reserve, thereby reducing errors associated with the social situation of testing. This procedure, long advocated by Irvine and others, has seldom if ever been adopted in research with Indians. Fourth, the Kainai testers were encouraged to put their knowledge of their culture into practice in the testing sessions, breaking the testing session when they felt the child's interest was flagging, explaining subtest instructions in Blackfoot when understanding of the English instructions was suspect, and rating each session in terms of how well the child's performance captured what the child was capable of doing. Finally, for our own reasons, minor modifications were made in some of the test procedures: the stopping criterion for some of the tests (for instance, Vocabulary) was increased by two, and the testers were told to allow children to go beyond time limits for other tests (for example, Block Design). This would permit clearer identification of items violating the difficulty sequence of the subtests. For all analyses presented here, however, items answered correctly outside the strict scoring protocol of the WISC-R were treated as incorrect.

INTERNAL AND EXTERNAL ANALYSIS

We have no reason to doubt that in clinical practice with Indian students the WISC-R is administered, scored, and interpreted without much question about its applicability. We have reviewed reports, sponsored by Indian bands or Indian Affairs, that have claimed 75% of the children assessed were "brain-damaged" or "learning disabled". When the WISC-R has been used to support such claims, no apparent attention has been given to evaluation of the psychometric or statistical properties of the scores.

The situation is little better in published material. Most of literature (McShane and Plas, 1984) either starkly reports subtest and composite averages as if such information is absolute; compares subtest and composite scores with other, presumably appropriate, reference groups; or derives popular but questionable composites of subtest scores and employs them as indices of disability. The N's in this research are generally miniscule, and psychometric data unreported (if calculated).

There are several more sophisticated reports that use subscale scores in factor analyses, but even these are subject to criticism: 1) the sample sizes are too small to trust the results; 2) the WISC-R has a theoretical structure (c.f. Kaufman, 1979) which should be tested explicitly and either accepted or modified; and 3) use of the subtest scores presumes each subtest is psychometrically well-behaved (Guilford, 1954). Ignorance of or inattention to the requirements of factor analytic procedures have generated a number of papers or conference presentations reaching questionable conclusions about the nature of Indian cognition.

There exits relatively few papers that, quite properly, have focused on the issue of whether subscale scores are psychometrically sound (Seyfort, Spreen, and Lahmer, 1980; Mueller, Mulcahy, Wilgosh, Watters, and Mancini, 1986; Mishra, 1982). In all cases, evidence has been found that the subtests examined perform differently in Indian samples, or are actually biased against Indians. While the work these researchers have started is incomplete, their results undercut the findings of those who have taken the WISC-R scores for granted.

It seemed to us that any reasonable examination of the Kainai WISC-R data required two kinds of analyses: analyses concerning the properties of the individual subtests (which we will call internal), and analyses concerning the relation between the individual subtests (which we will call external). Our terminology differs somewhat from Embretson's (1983), and indeed, we had hoped to do additional analyses relating WISC-R results to academic achievement, personality and motivational tests, etc., which would be more in keeping with her suggestions. However, we have not as yet been able to solve some problems associated with such analyses in our data set, and limit this report to examination of the WISC-R.

Methods for Internal Analysis. The psychometric properties of the individual subtests are readily examined by formal item analytic techniques. The WISC-R subscales are supposed to be unidimensional, with items ordered from least to most difficult. Our procedures examined these hypotheses in the Kainai data, as well as generating information on subtest reliability and item discrimination.

Three subtests (Information, Similarities, and Arithmetic) are composed of dichotomous items, and for these we used BILOG (Mislevy and Bock, 1986), fitting a two-parameter latent trait model. Details of latent trait theory may be found in psychometric textbooks, but for present purposes it is sufficient to say the model supposes for each subtest a single latent dimension, with the items having varying degrees of difficulty, and differing degrees of ability to distinguish students' status on the latent dimension. BILOG produces a test of the unidimensionality hypothesis, an index of how strongly each item relates to the latent dimension, an item discrimination index, and a reliability estimate (an internal consistency estimate similar to Lord's stepped-up reliability formula). It also generates scores for each respondent (based on the two-parameter model) which can be used for later external analyses.

The remaining subtests are composed of items with graduated scoring schemes. Although procedures exist to analyze such items via latent trait theory, they were only recently available to us. Hence, we employed Nishisato's (1980) dual scaling technique for multiple choice data. Nishisato's procedure is a version of the well-known Guttman (1941) scaling procedure, and generates item discrimination indices, internal consistency estimates, and scores for respondents. Guttman scaling is mathematically related to latent trait theory, and for our purposes no problems arise from conjoining the techniques.

Methods for External Analysis. Once we had some basis for believing that the subtest scores were not fictions (that is, that reliability was high enough to entertain the idea that the WISC-R was measuring something), the structure of the WISC-R for Kainai students was examined. While the correlated two-factor structure (implicit in the scoring rules) seemed a natural starting point, a recent paper by Kroonenberg and ten Berge (1987) provided an alternative, developed using normative WISC-R data and replicated in a variety of samples. The generalized structure Kroonenber and ten Berge (1987) suggested was essentially Kaufman's (1979) Verbal Comprehension, Perceptual Organization, and Freedom from Distractability solution, and their paper provided a technique (perfect congruence analysis) for comparing any WISC-R data set with their results.

It is possible that the scores obtained using BILOG and dual scaling could differ substantially from the scores obtained from the standard WISC-R scoring procedures. The comparability of scores was examined using LISREL (Joreskog and Sorbom, 1981) and found to yield indistinguishable covariance structures. For the rest of this paper we report analyses based on the standard WISC-R scaled scores.

Description of the Data Set. Responses were obtained for 332 students (189 female; 143 male) attending reserve schools in grades K through 12. WISC-R scale scores were obtained for all 12 subtests, but in the descriptive statistics reported here, Mazes results were uniformly substituted for Coding. Some of the Coding subtest results were suspect, in that some of the stopwatches being used required two full sweeps for a minute and some children were given insufficient time to complete the test.

Since Kroonenberg and ten Berge (1987) dropped Mazes from their analyses, our application of their technique was based on only those results where the Coding subtest was not suspect (N=309). Again, for the internal analyses reported, credit was not given for correct answers obtained by going beyond standard scoring protocols.

Although this sample is as large as any we have found in the literature on Indian IQ testing, we must empahsize that it is a small sample. It must be regarded as such because our analyses collapsed across age groups. If there is anything to the notion of age-related changes in cognitive structures, then our procedure would have blurred potentially important distinctions. Kroonenberg and ten Berge (1987) discuss this and similar limitations of many existing WISC-R studies.

We must also emphasize that these data are not comparable to anything done previously. Our selection of test administrators and the techniques they were trained to follow was designed to maximize the performance of the Kainai children. To the extent that such considerations have not arisen in previous research, our results are not comparable either to existing non-Indian research, or to other studies of Indian children.

RESULTS

Internal Analyses. Using the standard WISC-R scoring procedures, mean
Verbal IQ was 95.20 (s.d. of 16.67), mean Performance IQ was 108.37
(s.d. of 14.99), and mean Full Scale IQ was 101.46 (s.d. of 15.58).
These results are quite within expectations for normal children living
in a bilingual subculture.

The results of the internal analyses are summarized in Table 1.
The reliabilities are the BILOG estimates for the Information, Picture
Completion, and Arithmetic subtests, and maximized coefficient alphas
for the remaining ones. Problem items are listed for each subtest.

Table 1.

Internal Analysis of

WISC-R Subtests

Subtest	Reliability	Problem Items
Information	.897	8, 16, 17, 18(a,b), 19, 20, 21, 23, 24, 25, 26, 27, 30
Similarities	.893	14(b,c), 16(c)
Arithmetic	.828	8(a,b)
Vocabulary	.877	10, 20(b), 22
Comprehension	.855	12, 16, 54
Picture Comp.	.823	1, 6, 10, 12, 13, 17, 18(b), 25
Picture Arrang.	.822	10
Block Design	.866	
Object Assembly	.760	
Mazes	.736	

a = deviates significantly from 2-parameter model
b = low discrimination index
c = ordering of item option scores not incremental

Note: Reliability not estimated for Coding and Digit Span.

All items listed deviated by more than 2 places from their presumed rank (as given in the WISC-R manual), and additional information is provided concerning items that 1) deviated substantially from the 2-parameter model (when BILOG was used); 2) showed poor discrimination according to BILOG or dual scaling criteria; or 3) had a non-monotonic ordering of item response categories from the dual scaling analysis.

Overall, the WISC-R performed well in the conditions specified. Subtest reliabilities are comparable to those reported in the manual (although those are split-half estimates), and most items are well-behaved. An exception is the Information subtest, where nearly half the items demonstrate some problem. In general these difficulties are in the ordering of the items, and since standard instructions require stopping after 5 consecutive failures, it is possible that Indian children are receiving low scores because of being administered unfairly difficult items. Picture Completion also shows ordering anomalies, but the error is in the direction of being too easy for the Kainai children, rather than too difficult.

The reliabilities are low enough to suggest that the subtests are not "purely" unidimensional, but sufficiently high to warrant entry into factor analysis (Guilford, 1954). Examination of dimensionality of the subtests will be left for another time.

Again, we must point out that these results do not bear on either the quality or the advisability of previous research. We adapted procedures in the hope of achieving maximal performance from the Kainai children, and may have achieved this. Simply because we attained reliabilities of moderate size is no reason to assume that other applications of the WISC-R to Indian children have been as fortunate.

External Analysis. Results of fitting the Kainai WISC-R correlation matrix to Kroonenberg and ten Berge's (1987) general structure by perfect congruence analysis are presented in Table 2. The congruence analysis was performed using the GAUSS (Edlefsen and Jones, 1986) programming package.

First we give the loading matrix obtained by aligning the Kainai data to congruence with the generalized structure. The Verbal Comprehension, Perceptual Organization, and Freedom from Distractability components are clearly represented in the Kainai data. The variance explained by each of the components is comparable, in size and order, to the results obtained by Kroonenberg and ten Berge (1987) for the WISC-R standardization sample. Correlations between components were marginally different from zero, as Kroonenberg and ten Berge predict. In all, the Kainai results are indistinguishable from those obtained from the overwhelmingly non-Indian original sample. Like Kroonenberg and ten Berge, also analyzing data obtained from Indian samples, we find no reason to suppose that Indian cognitive structure, as reflected in WISC-R performance, is any different from that of any other group.

Table 2.

Perfect Congruence Component Loadings

for Kainai WISC-R Data

Subtest	VC	PO	FD
Information	.849	.261	.156
Similarities	.886	.281	.083
Arithmetic	.516	.269	.484
Vocabulary	.906	.224	.123
Comprehension	.886	.145	.054
Digit Span	.270	.052	.688
Picture Comp.	.325	.587	.097
Picture Arrang.	.328	.576	.266
Block Design	.204	.690	.392
Object Assembly	.082	.783	.187
Coding	-.013	.362	.646
Variance Explained	3.71	2.19	1.44
Percentage of Total	33.73	19.91	13.09

Some Practical Applications. A colleague of ours insisted that the Verbal-Performance discrepancy we found still lent support to the notion of racial differences. We dispute the utility of this index (c.f., Kavale and Forness, 1985), but in response have prepared Table 3, which gives an "overlapping averages" account of Kainai performance on the usual WISC-R composites. Data from the three youngest age groups were combined, and the means of the IQ subscores calculated. The youngest age was dropped, and the next age group added, and so on to the 14-to-16 age group. The moving average table gives more stable estimates than if each age group is reported separately, since N is larger.

As can clearly be seen, the V-P discrepancy is minimal at early ages, and increases eventually to an average 17 point difference in the 14-to-16 group. It is tempting to say that the discrepancy increases as a function of exposure to the non-Indian educational system (although located on the Blood Reserve, the school system is operated by the Department of Indian Affairs), but this is perhaps too flippant. Cohort effects and other factors undoubtedly play a role in these results. What is important is that a deficiency in brain "hard-wiring" is completely inconsistent with the clear trends in the data.

Table 3.

Overlapping Averages of Scaled WISC-R

Aggregate Test Scores

Age Group	N	Verbal	Performance	Full Scale
6, 7, 8	101	106	114	111
7, 8, 9	105	100	112	106
8, 9, 10	82	98	111	104
9, 10, 11	74	93	109	100
10, 11, 12	64	92	107	99
11, 12, 13	76	90	105	97
12, 13, 14	84	90	104	96
13, 14, 15	87	89	105	96
14, 15, 16	82	87	104	94

CONCLUSIONS

Whether or not our investigation has found out anything important about Indian cognition is, we feel, still open to question. What is significant is that, under the conditions described, Kainai children produced results indistinguishable from non-Indians. For us, this bears directly on previous research that has used WISC-R data to conclude Indians are inferior to non-Indians, and on unpublished studies characterizing Indian children as disabled or brain-damaged learners. As reviewed in Chrisjohn and Peters (1986a; 1986b), and in Chrisjohn, Towson, and Peters (1987), there are many latently racist viewpoints current in Indian education theory. Our results suggest that, when recommended procedures for cross-cultural assessment are practiced (Irvine, 1985), there is no Indian/non-Indian distinction to be made. To the extent that Irvine's procedures are not followed, adverse conclusions drawn are suspect. The WISC-R results are no more absolute than any psychological test.

It is a cliche to call for more research, but we are reduced to it here. We are uncomfortable with the obvious deficiencies of our own research (small N's, collapsed across age groups, for example), and hope for the opportunity to extend it, again, in accordance with principles of sound cross-cultural assessment. A formal items bias study, and more elaborate mapping of the age-related discrepancy trend, are two obvious studies arising out of the findings. We are also working on a formal examination of subtest dimensionality in our data. Part of the difficulty in continuing our line of investigation is the absence of modern, sophisticated analyses of WISC-R items, a task we gladly leave for others.

While our research may appear to bear more directly on the technical, rather than practical, side of psychometrics, we believe everyone working with Indian children has a commitment to fair and accurate assessments of a child's potential. Characterizing a child (indeed, a race) as cognitively inferior when he/she isn't is at least as damaging as the converse, and we urge applied psychometricians to take seriously Irvine's cautions about the social situation of assessment. Perhaps then such information will bear more securely on identifying what differences there actually may be between Indians and non-Indians, rather than fuel base prejudices looking for "scientific" justification.

NOTE 1: Thanks are due Dana Harrison, Mel MacLean, Paul van Katwyc, & Tanya Pace for their help in data entry and analysis. This research was supported by the Kainai Band Council, by whose permission this work is possible. Throughout the paper we use the terms "Indian" and "Native" rather than listing all possible names for the aboriginal nations of North America.

REFERENCES

Chrisjohn, R. D., & Lanigan, C. B. (1986). Research on Indian intelligence testing: Review and prospects. In H. McCue and R. Anthony (Eds.), Selected papers from the first MOKAKIT conference. Vancouver: MOKAKIT (U.B.C.).

Chrisjohn, R. D., & Peters, M. (1986a). The right-brained Indian: fact or fiction? Journal of American Indian Education, 25, 1-7.

Chrisjohn, R. D., & Peters, M. (1986b). The pernicious myth of the right-brained Indian. Canadian Journal of Native Education, 13, 62-71.

Chrisjohn, R. D., Towson, S. M. J., & Peters, M. (1988). Indian achievement in schools: Adaptation to hostile environments. In J. Berry, S. Irvine, and E. Hunt (Eds.), Indigenous cognition: Functioning in cultural context. Dordrecht: Martinus Nijhoff.

Crawford, M. S., & Boer, D. P. (1985). Content bias in the WAIS-R Information subtest and some Canadian alternatives. Canadian Journal of Behavioral Sciences, 17, 79-86.

Edlefsen, L. E., & Jones, S. D. (1986). GAUSS mathematical and statistical system. Kent, Washington: APTECH systems.

Embretson, S. (1983). Construct validity: Construct representation versus nomothetic span. Psychological Bulletin, 93, 179-197.

Guilford, J. (1954). Psychometric methods. New York: McGraw-Hill.

Guttman, L. (1941). The quantification of a class of attributes:

A theory and method of scale construction. In P. Horst (Ed.), The prediction of personal adjustment. New York: Social Sciences Research Council.

Irvine, S. H. (1985). What does research have to say about the testing of minorities? In R. Samuda & A. Wolfgang (Eds.), Intercultural counselling and assessment: Global perspectives. Toronto: C. J. Hogrefe, Inc.

Irvine, S. H., & Sanders, J. T. (1972). Logic, language and method in construct identification across cultures. In L. Cronbach & P. Drenth (Eds.), Mental tests and cultural adaptation. The Hague: Mouton.

Joreskog, K., & Sorbom, D. (1981). LISREL V user's guide. Chicago: Internation.Educational Services.

Kaufman, A. S. (1979). Intelligence testing with the WISC-R. New York: Wiley.

Kavale, K. A., & Forness, S. R. (1985). The science of learning disabilities. San Diego: College Hill Press.

Kroonenberg, P. M., & ten Berge, J. (1987). Cross-validation of the WISC-R factorial structure. Applied Psychological Measurement, 11, 195-210.

McShane, D. & Plas, J. (1984). Cognitive functioning of American Indian children: Moving from the WISC to the WISC-R. School Psychology Review, 13, 61-73.

Mishra, S. (1982). The WISC-R and evidence of item bias for Native American Navajos. Psychology in the Schools, 19, 458-464.

Mislevy, R., & Bock, R. D. (1985). BILOG manual. Mooresville, Indiana: Scientific Software.

Mueller, H. H., Mulcahy, R. F., Wilgosh, L., Watters, B., & Mancini, G. J. (1986). An analysis of the WISC-R items responses with Canadian Inuit children. Alberta Journal of Educational Research, 32, 12-36.

Nishisato, S. (1980). Analysis of categorical data: Dual scaling and its applications. Toronto: University of Toronto Press.

Seyfort, B., Spreen, O., & Lahmer, V. (1980). A critical look at the WISC-R with Native Indian Children. Alberta Journal of Educational Research, 26, 14-24.

Wechsler, D. (1974). Manual for the Wechsler Intelligence Scale for Children-Revised. New York: Psychological Corporation.

Part V

SOCIAL AND PSYCHOLOGICAL PROBLEMS

A CONTINGENCY APPROACH FOR
PROMOTING INTERGROUP RELATIONS

Y. Amir and R. Ben-Ari
Bar-Ilan University
Ramat-Gan, Israël

The purpose of this paper is to discuss the application of knowledge about intergroup relations in dealing differentially with intergroup conflict, thereby producing better intergroup understanding and perceptions.

The existing ways of dealing with change in intergroup relations stem from three major models: The contact model, the information model, and the psychodynamic model. The contact model is based on the belief that intergroup contact will lead to a change in mutual attitudes and relations of the interacting members. Underlying this belief is the assumption that contact among individuals from diverse groups creates an opportunity for mutual acquaintance, enhances understanding and acceptance among the interacting group members, and consequently reduces intergroup prejudice, conflict, and tension (Allport, 1954; Cook, 1963). The underlying rationale for the contact model is that during contact, members of one group may discover new positive information about the members of the other group.

In order to achieve these positive ends, prerequisite conditions should be maintained during contact (Amir, 1969, 1976), such as: Equal status between the members of the interacting groups, intergroup co-operation in the pursuit of common goals, contact of an intimate rather than a casual nature, and a social climate supporting the intergroup contact.

The underlined word is *information model* focuses on the information available to members of one group about the other one (Brislin, 1986; Triandis, 1975). The main assumption of this model is that ignorance and lack of information comprise the basis for the development of prejudice, stereotypes, and the consequent tension between groups. Therefore, members of one group must understand the cultural characteristics of the other group before being able to understand and positively evaluate individual members of this group. An obvious way to achieve these goals is to recruit the means of mass communication and/or the educational system for the dissemination of the new information about the target culture.

Controversy exists as to the necessary focus of the information. One approach stresses an emphasis on group similarities in teaching the history of the different groups in the society, highlighting their achievements and contributions. Concentrating on the similarities should enhance intergroup attraction and understanding (Stephan & Stephan, 1984). The second approach focuses on group differences. Misperceptions and dissimilarities are assumed to be the basis of conflict. Accordingly, the focus should be on explaining and legitimizing the differences between the groups rather than ignoring them (Triandis, 1975). Both approaches share the underlying assumption that members of one group lack important information about the other group and this disrupts their possible understanding and positively perceiving the latter group.

The psychodynamic model assumes that the negative reactions of the individual toward members of the other group stem from problems in the individual's psychodynamic process and not necessarily with the target group itself. Therefore, only the treatment of the individual's personal problems or conflicts will lead to a positive change in his or her reaction toward the other group. The implementation of this model involves programs which may help participants to understand themselves and their own mental set-up, such as personal treatment, T-groups, or "new culture groups" (Gudykunst, Hammer, & Wiseman, 1977).

The amount of work produced in the last 20 years in developing programs and techniques to promote intergroup relations is quite impressive (Bennett, 1986; Landis & Brislin, 1983). Still, its quality and scientific sophistication are sometimes far from satisfying. Many "change" programs have been produced, but most have not clearly defined their objectives or theoretical basis. Implementation usually takes one of two forms. In the first, training utilizes one specific approach or technique which, even when theoretically well-conceived and technically excellent, is not necessarily geared towards solving the major intergroup problem at hand. The second form involves workshops or training programs which employ pieces and parts of different approaches and techniques. The idea is that if one approach does not attain the desired change, another one will do the trick. This is a "cookbook" approach, mixing many ingredients in different shapes and quantities. As we have already pointed out, the quality of the final product is often questionable.

It seems obvious that a major consideration in constructing ways and techniques for changing ethnic relations concerns who it is one wants to change, only later can one address how to change it. One must specify whether program goals focus on learning about the other culture, changing the readiness for social acceptance, developing a more positive emotional orientation, changing attitudes or perceptions, or something else. Goal delineation is crucial because different goals require different methods for their attainment. Moreover, the relevance of specific goals and the probability of their attainment may not be the same for the different cultural and ethnic groups involved in a certain conflict situation.

These issues will be illustrated by examples from intergroup relations in Israel - between Israeli Arabs and Jews, between Middle-Eastern and Western Jews, and between religious and secular Jews. Special emphasis will be given to the possibilities for producing intergroup change among youth or in the schools.

ARAB-JEWISH RELATIONS

Historical Background. The intergroup situation of the Jewish majority and the Arab minority in Israel can be typified as two groups living side by side as distinct entities. Their relations are characterized by an almost total separation in most areas of life and by some pronounced negative feelings and attitudes towards each other. These conditions of separatism among adults are accentuated among youth. Although the adult Jews and Arabs have some contact in various work settings, no such opportunity for contact exists among youth who reside in different localities and attend separate educational institutions.

Jews are generally oblivious to the realities of the Arab sector and do not exhibit much interest in Arabs and their culture. The Jewish educational system also exhibits conspicuous neglect of the Arab issue. Among Israeli Arabs, there is a strong feeling of minority discrimination and a heightened sensitivity to their being ignored by the Jewish majority.

This state of affairs, unchanged since the establishment of the State of Israel, has been sustained and intensified by the continuous conflict and tension between Israel and its Arab neighbors. However lately, after more than 30 years of Israel's independence and probably as a consequence of the peace treaty between Israel and Egypt, some change in the attitudes of both sides appears to have taken place (Amir & Ben-Ari, 1985). Both Jews and Arabs have gradually come to realize that they will have to continue to live together in one country. Consequently, some readiness can be detected to act towards changing the existing status quo in intergroup relations (Peled & Bar-Gal, 1983).

Goals and Techniques of Change. It is conceivable that some of the goals to be achieved are identical for both Arabs and Jews, while others may be unique to each group. Among the common goals for both Jews and Arabs in Israel one could suggest the change in negative attitudes and stereotypes, and an increased readiness to get to know, accept, and tolerate each other. As for distinctive goals, it may be worthwhile for Arabs, for example, to learn to function effectively in the Jewish society. The Israeli Arab lives in a country with a Jewish orientation and he constantly interacts with Jewish institutions and authorities. In order to function effectively, he must get acquainted with the Israeli Jewish society, its orientations, customs, and needs.

We should also take into account that neither side is interested in attaining social and cultural integration or in promoting interpersonal relations of an intimate nature. On the contrary, both sides favor strict cultural pluralism and each group prefers to retain its cultural and national uniqueness, social and physical separation, as well as a distinct group identity. In dealing with Arab and Jewish youth in Israel, we have to recognize that their separate educational systems are usually geographically distinct.

In this context, it appears worthwhile to consider the informational model. This approach focuses on providing essential information and changing misconceptions about the other group. The attainment of the goals may be facilitated by relating to the cognitive aspects of the problem, i.e., to supplying relevant and accurate information on the issue at hand. According to theory, the factual content regarding the other culture is critical for modifying perceptions which have been based on the absence of correct information or on misinformation. Theories maintain that stereotypes stem from negative associations formed about the other group and any positive associative content would be expected to promote the establishment of more positive attitudes and perceptions.

It also stands to reason that the informational approach may be acceptable in the schools because it is directly applicable to the general orientation of these institutions. The choice of the specific learning material should be accommodated to the span of interest and the level of maturation of the child.

Some major difficulties may hinder an extensive implementation of the contact approach. As was mentioned earlier, the Arab and Jewish populations in Israel live in geographically separated communities, creating an objective barrier in establishing contact between them. In addition, close relations between the groups, especially on a bisexual basis, may be considered by both national groups as highly undesirable and even threatening. Thus, although the direct contact may be potentially powerful as a vehicle for promoting better intergroup perceptions, attitudes and relations, its applicability to this situation is limited, maybe even negligible.

The psychodynamic approach does not seem relevant to the present case. Developing self-insight and sharing of feelings is difficult to implement on large populations, since it is basically an individualistic approach and is carried out in small groups. Since our aim is to work with large student populations, this approach is not promising. Moreover, it is questionable whether this approach is at all applicable to young people who may not be mature enough to profit from interactions involving self-evaluaion and sharing of feelings.

On the basis of the above considerations, it seems that the optimal orientation for the development of educational programs aiming to promote intergroup understanding and relations between the Arab and Jewish youth should be based upon the informational approach, i.e., learning about the other group and its culture, (possibly combined with a minimal number of intergroup meetings). We should, however, be aware of the limitations of any, even an optimal personal or interpersonal approach: Without a solution of this intergroup conflict at the macro-political level, the effects of micro-interventions will be highly limited.

RELATIONS BETWEEN WESTERN AND MIDDLE-EASTERN JEWS

Historical Background. The intergroup dynamics between Jews from Western and Middle-Eastern origin differ from those arising between Arabs and Jews. At present, each group comprises about half the Jewish population. Differences in cultural background and considerable differences in educational and occupational level have resulted in a high correspondence between ethnic background and social class. Westerners acquired solid social positions, while most Middle-Easterners populated the bottom of the social ladder. In addition, the encounter was and still is accompanied by prejudice, stereotypes, social distance, and tension.

In spite of this social-cultural cleavage, members of both groups identify themselves as members of a common Jewish people and show a basic sense of identification with the land and people of Israel. Ethnic interaction and integration is generally accepted as a national norm. As such, there is broad acceptance of the goal of ethnic mixing at least on the level of public proclamations. No institution or group opposes this policy in principle.

It is important to note that the percentage of Middle-Easterners belonging to and regarding themselves as part of Israel's middle-class society increases from year to year. Another, down-to-earth expression of the tendency towards interethnic mingling is the percentage of "mixed" marriages, which rose from 9% in 1952 to 21% in 1984. These trends contribute strongly to a de-emphasis of ethnic origin, especially among children and youth. The latter represent native Israelis, two or three generations distanced from the ethnic origin.

<u>Goals and Techniques of Change</u>. What seems to be the major problem to be overcome through interventions with these two ethnic groups? Is it the cognitive aspect, such as the two groups not knowing each other and consequently distorting perceptions about each other? Is the root of the problem emotional-personal, such as a low self-esteem of the "minority" group? Or could it be based on prejudice - because of historical, economic or ideological reasons?

All the above may have played some role in the past. At present, however, when we are already dealing with second and third generation Israelis, these features do not seem to represent the major social problem needed to be solved. The main aspects that still divide these two ethnic groups seem to be: (1) The <u>status</u> difference between the groups; (2) Some <u>social</u> rejection of Middle-Easterners by Westerners.

Even with regard to status and social relations, much has changed for the better during the last two decades. Many of the Middle-Easterners previously labeled low-class moved economically into the middle-class and were accepted as equals by the Western group. At the same time a change in the orientation of the Israeli society has been taking place during the last 25 years, namely, from an ethnic - to a class-conscious society. Thus, when class differences between the ethnic groups narrowed, the salience of ethnicity decreased. Still, social acceptance of Middle-Easterners by Westerners, especially when the former are from low social strata, is as yet a problem. This phenomenon seems to keep alive the social-psychological aspect of this intergroup conflict.

In light of this background, the question arises as to the most effective approach for reducing tension and promoting understanding and acceptance between Jewish youth from different ethnic origins. Clearly, the optimal solution in the case of Jewish and Arab groups - <u>learning</u> about the other group - does not seem to address the main difficulties of the Jewish groups. The perceived differences between these latter groups are not very marked to begin with and both groups know each other quite well. Similarly, the psychodynamic approach would not be appropriate in this case because of the same reasons mentioned with regard to the Arab-Jewish conflict.

The approach which seems worthy of consideration is that of interaction. This approach is generally accepted to be promising when dealing with social acceptance and attitude change regarding social-emotional aspects. Social psychological research has clearly shown that these goals can effectively be achieved through cross-ethnic interactions, while other approaches seem to have only limited effect (e.g., Amir, 1969, 1976). This is especially important, as the main need and consequently goal for promoting intergroup relations between Jewish youth from Western and Middle-Eastern backgrounds lies, as already stated earlier, in the sphere of social acceptance (Amir, Sharan & Ben-Ari, 1984).

RELATIONS BETWEEN RELIGIOUS AND SECULAR JEWS

Historical Background. Since the start of modern immigration movement of Jews to Israel at the turn of this century, relations between religious (sometimes called orthodox) and secular Jews were strained. This problem has gained momentum since the formal establishment of the State of Israel about 40 years ago. During the last decade these relationships have even become at times extremely tense and violent.

The exact numerical ratio of these groups is hard to determine, since it depends on how one defines what constitutes being religious or secular. Still, about 50 percent of the Israeli population would define themselves as secular, about 30 percent as "traditional", and 20 percent as religious. Most research findings indicate that the traditional group feels "nearer" in numerous respects to the secular group rather than to the religious one. Thus, there is a general consensus that the secular group comprises a majority, while the religious are in the minority.

The severity of the conflict between these groups stems from its ideological basis. The two groups are divided on major aspects of daily life: What should or should not a citizen be allowed to do? What code of ethics and law should be adopted - religious or civil? These codes do determine the everyday way of life of each citizen and, therefore major importance is attributed to it. The difficulty is that these two ways of life have many unbridgeable components, each of which founded on some ideological or religious basis on which there is naturally no agreement between the groups.

From a social-psychological point of view, most members of the two groups live separately, physically as well as mentally. In terms of attitudes and feelings towards different aspects of life, the two populations are extremely apart from each other. It is as if they were living on different social-psychological as well as physical planets (Barnea & Amir, 1981). Prejudice, intergroup rejection and alienation, as well as hatred and occasional violence are a natural as well as the actual consequence of such a social situation.

What makes things even more difficult is that lately a trend can be observed in both groups towards extremism. This is especially noticeable among religious youth, where the direction is toward religious fundamentalism. This radicalism is generally supported by the major social institutions of the religious sector. Concurrently, tendencies in the opposite direction can be detected among secular groups, which are expressed by violent acts against religious people and institutions.

Goals and Techniques of Change. What goals should be achieved through social interventions? It seems that these groups are so far apart that any goal of bringing the groups closer would be worthwhile considering. Yet, is there any chance at all to achieve any meaningful goal through interventions at the micro-level?

Change in the cognitive or evaluative components of the attitudes towards each other is questionable. It stands to reason that these attitudes are based on highly significant differences in the mental and moral structure of the individuals involved (i.e., religious-ideological orientations and their behavioral consequences). Thus, even where these attitudes involve stereotypic thinking and have some prejudicial basis, there seems little realistic opportunity for change. The efficacy of treating the affective or behavioral components of the attitude also seems questionable. Each group actually questions the legitimacy of the other. There seems little chance for change in spheres such as interpersonal liking or social acceptance when another group's very existence threatens one's own social and ideological well-being and daily functioning.

In social situations like this, it may be difficult to set up goals for intergroup change that may be achieved through social-psychological techniques and manipulations. It may be more reasonable to assume that a real change will only come as a consequence of some events at the macro-level, such as major political or general ideological developments. These might include the attainment of a shared code of conduct by the leadership of both groups or the presence of a major outside danger threatening the physical existence of both groups. In the absence of change at the macro-level, social-psychological interventions at the individual or small-group level may be ineffective and thus not worth pursuing.

SUMMARY

This paper tried to emphasize the importance of evaluating and defining the socially relevant goals for intergroup change before launching on an intervention program in this area. Only after the goals that should and could be achieved are clearly defined should programs relevant to these goals be set up which are capable of achieving them.

This argument was exemplified by the three main intergroup conflicts presently prevailing in Israel. Comparing these three situations, it becomes apparent that each of them is at a different stage of development: The Jewish interethnic situation is at the most (positively) advanced stage, the Jewish secular-religious situation is at the least advanced, and the Jewish-Arab situation falls somewhere between the two. These stages of development can be characterized and ranked (from least to most advanced) as follows. First stage: Agreement between the groups on the principle of coexistence; Second stage: Agreement between the groups regarding the objectives to be achieved in the context of coexistence; Third (most advanced) stage: Finding ways and means of achieving these objectives.

An attempt was made to show that each of these situations should be treated differently. With regard to one of these conflicts - between Israeli Arabs and Jews - an informational approach would be the optimal to produce change for the pertinent goals. For the conflict between the different Jewish ethnic groups, the contact-interaction approach seemed preferable. Finally, to improve relations between religious and secular Jews, solutions should be sought at the macro-level rather than concentrating on micro-level interventions.

REFERENCES

Allport, G.W. (1954). The nature of prejudice. Cambridge, MA: Addison-Wesley.

Amir, Y. (1969). Contact hypothesis in ethnic relations. Psychological Bulletin, 71, 319-342.

Amir, Y. (1976). The role of intergroup contact in change of prejudice and ethnic relations. In P.A. Katz (Ed.), Towards the elimination of racism. New York: Pergamon Press.

Amir, Y., & Ben-Ari, R. (1985). International tourism, ethnic contact and attitude change. Journal of Social Issues, 41(3), 105-115.

Amir, Y., Sharan, S., & Ben-Ari, R. (Eds.) (1984). School desegregation: Cross-cultural perspectives. Hillsdale, NJ: Erlbaum.

Barnea, M., & Amir, Y. (1981). Mutual attitudes and attitude change following intergroup contact of religious and nonreligious students. Journal of Social Psychology, 115, 65-71.

Bennett, J.M. (1986). Modes of cross-cultural training. International Journal of Intercultural Relations, 10, 117-134.

Brislin, R.W. (1986). A culture general assimilator. International Journal of Intercultural Relations, 10, 215-234.

Cook, S.W. (1963). Desegragation: A psychological analysis. In W.W. Charters, Jr. & N.L. Gage (Eds.), Readings in the social psychology of education. Boston: Allyn & Bacon.

Gudykunst, W.B., Hammer, M.R., & Wiseman, R.L. (1977). An analysis of an integrated approach to cross-cultural training. International Journal of Intercultural Relations, 1, 99-110.

Landis, D., & Brislin, R.W. (Eds.) (1983). Handbook of intercultural training (Vol.2). New York: Pergamon.

Peled, T., & Bar-Gal, D. (1983). Intervention activities in Arab-Jewish relations: Conceptualization, classification and evaluation. Jerusalem: The Israel Institute for Applied Social Research.

Stephan, W.G. & Stephan, C.W. (1984). The role of ignorance in intergroup relations. In N.Miller & M.B. Brewer (Eds.), Groups in contact: The psychology of desegregation. Orlando, FL: Academic Press.

Triandis, H.C. (1975). Culture training, cognitive complexity, and interpersonal attitudes. In R. Brislin, S. Bochner & W. Lonner (Eds.), Cross-cultural perspectives on learning (pp. 39-77). Beverly Hills, CA: Sage and Wiley/Halstead.

EVALUATION OF NORM VIOLATIONS AND REACTIONS TO NORM VIOLATIONS BY MEMBERS OF DIFFERENT 'CULTURAL' GROUPS

Sandra G.L. Schruijer & Richard DeRidder
Tilburg University,
Tilburg, The Netherlands

Recently a theoretical framework on intergroup behaviour has been formulated, which focuses on the importance of norms and norm violations in interactions between members of different groups (Schruijer, DeRidder, Poortinga & Tripathi, 1986; DeRidder, Tripathi, Sinha, Poortinga, Schruijer, Ghosh, Kumar & Sinha, 1985). It describes how norm violations by an acting party and subsequent interpretations of this behaviour by a victim party can lead to (an escalation of) intergroup conflict. Since the model intends to predict escalation and/or deescalation of conflicts between existing groups in society, additional factors are incorporated. Existing groups have a historically grown relationship, reflected in power differences between those groups, intergroup attitudes, feelings of relative deprivation and the strength of its group members' social identity. Figure 1 presents the model.

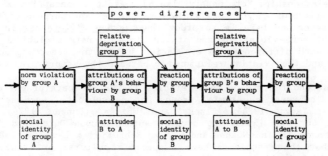

Figure 1: A model of norm violations and intergroup behaviour (Schruijer, DeRidder, Poortinga & Tripathi, 1986).

1   We are indebted to Ype Poortinga for comments on a previous draft of the present paper. Thanks are due to Peter Rutten, Ibrahim Ay and Lex Lemmers for collecting the data.

It is important to note that the central sequence of the model (norm violation -> attribution -> reaction) is formulated from the victim party's perspective. The sequence starts when members of either one of the interacting parties display a behaviour which the victim party evaluates as norm infringing. It will react with behaviour which is subsequently interpreted by the party initiating the sequence. The latter, who then finds itself in the victim position may consider this reaction as norm violating. The original victim party, it should be emphasized, might well conceive of its reaction as appropriate because it evaluates its own behaviour with reference to the other party's original norm violation.

For several parts of the model empirical support is found in the literature. Within an intergroup context norm violations are interpreted differently, depending upon the group membership of actor and of observer (e.g. Taylor & Jaggi, 1974; Duncan, 1976; Hewstone & Ward, 1985; Schruijer & Lemmers, 1987). Intergroup attitudes were shown to influence the kind of attributions made (Greenberg & Rosenfield, 1979; Schruijer & Lemmers, 1987). Elsewhere we argued that the victim party will match the intensity of the norm violation suffered (DeRidder & Schruijer, 1986). In that paper we presented evidence that Turkish and Dutch subjects expected members of their group to apply such a 'tit for tat' strategy towards members of the outgroup. In another study it was found that, according to Turkish subjects, victims of their in-group (Turks) are likely to react differently when an outgroup (Dutch) violated a norm directed towards them as compared to how an outgroup victim (Dutch) would react when suffering from a norm violation by a Turk (Schruijer, DeRidder & Poortinga, 1986).

All these studies have two features in common. First, the behaviour presented is embedded in an intergroup context, that is, actor and victim belong to different groups, one of them being the subject's ingroup. This implies that the results of these studies are partly determined by a group's conception of the outgroup and of their inter-group relationship. Yet, partly also by a group's conception of appropriate behaviour and/or norm violations per se. The purpose of the research described here is to study these group differences in evaluations of norm violations and of reactions to norm violations unconfounded with differences in evaluation due to the actor's group membership and the existing relationship between the actor's and victim's party.

A second feature of these studies is that members of one or more natural 'cultural or ethnic' groups act as subjects, such as Hindus (Taylor & Jaggi, 1974), 'Blacks' and 'Whites' (Duncan, 1976) and in most of our own intergroup studies autochthonous Dutch and Turkish allochthones in The Netherlands (e.g. Schruijer & Lemmers, 1987). We grant that these subjects have a specific cultural or ethnic background which is likely to affect their judgements of social behaviour. However, this 'cultural or ethnic' factor is a too global characterization of the groups' differences. Therefore it should be further specified (cf. Poortinga, Van de Vijver, Joe & Van de Koppel, 1987). Most often groups of different cultural background differ on a host of historical, economic, social and social psychological variables. These variables separately or in combination may account for differences in judgements obtained from these groups. This feature of research on groups with different cultural backgrounds explains the quotation

marks in the title of the present contribution. As a minimal requirement it calls for theoretical insight in important variables on which
existing 'cultural' groups differ (Lonner & Berry, 1986).
The present study is relevant for two reasons. First, it is
important to know whether groups with different cultural backgrounds
have different conceptions of norms, of norm violations and of appropriate reactions to such norm violations. Second, if differences do
occur, they have clear implications for the interpretation of reactions by such groups to norm violations. The latter is the object of a
large-scale study, partly reported earlier (Schruijer, DeRidder &
Poortinga, 1986). In this large-scale study, Turkish allochthones
living in The Netherlands and Dutch autochthones are the two different
cultural groups studied.
More specifically, the following research questions guided the
two studies we will report next.
1. Are norms and norm violations evaluated differently by a group of
   Turkish allochthones as compared to a group of Dutch autochthones?
2. Are reactions to norm violations judged equally (in)appropriate by
   these groups?
3. Is norm violation, both from the Turkish and Dutch individuals'
   perspective, an appropriate reaction to suffering of an initial
   norm violation?

STUDY 1: PERCEPTION OF NORMS AND NORM VIOLATIONS

This study addresses the first of the above-mentioned questions.
Sixty-six male Turkish allochthones living in The Netherlands and 30
male autochthonous Dutch subjects varying with respect to age (18 to
67 years old) and occupation were administered a preliminary version
of a Norm Perception Questionnaire (NPQ). In this questionnaire respondents were requested to indicate their personal evaluation of the
impact of social norms on their day-to-day life in general, to rate
the importance of a given set of norms and to judge the (in)appropri-
ateness of violations of those norms.
It was found that both the Turkish and Dutch respondents judged
the impact of social norms on their daily life as important to very
important. Out of 18 concrete social norms, 17 were rated as important
to very important by the Turkish and Dutch subjects. The means were
1.27 and 1.86 respectively on a 5-point scale (1=very important;
5=very unimportant). Violations of the same 17 norms were considered
as inappropriate to very inappropriate by them. The means were 1.22
for the Turkish and 1.67 for the Dutch respondents (1=very inappropriate; 5=very appropriate).
The results obtained, indicate that in the individuals' view social
norms are an important determinant of their social behaviour. The main
difference between the Turkish allochthones and the autochthonous
Dutch appears to be a matter of degree and intragroup variance. Overall, the Dutch individuals considered norms to be 'important' and norm
violation 'inappropriate', while the Turkish individuals' considered
norms 'very important' and norm violation 'very inappropriate'. Moreover, in most of the judgements of norms and of norm violations, the
variance of the group of Turkish respondents appeared to be smaller
than that of the Dutch. The evaluation of the importance of norms cor-

related highly with that of the inappropriateness of norm violations. (A more detailed description of Study 1 can be found in Rutten, 1987).

STUDY 2: EVALUATION OF NORM VIOLATION AND REACTION

This study addresses all three research questions raised and is a more elaborated version of Study 1.
The number of norms of the Norm Perception Questionnaire is extended to 36 in order to cover three behavioural domains: Social Contacts, Institutional Contacts and Social Responsibility. The behavioural domain of social contacts pertains to interactions between social agents acting from a private capacity. Institutional contacts refer to interactions in which the agents (are supposed to) act out of certain roles or role obligations. In social responsibility situations agents engage in irresponsible behaviour towards society at large or towards another defined person. Each domain is represented by 12 norm violations which are selected out of a pool of 69, on the basis of the following criteria. A majority of the population (both Turks and Dutch) is likely to evaluate the situation presented as a norm violation (as judged by Turkish and Dutch informants); the norm violating behaviour of the actor is likely to be attributed to internal factors and furthermore, the actor is expected to be aware of the norm violating character of his behaviour (again as judged by informants; see DeRidder & Schruijer, 1986, for a detailed description of the pilot-study and of the selection procedure).
In the Study 2 version of the Norm Perception Questionnaire respondents are requested to evaluate not only the 36 norm violations presented, but also the (in)appropriateness of 5 reaction alternatives belonging to each norm violation. In this version no evaluation of the importance of the norms as such was included, because results of Study 1 demonstrated that such evaluations would correlate very highly with those for the violation of these norms.

Subjects: Fifteen male Turkish and 15 male Dutch subjects living in The Netherlands, participated in this study. The age of the Turkish subjects varied from 19 to 49 years (mean age is 30.7); the Dutch subjects were 20 to 59 years (mean age is 28.3). The length of time the Turkish subjects are living in The Netherlands ranged from 8 to 21 years (mean length: 14.5 years). Seven of the 15 Turkish and 1 of the Dutch subjects are unemployed. The remaining 8 Turks worked as a factory-worker or as a mechanic. Of the Dutch subjects, 8 were students, 2 just finished their higher education, 2 were supervisors in industry and 1 was a teacher. Of one Dutch subject the profession is not known.

Method: A Dutch research assistant distributed the NPQ to the Dutch respondents and a Turkish research assistant was present when the Turkish respondents completed the questionnaire.
The format of the NPQ was as follows. On top of each of the 36 pages of the questionnaire a norm violation was presented. On a 7-point scale the respondents had to evaluate the norm violation in terms of appropriateness (1=inappropriate; 7=appropriate). Following this, five possible reactions by a victim were listed, labeled a, b, c, d and e. The subjects were requested to indicate their judgement of the (in)appropriateness of each reaction alternative by placing a tick

300

with a corresponding letter on a 10 centimeter long line with the end-points 'inappropriate' and 'appropriate'. To illustrate the format, one example of a norm violation and the reaction alternatives is presented below.

Someone plays loud music in the middle of the night.
a. Friendly ask this person whether the volume could be turned down.
b. Ignore the noise and try to fall asleep.
c. Lodge a complaint with the police.
d. Play loud music as well in the middle of the night.
e. Teach this person some manners in a violent way.

As the reader may notice in this example, the content of the alternatives provided are matched to the norm violation suffered. The more general scale which underlies the reaction alternatives to all norm violations ranges from a positive reaction to an extreme negative reaction. More specifically, the five scale points are:
a. a positive reaction;
b. no reaction at all;
c. a norm violation of a lesser intensity than the one manifested by the actor;
d. a norm violation of about equal intensity, and
e. a norm violation of a higher intensity as compared to the one committed by the actor.
For the 36 norm violating situations in the NPQ the alternatives were not presented according to the a priori underlying scale, but in a random order.

Results: Subsequently we will report the results for the ratings of the norm violations, of the reaction alternatives and of the relationship between both ratings.
We computed multivariate analyses of variance per behavioural domain with the subjects' cultural background as the independent factor and ratings of the 12 norm violations per domain as dependent variables. This resulted in a nearly significant effect for the social contact domain (F=2.38; df=12; p=0.058). Norm violations within the social contact-domain are considered to be less inappropriate by our Dutch subjects as compared to our Turkish subjects. For the other domains, each of which was reduced to 10 norm violations since two showed no variance at all on the part of the Turkish subjects, no effects were obtained. The means for the Turkish and Dutch subjects per behavioural domain are presented in Table 1.

| | Cultural background | |
	Turkish	Dutch
Social contacts	1.61	2.36
Institutional contacts	1.21	1.64
Social Responsibility	1.57	1.96

Table 1. Means of appropriateness ratings of norm violations for the Turkish and Dutch respondents per behavioural domain (1=inappropriate; 7=appropriate).

301

As might be expected from the means of Table 1, the actor's behaviour in almost all situations is perceived as being inappropriate by both the Dutch and the Turks. In fact, in only one situation the actor's behaviour is not seen as norm infringing, namely the situation in which a girl tells her parents that she is going to marry a foreigner. Analyses performed on each of the 36 norm violations separately show that the Turkish subjects consider them in a number of cases as more inappropriate than the Dutch subjects. This difference is significant for 11 situations at a .05 level and for 2 situations at a .10 level (t-test, corrected in case of a significant difference in variance of the Dutch ratings as compared to the Turkish ratings). Eight of the situations where a significant difference for the appropriateness rating is obtained, belong to the social contact domain, two to the domain of institutional contact (plus two differences p < .10) and one to the social responsibility domain (plus one difference at p < .10 level).

It should be mentioned that, in general, the appropriateness ratings are characterized by a small variance, which suggests that a high interindividual consensus exists about the inappropriateness of the behaviours included in the NPQ. However, the variance of the Turkish subjects' ratings is even considerably smaller than that of the Dutch subjects (in 14 out of 36 situations this difference is significant (F-test)).

In sum, the results obtained for the perception of norm violation are very similar to those found in Study 1.

How (in)appropriate are the reaction alternatives presented in the NPQ?

The appropriateness ratings of the reaction alternatives were analysed as follows. Per subject, the score for each reaction category (positive, neutral, less strong norm violation, equal norm violation, stronger norm violation) is added over 36 situations and divided by 36. This means that we have five scores for each subject: the overall appropriateness rating of the positive reaction alternative (R+), the overall appropriateness rating of the neutral reaction (R0), and the overall appropriateness ratings of the less, equal and more serious norm violating reactions (labeled respectively as R<, R= and R>) With the five newly created scores as dependent and the cultural background (Turkish or Dutch) as independent variable a multivariate analysis of variance was performed. This resulted in a significant effect for cultural background (F=4.82; df=5; p<.01). Subsequent univariate analyses of variance show no effect for cultural background on R+, R0 and R<, yet they do show an effect on R= (F=6.38; df=1; p<.05) and on R> (F=18.17; df=1; p<.001). The Turkish subjects consider the equally strong reaction alternative and the stronger reaction alternative (R= and R>) significantly more appropriate than the Dutch subjects. The means for the Turkish and Dutch subjects per reaction category are presented in Table 2.

```
                Cultural background
                Turkish        Dutch
                (n=15)         (n=15)

R+           6.75_a          7.07_a
R0           5.97_bc         6.22_bc
R<           6.27_b          5.81_c
R=           5.66_c          4.73_d
R>           4.47_d          2.83_e
```

Table 2. Means per reaction category and cultural background; column
means with different subscripts differ significantly from
one another (t-test for correlated data; $p<.05$, 1=inapprop-
riate; 10=appropriate).

Analyses of variance of the ratings for each of the 36 norm violations
separately for R= and R> as dependent and the subjects' cultural background as independent variables, result in significant differences in
14 out of 36 situations for R=. In 10 cases the Turks consider this
reaction as more appropriate than the Dutch, and in one case the reverse is true. In 21 cases Turks evaluate R> as more appropriate than
the Dutch.

We furthermore analyzed whether, within each of the groups (Turks
and Dutch), the means of the reaction categories scores differ significantly (t-test for correlated data, see Table 2). It appears that
for both the Turks and the Dutch R+ is always judged as significantly
more appropriate than a reaction with norm violation (R<, R= and
R>). Not showing any reaction (R0) is always seen as less appropriate
than R+. This absence of a reaction (R0) however, is not significantly
different from R< nor from R= in case of the Turkish subjects. Moreover, it may be noted that the mean range of the ratings of the reaction categories of the Turkish subjects appears to be smaller than
that of the Dutch.

In sum, these data indicate that given a norm violation by another
party, an attempt to solve the conflict in a positive way (R+) is
considered always as more appropriate than doing nothing or reacting
with a norm violation. However, when members of a victim party would
react with a 'tit for tat' norm violation (R=) or with one with exceeds the intensity of the norm violation suffered (R>) Turkish subjects consider such behaviour as more appropriate (or less inappropriate) than the Dutch subjects do.

How are, in the subjects' view, reactions to norm violation related to
the original norm violation suffered?

Inspection of the results of Pearson-correlation analyses between
the appropriateness rating of each individual norm violation on the
one hand and the appropriateness rating of each of the five reaction
alternatives separately, on the other (Turkish and Dutch data combined), show the following overall pattern. A negative correlation
exists between the appropriateness of the norm violation and the
appropriateness of R> (9 correlations are at a .05 level; 3 at a .10
level; only one positive correlation is found). That is, the more
inappropriate the initial norm violation, the more appropriate it is

to react with a stronger norm violation. Or, the less inappropriate the initial norm violation, the less appropriate it is not to react with a stronger norm violation. Negative correlations are also obtained for R=. Here 16 negative correlations are significant at .05 level and three at .10 (two positive correlations are obtained as well). The more inappropriate the initial norm violation, the more appropriate it is to react with a 'tit for tat' norm violation. For R< a similar pat-tern is found. Eleven negative correlations at .05 level and 6 at .10 (no positive correlations). The correlations of the appropriateness rating of the norm violation and the appropriateness rating of RO are positive (8 at .05 level, 3 at .10). The more inappropriate the initial norm violation, the more inappropriate it is to do nothing. The results with respect to R+ are inconsistent. Four positive correlations are found (.05) and two negative (.05).

Correlation analyses for the Turkish (except those four norm violation which produced no variance in the appropriateness ratings) and the Dutch subjects separately, resulted in the same overall pattern of significant correlations, although less pronounced (which is partly due to the smaller number of subjects).

Overall, these results suggest that in the minds of Turkish as well as of Dutch subjects norm violation and reaction are related in terms of appropriateness. More precisely stated, the more they consider a norm violation on the part of another as being inappropriate the more it appears to them as being appropriate to react with norm violation, either R< , R= or R>. It however appears more inappropriate in that case to show no reaction and it seems sometimes more sometimes less appropriate to react positively.

DISCUSSION

The results of the two studies reported can be summarized as follows. Both Turkish and Dutch individuals considered norms to be important determinants of their day-to-day life and the norms presented in the NPQ as important (Dutch) to very important (Turks). Violations of norms were perceived as more inappropriate by the Turkish subjects than by the Dutch. Moreover, although both cultural groups considered an attempt to solve a conflict in a positive way as the most appropriate reaction, the Turkish subjects considered reciprocation of norm infringing behaviour with a norm violation of equal or higher intensity as less inappropriate than the Dutch did. For both groups it appears, that they consider a norm infringing reaction as more appropriate the more they view the initial party's behaviour as inappropriate.

In short, the two 'cultural' groups involved in the present studies share a naive evaluation of the appropriate reactions to norm violation suffered. The main differences between the two groups are that (i) the variation of responses of the Turkish respondents is smaller than that of the Dutch, that (ii) they consider certain norm violations as being more inappropriate than the Dutch and (iii) certain norm violating reactions less inappropriate.

In order to understand these results and be able to outline their implications for studies on intergroup behaviour, the differences between the two 'cultural' groups need to be specified. Not only do the group employed differ with respect to their ethnic background, they differ on a host of other variables as well. Turkish allochthones in The Netherlands enjoy a much lower social and socio-economic status in comparison with the autochthonous Dutch, have less power (be it social, economical or political); and constitute in many ways a minority. Furthermore it can be argued that in the present studies the Turkish subjects' social identity was more salient than that of the Dutch subjects. Although no explicit reference has been made to the relationship between the Dutch and the Turks in the questionnaires administered, the Turkish subjects might have been more aware of their group membership, since the study was carried out under the responsibility of Dutch researchers. The questionnaire in Study 2 moreover, was phrased in Dutch. Other differences worth mentioning are the following. The Turkish subjects (in Study 2) completed the questionnaire in the presence of the research assistent, whereas the Dutch subjects filled it out alone at their homes. Also, the Turkish subjects (at least in Study 2) were largely unemployed and their education level was lower.

Each of these differences or combinations of them may account for the differences in evaluations obtained. It might be for instance, that an ethnic difference is the cause for differences in appropriateness ratings. Turkey scores high on the dimension of Uncertainty Avoidance (Hofstede, 1982), higher than The Netherlands. Hofstede argues that societies scoring high on this dimension are characterized by a need for written rules and regulations. From this might follow that our Turkish subjects consider norm violations more inappropriate than the Dutch subjects. (One should keep in mind, that the Uncertainty Avoidance Index is a national one and can therefore not be directly applied to individuals!).

The difference in majority/minority status between the two groups studied, is a factor which may have influenced the results with respect to the appropriateness rating of norm violations and reactions as well. First it might be, that minority members identify the actors in the situation descriptions as Dutch, since in daily life they are often confronted with majority actors. For the Dutch however, it appears to be farfetched to assume that they would identify the norm violating actors as belonging to an outgroup, and to identify them as Turkish actors is even more unlikely. This assertion assumes that the Turkish subjects, members of a minority, judge the other's norm violation as more extreme than the Dutch do, because the norm violation is in the Turkish subjects' view manifested by an outgroup member. Second, minority members might differentiate little between reaction alternatives, since in their view their past experience taught them that no reaction whatsoever to the majority's norm infringing behaviour proves to be effective. This line of reasoning can explain the smaller range of appropriateness ratings by the Turkish subjects.

A higher salience of the Turkish group members' social identity could explain the lower intragroup variance for these subjects. A heigthened salience of social identity might lead to 'typical' ingroup evaluations of (outgroup) behaviour and less personal judgements (cf. Turner, 1987).

Despite these differences between the groups studied, it is perhaps surprising that we find many similarities as well. We might infer from this that the norms covered in the questionnaire are important for groups with different 'cultural' backgrounds. Norm violations are perceived to be inappropriate and furthermore, the more inappropriate they are perceived the more subjects conceive of norm violating reactions as appropriate (and vice versa).

We must point to some limitations of the present studies. We confined our investigations to male subjects only, and our subject samples were not representative of the Turkish allochthones and the Dutch autochthones. The samples were small. Any generalization to a larger population is therefore extremely hazardous. Moreover, we want to emphasize that the data are of a verbal nature. The studies reported here do not show that e.g. norm violating behaviour leads to a norm violating behavioural reaction. Nor has it been demonstrated that people expect norm violating reactions to occur to initial norm violating behaviour (which, embedded in an intergroup context, is the focus of our large-scale study). We only have some evidence that people, belonging to different 'cultural' groups, consider norm violating behaviour as a reaction to an initial norm violation as appropriate.

From the number of plausible explanations suggested, it will be clear that hardly any study which investigates natural groups can provide clear-cut answers. In addition, if our explanations concerning the majority/minority status and salience of subjects' social identity explanation are correct, it implies that extracting personal answers from minority members is virtually impossible. This means that our attempt to 'degroup' the norm violating episodes might have failed for the Turkish subjects.

The results of the present studies will be helpful in interpreting other research done within the theoretical framework presented (see Figure 1), especially since we use the same norm violations (embedded in an intergroup context) in our large-scale study. We now know that a different baseline of appropriateness might exist for one cultural group compared to an other, for some norm violating situations. This has to be taken into account when an intergroup context is superimposed upon the norm violating episodes used.

REFERENCES

DeRidder, R., Tripathi, R.C., Sinha, J.B.P., Poortinga, Y.H., Schruijer, S.G.L., Ghosh, E., Kumar, R., & Sinha, D. (1985). Psycho-cultural determinants of intergroup relations: A project proposal. Unpublished manuscript, Tilburg University, The Netherlands; Allahabad University and ANS Institute of Social Studies, India.

DeRidder, R., & Schruijer, S.G.L. (1986). Norm violation, attribution and intergroup relations: A theoretical proposition and some initial data. Paper presented at the 7th East-West Meeting of the European Association of Experimental Social Psychology, Graz, Austria.

Duncan, B.L. (1976). Differential social perception and attribution of intergroup violence: Testing the lower limits of stereotyping of blacks. Journal of Personality and Social Psychology, 34, 590-598.

Greenberg, J., & Rosenfield, D. (1979). Whites' ethnocentrism and their attributions for the behavior of blacks: A motivational bias. Journal of Personality, 47, 643-657.

Hewstone, M., & Ward, C. (1985). Ethnocentrism and causal attribution in Southeast Asia. Journal of Personality and Social Psychology, 48, 614-623.

Hofstede, G. (1982). Dimensions of national cultures. In R. Rath, H.S. Asthana, D.Sinha, & J.B.P. Sinha (Eds.), Diversity and unity in cross-cultural psychology. Lisse: Swets & Zeitlinger.

Lonner, W.J. & Berry, J.W. (Eds.) (1986). Field methods in cross-cultural psychology. Beverly Hills: Sage.

Poortinga, Y.H., Van de Vijver, F.J.R., Joe, R.C., & Van de Koppel, J.M.H. (1987). Peeling the onion called culture: A synopsis. In C. Kagitcibasi (Ed.), Growth and progress in cross-cultural psychology. Lisse: Swets & Zeitlinger.

Rutten, P. (1987). Waarneming van normen en normschendingen door Turken en Nederlanders (Perception of norms and norm violations by Turks and Dutch). Unpublished MA thesis, Tilburg University.

Schruijer, S.G.L., & Lemmers, L. (1987). Explanations and evaluations of negative ingroup and outgroup behaviour by Turks and Dutch. Paper presented at the First Regional North American Conference of the International Association for Cross-Cultural Psychology, Kingston, Canada.

Schruijer, S.G.L., DeRidder, R., & Poortinga, Y.H. (1986). Norm violations and the relationship between the Dutch autochthones and the Turkish allochthones in The Netherlands. Paper presented at the 8th International Conference on Cross-Cultural Psychology of the International Association of Cross-Cultural Psychology, Istanbul, Turkey.

Schruijer, S.G.L., DeRidder, R., Poortinga, Y.H., & Tripathi, R.C. (1986). Norm violations and intergroup behaviour: A framework for research. In L.H. Ekstrand (Ed.), Ethnic minorities and immigrants in a cross-cultural perspective. Lisse: Swets & Zeitlinger.

Taylor, D.M., & Jaggi, V. (1974). Ethnocentrism and causal attributions in a South Indian context. Journal of Cross-Cultural Psychology, 5, 162-171.

Turner, J.C. (1987). Rediscovering the social group: A self-categorization theory. Oxford: Basil Blackwell.

MIGRATION PLANS AND THEIR DETERMINANTS AMONG PORTUGUESE ADOLESCENTS

Félix Neto
Universidade do Porto
Porto, Portugal

Emigration is not a phenomenon only in recent years of Portuguese history. It is an old tradition that goes back to when the country started venturing forth in the conquest of new worlds. In four centuries, the number of Portuguese residents abroad increased from 100,000/150,000 (Godinho, 1978), to more than 3.5 million today. This took place in a country with approximately 10 million inhabitants.

However, today the Portuguese migratory phenomenon is changing: in 1970 some 180,000 people emigrated, while in 1986 less than 9,000 left the country. Even if now the migratory flow is small, it still continues to affect us. Among the many social phenomena affecting Portuguese people, migration undoubtedly is one of the most significant. Today, many people directly live the experience of migration, while others have contact with it either through the emigrants themselves or by the mass media, or because they plan to eventually emigrate.

If one asks a German, a French or a Swiss youth, 13 to 16 years old, studying in high-school, what he intends to do in the future, there is one probability in two that he answers: I want to be a physician, a lawyer, a teacher ... or even an astronaut or a racing driver (cf. the problem of the pyramid of choices, Reuchlin, 1978). If one asks a Portuguese youth, about the same age and school level, what he plans to do in the future, there is a fifty per cent probability that he answers: I will be an emigrant. This statistic is one of the surprising results that appears in a survey among Portuguese adolescents resident in the North of Portugal. To fully understand the field of study now called "life project"[2], it is necessary to add to the concepts of "educational projects" and "career projects", the concept of "migratory projects" (Neto & Mullet, 1987a).

In this paper, our purpose is the assessment of the contents of the migratory projects of Portuguese youth and of some of their determinants. This goal is part of a larger study, in which we tried to comprehend adolescents' representations of the migratory phenomenon (Neto, 1986a, 1986b). The general idea underlying our study is that the intention of emigrating depends on a multitude of factors. We shall assess particularly three orders of factors: socio-demographic, socio-psychological and psychological.

METHOD

Sample. Our goal was not so much to obtain a representative sample of the population, but rather to obtain a reasonable cross-section of the population variation. We selected a stratified sample. The adolescents were chosen on the basis of geographical, sexual and sociocultural criteria, keeping constant the school grade (8th). Our sample is composed of 480 adolescents, distributed along a 2x2x2 factorial plan: half of the subjects of the sample are from rural areas, and the other half from urban areas; it includes as many boys as girls; half belong to a low socioeconomic status, and the other half to a middle socioeconomic status. While the sample is homogeneous, as far as the school grade is considered, we find a dispersion in ages, ranging from 13-17 years.

Data Collection Techniques. The survey can be used with many different aims. Debesse (1948) mentions the introspection survey, the reaction survey and the test survey. The techniques used with the subjects (a free association game, a questionnaire, the High School Personality Questionnaire) cover these three kinds of survey. The use of the free association technique will allow us, through the constitution of its semantic field, to discover the elements of the emigration representation. The questionnaire was designed to collect information on the components of the social representation of emigration and on the subject's identification. It includes 121 closed questions and 11 open questions. To assess the adolescents' personality, we used the H.S.P.Q. (Cattell & Beloff, 1966) which is composed of 14 dimensions.

Administration of the Survey. The survey was administered in groups in the schools where the adolescents studied during class hours, by their own teachers. Each session lasted for two hours. In the first hour the subject was invited to answer the free association and the questionnaire. In the second hour the personality test was administered.

RESULTS

First we will present some aspects of the contents of the students' migratory projects, and secondly we will present some of their determinants.

Students Migratory Projects. We will examine if the intention of emigrating is present in the Portuguese youth of the eighties, the temporal source of this intention, the motivations expressed by the subjects to depart, the host country and the length of stay considered and, finally, the belief in the possibility of achieving this project in the future.

The intention of emigrating allows us to perceive the conative component of the attitude towards emigration. It splits the sample by half: 47% of the adolescents express their intention of emigrating, and 52% do not. This cleavage is even more surprising if one keeps in mind that, although the sample is stratified, the intention of emigrating was not a selection criteria.

Of those intending to emigrate, 44% said they made the decision before age 13, and 21% made it after that age. The motives for migrating mentioned by those intending to emigrate are: employment, wages, education, living in another country, the limited possibilities of success in Portugal and the search for adventure. More than half of the sample considers the shortage of jobs the main cause for Portuguese emigration, but only one third of the ones intending to emigrate consider it the main motivation.

The absence of the intention of emigrating is justified in different ways, the most common being the difficulty or the non-necessity for leaving. Some even advance negative evaluations of emigration. For them emigration implies an escape to the resolution of problems. Others stress the administrative and adaptive difficulties that arise with the departure, or even the defense against the emergence of affects released by emigration, such as sadness and nostalgia. Finally, the migratory experience is also used as a motive for the absence of that intention: "I've been the son of an emigrant and I already know what it takes"; "my parents are emigrants and, given that fact that I live separated from them, I don't want the life of my children to be as tough".

Thus, in the justification of the absence of the intention of emigrating, the elements of migration appear coherently arranged: departure is surrounded with multiple difficulties, and there is an absence of motivations for emigrating. There is a protection against the emergence of affects that emigration might cause to appear.

Which are the countries of destination for the ones who intend to emigrate? The answers included 21 countries, spread over the five continents. Slightly less than two thirds of the subjects mentioned Europe. In decreasing order appear: France, Great Britain, Germany, Switzerland, Sweden, Belgium, Holland, Spain, Soviet Union and Greece. Less than one third are oriented to the Americas. One of the main countries of destination of historical Portuguese emigration

- Brazil - is no longer important. Countries in Africa, Asia and Oceania are rarely mentioned.

The choice of France as the first country of destination is essentially justified by two reasons: the phenomenon of group network and the positive attitude of France towards immigration. One of the youngsters summarizes it when declaring: "I choose this country because it is where more people emigrate to and probably the one that offers better conditions".

The choice of the United States, the second country of destination of the youngsters, is essentially justified by its development and culture: "what makes me choose this country for emigrating is the development it has"; "it is a superdeveloped country and you make more money"; "because they got very advanced technology and if I go there I can take a technical course"; "because I would like to be a scientist".

Great Britain, the third country of destination, is justified mostly by the attraction exerted by the language: "I choose Great Britain because I would like to learn the English language"; "because it is a country that I always wanted to know and because I think the people have a healthier way of thinking and because it is a very free country".

The choice of West Germany, the fourth country is justified by the phenomenon of group network and by its development: "I intend to emigrate to Germany because I've got friends and family there"; "because my father has already worked there"; "because it is a very developed country, in terms of industry, commerce".

Among those intending to emigrate, 88% consider it to be only temporary (for several years abroad), while 12% considered it to be for all their lives. Finally, 89% believe that their migration plans will be achieved.

<u>Determinants of the Migratory Process</u>. Having examined some components of the content of adolescents' migratory projects, we will now describe the relations of the migratory projects with socio-demographic and personality data, and with the representation of the migratory event. Last, we shall question if the migratory projects interfere with the adolescents' educational projects and their career projects.

To understand how the different socio-demographic variables structure themselves around the intention of emigrating, we turned to the factorial analysis of the correspondences (Benzecri, 1973). To perform this analysis in a disjunctive way, were used, as the main elements, the <u>population characteristics</u> (age, religion, residence

with parents), the _family_ characteristics (age of the parents,
marital status of the parents, type of relationship between the
parents, number of children), as well as the exposure of the subject
to _migration_ (through relatives, friends and neighbors still involved
in the migratory process, or already definitively returned, and even
through internal migration). As supplementary elements, besides the
intention of emigrating, were projected the perspectives of education
and career. Two axes appeared in the solution: Axis 1 seems to
oppose fundamentally the socio-demographic characteristics of a rural
society and of an urban society, whereas Axis 2 indicates the
cleavage between family constellations that are connected and
disconnected. The intention of migration appears better explained by
Axis 1 than by Axis 2, thus having to do more with the type of
society than with the family type. It is associated with population
characteristics whose modalities indicate rural residence, older age
(15-17 years old), active Catholic, intermediary position in the
family (or the youngest son), low socioeconomic status and large
families. All the variables of emigration are associated with the
intention of emigrating: experience of internal migration, and of
emigration and return from emigration of relatives, friends and
neighbors.

To learn if the intention of emigrating depends on personality
factors, we used the H.S.P.Q.. This test was used to ascertain the
relations of intention to emigrate with the second order factors of
anxiety and extroversion. Globally, the anxiety effect on the
intention of emigrating is not significant ($t=1.77$; $p=.78$).
Similarly the extroversion effect is not significant ($t=.77$; $p=.441$).
The extroversion is as much present in those who have the intention
of emigrating as in those that don't have such a behavioral
intention.

As a last question we tried to find out if the migratory projects
interfere with the educational projects and with the career projects
of adolescents. Questioned about their educational projects, 29% of
the adolescents express their ambition of going to college, 56%
secondary school only, and 15% don't know. These percentages are not
very different from those obtained in the answers of the adolescents
expressing their intention to emigrate (27%, 60%, 13%), or from the
answers of those who don't plan to emigrate (30%, 50%, 17%). The
same remarks can be made regarding the professional status intended:
22% of the adolescents state they want to reach a high professional
status, 55% a middle professional status, 23% don't know. Among the
adolescents wishing to emigrate, the percentages are 23%, 58%, 19%;
for those not intending to emigrate, 21%, 52%, 27%.

DISCUSSION

Migratory projects are in the future perspectives of a considerable
number of the Portuguese youth, particularly those from rural areas,
of deprived socio-economic classes, and male.

However, these migratory projects do not appear merely associated
with adolescents' dreams. The various motivations for leaving
(unemployment, low wages) are comparable with those that are
mentioned by migrant workers living abroad (Neto & Mullet, 1987b).
Concerning the socio-demographic characteristics, globally it seems
to be confirmed that what influences the emigration decision later in
life is also what adolescents mention as factors in their intention
to emigrate. The subjects who intend to emigrate value the migratory
phenomenon more. They stress the positive aspects more and do not
consider that migration will interfere negatively with their school
or career projects.

We should also point out that in another study with pre-adolescents
(Neto, 1986a), we found a proportion of those expressing their
intention of emigrating (46%) identical to the ones we have been
describing. Therefore, a large number of adolescents in Portugal
desire today to enter the world of grown-ups tomorrow; it is a sign
of the dissatisfaction with local living conditions and fear for
their future prospects at home. On the other hand, in two other
surveys performed in France (in 1977 and 1983), with first generation
Portuguese migrants, we found plans for returning to the home
country. Considering the large number of projects both for leaving
in the adolescents and in the pre-adolescents, and of returning in
the emigrants, we found complementary references to socio-economic
factors internal to emigration that are long lasting. These are
convergent modes of viewing our chronic incapacity to stop the
migratory haemorrhage. They emphasize our lack of collective
imagination that will be required if our country will truly become
the homeland of the Portuguese people (Malpique, 1986).

REFERENCES

Benzécri, J.P. (1973). L'analyse des données. Paris: Dunod.

Cattel, R., & Beloff, H. (1966). Manuel d'application du H.S.P.Q.
    Paris: Editions du CPA.

Debesse, M. (1948). Comment étudier les adolescents. Paris: PUF, 3 éd

Neto, F. (1986a). A migracao portuguesa vivida e representada. Contribuicao para o estuda dos projectos migratorios. Porto: Secretaria de Estado das Comunidades Portuguesas, Centro de Estudos.

Neto, F. (1986b). Social representations of migration in Portuguese adolescents. Paper presented at 8th Internat. Conference of Cross-Cultural Psychology, Istanbul, Turkey, July 6-10.

Neto, F., & Mullet, E. (1987a). Orientation: migrant. Berufsberatung und Berufsbildung/Orientation et Formation Professionnelle, 72,2, 53-58.

Neto, F., & Mullet, E. (1987b). Aspects quantitatifs du vécu des travailleurs portugais en région parisienne. Porto: Faculdade de Psicologia e de Ciencias da Educacao, Centro de Psicologia Social.

Reuchlin, M. (1978). L'orientation scolaire et professionnelle. Paris: PUF.

Notes

1   The participation in this Conference was supported by funds from "Secretaria de Estado das Comunidades Portuguesas", and from grant no. 51/86 (University of Porto).

2   The study of the "projects" of individuals has come to the fore recently in European psychology: individuals are considered to have "life projects", which are a set of goals or plans they have laid out for themselves for their lifetime. While the term "plans" was used in the title of this chapter, the notion of "projects" will be employed in the body of the text.

BEING A BILINGUAL THERAPIST

Richard Ruth
Arlington County Department of Human Services
Arlington, USA

There is a surprising lack of psychological literature on the process of doing psychotherapy with bilinguals. There are growing litera-tures on the barriers and architectures of service-delivery systems (cf., e.g., Garrison, 1978, and Acosta, 1979) and on microcounseling techniques (cf., e.g., Sprafkin et al., 1987). There are also a small number of classical articles (e.g., Velikovsky, 1934; Buxbaum, 1949; Greenson, 1950; Krapf, 1955; Lagache, 1956; Marcos, 1976; Marcos and Alpert, 1976; Marcos and Urcuyo, 1979), written from a psycho-analytic more than a psychotherapeutic perspective in most cases.

In no case, however, do these writings discuss the phenomenology from the psychotherapist's point of view, except incidentally to descrip-tions of the patient's phenomenology. It is as if there is an implicit assumption that the processes of becoming a therapist for bilingual clinicians and securing access to treatment for bilingual patients are the heart of the matter (and they surely are formidable challenges). Thus, once the therapist has arrived at a professional identity and has begun the therapy with his/her bilingual patient, there is nothing left to say. What we do (again, by implicit assumption) is no different from what our non-bilingual colleagues do.

The fallacy, which seems obvious once such a thought is articulated in words, is that what we feel is not what our majority-culture, monolingual colleagues feel.

This paper, then, is an initial attempt to describe some of the critically meaningful phenomena that occur when one works as a bilingual therapist. A proviso at the outset is that this will be a clinical paper, a reflection personal experience and the shared experiences of colleagues, and not an attempt at empirical validation. Also, this paper is very much grounded in experiences as a bilingual/ bicultural therapist working with Hispanics in the United States;

the commonalities and differences with other cross-cultural
therapeutic combinations will not be explored. The limitations
of such an approach are obvious, and no claims of generalizability
of the data are offered. Still, given the lack of prior investigation in this area, the approach seems reasonable as a starting
point.

CONCEPTUAL ISSUES

Bilingualism is often used incorrectly as a euphemism for "speaking
a minority language"; thus the nonsequiturs of "bilingual education"
meaning education in Spanish, or "bilingual workers" meaning para-
professionals who speak Spanish. However, the term actually means
"the capacity to speak two languages". This distinction is important
to bring into a discussion of this nature at the outset, because it
is the embodiment of the capacity to cross and bridge languages and
cultures within the mind and person of the therapist that brings
dynamic shape to the unique experiential phenomena when a bilingual
does psychotherapy.

A useful analogy can be made to the concept of transference. Transference phenomena acquire their power in dynamic therapies because
they recreate -- within the consulting room, where they are amendable
to examination and change -- key unresolved conflicts and dysfunctional
emotional and behavior patterns from the past. Along similar lines,
the therapist's bilingualism can recreate within the field of the
therapeutic encounter the experience of culture-bridging that is often
key to the origin, shape and/or course of the patient's difficulties.

What happens, however, when the therapist becomes aware of this? It
is complicated enough to learn how to use oneself as a therapeutic
instrument -- to develop even-hovering attention, to become sensitized
to transference and countertransference phenomena, to develop the
"split-screen" ability to listen and plan strategic interventions at
the same time. When bilingualism is grafted onto this, the difficulty
becomes geometrically more complex. To extend an inexact analogy,
one develops "split screens" in two languages and two cultures, two
systems of conceptualizing and thinking. A patient's comments, in
English, will resonate with a core, revealing personal experience of
the therapist encoded in Spanish. Or a patient's comment in Spanish
will be understood with the help of a technical formulation the
therapist has learned and encoded in English.

Actually, there are several variants of a bilingual psychotherapeutic
encounter. The therapist can be of the majority or minority culture,
as can the patient. The treatment can be conducted in the therapist's
native or acquired language, which may or may not be the native
language of the patient. The language of treatment may oscillate
back and forth within sessions, or change serially over time, and

perhaps with meaningful specificity to the developmental stage of the therapy. The therapist can be a coordinate or a compound bilingual. The therapist's professional training may have been transacted in the native or acquired language. The differences are as many, and as complex, as the facets of a gem, and different meanings and phenomenology inhere to each.

Deep sociopolitical meanings, and deep personal meanings, attach to the choice of the use of the dominant-culture language or the minority language in therapy. Key to this is deciding which, psychodynamically, is the language that facilitates regression (often the native language) and which is the language of adaptation (often the acquired language); this then needs to be matched to the developmental task or stage of treatment.

The bilingual therapist faces a meaningful choice not only in picking the language of therapy, but in deciding whether, and when, to allow feelings and conflicts about the language choice to enter the process of therapy as a dynamic issue. The therapist needs to examine for him/herself as well as the patient the meanings and dynamics of the choice. This falls in the category of what Langs (1973) calls a ground-rules issue. The clarity and security with which this issue is resolved and handled may affect whether the entire therapy works or not, in line with the general rule that ground-rule issues must be securely resolved before dynamic material can be validly interpreted. Failure to do so may block or skew the development of an empathic-enough relationship, and remove the interpretability of the therapeutic field.

COMMON PHENOMENA IN BILINGUAL THERAPY

Beyond the field of rules, certain phenomena appear to appear across the range of bilingual therapeutic situations. Let us begin to examine these.

First, an intuitively aware bilingual therapist never loses consciousness of the "split screens". Majority-culture therapists take for granted the hearing and speaking of their own language while they do therapy. A bilingual therapist never has this possibility. Speaking in an acquired language, there is a hovering awareness of the historical struggle and meanings of the acquisition. Depending on the valence of the therapist's cathexis, this can either pull toward countertransference or push toward insight. Such awareness, for example, can be invaluable in attempting to work empathically with children struggling to develop identities, to learn and to acculturate while they acquire a new language. Speaking in a native language, perhaps especially when this is a minority tongue, there is an awareness of the different-ness of this act that cannot help

but imbue the therapeutic ambience. It is difficult to do therapy
in Spanish in the U.S. without being almost constantly aware that
one is indeed doing therapy in Spanish. The signs in the corridor,
the chart, the language in which the secretary answers the phone,
the materials on one's desk are in English; the therapy is in
Spanish. One cannot help but acquire a particular awareness of
the language, to wonder how that fits into the patient's scheme of
things, to preconsciously translate ideas back and forth, in both
the linguistic and the cultural senses. One can also find oneself
oscillating between developmental moments - between the formative
moment, associated with language acquisition, and the adaptive
moment of language practice.

If one cannot give a name to these experiences, they become disconcerting and distracting. I can recall being in supervision,
presenting material on a Spanish-language therapy to an English-
speaking supervisor -- and parenthetically, this is the most usual
type of supervision beginning minority-language therapists receive.
I had the usual load of anxieties and terrors beginning therapists
had, but I also had others: was the supervisor a racist, and what
might that mean for my career; how could he help me, if he was
foreign to the language of the treatment, and to the Hispanic
culture; what would I do about the fact that he was combing through
the material for oedipal issues, while my attention was focused
on how to accurately translate controlar, in the careful manner
that one speaks in supervision; if he were oblivious to the stresses
and tensions of the linguistic phenomena, what did it mean that I
was not oblivious? Could I ever fully relax with him, in the way
that we think the patient truly relaxing and associating freely is
essential to therapy, and that the supervisee speaking freely is
essential to the supervision? How would I handle this gap between
us, of which I was constantly and acutely aware, but which he seemed
to not see?

In retrospect, it seems remarkable that I met with this man weekly
for a year, and never did either one of us talk about what it meant
that I was translating the patient's material, and my interpretations,
before presenting them to him. Neither one of us could identify this
as a meaningful phenomenon.

Bilingual therapists experience regressive pulls in a different
manner from monolingual therapists. Because the use and choice of
language become conscious and meaningful, and the development and
acquisition of language are such primally meaningful, and powerful,
psychological phenomena, two things can happen. Speaking in a
therapist's role in an acquired language, libidinal energy gets
channeled into the use of language that otherwise would go into the
struggle to understand. This is demanding and exhausting, and can
lead to pulls to swerve away from challenging or painful material;

one is semiconsciously wary of exposing one's raw edges in a
"foreign" language, or that one may accidentally arrive at a con-
vergence between one's own conflicts and those of one's patient in
a less defended way than would a native speaker. Use of the
acquired language may also lead the therapist to over-emphasize
adaptive strivings and resist the necessary exploration and dis-
section of primitive affects, personal meanings and conflicts,
and character defenses, as such exploration may threaten the
therapist's own defensive adaptation.

Speaking in one's native language, when it is also the minority
native language of the patient, there are different regressive
pulls. Grateful for the relief from having to perform in an
acquired language, and related to a sense of cultural solidarity,
a feeling can develop of being "at home" with the patient that
creates blind spots to the patient's conflicts and distortions.
The warmth and pleasure of working in one's own culture can be
seductive,.and can pull the therapist away from necessary challenges
or confrontations. Hearing the patient speak the native language
may evoke regression and guilt in a therapist who has "abandoned
the mother tongue" to become proficient in the language of the
dominant culture. Associational streams and evoked affects may
become skewed because of the cathexis of the use of the language.

There are other transformations of pace and affect. I have
experienced, and several colleagues and supervisees have also
described to me, a sense that a stacatto rhythmic feel often develops
when one is a bilingual doing therapy. The analogic aspects of
language - tone, pitch, timbre and prosody - can conflict with the
digital aspects. This is particularly the case when therapist and
patient have different first languages, but it can also be the case
when both therapist and patient are speaking in a common minority
language: the relief of having a safe space to communicate in the
mother tongue can subliminally produce disconcerting experiences of
rushing or of slowing down.

The affective changes when bilinguals are in therapy as patients have
been described in the literature (cf. Marcos, 1976) -- anxiety may
flow from the effort to speak in an acquired language, or blandness
may flow from the use of strange words to describe intense feelings.
(As an aside, there is an interesting variant of this in immigrant
children, who have not learned in school, in English, words to
describe intense feelings that they have developmentally yet to
acquire words for in Spanish.) How is this different when it happens
in the therapist? Simply put, it increases the workload, producing
tensions and stresses that, if unattended, can get in the way of
being a well-oiled therapeutic instrument.

As a bilingual therapist, one is structurally compelled to be aware of political and social context in a way that majority-culture, monolingual therapists are not. Language is the first great achievement of ego, and then it subsides to background, for a monolingual. This is never the case for a bilingual; speaking Spanish in the U.S., or speaking English with a Spanish accent, or speaking English when one would rather speak Spanish, are acts with political meaning and depth-psychological resonances. Politics thus enters the consulting room in an unaccustomed way. For a therapist whose subjective preference is to split off political concerns and focus a strong lens on intrapsychic phenomena, this becomes not completely possible.

CASE EXAMPLES

It is important to describe these phenomena because once they can be named they can be mastered, and harnassed as powerful therapeutic tools. Two clinical vignettes can give a sense of this.

I was running a psychotherapy group in Spanish in a partial-hospital program. My fluency in English, and my acculturation, were greater than those of my patients. Responding to a comment of an intelligent, articulate patient, who spoke a rich and careful Spanish, I inadvertently used an anglicism. His correction was immediate and caustic, and I did not immediately reply. In the moment between his criticism and my silent containing, imbued with my unspoken awareness of the potency and relevancy of what had just happened, the patient caught an important psychological glimpse of himself: his rage at his cultural displacement; the impotence of having to speak in a new language, where his treasured eloquence eluded him; his difficulty asking for help, sharing his hurts; his defensive tendency to project his terrors unconsciously onto others. I was pleased, later on, with the productivity of the session. And yet it was not until months later that I realized my smug pleasure was my own defensive denial of how close I felt to his experience -- there but for the grace of God went I.

The second example comes from the treatment of a 5-year-old boy, a Puerto Rican, English-primary, in New York City. As a 2-year-old he had watched his parents be murdered in a drug transaction, and he was subsequently raised by an overwhelmed and thus inept grandmother. Her inability to contain his trauma and rage led him to become a wild, almost ferral child. After establishing that I in fact knew Spanish, he did his therapeutic work almost entirely in English. One day he came into the playroom in a rage. There was no speaking with him, and no protecting the materials, or in fact myself, from his assaults. I had to physically carry him out, something quite different from anything that had transpired between us before. I subsequently learned that he had heard that day that his grandmother was going to be hospitalized for a serious illness; he was afraid she would die, and he would be abandoned again, something completely beyond his capacity to tolerate. He came in the following week for his regularly scheduled session, with neither of us knowing how to begin or what to say. Then, in one of those serendipitous moments that strike us from time to time as therapists, I said to him, in Spanish, "Dime que paso," "Tell me what happened." He cried, and he began to speak. That was not simply a tactical accomplishment, but a turning point in his therapy; he began to trust, to express, and to open up, and it seemed in retrospect that a developmental blockage began to budge.

It was also a turning point in my development as a therapist. Intuitively I knew what to do. I unconsciously knew that here was a linguistic and cultural shift of focus that needed to be made, and I was able to make it, facilitating and not mischanneling the flow of the therapeutic process. The incident gave me a sense of the range of my own awareness and expertise, a sense that I could move with some sureness in the realm of the unconscious and the unaware, across languages and cultures. Why was it that an encounter with bilingualism would do that for me? In fact, because I had been there; and there were present in the experience important lessons about personal integration, and about consolidation of a professional inner identity as a bicultural therapist, as well.

CONCLUDING COMMENTS

I return to the observation that the bilingual psychotherapeutic encounter recreates, for therapist as well as patient, critical life experiences of cultural dissonance and cultural bridging, but now within the accessible-to-change context of the therapeutic field. The focal issues of cultural conflict are often key determinants both of the patient's presenting problems and of the therapist's struggle for professional identification and personal meaning. When the phenomenology of bilingualism enters the consulting room, there is both the opportunity and the danger of deep empathic identification. These issues must be actively examined and worked through by the therapist and not treated as background. The rewards for doing so are rich; the dangers of not doing so include the undermining of one's therapeutic leverage.

This paper has attempted to name, map and describe some of the phenomena that occur, for therapists, within the field of bilingual therapy. These phenomena are probably as inexactly described as those of any primitive map; perhaps they are also as meaningful. Others are encouraged to explore the same territory.

REFERENCES

Acosta, F. Barriers between mental health services and Mexican Americans: an examination of a paradox. American Journal of Community Psychology, 1979, 7, 503–520.

Buxbaum, E. The role of a second language in the formation of ego and superego. Psychoanalytic Quarterly, 1949, 18, 279–289.

Garrison, V. Support systems of schizophrenic and nonschizophrenic Puerto Rican migrant women in New York City. Schizophrenia Bulletin, 1978, 4, 561–596.

Greenspan, R. The mother tongue and the mother. International Journal of Psycho-Analysis, 1950, 31, 18–23.

Krapf, E. The choice of language in polyglot psychoanalysis. Psychoanalytic Quarterly, 1955, 24, 343–357.

Lagache, D. Sur le polyglotisme dans l'analyse. Psychoanalyse, 1956, 1, 167–178.

Langs, R. The technique of psychoanalytic psychotherapy. New York: Aronson, 1973. 2 vols.

Marcos, L. Bilinguals in psychotherapy: language as an emotional barrier. American Journal of Psychotherapy, 1976, 30, 551.

Marcos, L., and Alpert, M. Strategies and risks in psychotherapy with bilingual patients: the phenomenon of language independence. American Journal of Psychiatry, 1976, 133, 1375–1378.

Marcos, L., and Urcuyo, L. Dynamic psychotherapy with the bilingual patient. American Journal of Psychotherapy, 1979, 33, 331–338.

Sprafkin, R., et al. Structured learning: its cross-cultural roots and implications. In P. Pedersen, ed., Handbook of cross-cultural counseling and therapy. New York: Praeger, 1987.

Velikovsky, I. Can a newly acquired language become the speech of the unconscious? Psychoanalytic Review, 1934, 21, 329–335.

PATTERNS FOR ALCOHOL AND DRUG ABUSE ACROSS ETHNICITIES: A MULTI-FACTOR INVESTIGATION

Jeffrey J. King, and Julian F. Thayer
The Pennsylvania State University
University Park, U.S.A.

Research is rapidly increasing in the area of alcohol and drug abuse among ethnic minorities in the United States. However, most studies in this area tend to focus on only one or two ethnic groups--usually a minority group compared to an Anglo group. The problem with this approach is that norms may be different across groups. Another problem with these studies is that they usually focus on a single factor, such as depression. Consequently, other possible interacting factors, such as alienation and/or socioeconomic status, are ignored.

This study employs multiple measures to examine psychological distress and well-being factors within and across three ethnic groups: Black, White, and American Indian. This study examines factors which influence psychological distress, well-being, and alcohol and drug use. Because this study is exploratory, Black, White, and American Indian college students in Oklahoma have been examined.

Our study addresses the following four questions: (a) Are there culturally-distinct patterns for psychological well-being and/or distress? (b) What role does acculturation play in psychological health or distress, of alcohol and drug use, or cognitive style? (c) How does socioeconomic status affect psychological well-being and distress? (d) How do these factors relate to level of alcohol and drug use?

PSYCHOLOGICAL AND COPING FACTORS

High levels of psychological distress have been found to relate to loneliness (Weeks, Michela, Peplau, & Bragg, 1980), coping styles (Coyne, Aldwin, & Lazarus, 1981), legal drug use (Aneshensel & Huba, 1983), and drinking behavior (Jones-Saumty, Hochhaus, Dru, & Zeiner, 1983). This study simultaneously assesses these areas to get a more global view of the interactions and/or patterns displayed by these

factors in relation to alcohol and drug use. Patterns of
psychological health and distress are assessed across groups.

DEGREE OF ACCULTURATION

Degree of acculturation may largely influence manifestations of
psychological distress, as well as contribute to psychological
well-being (Berry, 1980). The acculturation process itself has been
shown to involve psychological distress, usually called
acculturative stress (Berry, 1980; Padilla, 1980). For the purpose
of this study, the degree to which a minority person identifies with
his or her own culture is measured. It is hypothesized that
different patterns of distress, coping style, cognitive style, and
alcohol use are displayed depending on level of acculturation.

SOCIO-ECONOMIC STATUS

This study will also view the role of socio-economic status
(SES) in psychological distress and alcohol and drug use. Low SES
has been consistently and reliably linked with higher rates of
psychological distress in the general population (Cervantes &
Castro, 1985). Furthermore, many studies initially finding
psychological distress differences across ethnic groups noted that
when SES was controlled, these differences became nonsignificant.
Thus, observed differences across cultures may not be due to
minority status or culture, but rather SES.

COGNITIVE STYLE

Neuropsychological measures of cognitive style are employed in
order to assess the influence of cognitive style on psychological
distress, as well as its relationship to degree of acculturation.
Research in this area suggests differences in cognitive styles
across some ethnic groups. (Scott, Hynd, Hunt, & Weed, 1979; see
also McShane & Plas, 1984). Two cognitive style measures are used
in this study: the Preference Test (Zenhausern, 1978) and the
Verbal-Visualizer Questionnaire (Richardson, 1977). These measures
will assess left brain-right brain information processing styles.

ALCOHOL USE

Alcohol use and/or abuse is evaluated by this study in relation
to coping strategies, psychological distress and well-being,
cognitive style, and acculturation. Previous studies have linked
alcohol usage with distress (Jones-Saumty, Hochhaus, Dru, & Zeiner,
1983). Other researchers have found evidence that alcohol usage has
a stress-buffering effect (Neff & Husaini, 1982). This would
suggest that those people manifesting high levels of psychological
distress would also tend to use alcohol or drugs more frequently.

Ethnic groups seem to display varying reasons for alcohol usage
(Marshall, 1979). Leavitt (1983, p. 171) cites studies that
demonstrate relatively higher rates of alcohol usage among Whites as
compared to Blacks. Studies involving American Indian groups report
vast differences between tribes in alcohol consumption (Mail &
McDonald, 1980). This study examines whether these previously
displayed differences in alcohol usage can be accounted for by the
patterning of these factors.

METHOD

Subjects. Black, White, and American Indian college students in
Oklahoma were selected for this study. The total number of
participants was 288. There were 59 Black students, 82 American
Indian students, and 147 White students. Further data for each
group are provided in Table 1.

TABLE 1.   Demographic description for each group

	American Indians	Blacks	Whites
Number(N=)	82	59	147
	(22 males)	(30 males)	(70 males)
	(60 females)	(29 females)	(77 females)
Age Range			
17-23	32 (39%)	44 (75%)	118 (80%)
24-30	28 (34%)	12 (20%)	16 (11%)
31+	22 (27%)	3 (5%)	13 (9%)
SES			
$10,000			
or less	62 (75%)	11 (19%)	20 (14%)
10-24,000	16 (20%)	23 (39%)	40 (27%)
24,000+	4 (5%)	25 (42%)	87 (60%)
Degree of Acculturation			
High	37 (41%)	39 (67%)	
Moderate	18 (23%)	--------	
Low	25 (36%)	20 (33%)	

Measures. The assessments are listed below in the order they
appeared on the questionnaire.

1. Multiple Affect Adjective Checklist (MAACL: Zuckerman &
   Lubin, 1965).
2. Demographic sheet.
3. Preference Test (Zenhausern, 1978).
4. Self Rating Scale (SRS: Fleming & Courtney, 1984).
5. Mental Health Inventory (Viet & Ware, 1983).
6. Beck Depression Inventory (BDI: Beck, 1967).
7. Revised UCLA Loneliness Scale (Russell, Peplau, & Cutrona,
   1980).
8. Verbalizer-Visualizer Questionnaire (VVQ: Richardson,
   1977).

9. Ways of Coping Scale (WCS: Lazarus & Folkman, 1984).
10. State-Trait Anxiety Inventory (STAI: Spielberger,
    Gorusch, & Lucerne, 1970).
11. UCLA Alcohol and Drug Questionnaire (UCLA/NIDA Center for
    Adolescent Drug Abuse Etiologies, Los Angeles).
12. American Indian Acculturation Scale (part I of the
    American Indian Mental Health Comparative Treatment
    Project form: Trimble, 1985).
13. Black Nationalism Scale (Harrell, 1979). This measure
    examines coping styles Black people use to relate to White
    culture.

For our analysis, the measures used to assess well-being were
the Mental Health Inventory; specifically the subscales of "general
positive well-being," and "positive emotional ties," and the Self
Rating Scale. Measures used for psychological distress were the
Beck Depression Inventory, UCLA Loneliness Scale, the State-Trait
Anxiety Inventory and three subscales of the Mental Health
Inventory: "depression," "lack of self-control," and "anxiety."
Coping styles were assessed via the subscales of the Ways of Coping
Scale. These are "confrontive coping," "distrust," "self-control,"
"social support," "accepting responsibility," "escape-avoidance,"
"planful problem solving," and "positive reappraisal." Alcohol and
drug use were assessed via the UCLA Alcohol and Drug questionnaire.
Degree of acculturation for the Indian and Black groups was examined
by the American Indian Acculturation Scale and the Black Nationalism
Scale, respectively.

It is important to note that item #10 of the UCLA Alcohol and
Drug questionnaire was used as our "rate of alcohol use" criteria.
This was selected after reviewing the frequency of responses given
on all the alcohol and drug items. This item represented each
group's drinking behavior more than any other item or items
combined. Also, due to the low N for high users, we had to modify
what constituted "high" and "moderate" use. Those who rarely drank
were assigned to the "low" group. Those who reported drinking once
a month to once a week were assigned to the "moderate" level. Those
who drank two to three days a week up to every day were the "high"
group.

Procedures. Subjects were selected through an announcement made by
an instructor in one of their classes. American Indian students
were told that they must be at least 3/8 Indian (blood quantum) in
order to participate in the study. At each campus, subjects were
administered the questionnaire in a large classroom. Subjects
received extra course credit for their participation. The American
Indian acculturation scale was included in the questionnaire packet
for Indian students, and the Black Nationalism scale was included in
the packet for Black students. The first administration of this
study took place in April 1986. Due to the low number of American
Indian participants, a subsequent administration took place in

February 1987. This time students were paid five dollars for their participation.

RESULTS

Scores were computed for each of our twenty-one dependent measures and multivariate analyses of variance (MANOVA) were performed initially using age and gender as independent variables. The MANOVA with age as the dependent variable was significant (approx. $F(88,890)=1.58$, $p=.001$). However, follow-up univariate tests indicated that SES was the only dependent variable that distinguished the age groups (approx. $F(4,245)=10.23$, $p<.0001$), with younger subjects having higher SES.

MANOVA results using SES as the independent measure came close to significance (approx. $F(2,173)=1.39$, $p<.06$). A follow-up univariate test revealed loneliness and lack of positive emotional control to be the distinguishing factors among SES groups. No differences in alcohol use emerged.

The MANOVA using ethnic group as the independent measure was significant (approx. $F(46,450)=5.96$, $p<.0001$). Because of the exploratory nature of this study a liberal criteria was adopted for the follow-up univariate tests. However, even a very conservative criteria would not alter the most robust of our findings. Follow-up univariate F tests revealed significant differences among our groups on SES, alcohol use, the coping styles of positive reappraisal and confrontive coping.

Scheffe post-hoc tests on these differences showed that: (a) Whites drank significantly* more than Indians or Blacks, (b) Blacks employed confrontive, positive reappraisal, and distrust coping strategies more than Whites, (c) Blacks also utilized escape-avoidance coping strategies more often than Whites or Indians, and (d) Blacks relied more on social support more than Indians.

We then looked at groups individually to determine within-group factor patterns related to alcohol and drug use. Results are listed first for Blacks, then for Indians, and finally for Whites.

Blacks. Univariate results showed that high SES Blacks used alcohol more frequently than moderate or low SES Blacks. A multi-regression of cognitive style, distress, well-being, and coping factors on alcohol use found four factors significantly related to increased alcohol use: state anxiety ($p<.000$), loss of behavioral and/or emotional control ($p<.000$), increased use of a positive reappraisal coping style ($p<.01$), and high SES status ($p<.05$). Together, these factors account for almost 40% of the total variance ($r^2=.39$). Within-group patterns for Blacks were further elaborated by using more items from the drug and alcohol questionnaire in relation to

*$p<.05$

the distress, well-being, and coping factors. Canonical correlations* yielded interesting relationships among these sets of factors. When we compared "reasons to drink" items with "recency," "amount consumed," and "total alcohol use" items, we found significant relationships between these sets accounting for much of the variance. The first function in our canonical correlations showed amount of alcohol use to be highly correlated with "not drinking with peers," "drinking to escape," and "drinking to relax" ($r^2=.62$, $p<.000$). The second function displayed "recency of use" to be moderately correlated with "drinking for excitement" and "drinking for kicks" ($r^2=.32$, $p<.06$). Degree of acculturation did not have any effect among these factors.

American Indians. Univariate results showed Indians who drank more also utilized certain coping strategies: seeking social support ($p<.05$), accepting responsibility ($p<.05$), and positive reappraisal, which approaches significance ($p<.06$), more than their Indian peers. Also, high users exhibited more of a right hemispheric cognitive style (VVQ, $p<.05$). There were no differences in alcohol use across SES levels nor degree of acculturation. Canonical correlations yielded a significant negative relationship between "recency of use" and a set containing "drinking to overcome depression," "drinking to relax," and "drinking to escape" ($r^2=.30$, $p<.004$). A non-significant relationship, yet one which may account for up to 40% of the total variance is "positive well-being" correlated negatively with "total use" ($r=-.63$, $r^2=.40$).

Whites. Univariate results showed that Whites who drink more frequently utilize coping strategies of: planful problem solving ($p<.05$), and positive reappraisal ($p<.05$) more than those who drink less often. There were no SES differences in frequency of alcohol use. Non-significant canonical correlations show coping strategies of "escape-avoidance" and "confrontive coping" to be moderately correlated with multiple reasons to drink--"pleasure," "to escape," "for satisfaction," "for kicks," "for excitement," "peers," and "to relax" ($r^2=.26$). A second correlation linked well-being factors of "not depressed" and "exhibiting self-control" with multiple reasons to drink--"to escape," "for kicks," and "peers" ($r^2=.26$).

Due to the low N in each group, these results must be interpreted cautiously. The intent of the study was to get a general idea of factor patterns, and not to view our results as final. Rather, we see these results as indicators of areas to study more specifically.

*(The purpose of canonical correlation analysis is to derive a linear combination between each of two theoretically meaningful sets of items in such a way as to maximize the correlations between the two sets. The squared canonical correlations (r^2) is a measure of variance explained in one set of items by the items in the other set.)

DISCUSSION

The discussion will be along the format of our four initial questions. However, before listing and discussing these questions, we note that there are several problems related to our population samples. We wonder how representative our sample is of their respective groups. Each of our groups scored in the "healthy" ranges of our measures. In fact, in order to use the MANOVA procedures for examining levels of alcohol use, we had to lower our cut-off points in scoring what constituted high, moderate, and low use in order to fill our cells. There simply were not enough subjects who reported high alcohol and/or drug use. It is our opinion that there were high social desirability effects.

A second problem was that our groups were not matched (see Table 1). The Black and White samples were fairly similar, while the Indian subjects were predominantly female, older, and poorer.

A third problem is that perhaps these measures were not reliable for the non-white groups. However, because of our low sample size we could not assess this.

Now to address our initial questions. We first asked, "Are there culturally distinct patterns of psychological distress and well-being?". For the most part, these groups were quite similar. However, the ethnic minority groups utilized confrontive coping, positive reappraisal, distancing, and distrust more frequently than Whites. This would make sense, given that minorities must cope with more non-group issues than Whites.

Our second question, "What role does acculturation play in relation to health, distress, coping style, cognitive style, and alcohol use?" can be answered by stating that it does not play a significant role in any of these domains. This was a surprising result to us. A possible explanation for this lack of effect is that ethnic minority persons attending college may not be dealing with the issue of acculturation as much.

The third question, "What is the role or influence of socioeconomic status on these factors?" has yielded some interesting results. In contrast to the reports of Castro and Cervantes (1985), SES did not account for the differences in psychological distress. Rather, coping style differences emerged--which may suggest that these coping styles are working. There were no differences in alcohol use across SES levels.

In answer to the fourth question, "How do these factors relate to alcohol and drug use?," we now have some general ideas. Culture, in this case, seems to be the major influence for rates of alcohol use. (There were not enough drug-use responses to assess anything about substance abuse among these groups.) The fact that Whites drink more often than Indians or Blacks supports the findings by Leavitt (1982) that Whites drink more than Blacks. This finding runs contrary to the Indian literature which suggests Indians drink far more than Whites (Lewis, 1980). Within groups the factor patterns related to alcohol use are varied. It appears that low SES Black college students utilize alcohol as a means to reduce stress. For Black students in general, there seems to be a pattern of distress which involves anxiety, and loss of personal control, as well as attempts at positive reappraisal coping. Also, Black persons who do not confront their problems, but rather distance themselves, appear to use alcohol more often.

Indians who drink more often utilize certain coping strategies of getting social support, accepting responsibility, and positive reappraisal more than their cohorts. Indians who drink less tend to score much higher on well-being items.

For White college students, high users also use certain positive coping strategies of planful problem solving and positive reappraisal more than other White students. Their reasons for drinking are varied, and those students who feel the most healthy report they drink to relieve stress.

In sum, our questions were given tentative answers, giving a general impression of pattern differences and similarities across Black, White, and American Indian college students. As an exploratory study, it has provided a rough framework in which to direct further research. Given the limitations of the study (low N, non-matched groups, primarily healthy populations) much was obtained. Future studies in this area should include much larger samples from more generalized populations, should try to match the populations more closely, and should contain at least one scale assessing social desirability. A larger sample would allow for the statistical procedures to be interpreted more confidently. Plus, factor analyses and confirmatory analyses could be used both to assess the reliability of these measures in non-white populations and to develop models for well-being and/or distress across ethnic groups. Finally, the methodology employed in this study provided a structure which allowed for: (a) assessing multiple factors simultaneously; (b) multiple measures on single factors which allowed convergent validity results; and (c) identification of factor patterns within and across ethnic groups.

REFERENCES

Aneshensel, C. S. & Huba, G. J. (1983). Depression, alcohol use, and smoking over one year: A four-wave longitudinal causal model. Journal of Abnormal Psychology, 92, 134-150.

Berry, J. W. (1980). Acculturation as varieties of adaptation. In A. Padilla (Ed.), Acculturation: Theory, models and some new findings. Boulder: Westview Press.

Beck, A. T. (1967). Depression. New York: Hoeber.

Cervantes, R. C. & Castro, F. G. (1985). Stress, coping, and Mexican American mental health: A systematic review. Hispanic Journal of Behavioral Sciences, 7, (1), 1-73.

Coyne, J. C., Aldwin, C., & Lazarus, R. S. (1981). Depression and coping in stressful episodes. Journal of Abnormal Psychology, 90, 439-457.

Fleming, J. S. & Courtney, B. E. (1974). The dimensionality of self-esteem: II. Hierarchical facet model for revised measurement scales. Journal of Personality and Social Psychology, 46, 404-421.

Harrell, J. P. (1979). Analyzing Black coping styles: A supplemental diagnostic system. The Journal of Black Psychology, 5, 99-108.

Jones-Saumty, D., Hochhaus, L., Dru, R., & Zeiner, A. (1983). Psychological factors of familial alcoholism in American Indians and Caucasians. Journal of Clinical Psychology, 39, 783-790.

Lazarus, R. S. & Folkmann, S. (1984). Stress, Appraisal, and Coping. New York: Springer Publishing Company.

Leavitt, F. (1982). Drugs and behavior (2nd ed.). New York: Wiley.

Lewis, R. G. (1980). Alcoholism and the Native American: A review of the literature. Alcohol and Health Monograph, No. 4., Special Populations Issues, NIAAA, Rockville, MD.

Mail, P. D. & McDonald, D. R. (1980). Tulapai to Tokay: A bibliography of alcohol use and abuse among Native Americans of North America. HRAF Press.

Marshall, M. (1979). Beliefs, behaviors, and alcoholic beverages: A cross-cultural survey. Ann Arbor, University of Michigan Press.

McShane, D. A. & Plas, J. M. (1984). The cognitive functioning of American Indian children: Moving from the WISC to the WISC-R. School Psychology Review, 13, (1), 61-73.

Neff, J. A. & Husaini, B. A. (1982). Life events, drinking patterns, and depressive symptomatology: The stress-buffering role of alcoholic consumption. Journal of Studies in Alcohol, 43, 301-308.

Padilla, A. M. (1980). Acculturation: Theory, models, and some new finding. Boulder: Westview Press.

Richardson, A. (1977). Verbalizer-Visualizer: A cognitive style dimension. Journal of Mental Imagery, 4, 109-126.

Russell, D., Peplau, L. A., & Cutrona, C. E. (1980). Developing a measure of loneliness. Journal of Personality Assessment, 42, 290-294.

Scott, S., Hynd, G. W., Hunt, L., & Weed, W. (1979). Cerebral speech lateralization in the Native American Navajo. Neuropsychologia, 17, 89-92.

Spielberger, C. D., Gorusch, R. C., & Lucerne, R. F. (1970). Manual for the State-Trait Anxiety Inventory. Palo Alto, CA: Consulting Psychologists Press.

Trimble, J. E. (1985). American Indian Mental Health Comparative Treatment Project. Acculturation portion, pp. 2-4.

Trimble, J. E. (1981). Value differences and their importance in counseling American Indians. In Pedersen, Draguns, Lonner, & Trimble (eds.), Counseling across cultures, The University of Hawaii Press.

Viet, C. T. & Ware, J. E., Jr., (1983). The structure of psychological distress and well-being in general populations. Journal of Consulting and Clinical Psychology, 31, 730-742.

Weeks, D. D., Michela, J. L., Peplau, L. A., & Bragg, J. E. (1980). Relation between loneliness and depression: A structural equation analysis. Journal of Personality and Social Psychology, 39, 1238-1245.

Zenhausern, R. (1978). Imagery, cerebral dominance, and style of thinking: A unified field model. Bulletin of the Psychonomic Society, 2, 381-384.

Zuckerman, M. & Lubin, B. (1965). Manual for the Multiple Affect Adjective Checklist. San Diego, CA: Educational and Industrial Testing Service.

published in the series CROSS-CULTURAL PSYCHOLOGY:

volume 1   Applied Cross-Cultural Psychology
            2nd International Conference, Kingston, Ontario, 1974
            Editors J.W. Berry and W. Lonner
            1975, 340 pp. isbn 90 265 0214 1 Hfl 45,00 / US$ 21.00

volume 2   Basic Problems in Cross-Cultural Psychology
            3rd International Conference, The Netherlands, 1976
            Editor Y.H. Poortinga
            1977, 386 pp. isbn 90 265 0247 8 out of print

volume 3   Cross-Cultural Contributions to Psychology
            4th International Conference, Munich, Germany, 1978
            Editor L.H. Eckensberger et al.
            1979, 452 pp. isbn 90 265 0300 8 Hfl 73,00 / US$ 34.00

volume 4   Diversity and Unity in Cross-Cultural Psychology
            5th International Conference, India, 1981
            Editor R. Rath et al.
            1982, 380 pp. isbn 90 265 0431 4 Hfl 70,25 / US$ 32.75

volume 5   Expiscations in Cross-Cultural Psychology
            6th International Conference, Scotland, 1982
            Editors J.B. Deregowski et al.
            1983, 460 pp. isbn 90 265 0450 0 Hfl 76,00 / US$ 35.50

volume 6   From a Different Perspective
            7th International Conference, Acapulco Mexico, 1984.
            Editor I. Reyes Lagunes and Y. Poortinga
            1985, 396 pp. isbn 90 265 0672 4 Hfl 73,00 / US$ 34.00

volume 7   Growth and Progress in Cross-Cultural Psychology
            8th International Conference, Istanbul Turkey, 1986
            Editor C. Kagitcibasi
            1987, 418 pp. isbn 90 265 0852 2 Hfl 76,00 / US$ 33.50

available in USA and Canada from: in other countries available from:

Taylor and Francis   Swets & Zeitlinger b.v.
242 Cherry Street   Heereweg 347
Philadelphia, PA 19106-1906, USA   2161 CA Lisse, the Netherlands

also available:

ETHNIC MINORITIES AND IMMIGRANTS
IN A CROSS-CULTURAL PERSPECTIVE

Selected Papers from the Regional IACCP Conference:
held in Malmö, Sweden, 1985.

Edited by Lars H. Ekstrand
Published for the International Association of
Cross-Cultural Psychology

Efficient and increasing means of communication have made nations
come closer, even in spite of severe conflicts. Behavioral research –
especially cross-cultural research and research on cultures in contact – is
one of the care areas for bringing out results that can help in guiding a
development towards mutual understanding and, ultimately, peace. This is
clearly shown in this volume.

Contents:

1986, 264 pp. isbn 90 265 0725 9   Hfl 64,00 / US$ 28.50

available in USA and Canada from: in other countries available from:

Taylor and Francis   Swets & Zeitlinger b.v.
242 Cherry Street   Heereweg 347
Philadelphia, PA 19106-1906, USA   2161 CA Lisse, the Netherlands